Change
The
Game!

*The Independent Hip Hop Label
Guide to Success in
the NEW Music Industry*

by Walt F.J. Goodridge

Published by a company called W, New York

Marketed and distributed by

THE PASSION PROFIT COMPANY, INC.
P.O. Box 618
Church Street Station
New York, NY 10008-0618
online at http://www.PassionProfit.com
email: orders@passionprofit.com

Retail Cost: $49.95
ISBN:0974531308
Library of Congress Catalog Card Number:

This book was originally published in July, 1992, under the ISBN: 0962920290
This Revised Millennium Edition is copyrighted May 2003, ISBN: 0974531308

Printed in the United States of America

Table of Contents

PART 1: Pre-GAME Warm-up

PART 2: THE GAME

PART 3: HALF-TIME

PART 4: BACK TO THE GAME

PART 5: POST-GAME WRAP UP

WE RECOMMEND THAT YOU GET:
The Change the Game Supplement: Hip Hop Lists of Exposure (Order separately)
 • All Black Radio • Hip Hop Chartmakers • Distributors • Manufacturers • Magazines & Media • Video Programs •

What People Are Saying About Change The Game:

"Carry this around with you and treat it like your Bible!"
-- Chuck D, PUBLIC ENEMY & Rapstation.com

*"Your book **Change The Game** is great!
It helped me sell my first 5000 units."***--Fred Jarmon**

"As the Hip Hop world gets more crowded, it's more difficult for you to make your project stand out. "This Game..." is an invaluable guide to the inner workings of the Rap industry. To succeed, you must know the rules of the game, and this book tells it all like it is!" **-- Jon Shecter, Editor-in-Chief, SOURCE MAGAZINE**

"A must-have for anyone who wants to know the business of Rap Music!" **--Sheena Lester, Editor, RAPPAGES MAGAZINE**

" I would be happy to include a link to your site...I'll even include it in my banner section...
When I first began my independent label it was after reading the inaugural version of your book...remember, the spiral bound copies? I've still got it...The Ultimate Hip Hop Directory

" *Change The Game* is the most comprehensive Hip Hop publication to date. It defines every aspect necessary in the business!" **-- Meshaq Blaq, Editor, NO SELLOUT MAGAZINE**

"...packs a lot of information...everything...!" **-- Havelock Nelson, BILLBOARD MAGAZINE**

"The Change The Game is the definite source for those aspiring to get into the music industry.. and not get jerked!" **-- Gabriel Tolliver, Associate Producer, YO! MTV RAPS**

"Walt Goodridge's step-by-step guides are fundamental for all Rap entrepreneurs. ....clearly illustrates the basics for starting your own record label. .... comprehensive reading, and an ideal roadmap for success in the music industry!" **--Kathy Danniels, UPSCALE MAGAZINE**

"To the point, easy to read. If you're putting a business together in the music industry, you must have this book!" **-- Wildman Steve, WBAU-FM, NY**

"On Point! It's truly one stop shopping for info on the Rap Industry!" **-- Wendy Day, RAP COALITION**

".... shows great caring and depth and foresight.....a great instrument for anyone, young or old interested in the music industry!" **-- Rev. Mariah Britton, Riverside Church, RAP WRITERS & PERFORMANCE WORKSHOP**

"...this is really giving a lot of love for Hip Hop!" **-- N. Robinson, CUSTOMER (WA)**

Dedication

This book is dedicated to Isolene Rebecca Golding
1907-1988

Acknowledgments

Special thanks to the true few who have supported, guided or joined me on my passion to profit journey:
My mother Thelma Rose Goodridge, Christine St. Hilaire, Reina Joa, Courtney Munroe,
Wayne Wright, Gurdeep Singh, Kenneth McRae, Courtney & April Gibson, Nicole Drew, Diamond Davis,
Ernest Capers, Erroll Paden, Carlton Gambrell II, Tony Cordoza, Nava Parker, Gary Ervin,
Dawn Greenidge, Marilyn DeFreitas, Stacey Spencer-Willoughby, Aaron Willoughby, Anika Moore,
Zelda Owens-Waters, Andrew Morrison, Kim McNeil, Odette Flemming, Maasai Kush,
the ACN family, and TagTeam Marketing!

What's New in Change The Game:

This updated edition of *Change The Game* will attempt to make sense of and help you keep pace with recent changes in the music industry as well as provide cutting edge business and personal development information and strategies. You'll get:

½ Answers to 10 years' worth of Frequently Asked Questions
½ A beginner's introduction to the Internet
½ Updated chapters with even more details and step-by-step guidance
½ How to launch your label online for the least expense!
½ Expanded contact information including website URLs and email addresses
½ An updated chapter on choosing the right business structure (with LLC)
½ My new philosophy on which business structure to choose
½ A sample producer contract
½ New tax forms and tips for the new business structures
½ Success Stories of other Hip Hop Entrepreneurs
½ Information on our new Associate/Affiliate Program
½ How to improve conditions in your life and business
½ An updated Comprehensive Game Plan and Task Checklist
½ A Record Label Trouble Shooting Guide

I'm going to help you start your own record label and release your own music. I'll take you through the entire process giving you tips and suggestions for doing things efficiently and at the __lowest possible cost__. And, even though the landscape will continue to change, this new edition will hopefully be useful in guiding another generation of Hip Hop Entrepreneurs for at least the next 10 years!

Thanks for your support, and remember:

Success is a journey, not a destination!

Walt F.J. Goodridge
"The Passion Prophet"
"I share what I know,
so that others may grow!"

HipHopBiz.com Founder and CEO of
The Passion Profit Company

PART ONE: PRE-GAME WARMUP

"Walt F.J. Goodridge, in his books Change The Game,
and This Game of Artist Management names all the areas that
need to be covered in the music business. He not only names all 25 areas,
but he also tells you what keeps you in business if you're in one of those areas.
If you don't build anything, then you have nothing. If you don't build anything,
you always have to be a part of somebody else's s—t. To be a part of white people's
structures is whack especially when it comes to Rap,
because they're not fully down with it!"
—Chuck D.
Public Enemy,
RapStation.com
[excerpt from *Fight The Power*]

The Game Plan:

To successfully start, run, succeed, grow and change the game of being an independent record label, you will need to:

► **Monitor your OPERATIONS**

½ **Find, sign and develop talented ARTISTS**

► **Create your PRODUCT on CD or other media**

► **MARKET, Promote & Advertise it…**

► **SELL IT to stores, distributors and to the public**

► **Maximize additional streams of INCOME**

► **RECOUP your expenses**

► **PAY the players**

► **Make a PROFIT**

½ **GROW your business**

Everything that we'll cover in the over 300 pages that follow is intended to help you successfully accomplish each of the steps above.

CHAPTER 1
"About This Book"

Welcome to the New Game!

If this is your first time reading *Change The Game* (the book formerly known as *Rap! This Game of Exposure*), welcome! If, on the other hand, you're reading this revised edition after having read the original, then welcome back! Since the original publication of *Rap! This Game of Exposure* in 1992, quite a lot has happened in the world of business, in the music industry, and in my own life. However, before we get to the new stuff, here's a recap of how it all started to bring you newcomers up to speed.

It was the summer of 1992. I was actively running an independent record label in New York City. I was also employed as a civil engineer, earning a living designing roads, tunnels and bridges. While running my label, I would often find myself sharing my experiences, knowledge, tips and advice with other Hip Hop Entrepreneurs who would call me up, requesting advice on how to start and succeed with their own labels. They may have seen my artists' videos playing on BET (Black Entertainment Television), or they may have come across the product in stores around the country. These were the days before the Internet, so while the avenues of exposure were not as abundant as they are today, we did a pretty good job with what we had.

One day, Arlington E., a recent associate whom I had met at the *New Music Seminar* a few months earlier, called with "Joe", a partner of his, on the line. Joe was based in Texas, and after having just launched his own indie label, was interested in getting distribution for his releases. I was happy to help, and after we'd been talking for close to an hour, with me sharing distribution tips, marketing dos and don'ts, and answering his questions, he said, "Thank you, for all that information, Mr. Goodridge. I really appreciate it. I would have been willing to pay you for it, y'know, if you had asked me."

I paused for a moment. Intrigued, I asked him, "How much would you have been willing to pay?" He replied with a very arbitrary figure, "Oh, I don't know, $179!" I remember that phone call as if it were yesterday. It was then that a light bulb went on over my head, and I had an epiphany that took my life on a significant detour at that exact moment. It didn't take me long to recognize the opportunity that had been presented to me. At that time, no book existed that showed young, Hip Hop entrepreneurs how to start their own record label and promote their own record. I had that knowledge! The timing was perfect. I had been looking for a new idea to pursue since, though fairly successful, my label wasn't giving me the fulfillment and satisfaction I really wanted.

At that moment I made a decision to embark on a project that would change my life forever!

While juggling the demands of a full-time job and running my independent label, I set about creating, compiling, typing, cutting and pasting all the information I had in my head and heart that I had been sharing with others for the past year. I was rushing to complete the book in time for a major event that was coming up: The *Jack the Rapper Music Convention* in Atlanta. It would be the perfect venue. Thousands of music industry upstarts, hopefuls, veterans, tastemakers, reporters and onlookers would be there at the annual event. I planned to debut it at that event, distribute fliers, and see what sort of interest I could generate.

It took me four weeks of non-stop writing to do it, but, working at a feverish pace up until the very last hour, I completed the 250-page first draft of my book at about 4:00AM on the morning of the event. I hopped into my Corolla and drove the silent and deserted roadways from the Bronx to Manhattan to find a 24-hour copy center. And, at about 5:00 AM on a summer morning in 1992, the spiral-bound edition of *Change The Game* was born. Exhausted, excited, I returned home, packed for the trip, got an hour's sleep and was then off to catch a flight to Atlanta for the convention.

So, amid all the excitement, schmoozing, auditioning, griping, partying, deal-making, and milling about that happens at such industry gatherings, I distributed fliers, practiced my pitch to anyone who would listen, and even made an announcement about my "new groundbreaking publication" during one of the workshops. When the workshop ended, I was mobbed in the back of the room by people interested in taking the book home with them right then. (OK, maybe 3 people wasn't exactly a mob, but it was enough to demonstrate a real interest in what I was selling.)

It was at that event that I met Sheena Lester, then editor of the now defunct *RapPages Magazine*.
We met at a coffee shop near the convention. I showed her the book, she liked it, and true to her promise, a few weeks later, when I sent her a copy, RapPages became the first major media publication to review *Change The Game*, exposing it to a national audience.

To top it off, by the time I got back to New York three days later, there was a check in my mailbox from someone who had received a flier at the event! I was on my way!

Wow! I now had my first real, legitimate order for my first book! There was only one little "situation" I had to deal with: THE BOOK DIDN'T EXIST! I only had that one spiral-bound master copy I had created for the convention. In order to fill the customer orders, I had to take the master in to work with me early in the morning, photocopy all 250 pages, take it home, spiral bind it, and send it off. Many of you reading this are probably among the first hundred or so customers whose copy of *Change The Game* is that same spiral bound, blue cardstock cover version--what I like to think of as a "collector's first edition.

And that's how it all started! My adventure into the world of publishing, mail order selling, information brokering, and niche marketing began in the Summer of 1992. With ads placed in the Source, the now defunct Rappages, and RapSheet Magazine, more orders soon started pouring in!

Since then, I've received an overwhelming amount of support from people all over the world who appreciated the book and the work I was doing. I have filing cabinets full of correspondence, several 1000-page computer files of saved emails from fans around the world. As a result of the book, I met and formed an unofficial alliance with Chuck D. He provided the powerful quote that we still use to this day. He, along with Yusuf Jah mentioned me and my books in the book *Fight The Power*. I met and bonded with Wendy Day, founder of Rap Coalition, and, most gratifyingly met and networked with thousands of customers who bought *Change The Game* and used it to launch their labels.

Soon, due to popular demand, I created several more books like *This Game of Artist Management* featuring Chuck D., and then incorporated other authors' books and videos to create a catalog of "success tools for Hip Hop entrepreneurs". I had become a resource for Hip Hop entrepreneurs. Within a few months, I was making the same amount of money in mail order as I was as a civil engineer! So, I put the record label on hold, and continued down that path creating more unique products based on my business experiences and my desire to help others succeed. I had found a niche! In 1995, three years after writing my first book, I walked away from my engineering job to be a fulltime entrepreneur.

In any event, back to my original point. Some of the specific changes that directly affect the music industry and your success are:

½ A new business structure, the LLC has gained popularity
½ The Internet is upon us!
½ MP3 is the "next big thing"
½ Napster came and went
½ Hip Hop Entrepreneurs make the Forbes 400
½ Major label video budgets are ridiculously high!
½ Technology has progressed to bring film-making/video into the hands of just about anyone

These developments, and more, represent, in some way shape or form, paths to follow, roadblocks to avoid, directions to heed, alternate routes to consider, examples to emulate, roads less traveled or vehicles to utilize in your own journey from passion to profit as you start and grow your independent label.

Why I Wrote This Manual

As the former president of an independent Rap Label, I've been approached over the years by many artists, producers and fans who want to know simply, "How did you do it?" and "How can I do it, too?" Many of these men and women are potential entrepreneurs, who simply lack the access to the information, or the finances to re-invent the wheel. Others may have already started labels, and have come upon some obstacles in keeping the promotion pressure on and focused. It is for both these groups of people that I wrote this manual.

The sale of recorded music in the U.S. generates approximately $14.3 Billion* annually. At estimated sales of $1.63 Billion*, Rap accounts for approximately 11.4% of this figure, making it the third most popular genre. Consequently Rap has gained more respectability as a viable music form. Many larger labels have jumped in to take advantage of this profit potential. In some cases, the executives of these labels have little or no "feel", basic understanding, or even respect for the art form. As a result, many of those closest to the source worry about Rap maintaining its credibility within the very culture it came from. It is for the individuals who want to keep the music alive, help it grow, while keeping it pure; those individuals who wish to be more actively involved in the control of Rap's direction for whom I wrote this manual. Control starts with awareness and information.

If you've always thought that starting a business or promoting a record was a Herculean task requiring a lot of money, prime office space, and a huge staff, this manual might begin to dispel some of the myths. Just for the record, in 1984, Rick Rubin (later in collaboration with Russell Simmons) started and ran Def Jam Records from his college dorm room. It's also worth mentioning that Sylvia Robinson's Sugarhill Records, an independent label, was responsible for releasing THE milestone in the record industry's contact with Rap music, Rapper's Delight by The Sugarhill Gang. Admittedly, times have changed the rules of the game since then. Now you have to be a bit more sophisticated and business conscious in your approach in order to take advantage of today's opportunities. But the opportunities for success are there! So, whether your label grows to greatness from humble beginnings like Russell's, or it becomes a stepping stone towards other ventures, like Sylvia's, the basics of business startup and the experience gained in operating your company can be useful in any venture. The information I've included is also a great business primer with tons of explanations of business concepts for anyone who is considering launching their own business. So, whether artist or non-artist, *Change The Game* has vital information that you can use to get the most of your career in business in general and in the Rap music industry specifically. I wrote this manual for those individuals who might be a little intimidated by the whole idea of being an entrepreneur, and who need that extra push to jump right in!

Source: Recording Industry Association of America

"Can this book REALLY help YOU??"
This book does several important things...

....First it answers some very important questions

In creating this book, I asked myself a very important question. If I were reading it, what information would make my investment worthwhile to me? What would I need to come away with after reading such a book? What would it need to teach me? Here are the answers I came up with.

-It would first help me get a realistic picture of what I'm about to embark on.

-It would answer ALL of my questions about the industry, or tell me where to go to find the answers.

-It would explain music industry concepts from the independent label's perspective.

-It would show me how to start a label in ANY state in the US, Canada and other countries.

-It would help me decide on what structure to choose for my company and provide the paperwork to do it.

-It would provide a sample contract for me to use to sign my artist.

-It would show me how to get my record in the stores.

-It would show me how get radio play.

-It would give me options for selling my product with or without a distributor.

-It would explain the day-to-day operation of my label (how much time to devote and to what and whom).

-It should provide real-live contacts I can call to take things out of theory and into practice.

-It would provide information I can go back and reference as certain challenges arise.

-It would help me play the game on a professional level.

-It would help me create a viable business entity with long term potential and resale value.

-It would help me sign my label to a deal with a major or a larger independent.

-It would help me turn my passion for Hip Hop and Rap music into profit!

*"Most industry books are written from the artist's perspective. This is a good thing as too often artists get the short end of the stick, the bad of the deal. **Change The Game** is written from the label owner's perspective. At the very least, it will help to explain what options exist for you in starting and operating your own label, so you don't duplicate and perpetuate the same exploitation. I believe there is room for equitable agreements, fair practices that respect and honor the creativity and humanity of the artist. If you believe that too, then this book can definitely help you."--Walt*

Next, it fulfills my commitment to you

The best help that I can offer you is the ability to know how to think. The next best thing is for me to teach you what to do. But, teaching you how to think will lead to you knowing what to do in most situations. From the moment that you say you want to start a record label, there are certain things that you have to know. Many of these things have nothing to do with the music industry, per se. They have to do with concepts of success, commitment, perseverance, critical thinking, and passion. They have to do with issues of personal growth which, in truth, are the real keys to success. This game is won or lost long before you ever sign your first artist. It is won or lost long before you experience the thrill of hearing your record played on the radio. It is won or lost years before your artist makes a name for himself in industry magazines. It is won on the first day you set a goal for yourself and fully believe and expect that you'll be successful. In truth, the game is won first in your mind. Then on the charts, on the radio, on video programs or in magazines. Once you understand and accept that, then the fact that you chose a record label as the means to express that, success is really secondary.

And, it answers YOUR Questions

Well, you'll be glad to know that I wrote *Change The Game* to be the answer to those personal expectations. But, I also wanted to make sure that I had input from the people who would actually be purchasing, reading and using it. So, in January of 2003, before I sat down to add the finishing touches to this revision, I posed the following questions to the two thousand members of the Hip Hop Entrepreneur Network.

1. *What specific topic(s) and questions would you want to see covered in detail?*
2. *What issues have you PERSONALLY encountered in starting your own label.*
3. *How can I best help YOU succeed at your own record label or other hip hop related business?*
4. *What other "This Game of" book topics would you be interested in purchasing?*

What I found was that whether you're in South Africa or South Central, or the South Bronx, many of the questions and concerns of Hip Hop entrepreneurs remain the same.

Question: How do I get the right funding without a loan?

Question: How do I get the right training to be a business owner in the music industry?

Question: What does a recording contract look like?

Question: How can I get my artist's music on a movie soundtrack, TV show, etc.?

Question: Can you explain how to go about licensing music?

Question: How little money do you need to start a label?

Question: Can you be successful without airplay, i.e. .as a strictly underground label?

Question: Where can I find examples of women working behind the scenes?

Question: Can you give me a good explanation of publishing, contracts, touring, college radio airplay?

Question: Can you tell me how I can find out about appropriate conferences for those starting a label?

Question: What can I do if deejays don't want to listen to my music; if geographically I'm in a bad location for Hip Hop; if there's no local support of my artist and his music?

Question: Provide up-to-date contact information as well as techniques on how to develop relationships with music business people.

Question: How can I get attention from the majors if I want to go that route?

...It even answers "Frequently Asked Questions" from the Answerman Files

[from the Answerman Files at www.HipHopBiz.com]

From: Tommy B. Barbell Records, LLC
Question: What up Walt,
I have a question referring to royalties. Do you know usually how the royalties are separated between the record label, producer, writer, artist, and publishing company? Because when I sign my first act I want to know everything that's going into the contract. If the producer is signed to a different label and he gives me a track to use how does his royalty rate usually work. One more question, I will be starting my own production company a long with my label. Do the producers on my production company get paid a salary, or just depending if I use one of their tracks. I know Puffy and all of the big labels that started out small have their own production labels, But why does he call it HItmen Management if it is a production label? Thanks for your advice.

****

Email From: Brenda N-B
Question: Hello Walt, I'm trying to help my husband put together his own label and make up some kind of contract, but we are not sure what we should tell the people we are currently working with about getting paid if we do end up making some money. First of all he is the only one who will be paying for the equipment and studio time how much in percentage are they (rappers/vocalist) entitled to? Also I was wondering if they are free to go to other labels and be featured on some other person CD and will we make any money off that?

From Tony G.,
Question: 1) What are the steps that I need to take into making my rap lyrics?
2) How do I find beats to the songs that I am making?

****

From: *L.P. Blaque Lyght Entertainment, Inc.*
Question: I am very interested in purchasing the "start your own record label", but I have a couple of questions. Does it provide any information about royalties? for example, How do you pay out royalties? When do you pay out royalties? How do points on a album work? Also if I'm seeking a distribution deal would this help prepare myself to go motivate and convinced major labels to give me a deal, considering it's not a guarantee but is the information helpful and offers proper knowledge and covers the ins and outs of getting that distribution deal? Is there a specific length of time that needs to past before you're certified gold or platinum?

****

From: *From: silkyslim2001 (Wade Simuel)*
What's Happening,
I think that your book should really get into detail a lot about how a person can start their own independent distribution company and also how some one can start their own publishing company without writing their own music, I am not talking about co- publishing I am talking about starting a publishing company straight up. Artist development is a very important part of this industry, explain what it is, what can a person do to really get involved with development how to get experience, how much experience do you need? Also I would like to talk about how people can find employment within the industry whether its through internships or getting a regular job. Some people want to get into becoming a booking agent or really get into artist management. Who can a person contact for advice and mentoring, this is important because a lot of people are not willing to give up this advice because they fear that someone is going to blow up bigger that themselves. Also explain to people that the music industry is not only for people who are in their teens and early twenties, there is room for people of all ages. The reason that I say this is because life experience a lot of times is the best experience. People during these times are looking for career changes whether they are in their late twenties or up, we need more older people involved. Talk to you later. Peace!

****

Finally, it offers 3 parts of the Formula for Music Industry Success

What you now have in your hands is part of the formula for success: INFORMATION. However, information without the will to succeed is practically useless. Information without a product that the public wants is equally useless. The lists and contacts you now have come from time spent on the telephone, in the library and on the streets. The advice comes from real time spent out "in the field" learning things the hard way.   Whether you are an artist looking to market and sell your music, or a music-minded entrepreneur seeking to market and sell other people's music, this manual gives you the information to help you in 3 important ways.

First, you now have the means to set up a legitimate structure around your music. Since you've already made the decision to take control of your music and your future, you should also make the decision to do so interacting and communicating with the industry and the public in the language of America: Business. Business is the language by which success in America is defined. Before you can expect to take control of your creation and compete with others who are doing the same, you have to know the basics of how the game is played.   Once you're in the game you stay in it by keeping up with the rules and strategies others are playing by.   You probably have many questions as to what needs to get done, when it should be done, and how it should be done. Many of these answers, as well as the "MindChecks" (suggested ways of thinking), can be applied to the start and maintenance of any business. Learn these concepts well. They are of extreme value in ANY business you start. Once you establish the tools to construct your house, you can build any type you wish. You'll learn how to get your record company up and running. You'll get facts, forms, suggested courses of action, advice and a step by step timetable for setting up your company and releasing your record.

Second, you now have the means to target your promotion efforts more effectively. *Change The Game* provides a more complete "who to" list for promoting Rap than you'll find anywhere. The wealth of information you now have will save you the task of reinventing the promotion wheel. You won't have to send your record to 100 radio stations, for instance, to find out that only 20 of them play rap. You'll know which are the key stores to target in your promotion. If you do a video, you now have a list of over 120 video programs across the country which play rap.

Industry Rule No. 4080 subsection 7; paragraph 1a:
"Things don't HAVE to be as shady as you might have been led to believe.
You don't have to become evil to succeed in the music industry!"--Walt

In the first several sections, I'll be painting a picture of what the music industry currently looks like. The information was gleaned from several sources including Rap Coalition, The Recording Industry Association of America, and my own research. It includes excerpts from articles and industry reports. Some of the articles excerpted, as well as the books and source referenced paint a dismal story of the financial situations of artists who have signed to major labels. They contain horror stories of the deceptive practices of many major labels. Now, it doesn't mean that entire industry is "bad" or "evil". It simply means it's currently structured in such a way that is not always the most lucrative for the artist who's not in control. But, don't be discouraged. It doesn't mean that YOU have to be equally deceptive in order to succeed as a label. It is specifically for this reason that I have always advocated starting your own label, and why I wrote *Change The Game* to be a remedy, treatment and antidote for this malady. And the first thing that has to change is the concept of being "discovered" "hooked up", or "put on" by someone as the ticket to success. This manual is designed to help you do one thing only: start your record label and release your own music…on your own!

Thirdly, remember always that this is a "How To" book. It's not a "Look What Happened To" book, a "When Will Things Change", or an "Isn't it a Shame" book. This book will not go too deeply into an analysis of why things are the way they are, who the culprits are, or what needs to be done to change things. In fact, we might even be accused of being too naïve and optimistic in our assumptions. This book will help you deal with reality and create something DESPITE what others see as obstacles.

A PERSONAL NOTE: This book will equip you with the steps required to succeed based on the proven belief that in life you pretty much get what you expect. Let me explain specifically what I'm referring to. One of the often-expressed concerns that aspiring artists as well as label owners have is the fear that they won't have the financial means to make things happen the way they should. Specifically, they've heard that everyone from radio DJs, promotion companies, A&R people, and mailroom attendants are "on the take", (ie. interested in taking bribe money in order to promote, support, play, sign and boost label's product and artist's career) and that such bribery and "payola" is such an accepted part of doing business that you can't get your record played without bribing several people…constantly. There are those who will dispute what I'm about to say. And I'm not naïve enough to believe that such "mutual back washing" doesn't occur. However, what I'm here to tell you is that you most absolutely CAN get your record played on the radio, in clubs, and advance your label and artists' careers WITHOUT having to resort to bribery. In fact, one of my coaching/consulting clients just recently scored a half-hour interview on one of the major stations here in NY just on the strength of his music, and the relationships he's forged.

So, can this book help you? Yes, I believe it can; provided you also use it the right way!!

How to Use This Book

Content

This is no ordinary book. It was divinely inspired, hastily conceived, rushed through its gestation, prematurely birthed. And has been kept alive despite my own neglect marketing it effectively these past years as I venture off in new directions and embark on new projects. Even with all its imperfections and typographical errors, it had an energy which has kept it my most consistent best seller. In revising it for the new millennium, I've made sure not to tamper with success. I've added to, rather than taken from the content. You may see certain references that seem a bit outdated. Rather than take out references to Latifah and Russell Simmons and replace them with Lauryn Hill or Master-P, I've left the older references in, and added to them.

"If you find yourself thinking I'm taking too long to make my point,
you're probably missing the point I'm making."

I like to think of myself as an efficient person. My mother tells me that as a toddler, I didn't speak much. I've told her it's because until I felt I had something meaningful to say, I wasn't going to waste any words! And though, even now in fact, you might think that I have a lot to share in these 200 plus pages, very few are wasted. You'll get much more out of this book if you read it knowing that every word can represent or result in a lead, I'm guided by Spirit to say the things I say. And, I'm not always sure for whom they're meant. I always know, however, that every thought, every choice of word has the potential to inspire someone else. Heck, even the very fact that the original publication of this book exists and was written in four weeks over 10 years ago can serve to inspire budding writers and poets who are considering publishing their own work. So, as you read, know that every personal accomplishment of mine exists as a roadmap for you to follow. Every statistic I quote represents a trend you can spot and capitalize on. Every personal belief I express represents an alternate reality you can choose from. Every challenge the industry presents represents an opportunity for you to solve and make money doing so. Every mention of another person's success represents what's possible for you. Everything you learn becomes that which you yourself can now teach. Even my self-authored "Friday Inspirations*" force a shift in your brain from left-brain to right brain thinking in the middle of what might otherwise be a strictly technical exercise.

This book also teaches on many different levels. Not only will you learn things from what I say, you can learn techniques from how I say it. For example, even the techniques of persuasion and marketing that form the basis of my work are yours to copy, use and master as you build your dream. My goal is to get you to believe in, aspire towards, and create your success in business as a record label. I want you to take action doing the things that I outline in the book. I know from my own years in Network Marketing that in order for someone to be moved to action outside of their comfort zone, that they must make three statements to themselves in their minds as they evaluate the information they're presented with.

1. Me too
2. This makes sense
3. I can do this!

If you can relate to the client (share an interest, speak on a common background or experience so that they're subconsciously saying, for instance, "I like golf, too!"), you've accomplished step one. If you can present your argument asking for agreement in such a way that gets them in the habit of saying "yes, I agree" or "yes, this makes sense", then you've accomplished step two. And finally, if you can physically demonstrate, or verbally paint a picture of their involvement, participation or performance of the desired activity, so that they see or feel themselves engaged in the way you wish them to be, then you've accomplished step three. And in many ways, that 's what I do in my books and workshops. In other words, I teach not just to educate. I teach so you can emulate.

Here's the perfect example of the previous two points I made about reading between the lines of this book.

Gold in Words

Everything you see me do
exists as possible for you

Every choice you see me make
becomes a path you too can take

In every thought and every rhyme
Its value is revealed in time

So listen well, now that you've heard
there's gold within each written word

Format of the book

Have you ever read a book packed with information, and gotten overwhelmed by the sidebars, colored text boxes, and other information on the page. Well, I have. When I'm reading, and I see a sidebar, I just don't feel like stopping in mid sentence and going off on a tangent. So, I frequently make a mental note to myself to return to the sidebar when I'm finished with a section. Of course, I get so caught up in finishing the idea I'm reading, and getting more, that I rarely remember. The result is that I continue reading from one section to the next with this nagging feeling that I've missed something that I need to go back and get.

Therefore, unlike many great books with sidebars and anecdotes, my sidebars, called "Mindchecks", are placed and formatted in such a way as to be read right when and where they appear in the flow of the page. That way, you never feel like have to make a choice as to what to read and when, and your reading experience is more satisfying, with nothing you have to "go back and get". Having said that, here is our first, timely and appropriately, placed Mindcheck.

MINDCHECK

How to Read a Book

One of the more significant ideas I picked up from my Scientology experience was the following advice, which is repeated in all their literature:

"In reading this book, be very certain you NEVER go past a word you do not understand.

The only reason a person gives up a study or becomes confused or unable to learn is because he or she has gone past a word that was not understood.

…If the material becomes confusing or you can't seem to grasp it, there will be a word just earlier that you have not understood. Don't go any further, but go back to before you get into trouble, find the misunderstood word and get it defined."

This advice might be of great importance when faced with any conveyance requiring your endorsement.

The Record Label Trouble Shooting Guide

I wanted to make *Change The Game* an indispensable tool for repeated use and reference rather than simply a one-time read. But, the question was, how could I do that effectively? Sure, I knew I already had the timetable and master checklist, and the tax forms are always a great reason to open up the book every few months. But I wanted something else.

Now, one of my strengths as a coach/consultant that helps me achieve success for my clients is that I'm able to extrapolate successful ideas from one setting for use and application in another. I thought to myself, "what types of books have value such that people keep them around and reference them for years and years? "Of course," I thought, "owners manuals!" Think about it. When you buy a new electronic gadget, computer, or automobile, for example, you usually find a special place to store the owner's manual. Why? Because you know that it has valuable information you'll need if something goes wrong. You know that in the back of the manual, is a troubleshooting guide that can help you diagnose what's wrong with the darn thing so you can fix it yourself or take it in for professional help. It occurred to me that one thing that makes a manual worthwhile is the Trouble Shooting Guide. Why not create a trouble-shooting guide for a record label?

We've even said before that your record label business is a "vehicle." So, taking that analogy a bit further, your label is a money-making machine that's supposed to get you where you want to go. It has a purpose to fulfill and a certain way it should be operating. And either it's working right, or it isn't. If it's not, then you'd better find out why and fix it, because it'll only get worse or may even break down when you really need it most!

Admittedly, there are many things that can go wrong with a business that could never be anticipated in a book. The best diagnosis and treatment for any ailing business is done in real time, with a real person who can analyze the impact economy, inflation, the national mood, current events, industry standards, and even the weather may be having on consumer spending or marketing effectiveness.

The Record Label Trouble Shooting Guide is my best attempt to give you a global perspective to address why things may not be working right with your business at any given moment, and offer you solutions or directions to head in order to fix it!

A Quick Test

By the way, what do the following words "conveyance", "extrapolate " and "predilection" mean? If you don't know, then you must have read past them and didn't follow the advice in Mindcheck #1 (Remember? "In reading this book, be very certain you NEVER go past a word you do not understand…" If you DID stop and look them up online or with a handy dictionary, congratulations! You follow directions and are coachable. You've passed the first test to determine if you're qualified for the success you seek.

<u>SUMMARY of Chapter 1: *"About this Book"*</u>

Did you pass the test?

Let me ask you something. Did you read this chapter, or did you skip it to come here to the summary page? Did you read the testimonials page? If you did, did you notice that some websites, organizations and programs were listed after the names of those quoted? Did you take the time to note them as avenues of possible exposure for your label? I suggest to you that if you're not patient enough to read these introductory sections including the "Why I wrote this manual", and "Can this book really help you?" sections that don't appear to be directly related to your success in the music industry, that perhaps you're not quite ready to devote the similar pre-game time to understanding the game, improving yourself, your mind, your body, your spirit, understanding and grooming your artists. Remember, everything is a test.

In elementary school, all the way through to college, before you can proceed to the next grade level, you're required to pass the tests for the level you are currently. Life is the same way. Everything that you will ever experience that seems to challenge your forward motion is merely a test to see if you're ready to move forward. Be very careful, therefore, how you respond and react to the things that happen to you. How can you be ready for level 3 life and its tests if you let a level 2 test stop you? How can you even think of playing the game on the pro level, if you can't win at the amateur level. How can you even think that you're ready for world of fame, and financial success, along with the scrutiny, rejection and the pressures that go with it, if you allow one rejection from a local club DJ or a magazine or distributor to throw you off balance? I remember reading the story of one entrepreneur's challenge of taking his company public. He described it as the most intense, nerve racking, pressurized, time consuming, labor-intensive, detail oriented process he'd ever been through, a process in which any one of a thousand little details could derail the entire venture at any time. He described the late night meetings, the teams of lawyers, the SEC (Securities and Exchange Commission) and government scrutiny, the public attention, the traveling to pitch the company to investors and investment companies, the bank involvement, the mounds and mounds of paperwork, and the waiting. Just from that one description, I realized that anything else I was doing was an amateur's game compared to life on the pro circuit.

The Real SUMMARY of Chapter 1: *"About this Book"*

- A Game is an activity defined by freedoms, obstacles and goals. Every area of life can be likened to playing a game. The object of *Change the Game* is to help you maximize your freedoms, overcome the obstacles and reach your goals. Towards that end, we've created a Record Label Game Plan.

- The RECORD LABEL GAME PLAN includes the following 10 steps:
    - ½ **Monitor your operations**
    - ½ **Find, sign and develop talented artists**
    - ½ **Create your product**
    - ½ **Market, Promote & Advertise it**
    - ½ **Sell to stores, distributors and to the public**
    - ½ **Maximize additional streams of income**
    - ½ **Recoup your expenses**
    - ½ **Pay the players**
    - ½ **Make a profit**
    - ½ **Grow your business**

- The Music Industry has gone through some significant changes in the 10 years since the initial publication of this book! In order to address how these changes affect the Hip Hop artist & label, *Change The Game* is back! Bigger! More thorough! And ready to provide step-by-step guidance to another generation of Hip Hop Entrepreneurs for the next 10 years! It has been painstakingly re-created to address the frequently asked questions of new and experienced record label owners! This manual was written to answer questions, provide guidance and offer the tools and techniques required to conceptualize, launch, operate, profit from, grow and eventually sell your record label! Written by someone who owned and operated an independent label, it is written from the label owner's perspective. It's the combined result of over ten years of research, the answers to thousands of questions posed over the years, and the archives of the HipHopBiz.com website's "Answer man" feature.

- Understanding is the key to getting the most out of *Change The Game*. As you read through it, make sure you do not go past any word or concept you do not understand.

- Enroll others in your vision. Whenever anyone can say "Me Too", "This Makes Sense", and "I can do this" in relation to embarking on a new venture or way of thinking, their participation is almost guaranteed. Use this valuable information in your own efforts to build and grow your company/

- There's value in the both the content and format of *Change The Game*. Pay attention. The Mindchecks, Trouble Shooting Guide, Chapter Summary, Resources, and Right Questions all provide invaluable information and techniques for getting your record label to succeed.

- There's a certain amount of preparation and groundwork that is necessary for your success. This groundwork requires patience; the patience to read the right books, ask and answer the right questions in the right order; the patience to read this chapter thoroughly rather than simply jump here to the summary page. the patience to prepare your mind and your life for the wealth that you seek

- This book, like the very life you lead, will give you tests to determine if you're ready to proceed to the next level.

Chapter 1 RESOURCES: *"About this Book"*
BOOKS, AUDIO PROGRAMS, MAGAZINES, ORGANIZATIONS & WEBSITES

½ To learn more about Walt, his books, websites, and Passion Profit philosophy
- *Turn Your Passion Into Profit* by Walt F.J. Goodridge
- *The Tao of Wow: Ancient wisdom. Modern Success* by Walt Goodridge
- *This Game of Hip Hop Artist Management* by Walt Goodridge-
- Request a copy of the Passion Profit Catalog at www.passionprofit.com or www.hiphopbiz.com

½ For inspiration from other Hip Hop Entrepreneurs
- *Fight the Power* by Chuck D. with Yusuf Jah
- *Life and Def: Sex, Drugs Money and God.* by Russell Simmons; Nelson George
- *The Men Behind Def Jam:* The Radical Rise of Russell Simmons and Rick Rubin by Alex Ogg
- *Bad Boy: The Influence of Sean ""Puffy"" Combs on the Music Industry* by Ronin Ro

½ The right questions to ask to create a task list to get the most out of this chapter
- What are my 20 frequently asked questions about starting and operating a record label?
- What do successful people know that I need to learn?
- How did Russell, Puffy and Master P succeed?
- Whose success can I model?

CHAPTER 2
PREPARATION: What Game Are You Playing?

"Meet me down at the label..!"

What does a record label look like? What does it smell like? Where is it located? How many people work there? When you think about owning your own record label, what images and feelings come to mind? Perhaps, in your mind's eye you see a physical office space; with marble walls; in a building downtown amid the hustle and bustle of a big city; there's receptionist at the front desk greeting visitors and instructing the wide-eyed rappers from Cleveland to "Please have a seat, someone will be with you in a moment"; maybe there's a television tuned to a national video program for the distraction of the receptionist and visitors; or maybe there are gold and platinum records on the wall commemorating past successes; the sound of demotapes playing in the background; messengers darting through the hallways delivering tapes, posters and t-shirts for the new album promotion. music; the sound of laughter and merriment comes from a back office as groups of A&R, assistant celebrate a jump in chart position; As you're escorted down the hallway to meet the A&R rep, you pass an office and from within, you hear someone of authority screaming, "...absolutely not!! We can't wait that long, we've gotta have it on the streets and playing on the radio at the same time!"

Or maybe you'll run a home-based record label, so, if you ever did utter the words "meet me at the label," it would mean "meet me at my crib" Maybe your record label will never really exist anywhere but in the minds of those associated with it. And so therefore, as the owner, it will be located wherever you are at any given moment. So, sometimes "the label" will be at the artist's house this week, and in the producer's basement the next. Exist nowhere and everywhere at once. Never actually occupying any space in the real world except a few lines on a document, a mention in a magazine, a few spaces next to the name of the single rising up the charts, on the back and spine of the CD sitting on the shelf in a record store in Detroit.

Or maybe your label is nothing more than your intention to make money with your music however you can. Maybe your concept of a label hasn't really taken shape in your mind other than in the form of the freedom, the fame, the toys that you associate with the success you envision for yourself and/or your artists. Maybe your label is a feeling you g et when you look at your corporate checking account, your logo, your letterhead, your business cards, or that feeling of responsibility that arises based on your artists' trust, and their expectations of you.

Well, exactly what the term "my record label" means to you is unimportant. What matters, however, is that you have some sort of clear picture, at least at the start, that you are striving towards. As you prepare to play the game, that picture of success will be what drives you. To help you develop that picture in your mind, let's ask a very important question.....

Why Do You Want To Start A Record Label?

Whoa! Now where did THAT question come from???? Bet you never thought you'd be asked that one, did you? Well, having the answer to that question may be the single most important thing you do as you embark on this journey, and may be the most critical factor in your future success. So, go ahead, give yourself an answer. Why do you want to start and independent record label? Is it for the money? Is it for the fame? Is it because music and/or the culture of Hip Hop specifically is your passion? Is it simply to free yourself from the restrictions of working for someone else? Or, perhaps, is it simply as a strategic step on a journey towards other goals? Having the answer to this question clear in your mind BEFORE you begin this journey is essential to your success. So, I'll give you a chance to think about it while I share some more information with you.

The REAL Game of Business

When I was younger, my brother and I lived with our grandparents for a while. One of the rules Grandpa had was that we should never leave the yard to go out walking on the street unless we had a specific purpose. As it relates to building and growing your record label, I'll borrow from his philosophy. Never even think about starting a business journey without knowing where you want the business to take you. I'll also add a very critical piece of information I learned from reading Michael Gerber's best-selling book, *The E-Myth*.

That concept—which still takes some getting used to—is worth elaborating on. According to Gerber, "The only reason to start any business is with the express purpose of SELLING IT!

I suggest you read his book while you build your business to save yourself countless of hours of misguided efforts. But, in the interim, I'll summarize it here.

According to Gerber, the mistake that many business owners make is that they create a business that tends to consume all of their mental, emotional and physical energies. They become the business. They make decisions that trap them into being the soul of the business, and that makes them too critical a factor in the day-to-day operations and maintenance of the business. In other words, they structure things in ways that make them indispensable, such that a common refrain from these business owners include, "it's overwhelming me" "If I don't do it, it won't get done", "I can't find competent people" "No one does as good a job as me, so I end up doing everything!" It's a common mistake among entrepreneurs resulting in burnout, and the eventual failure and crash of the business.

Instead, Gerber advises that if you start your business with a different goal—i.e. the goal of selling it—you'll make different choices, and thus produce different outcomes. And, he shows in impressive and enlightening detail just how to do that. He uses the model of a successful franchise (i.e. McDonald's) to illustrate the type of business-building concepts and practices that make for a successful outcome. If you're building a business to sell to someone who wants to open and run their own version of your business (what franchisees do every day), or if you build your business knowing that someone will be required to take over from you one day, then you would build it in ways that differ significantly from someone who's not thinking that way. If you knew that in five to ten years you'd have to demonstrate to a potential buyer how your business will generate income for him or her, you'd make plans for that day from the day you launched. You'd set clear policy and procedure. You'd document the daily operations. You'd create accurate job descriptions. You'd hire competent people, rather than simply who's available. You'd create an organizational chart with clear delineation of roles and responsibilities as well as accountability. You'd work yourself into and then out of each position so that you understood the skills required, and were better able to fill them with the right people after you leave. In other words, you wouldn't simply be creating a venture, but a vehicle that will take you where you wish to go. And, because you'd have built it in such a way to create that same result even in your absence, you'd have something you could sell to anyone else looking to duplicate your success. As a result of this sort of thinking, you'd BEGIN with a clear separation of yourself and your business. You'd begin with different goals. And, you'll make different decisions. You'll see the business as something you're working ON, as opposed to something you're working IN.

When it comes time to sell such a vehicle. You'd be able to say proudly, "This is my vehicle. Here's how it works. This is what it can do. This is what it did for me. This is what it can do for you, too. Here's its potential. And, if you want it to do the same thing for you, then this is my asking price."

In this game of business, your goal should be to create an entity which not only makes money and turns a profit, but which can then free you to do the things you enjoy doing, even if what you enjoy doing is…running the business. In other words, it should be seen as a vehicle, a means to an end, a tool that can help you build something greater for yourself. It should be a machine, if you will, an invention, a separate, well-functioning, self-sustaining entity that either works or it doesn't. And, if it doesn't, it needs to be fixed so that it can do what it's supposed to: make you money, set you free and fulfill whatever mission you've set for yourself in life.

Think of all the great business success stories of people who've grown great companies from their ideas. People like Robert Johnson of BET, Russell Simmons of DefJam and Berry Gordy of Motown, understood this concept. As you may know, these individuals no longer own their respective companies. However much they had a passionate commitment to the values, dreams and significance of their ventures, they didn't let those emotional considerations cloud their decisions to "sell to the highest bidder" when it was economically advisable. Of course, they can and should exercise their best judgments in deciding whom to sell to, choosing some individual or some company that will maintain their companies' visions and operating cultures. But, at the end of the day, the winners in the game called Big Business are those with the financial freedom—operative word, freedom—to do the things they dream of.

Which Game Are YOU Playing?

Now, there's no reason why you have to accept ANY of what I'm saying. You are free to play whatever game you wish. After all, it's your company. You don't have to play the game called "Big Business." You can play the game called "This Business is my Life, " or you can play "Keep this Business in the Family," or the "Keep it Black-Owned " game. It's your choice. Keep in mind, however, that with each game comes a different set of rules, obstacles, freedoms and goals. Think about it. If Russell Simmons had been playing the "This Music Business is my Life" game, he'd still be running Def Jam, and may not have branched out into film, clothing and other ventures that are now part of the Rush empire. If Robert Johnson had been playing the "Keep it Black-Owned" business game, he wouldn't have sold to Viacom.

I'll readily admit that I've just recently started playing the "Big Business" game. I started out playing the "This is What I Know so it Might As Well be the Music Business" game, having been a radio DJ with relationships in that industry.   In my efforts to redefine myself from being a civil engineer, I played the "This Business is My Life Game." That game ended when the relationships in that first label took a turn that had me question my involvement with my partners at the time. I had to go my own way, but I couldn't take the company name—a name I had been using to define myself. It was then, when forced to detach from a label I had helped build from scratch, that I was also forced to reinvent myself, or, more accurately, rethink my invention of myself. I realized that I wasn't my business name, or its identity. I realized that I was separate from the things I created, and that I could create again another separate entity called a record label to accomplish the same goal I had expected to achieve with the first label.

So after many ups and downs, I settled into the "Me Against the World One-Man Business" Game. And that story was never challenged until my cousin confronted me on it. But that's another story.

That's My Story! And, I'm Sticking To it!

My cousin, who's also involved in the entertainment industry, with his own label and film company, once suggested that I approach some companies with "deep pockets" in order to get some major monetary muscle for my venture. It was a good idea. But, I thought about for a while and replied, "Yeah, but that's not the story I want to tell." And what I mean is this. In my mind, I see myself as a teacher. As the "Passion Prophet" it's my calling to help people turn their passions into profit. As I say as a statement of my personal mission, "I share what I know, so that others may grow." I'm not only teaching people, but I'm offering myself as a real-life example of what I teach. I only refer books, companies, organizations, workshops I've personally read, used and experienced. It's also critically important for me to be able to reach the greatest number of average people just like me with a concept and process that's doable by the greatest number of people. In other words, on the road of success, not everyone will be able to run into Russell Simmons at a vegetarian restaurant in New York (as I have), and have the opportunity to pitch a business idea. Everyone won't have the chance to get to know Chuck D personally. And, while success is all about forging mutually beneficial relationships, I didn't want my "rags to riches" story to be *I struggled for 5 years, then I met Russell, and now I'm rich.* That's NOT a story that everyone will be able to duplicate. It's important for me to be able to show a method that can be duplicated effectively and successfully by just about anyone. Make sense? In other words, if what I'm teaching isn't practical, then I'm not being a good teacher.

Sure, there will be people whose stories will include being rescued by their wealthy friend, contact or relative. And there'll be nothing wrong with that. However, just for my own credibility as a teacher of business skills and passion to profit possibilities, my story must be different and duplicable.

My story, as it stands on January 1, 2003, reads this way: *I was unhappy working for someone else, so I pursued my goal of freedom by looking first at my passion for music. I started my own label. Then ,by listening to the needs of others, and capitalizing on my innate teaching skills, I wrote a music industry "how to" book, and sold it by taking out small classified ads in music industry magazines. I was soon able to match my civil engineering income. Then, based on that success, I walked away from corporate servitude. I was evicted several times as I struggled to build a business that now sustains me. I now work from home. I have the freedom to go see movies in the middle of the day. And I generate 90% of my income through online websites that I've built myself, with knowledge I gained from books and audiotapes borrowed from the library or read in bookstores. No rich uncles. No major label deals. No major publishers. No buyouts, mergers and acquisitions. Just my own creative resources, along with friends and family who helped me out through the ups and downs (see dedications).*

I'm proud of that story. I wouldn't change a single character or chapter, and I feel good that it can inspire others who have "less" and those who have "more" to do even greater things. This is the story I wanted to tell. This was the game, therefore, I chose to play. In 1992, I titled this book, *Change The Game*. If I were to choose a title today, 10 years later, I might call it *The Game of Freedom*. Now, don't get me wrong. I'm open to the fact that this perspective can change at any moment that I change my focus, my goals, my own personal vision of what constitutes my own success and effectiveness to others. But right now, that's my story, and I'm sticking to it! And that's the game I choose to play!

So, your key task, before you read another word, is to decide which game you are playing. Are you going to play the

- "Help-a-Few-Friends-get-Noticed" game
- "Create-the-next-Motown-and-be-an-Icon-of-Independent-Black-Music" game
- "Make-tons-of-loot-and-flip-it-into-bigger-ventures" game
- "Make-a-statement-to-the-world-that-I'm-the-ONE!'" game
- "Generate-wealth-for-my-family-and-future-generations" game
- "Create-an-empire-to-rival-the-magnates-of-our-time" game, or the
- "Create-a-lasting-tribute-to-Hip-Hop-that-stays-in-our-community-and-helps-thousands" game?

You can choose any game(s), and any name you wish. You can play an established game, or one of your own creation. You can play by established rules, or you can make them up as you go along. You can switch games at any time you choose. The only thing to remember is that every single one of your decisions has consequences. If you choose to play Game "A" in an industry where most people are playing Game "B", then that choice will have a unique set of consequences. It won't make playing Game "A" impossible, but it may present more challenges than most others would experience. Hopefully this is making sense to you.

The rules will be determined by the specific goal you wish to accomplish, the commitment you wish to uphold, and the statement or story you wish to tell. So, the next logical question is, "Ok, Walt, so what are the rules of the game I choose to play?" Funny you should ask, cause I've thought about that, too!

Fame, Fortune and the Rules of the Game.

Ask yourself, would you rather be rich, or famous? In my observations of people over the years, I've noticed that entrepreneurs are playing one, or both of following two types of games: Games of Ego or Games of Economics. You can think of them as the "Fame Game" or the "Fortune Game." Some people are driven by fame and notoriety, while others are driven by money. Some just want cash, while others are more driven by some inner ego need to be known, to make an impact, to create something lasting, to prove themselves to themselves, to the world, or on a subconscious level to a parent, in an effort to remove some such deeply imbedded emotional baggage. In either case, the decisions a Fame Seeker makes differ significantly from the decisions a Fortune Seeker will make. The rules that govern these two different types of games fall into one of three categories:

1. Ethics,
2. Emotion
3. Everything Goes.

In other words, whether you choose to play the Fortune Game or the Fame Game, your choices and decisions will probably be based on your personal sense of ethics, based on emotions, or based on rules that change from minute to minute dependent on what's needed at that moment, in other words, "Everything goes!" Let's take a look at a quick example based on a situation we can all imagine, and one which often causes much debate in entrepreneurial circles.

John, Jay and Judy are three individuals who've started record labels. They have all been presented with the opportunity for their artist to be the spokesperson for a Malt Liquor company. How will they respond to the offer? If they're each playing different games with their own personal rules, how will this affect their responses? Let's find out!

John is playing the Fame Game and is governed mostly by a sense of personal ethics. He declines the offer based on his belief that it's just wrong to support a company whose product is such a historical blight on his community. As he says, "I couldn't live with myself knowing my company is associated with and indirectly benefited from the destruction of our people."

Jay, meanwhile, is also playing the Fame Game, but his decisions stem mostly from his emotional commitment to putting food on his artists' tables. He's conflicted, as he shares some of John's sentiment on corporate exploitation, but he's concerned he might not have another chance to do right by his artists who are looking to him for their success. He accepts the offer. And, as he says in justifying his decision, "It's kinda true about them being a negative in our community, but that's where the money is, and this game is about money, right? I mean we can always do positive things with the money once we get it."

Judy, on the other hand, is playing the Fortune Game. In her mind, everything's fair in business and war! She believes that it's the very fact that liquor companies benefit from marketing predominantly to their neighborhood that justifies her taking their money. By doing so, her label is simply making sure the liquor company puts money back into the community from which it reaps benefit. She gladly accepts the endorsement offer. She says, "Look, they've been taking, and taking for so long, it's about time they gave something back!"

Admittedly, the example is a bit simplistic. Most everyone's game has some element of all three types of rules dictating their choices. (Pose that hypothetical question to your friends, family or business partners, and note the range of responses, reasons, and emotions that arise). One or two types of rules, however, tend to dominate in a person's perception. But it's a good example of how the rules of Ethics, Emotion and Everything Goes affect the decisions you'll be confronted with in running your record label.

Your success as the owner of a record label, faced with similar decisions every day will be a result of what game you believe you're playing, and the rules you are likely to follow. There's no right or wrong in the game, just choices and consequences. Some people play the Fame Game with absolutely no sense of "Ethical Rules" and appear to do quite well. Some people play the Fortune Game, playing by only the highest set of personal values, and "Ethical rules", and do extremely well too. Some people make all their decisions based on "Emotional Rules" and end up sabotaging their businesses. Some people make all their decisions based on "Everything Goes Rules" and end up losing their values. Now, here's some advice: Don't make the mistake of associating ethics with poverty. In other words, don't think that you HAVE to sacrifice your ethics in order to make money. Both types of games—Fame or Fortune--can be played ethically. Both can be equally profitable. Based on stories in the industry, the biggest mistake many people make is to assume that they have to give up their ethics in order to play the economic game. They thought that was the choice they had to make. Not true. As we said earlier, the industry doesn't necessarily have to be as "shady" as you've been led to believe.

On the other hand. In any journey you embark upon, there's the potential for corruption. Not just in running your record label, but in life in general, you need to be careful. But there's another reason to be very careful about the choices you make. As I've said, every choice has consequences. And some, are not always easy to bounce back from. In the process of "going for the gold", or the "gold record" you've got to be very sure you don't lose yourself.

Don't Lose Yourself

It's quite simple. Let's take this discussion out of the setting of the music industry for a moment, and speak simply about human nature. When you really distill things down to their essence, the only thing you really have here on the planet is what you think of yourself. Your self-image. Your sense of yourself. Who you know yourself to be. You must maintain that at all costs. That's the deciding factor, the "ball" if you will, in this game. In my opinion, if you compromise that—if you lose it, if you drop it--you've lost the game. How ultimately fulfilling will the riches be if, in acquiring it, you've lost the only thing that really matters. As it says in the Bible, "What profit a man if he gains the whole world, yet lose his own soul?"

Think about this. If asked to describe yourself, you can choose any number of descriptive characteristics. You can describe your physical form (I'm tall, short, fat, skinny, etc.). You can describe your mental skills (I'm smart, not good with numbers, etc.). You can describe your religious, political, psychological leanings (I'm Protestant, Republican, Vegetarian, Type A personality, etc.) You can choose from any number of personality traits, talents, (I'm honest, good with my hands, I can build things, etc.) And you can choose from your likes and dislikes, dos and don'ts wills and won'ts (I don't like cigarette smoke, I always say thank you, I never lie, curse, drink, smoke or do drugs). At the end of the day, in addition to the profits and sales, there's also another very important question you should ask. But, before I tell you what that question is, let me make a point.

A VERY IMPORTANT POINT:

At some point most entrepreneurs realize that what they're really striving for is not the money, but a feeling they associate with the money. Think about it. You're starting a record label not because there's something intrinsically soothing about sitting around your apartment with piles of hundred dollar bills covering the furniture. The money in and of itself doesn't emanate some healing force that cures unhappiness, cancer or makes you live forever. It does, however, afford you the means, in certain economies, to purchase the things you think you need in order to heal your body, suppress unhappiness, or feel like you could live forever. There's no doubt about that. With all of your earthly concerns taken care of, you believe you are then able to feel happy, healthy, youthful, energized, free, or what ever feeling you seek.

Yes, we're ultimately chasing a feeling. And the money is merely means to an end. If you aren't convinced of this yet, then just keep asking yourself why you're doing what you do, and eventually you'll arrive at a bottom line feeling that you're searching for. Here's an example:

Question: Why do you want to start a record label?
Answer: So I can make a lot of money.
Question: Why?
Answer: So I can buy my mom a house.
Question: Why?
Answer: So she can live in more luxury.
Question: Why?
Answer: Cause she deserves it.
Question: Why?
Answer: Cause she struggled to do right by her kids.
Question: Why?
Answer: Because I want to do right by her.
Question: Why?
Answer: Because it's the right thing to do.
Question: Why?
Answer: Because I want to feel like I'm giving back .

Bingo! So given enough self-inquiry, you'll find too that there's an image of yourself, and a feeling associated with it that you're striving to achieve. Whether it's freedom, success or happiness, there's a feeling that you seek that is the basis of this entire pursuit.

So, now. If feelings are the most important goal we seek, then it follows that how you "feel" about yourself during the journey is much more important than you may realize.

So, back to that important question I talked about before. If at the end of the day, in addition to "how much money did I make?", you ask yourself, "What did I have to do to get it?" you'll come up with an answer. Based on that answer, you should then ask yourself, "How do I feel about myself having done this or that to achieve my goals?" This is very important. You've got to ask that question every step of the way. After every triumph. After every setback. Every time you make a decision and take a step closer to your goals, you should ask and answer that question. And especially before you make any decision and choose a course of action in response to a challenge, setback or opportunity. Why? Because the answer may save your soul, and your life.

It's important to ask yourself that question *before* you justify your actions. It's always easy to justify our actions. That's what humans do best. Psychologists say that no one ever does a thing they know to be wrong, so before a person commits any act, they've had to justify it as necessary, forgivable, or acceptable in some way. And we all know that the jails are filled with innocent people.

It's important to ask yourself that question before you make your choices because every time you do something, it changes you. Every action you've ever done and will ever do in your life expands your image of yourself in some way. It either raises it and gives you a higher perception of yourself. Or it lowers it and results in a lowered perception of yourself. That all-important self-image, who you know yourself to be, is affected by all that you do. Once that starts to deteriorate, you'll do just about anything that's consistent with the new self-image. For example, once you speak in front of a large group for the first time, it becomes a part of your perception of yourself. You've instantly become someone who can speak in front of an audience, and that self-image is now yours to keep. Once you cut a $500,000 deal, you become someone capable of making that sort of deal, and you may even push yourself to outdo yourself.... Again, "million dollar deal maker" is now a part of who you are, and who you know yourself to be.

Similarly, however, the opposite is also true. Once you cheat, you now see yourself as a cheater, and cheating becomes a more acceptable option in future decisions. Once you lie to get your way, then you now know yourself to be a liar, and lying becomes a more acceptable option in future decisions.

Sure, money can do a lot of great things. But, if at the end of the day, you see yourself as less than who you were when you began, then you may end up being unhappier, and may think its because you don't yet have enough money. Then, you may then mistakenly look to acquiring MORE money as the solution. Let me repeat that: That lingering sense of unhappiness that often comes when we've achieved a great milestone and are either disappointed that "I didn't feel as happy as I thought I would", or perhaps in achieving the goal. Some of that stems from the lack of a solid spiritual grounding that seeks self definition in the material world, but some of that unhappiness stems from the fact that you may have had to compromise some image of yourself in order to achieve your goal. Your unhappiness is subtle grieving for the part of you that was lost.

That, my friend, is what I call "The Trap" that many seekers fall into.

I've rarely heard this point discussed. But the reason why wealth corrupts, and ultimately fails to fulfill us, is that we're often faced with choices as we pursue it and we don't always set and keep a code of ethics to adhere to that guides our decision-making. We end up spiraling downward into a lower and lower self-concept from which no amount of money can ever pull us free.

There is a subtle shift in self-perception that occurs each time you compromise your values. It results in a slight movement and a downward spiral towards a new self-perception. The frightening part of it all, is that it's sometimes so subtle, that you literally "wake up one day" and your world is completely alien to you. It then becomes a great challenge to lift yourself back up for the simple fact that you've spent the last few months, years or decades practicing, developing mastering and become acclimated to the very behaviors, perceptions, skills, talents, outlooks and self-concept that got you there. For ever action you took that brought you closer to where you now find yourself, you've had to convince yourself that it was OK, so now you have a warehouse full of justifications, rationalizations and reasons why, but no reasons why not.

"You'd think that with all his money, he wouldn't have to _______________"

How many times have you heard, thought or uttered those very sentiments about a particular celebrity? Too often, I imagine. And it seems to make sense to us that, "he or she could have anyone, do anything, go anywhere, etc., Why is he making those particular choices and destroying himself, his reputation and everything he's spent years building?"

Well, now you can finally understand that what Joe Celebrity thinks of himself today is the end result of choices he's made along the way that changed how he saw himself, and this self-perception is a reality that is neither improved nor remedied by having or acquiring more money. In fact, the saddest part about wealth is that it is the great enabler, allowing us to continue feeding our fantasies, indulging our indiscretions, satisfying our sickness, and delaying dealing with our dysfunctions. He's been busy building a self-concept, AND he's been building a pile of money.

If you have no guiding principles to determine what to do in a situation, then you have no means of determining good deals from bad deals. If you have no moral guidelines from which to draw, then you have no means of choosing people who will be able to keep those principles in tact as you build your business. The result is that you may surround yourself with people and circumstances that are building one reality while you're building another. You may find yourself in situations not of your direct choosing, but yours by default based on the people with whom you surround yourself. You may end up

So how do you avoid "The Trap?'
ANSWER:
Define who you are.
Define who you want to be.
Define who you wish to be seen as and known for.
Write the story you want to tell. Do it NOW, before the game begins.

Now you know. The pursuit of money doesn't make you noble by default. It's simply a pursuit. How you define yourself from day to day as you pursue it, is what you'll become and what you'll be when you get the money you seek. Again, your sense of who you are is what dictates what you'll do in a given situation, and eventually who you become. One compromise invariably leads to another and another, and changes the course and destination of your journey. Of course, if you're of the mindset that , as Bob Marley said in Running Away, "some people think life is a dream, so they make matters worse," then you won't feel any particular need to act in any socially redeeming, or noble way. You'll define yourself in any way that suits you at the moment. On the other hand, if you cultivate a definition of yourself consistently from day one, and act according to that definition when faced with decisions. You'll arrive at the destination you seek with your sense of self intact.

I believe that I've done just that. I always considered my label, and any company I start as an extension of who I am. So, I have my own set of guidelines for myself and my company. Of course, you're free to set your own. I can only tell you what works for me. In my world,

- Everyone I deal with should benefit from our interaction.
- I'm not such a slave to money that I can't walk away from a deal I feel in my gut is bad
- My company will be perceived as honorable.
- I never take advantage of anyone.
- I never speak badly about anyone.
- I will not endorse these [products or companies].
- I will not compromise my values.
- I will not release music that compromises those values
- I don't drink or smoke or do drugs
- I always play fairly with others.

If you want to play the Big Business Game by ethical rules, find role models who do just that. Define who you wish to be. Set the rules. Stick to them. Arrive in tact.

Who you will need to become:

"One T'ousand Job!"

Many of the aspiring, current and future record label executives to whom this manual is targeted, will be living two or more lives for some time while their new company grows. Many will be holding down a day job, or as it is sometimes called, a "suit and tie", while taking care of their "dream job" pursuing their passion during lunch hours, on weekends and on days off.   It is a fact of the industry, that many of the individuals with whom you will be dealing will also be in the same situation. A committed few get to make the final leap into independence after months or years of maintaining this dual lifestyle. Until things fall into place, however, all the responsibility and the tasks which come with it will be yours. These tasks may be unpleasant, but they have to be done. They should be put in place now, while the company is still young and manageable. As a one-man or one-woman record company executive, you should be prepared at the beginning to wear many different hats. Just like the Headleys of the old TV show "In Living Color", you may find yourself holding down as many as "One T 'ousand Job!" to keep your company running. Some of the jobs you'll have to add to your "resume" are:

Visionary	Tax specialist
CEO (Chief Executive Officer)	Graphic Designer
COO (Chief Operating Officer)	Event Promoter
Manager	Salesperson
Team Captain	Legal Representative
Motivator	Secretary
A & R Rep (Artist & Repertoire= talent scout)	Mailroom Clerk
Accountant	Inventory/stock person

[See Record Label Org Chart for the structure of your label, as well as job descriptions]

Make no mistake about it. These roles are every bit as important as the CEO, A&R Rep, as well as the artist responsibilities.   In determining how you will fill these positions, take stock of your strengths and weaknesses, and those of any partners you may have. You must prepare yourself for the reality of what lies ahead if you are to keep the business running efficiently and growing smoothly. The truth is, starting your company will be the easy part. Keeping it going will require long days and even longer nights. It will mean sacrifice, hard work and a level of commitment you might never have given to anything else before. It will mean developing and becoming confident in all the skills necessary to manage, communicate, analyze, make sound decisions, and set goals for your business. It will mean learning how to be a self-starter, taking risks, being creative, being calm amidst chaos, and taking responsibility for your actions and decisions.

As your company grows, you'll also need to practice the ability to train others and delegate tasks in order to free yourself from shouldering all the responsibilities and minute details of keeping a multi-million dollar enterprise operating. You wouldn't want to be the only one who knows how to run the mailroom when your company is making millions and being traded on the stock market.

If you are going into business (any business) with someone else, it's best to be realistic about what each of you is bringing into the venture. There's a reason why an artist is an artist, and why a manager is a manager. It takes different personality types, talents, skills and "brains" to succeed at each job. Accept this fact, and use it to your advantage. Business decisions need to be made with a business mind (known as the left brain). Creative decisions need to be made with a creative mind (right brain). People on the business side usually justify their decisions with words like "expense", "feasibility", "revenue", "evidence", and "profit". Those on the creative side usually find themselves standing behind decisions with words like "feel", "sound", and "mood". Both sides should respect the reality of the other and practice flexibility by reaching compromise. If one side always makes the decisions, you may find yourself bailing out of business the minute a venture doesn't turn a profit, or putting out music which only an artist can understand—an equally disastrous reality.

If you are the artist looking to launch your own label, or if you are a non-artist going into this with an artist, there are a few things you should keep in mind. It's the rare artist who can function alone and effectively as business person without some conflict with their creative side. It's not impossible, and there are a few who do it. However, the very qualities that make one the most sought after writer, producer or musician, in town may spell difficulties when applied to running a business. Running a record label, like any venture requires a balance of opinions, perspectives and talents that draw heavily on the left brain. It often requires a point of view and appreciation of the other less creative aspects of the business that the artist may not be as skilled in.

If nothing else, the non-creative partner can offer objective critique of the artist's work. The non-creative may excel within the same sort of structured lifestyle, adherence to rules, salesmanship, and diplomacy which characterizes many businesses and which many people with that creative spark tend to avoid. If at all possible, the roles each individual will play should be clearly defined IN ADVANCE with as little ambiguity or overlap as possible. In other words, decide on the roles, then let the artist do what she does best, and let the manager/label owner do likewise.

Left Brain	**Right Brain**
Business	Creative
Structured	Artistic
Logical	Random
Sequential	Intuitive
Rational	Holistic
Analytical	Synthesizing
Objective	Subjective
Looks at parts	Looks at wholes
Thinks in words	Thinks in pictures
Reality	Fantasy

According to scientific studies, it's been revealed that different hemispheres of the brain control different modes of thinking. the chart above, we see that artistic, creative people (artists), tend to be "right brain" thinkers. While more logical, rational thinkers (business people), tend to be "left brain" thinkers. Individuals who appear to function equally adept at using both sides are called "whole brain" thinkers. Of course, whole brain thinkers are rare, as most of us tend to prefer and excel in one or the other modes of thinking.

Your key to using this information in succeeding with your record label is in understanding that there's no "right" or "wrong" when it comes to modes of thinking, and behavior. A person simply is one way or the other, and the world as well as your label needs both types of thinkers in order to function optimally. Once both types of thinkers understand this about each other, it will breed tolerance, and do away with the expectation that one way is superior and another inferior.

On the other hand, knowing that a balance of the two modes of thinking is key to success will encourage both types to work on improving use of the side of the brain they are less used to functioning in.

What You Should Know About People

Remember: No one does anything in life without personal gain.

That isn't as selfish a statement as it sounds. It means simply that everyone who you run into in life has something that they are pursuing with as much dedication as you are.   In business, it means that everyone wants and needs something from the next guy. If you are a DJ, you want slammin' music before anyone else. If you are a distributor, you want music that will sell. If you are a magazine editor, you want stories that people want to read about, as well as advertisers. The more you know about what motivates the individuals with whom you do business, the more likely it is to create win-win situations in all your dealings.

In addition, there's also a certain personal fulfillment that everyone searches for. Different people are driven by different desires, but behavioral psychologists have identified several basic needs that motivate the majority of the people on the planet: The desire to be in control; the desire to be safe; the desire to be comfortable are just a few. People also want affection, beauty, comfort, companionship, convenience, ego satisfaction, enjoyment, entertainment, friends, good health, happiness, knowledge, love, money, peace of mind, pleasure, praise, recognition, security, self-actualization, self-confidence, self-esteem, self-improvement and spiritual well-being.

Keep this in mind when you create your products for sale, when you develop your marketing materials—brochures, fliers, etc.—and especially when you recruit anyone to "join" your company. Think to yourself, "What is this person getting out of being part of my dream?" If you can't find the answer, find a tactful but direct way to find out My technique was simply to say something like this: "I want us to work together, but first I want to make sure that we both get what we want from this. What are your goals? What does success look like for you? My goal is to have my own record company. What's yours?" At this point you have to listen carefully to what the other person says.   Your goal here is to make sure the people you're dealing with are motivated by more than just money. They should have their own dreams of success that don't necessarily include or require your direct participation. You should be just one avenue of success for them, not the only one.

Things to look out for: If the other person doesn't seem to have a clear idea of what they want, it might be cause for concern. While it could indicate a willingness to be part of a bigger dream, and an openness to new ideas, it could also mean he or she is simply floating from one opportunity to another, bailing out when the going gets tough, or when something better comes along. Also, if the other person you're considering wants exactly the same thing you want, it could lead to a few ego challenges down the road. Two people who've always wanted "to be President of a record label" are asking for trouble by working together if their roles aren't clear in their individual minds.   While I always prefer to work with people who want to be their own boss, it's important that their area of interest and expertise complements and doesn't conflict with my own. One of the most profitable "partnerships" I was involved in was with Lance Cain, the video producer who did our first three videos. My label was the first he'd worked with, and wanted to use the assignment to start his own reel (that's video talk for what amounts to a video resume). He wasn't looking to me to put him on my payroll as the official company video producer. He had his own dreams that he was pursuing, and use our collaboration as a starting point. This producer worked long hours, weekends, and generally was there whenever I needed him.   The sort of commitment that he had didn't come from him counting on MY success, it definitely didn't come from what I was paying him, it was the commitment of a man who had set and was pursuing his own goals. That's the sort of partner, intern, volunteer, employee that you want!

Getting Information And Solving Business "Challenges"

Many new businesses falter for a number of reasons: lack of capital, poor planning, and poor record keeping. For a record company, you can add to the list: ineffective legal counsel, poor artist management, bad promotion, and bad music. For many new business owners, it simply boils down to a lack of the correct information to deal effectively with the challenges facing the business. It is my belief that the solutions to most challenges to business success fall into two categories: financial and informational. However, many business owners tend to believe that most of the solutions they require are financial rather than informational. In other words, they believe that 90% of what holds them back has to do with not having enough money. Many of you who have purchased this manual, for example, may have believed that there was no way you could do an effective job of promoting your record without tens of thousands of dollars to pay promotion companies. Now, while it does take some money to do things right in many cases, with the information you now have, you are better equipped to make the decision as to how to promote, and now have the means to launch a formidable self-promotion campaign tailored to your own needs and bank account. Hence, with the right information, you've changed a challenge that seemed 90% financial into one which may now be a bit more manageable.

Let's take a look at three commonly cited reasons for record label failure, and see how simply having better information might actually be able to remedy them. For example, "lack of capital" may be remedied by knowing 1) that venture capitalists exist who might be willing to invest in a new company, and 2) where they are, and how to get to them. "Poor planning" may be remedied by knowing that industry organizations exist which provide advice and support to new companies. For example, there is even an association of retired business persons who volunteer to provide consultation for new business owners. "Ineffective (or non-existent) legal counsel" dilemma can be reversed if you know, for example that many states have a Volunteer Lawyers for the Arts organization which provides free legal counsel to individuals in the performing arts. It is rarely a lack of enthusiasm and drive which threatens an entrepreneur's success.   The biggest challenge is often channeling that enthusiasm and drive into getting the information to solve the challenges.

Platinum Update: Getting Information in the Information Age

Virtually everything that has ever been thought of or done has been written down. Once it's been written down, it can be found and read by practically anyone else. Even the documents and correspondence within the U.S. government are available to the public by way of the Freedom of Information Act. Lack of information should never be an excuse for lack of action. It doesn't matter if you don't have an extensive personal library, access to a public one, a set of encyclopedias, a dictionary, a thesaurus or even a telephone directory. All you need is a telephone (every home or street corner should have one), a voice, and the ability to ask a question.

When I first wrote the preceding section, the Internet did not exist. Imagine that! Actually, it did exist, but it wasn't the ubiquitous tool it is today having gained widespread popularity in the mid to late 90's. Today, just about anything you want, from phone numbers, social security numbers, credit histories, email records, sample contracts, artist CDs, books in electronic format and contact information can be obtained by doing searches on the internet. Search engines, industry websites, government databases all exist in some form, and are accessible free or at charge for you to browse and collect the information you need. But as vast a repository of information as the internet is, there is still some information that remains accessible only to those individuals who are willing to use one of the greatest inventions that has remained virtually unchanged since its invention.

The Cold Call: Phone Power!

The telephone is one of humankind's greatest inventions. There really is no way to say that without sounding corny, but it's true. (The phone, mail service, and now the fax machine have put the potential for real power at practically everyone's fingertips.) There is virtually no limit to the influence, reach, and access one has through the telephone. Just pay the bill every month and you'll be set!

The value of the telephone is something many people tend to overlook and take for granted.   Your telephone is one of the most reliable avenues to get information and answers to practically any question. Many people are frightened into passivity at the thought of making "cold calls" for information. However, once you master this simple concept, and add it to your repertoire of information-gathering techniques, you'll achieve mastery of your environment and of situations to a degree that might astound you. The "cold call" is not a new concept. Salespeople use the same term to describe their method of soliciting sales over the phone. The cold call technique for getting information is simple:

1. Think and plan for a minute.
2. Pick up the phone.
3. Dial a number.
4. Ask a question.

Actually, a cold call isn't really 100% "cold", or out of the blue. You should usually spend a little time planning beforehand so that you will have an idea of where best to start looking for the information you want. Remember, for every piece of information that exists, there is usually a chain of people or companies with access to it. Your job is to find the person or company in that chain most likely to let you in on it as well. Many business operators, receptionists and employees are used to getting calls for information, so there's no need to be shy. If you call another company looking for some specific information known only to a few, expect that you'll be transferred around a few times before you find that person who might either tell you what you need to know, or tell you where you might be able to find it. However, you need not limit your cold calls to businesses. Schools, churches, anyplace that can receive your call might have someone at the other end with an answer to your question.   My cold calls have been as outrageous as calling random names in out-of-state phonebooks to ask about radio stations in their communities.

For calls to businesses: call, explain what you're looking for, and suggest a department (make something up) which might handle that kind of information. Let's say, for example, you're trying to find out which are the best pressing plants around. You figure that whichever plants the major labels use must be good, so you phone Big Time Records. Your approach: "Hello, I'm trying to get some information on the different pressing plants that your company uses to press your records, would you be able to help me? or, is there a production department that handles that?   The possibilities are that the person on the other line says "yes", "no" or "I don't know". If they say yes, you're set. If they say "no", or "I don't know", ask politely if they might know of someone else who might be able to help you. No call is or should ever be wasted. There's a good chance you'll come away with a bit more information than when you started.   You might want to try my patented "Hi, I'm doing some research for a report/school paper/my company, and I wanted to know...." approach. Said with the right amount of confidence, sincerity, and pleasantry, this approach is difficult for most business people to pass up. (Just in case, make sure you have a plausible response for any inquiries they may make as to the nature of the report, school, or company!) Books have been written teaching "cold call" techniques to maximize sales. Perfect your own technique to maximize information gathering.

If you literally have no idea where to start in your search for information, ask the operator. He or she does this sort of thing for a living. You can have access (24 hours a day) to their years of experience tracking down information for free (from pay phones "411" and "0" are free!) Also, if you're trying to get in touch with a company and all you have is a name, but no address, phone the "800" operator. If the company has an "800" number, and many bigger companies do, even though they may not make it known to the general public, you'll be able to track them down.

A Quick Story: "Once Upon A Time, During A Search For Information..."

The following anecdote from personal experience shows a bit of what I went through to get hold of some needed information. The entire process took about a week and about 2 dozen calls.

Have ever gone into a stationery or office supply store and seen those thick catalogs on the counters which offer office supplies, furniture and cabinets? Well, I once had an idea for a product that I thought would be perfectly marketed to the public in these catalogs. My goal, therefore, was to get my product featured in these catalogs that would sit on the shelves of every stationery store in the country. I figured that I needed to get in touch with whoever was actually publishing those catalogs to see about getting my product included in its pages. I did some research and noticed that literally every store I visited had one of these catalogs, and that many looked exactly alike except for the name of the particular local store custom printed on the front in a white space which seemed obviously pre-designed made for that purpose. (Are you with me?)

I was clueless about how the office supply industry worked, at the time, but this much I was able to figure out: Mrs. Smith's Corner Stationery store must just be an agent for a bigger company. She apparently took the orders, placed them with the catalog supplier, and got her cut in return for providing the bigger company with customers. So, I got a hold of one of those catalogs. Checked the fine print, scanned the spine, skimmed inside, front, back and middle, and couldn't find any other name, address, or number that might lead me to who that major supplier was. Usually, a (P) 1991, or copyright notice © Some Company, Inc. would be discretely located somewhere on the catalog. It seemed, that the publisher's anonymity was intentional.

Never one to give up so easily, I "cold-called" several local stationery stores and asked for what I wanted. I made the mistake of asking for the name of the company whom they dealt with via the catalog. Many of the clerks I spoke to didn't know where the catalogs came from either (some of those stores were agents for still larger agents, and as a result were just as clueless as I was). Further, the occasional manager I spoke to, was always reluctant to tell me anything, insisting instead that his store was indeed where the buck stopped and that anything I needed to order I could get through them. I realized later that his fear was that I would threaten his income by ordering directly from his main supplier. (I learned a lesson from that approach.)

I asked around at my own 9-to-5 job, and got some seemingly better known names from the clerks and secretaries who ordered supplies. They showed me the catalogs they used. The catalogs were getting bigger, but that telltale white space was still there identifying the companies as agents. I phoned these companies and confirmed that although they were evidently more established, they were still merely agents, and (as I found out) unwilling to part with any information.

Ultimately, I mentioned to a friend what I was interested in accomplishing. She worked at a major utility company, and also just happened to be the person in her department responsible for ordering huge amounts of supplies for the company. I asked who she placed the orders with. She mentioned the names of three companies and added that there were only about 5 or so in the whole country who actually put the catalogs together. Just like that I was on my way! I tracked down the numbers through the "800" operator.

Interestingly, just as an experiment, I phoned an individual at one of the same middleman companies I had tried earlier, who had been a bit cold in responding to me. This time I told him that I was trying to get in touch with the five or so of the top office-products suppliers. I told him I had already contacted "A" and "B" and "C" and wondered if he knew of the others. Right on cue (forgetting that I had asked him virtually the same question several days earlier) he rattled off the name of the other two names I was missing. I thanked him for being such a nice guy and for taking time out to help me. Having access to some of the same information he had, magically put me on par with him, removed some of the threat, and loosened up the channels of communication. Often, the rules of interaction change when a business owner knows he is dealing with another business. Be careful, however. As I learned, mentioning my business status at the wrong time just as easily put an unbreakable lock on the information I was seeking.

So the point of this anecdote is: there's always someone, somewhere who will have the answers to your questions; and someone, somewhere who will be willing to give it to you. Sometimes all you have to do is ask. Remember, there's nothing known by someone else, that you can't gain.

P.S. The name of the major office supply company is Boise Cascade, now known as Office Max.

How to Find Anything on the Internet: The only tip you'll ever need

Being known as an information guru has it's pluses and minuses. A plus is that I do, in fact, have a very helpful knack for being able to locate any sort of information I desire. A minus, is that everyone else knows this about me, too!

Recently a friend of a friend—an actress--called to ask for information on learning how to buy the rights to a book she'd recently read and enjoyed. She said she looked online and couldn't find anything, and wondered if I'd be able to help her. Well, the truth is, I knew without even knowing what she was looking for, that I would be able to help her thanks to the wondrous power of the Internet!

I rank the Internet as probably THE greatest tool developed in the past 100 years. Especially as one who sells information, it's one of my most used tools. I research my promotion lists, write books, create products, support my consulting, find rhymes, access dictionaries, thesauri, etc. all from my home computer. I've always been good at tracking down information (see cold calling techniques), but the Internet just took my abilities to a whole different level. In fact, I sometimes feel guilty selling information that I know is equally accessible to anyone willing to invest the time in the search. (But, of course, that's exactly the value that I offer through my company's products and services: the time-saving benefit of you not having to invest the time yourself, but simply paying me for the results of me having already done it.)

If I felt empowered before, then I'm pretty close to omnipotent now, since the arrival of the Internet. And I'm not even an expert! There are people who search for information every day, (researches, private investigators, etc.) who could write books, and many have, showing how quite literally every piece of information that exists on a person, for example, can be tracked down with a few simple keystrokes on a keyboard while connected to the World Wide Web.

But just for your garden variety searches that can save you a few hours, and save a trip to the library, this one tip will help you cut through the millions

The (unfair) Writer's Advantage

Here's the one tip that I discovered that's responsible for the confidence I have that I can find just about anything I'm looking for online. It has to do with how search engines retrieve the information contained on the pages that are archived in their database.

Many people may make the mistake of treating the search engine like a person and ask a question "How do I find information on buying the movie rights" However, search engines are not like people, and they use a technology more similar to the "find" feature on your computer that allows you to search for files "containing a specific string of text" (a string is simply a sequence of words)

So, the single most important question to ask yourself when doing a search is "How would the information I'm looking for appear in an article or webpage that's already been written?"

As a writer, and someone who's read a fair amount of books, I have a natural feel for how information is presented in written form. In other words, as a writer, I know how other writers write. So, in launching my search for the movie rights information, I reasoned that the information I'd want would probably appear as full-length article on the subject, or as an excerpt from a "how to" article, and because I'm a writer, I know a typical writer's line might read something like

"...for anyone wishing to **buy the movie rights** to..."
"...New Line Cinematics **purchased the film rights** to...."   ← *When using a search Engine*
"...Johnson **sold the movie rights** to his 1995 bestseller..."

Now, if you enter the term "sold the movie rights" (including the quotes) into a search engine form, what you'll get are all the pages in their database that have that exact wording (i.e. as quoted) in the text. So whether it's a "how to" article, a book excerpt, an interview with an author, the engine actually scans the text of every webpage archived and finds all the pages that include those words in that order.

Pretty simple, isn't it. Simple, but on one hand using it requires developing skills you may never have thought important. For most people, reading is a process of discovery. The writer's thoughts get revealed to them, the reader, step by step, and what happens from one sentence to the next is not often anticipated, so it comes as a surprise. And, if you're like most people, you've never thought about how a writer's thoughts get strung together, and what words and sentence structure the writer is likely to use. In order to search more effectively, however, you must become as a writer.

Whenever you launch a search for information, ask yourself, "If I were already in possession of and reading the sort of article or book excerpt that I'm searching for, how would it flow? What standard words and phrases might appear in such an article?" Is it a "newsy" tone? If someone were reporting or explaining details of the subject in question, how might it be approached by a writer

But, trust me, a subtle point overlooked by the masses who search for information online. Now it's yours. But use it wisely, dear student. This sort of power used for the wrong purposes can prove disastrous!

So, boys and girls, what have we learned today that we can apply to running our record label? Answer:

The answer to any question you ask, the completion of any project, the agreement with any distributor, the achievement of any sales goal you set, every chart position, every pressing and distribution deal, every artist signed, every single that goes "gold", as well as every other major and minor victory involved in running your label, presents itself as a challenge. The solutions come as the result of a question asked, information received and the resulting wisdom applied.

Why this may be the most important skill of all

Think about it. As described so eloquently in Entrepreneurophobia, inaction is all about fear. Fear is all about not knowing. We fear the things we don't know and what we don't understand. Once you remove the "not knowing", then you act with confidence. Many of the reasons business in general--and record labels specifically--fail to prosper has to do with failing to act, or acting incorrectly. Passivity, procrastination and poor choices, all have fear, confusion and doubt as their root causes, some fear that causes us not to act, or to act ineffectively. When you can remove the doubt of a situation, you tend to act more decisively and with confidence. You remove doubt by having knowledge that you're sure of. That knowledge comes from information.

Therefore, your ability to ask for, listen to, seek out and apply information is the single greatest skill set you can develop. Start training to develop your own techniques for rising to life's challenges and getting information. Decide what percentage of the challenge is financial and what percentage is informational. Trust me, every challenge can be solved without ever having to be defeated by the lack of your own money. Look for ways to change the Information/Finance ratio of the challenge. Keep in mind that many challenges aren't as financially based as they may seem, and that any information that isn't readily available from your bookstore or library can still be yours if you know how to get it. There shouldn't be any information that you feel is necessary for your success that you can't track down given the right combination of Persistence, thinking quickly on your feet, and preparation…

It's the "not knowing" that gets you!"

How you become great and build a great record label

With the ability to seek and find information at our disposal, you're now ready for greatness! So, the right question is: how do you become great? How do you duplicate the success of a Russell Simmons, or a Master P? How do you grow your enterprise to become a fixture on the Forbes 400 list of the wealthiest individuals? How do you diversify and launch businesses inside and outside the music industry that create wealth for you and your family, and community? The answer might surprise you. You might think it involves having the right Rolodex® of contact people, partners and friends that Russell or Percy do. You might think it involves luck. You might think that it requires having a charming personality, good looks and an education. And while all these things are indeed helpful and important, they are actually the results of something much more basic. They, and your greatness are the result of an attitude that you cultivate, beliefs that you commit to and habits that you develop. In other words, your greatness is a result of the way that you think.

This new way of thinking is compiled into something I've called New Thought Practices. My book, *Turn Your Passion Into Profit* explores the new thoughts in greater detail, so I won't repeat them here. Find new ways of being, new ways of doing, and you will experience new ways of having.

Remember, you are where you are right now and have what you have right now as a result of all the thoughts you've had up until this point. In other words, the way you think is what got you here. So, if "here" is not exactly where you'd like to be, and if "there" is more appealing, then the thing that must first change is your way of thinking. It's that simple.

So, how do you change the way you think? You read, listen to and practice the ways of thinking that have been shown to produce the results you desire.

And, where can you find those proven ways? Well, the nice thing about life in this information-rich society is that the knowledge to be, do and have anything you desire, exists in many different formats for you to acquire. You can be coached by a mentor. You can listen to audio programs, read books, take workshops and courses, or simply befriend those who would teach you.

You become great by first expecting greatness of yourself. You become great by being a student of the game. You become great by asking the questions a student should ask. You become great by questioning the answers that you receive. You become great by accepting the answers of only those who have shown they know the correct answers. You become great by modeling yourself after those who provided those answers.

You become great by showing others the way to greatness. You become great by becoming in thought and deed like those who have achieved greatness. You become great by following the example of those who've done it. Not those who want to do it. Not those who say they can do it. But those who've actually done it, and can show proof. In other words, as a mentor of mine is fond of saying, "Don't take real estate advice from your Uncle Larry who lives in a trailer park. This is important because more than likely, these new thoughts won't come from those in your immediate circles. If the people you associated with were able to think in ways that created wealth and prosperity of the degree that you desire, then they'd already be wealthy and prosperous. It most likely won't come from your parents and relatives, again for the same reason. Though they may have the wisdom that comes from observation, and the desire to help you, they don't have the road map that comes from making the journey. And, what you need is a roadmap.

The roadmap is what will get you the right Rolodex® , change your luck, attract the education you need, and hey, you never know, it might even make you more attractive! Here is your roadmap to success in three easy directions.
1. Commit to personal growth
2. Ask the right questions
3. Keep moving forward.

Let's take a closer look at each phase of your journey.

"How to Become Great" Secret #1: Commit to Personal Growth

What is personal growth? The simplest practical description I can come up with for personal growth without writing a whole new book is that personal growth is based on the following beliefs.

1. Thoughts create reality
2. Be, Do, Have is the order of creation
3. You grow by conquering fears

First and foremost, committing to personal growth means understanding that your situation and success in life is a direct function of the thoughts you keep. Your thoughts are a function of your mental, emotional and physical state. Therefore, the only way to be successful is to improve, or "grow" mentally, emotionally, and physically as a person, which will, in turn, improve the nature and potency of your thoughts, which optimizes the results of your decisions, choices and actions. It means developing your Wow! Factor, that unique combination of thoughts, skills, talents, experience that sets you apart from everyone else on the planet. It means understanding that the only thing you have complete control over in life are your reactions, and that your thoughts about reality determine the reactions you choose.

It means knowing the order of creation is: 1. "BE". Then 2. "DO". And finally, 3. "HAVE". In other words to achieve anything in life, you must FIRST become in thought, word and deed, the very person you aspire to be. Most people believe that if they *have* more money, they would be able to *do* certain things and they would then *be* happy. They've put having, before doing before being. The truth, however, is that you must first assume a "being-ness", in order to accomplish a "doing-ness" in the direction of "having-ness". (That's more stuff from my Scientology exposure.) In this example, therefore, our happiness is a state of being that we must create for ourselves first. We must then act and do the things we would do were money in our possession, in order to bring it into our possession. As spiritual author, Neville says, that just like on any road that you travel in the physical world, "signs precede, they do not follow." In other words, the "signs" that show you're on the road to wealth and happiness (i.e. the wealth walk, talk and mindset) must precede the reality.

[*For a full exploration of how thinking differently is the key to success, read "And Things Will Never Be the Same Again" the second chapter of Turn Your Passion Into Profit*]

Committing to personal growth also means accepting that life is about the never ending process of the conquest of each successive fear. (What the heck does *that* mean??) It means moving through life with the understanding that every milestone you will ever achieve in this journey lies waiting for you beyond the conquest of a specific fear. A fear is nothing but a perceived boundary to your potential. So removing that boundary expands your comfort zone and sphere of influence, and creates a new, bigger self-concept which now naturally includes more possibilities than it did before

Committing to personal growth also means believing some principles, knowing some specific concepts, following some specific advice, and developing some specific habits s Here are some tips, excerpted from my Web-Renown article "Entrepreneurophobia: Conquering the Fear" to help your commitment.

TIP 1: Start small:

Building up the courage to tackle your fears takes practice. Start with the easier challenges and work your way up to the bigger issues.

TIP 2: Do daily affirmations:

An affirmation is a statement of a desired outcome stated in the present tense. "I am a successful entrepreneur." "My company is making enough money to support me." These are examples of effective affirmations that you can write on 3"X5" index cards and read them to yourself in the mornings and in the evenings. What you'll be doing is reprogramming your mind to think in terms of success!

Decide that you'll focus on the times you acted and got good results, rather than the times things didn't quite work the way you planned. In other words of mine:

Live in the thoughts of your most treasured experience
not in the pain of your last
See from the heights of your loftiest dream
not from the depths of your past

Judge and be judged from your best creation
not from what you didn't do
Your power in life comes from which thoughts you keep
and which you let pass on through

Which ones to keep
Walt's Friday Inspiration #23

As you go through life, it's normal that your energy level will fluctuate. Several good books exist which can help you keep the motivation high. They can usually be found in the self-help or psychology sections of your local bookstore. Check the chapter Resource page for a list of books, including *The Psychology of Achievement* by Brian Tracy, *Unlimited Power* by Tony Robbins, *Live Your Dreams*, by Les Brown, *The Master Key to Riches* and *Think and Grow Rich* both by Napoleon Hill.

Misery (and failure) loves company! Stay away from negative thinkers and align yourself with people who are on their way to or are already where you want to be! The people you keep in your circles have a tremendous effect on who you will become. Hang out with people who challenge you. Seek out people whose ideas help you to think differently, and whose lives give you something to aspire towards. It's well known that:

The people who affect us most
are those who make us think
For growth comes from the gusts of thought
that push us to the brink

In thought is where we find ourselves
if lost or on a quest
from thought is where the visions come
that make us act our best

Think long and hard on who you are
and what you've come to be
and trace it back I'm sure you will
to one who helped you see

they made you think in different terms
life's tide through them did shift
they changed your thoughts of who you were
direction was their gift

These people were your signposts
offering what can't be bought
Life's turning points are people
who change the level of your thoughts!

Turning Points
Walt's Friday Inspiration #104
© Walt Goodridge

Your "gut", what scholars refer to as intuition, is an important tool for success. Your feelings of fear are gut messages that you need to recognize. They indicate that there is a lesson to be learned; new ground to be covered; a challenge to be met. Seek out those feelings and move in their direction.

Eventually, with enough practice, your gut will send you messages not just of situations to avoid, but of the dreams you wish to pursue. For just beyond the feelings of fear are equally powerful feelings of excitement that indicate when your dreams are about to come true.

How to Become Great Secret #2: Ask the Right Questions

Recently, a friend and I were standing on the Howard University Washington D.C. campus discussing business, life, people and the universal subconscious mind. (no, really!) It was during the Howard homecoming weekend and there were hundreds of people from all over the country who had convened there for fun, socializing, food and more.

A group of young people came up to us and a young man asked, "Do you go to school here?" I answered no, and my friend made a comment that there were probably more people on the campus at that moment who didn't attend Howard, than there were who did. As we shared a chuckle, the young man, who didn't quite know where to take it from there, looked puzzled. I then asked, "What are you looking for?" To which he replied, "The BlackBurn Center. Well, it turns out both my friend and I did in fact know where the BlackBurn Center was. We pointed it out to him and he and his group thanked us and went their way.

As they departed, I commented to my friend what had happened was an example of asking the wrong question. Our young friend started his quest for directions by asking a question based on a faulty assumption. He assumed that in order for us to know where the BlackBurn Center was located, that we had to be students at the university. Having asked the wrong question, he was given an answer that didn't really serve his needs, and which took him in an entirely undesired direction.

Had we not asked him what he wanted, he may have continued in search of direction always asking the wrong question. Had he asked a more direct, more pointed, simpler question, (i.e. "Excuse me, where's the BlackBurn Center?") he would have been much better served.

The Moral: In every aspect of life, particularly in discovering your passion and creating a business around it, it is very important to ask the right questions.

In fact, I believe the question is often more important than the answer! Here's why:

The question is what sets things in motion. It's in the search for the answer that you find the success you seek. Everyone's answer will be different.

Let me give you an example. Let's say two labels each have an artist with potential that they want to make famous and successful. "Label A" is based in New York, while "Label B" is in Los Angeles. Let's suppose that the first question each label owner asks is, "Who do I know who's already in the music industry?"—a very important "right question." The New York label's artist has a brother who now lives in Texas and who used to do a radio show at Columbia University's radio station in NY. Turns out his circle of friends and associates he made while in radio in New York includes the current program manager for a New York station that plays Hip Hop. The artist's brother calls up his old friend, and the relationship leads to a guest spot on an afternoon show, which leads to other exposure, etc. You get the picture.

Meanwhile, in California, Label B's owner, doesn't know anybody directly, but has the confidence in his own strength of character and personality, that he can charm anyone he wants to. So, he starts hanging out at the spots frequented by label executives and A&R people. He strikes up conversations. He buys people drinks. He invites them to listening parties. He becomes a regular in their lives and daily routines, and eventually wins friends and influences people in high places. Can you see where this is heading?

So, the point I'm making is that both these labels asked the same question, but came up with different answers, that got them both heading in the same direction towards the same goal. The chain of contacts, the sequence of events, the people involved are going to be different for you and for your neighbor down the street. The person, the relationship or circumstance that plays the pivotal role in their answer can and often is quite different from one label to the next. Even if your boy next door is asking the same question, his answer may be different than yours simply because of different relationships, different experiences, different expectations, different strengths, weaknesses, etc. Who knows, his answer may include YOU, his next door neighbor, as the key player!

The Right Question

Your life is the answer to a question
you'll find responding is not the real task
No, the trick to living life with purpose you see
is knowing which question to ask

Some ask "Why me?" in frustration
and respond with a life filled with pain
Some ask "What's next?" with elation
and on happiness they seem to make gain

"What's in it for me?" others query
and seem forever on a self-centered quest
"What more can I be?" a small few wonder
and show others their personal best

"What's wrong with the world? Oh, how tragic!"
Some see with eyes of woe and despair
"What's wrong with the world? Let me fix it!"
And those strive always to heal and repair

All in all it's a question of answers
that determines if you win or you lose
For when life is an answer to a question
your life depends on which question you choose...

In this game, the right questions usually begin with "How…" Most people who are playing, choose to play the victim game and begin their questions with "Why…" as in "Why does this happen to me?" Why can't I get a record deal?" Why won't they help me?" Success stories, on the other hand, begin their questions with "How.." as in "How can we get this done despite the obstacles?" "How can I create the product, elicit the response, market the product so as to maximize my returns?" If you must begin your questions with "Why…", then make it a "Why NOT?" as in Why NOT shoot for the stars?" Why NOT become the next Motown?

Therefore, at the end of each chapter are key questions you should be asking yourself in order to move yourself and your label towards success. Which brings us to the final key to creating a successful record label.

How to Become Great Secret #3: Keep Moving Forward

In my experiences in business ventures, and in various organizations, I've seen hundreds of people come and go. I've seen people rise to the top in record time, and I've seen others jump ship in utter frustration. I've had a chance to meet people from a wide range of backgrounds, skills, motivations, and talent. It's true that we may never know why some people are more successful than others. We may not be able to pinpoint the single pivotal moment, or the unique sequence of events in that individual's development that are responsible for their success. However, we do know the things that they do which result in their success. We hear of successful people's "work ethic", their willingness to help others and their persistence despite setbacks. In order to succeed, you simply need to be committed to success.

Being committed to success means you have to set yourself to a higher standard than most. It's said that 97% of the people in the United States will retire dependent on family, friends or the federal government for survival. If that's true, then you need to consider yourself what I call a "3-percenter." That being the case, you're going to run into people from the other 97% more often than you will meet others like you. Therefore, to determine who you need to be in order to succeed as a 3-percenter, you cannot rely on what the 97% of the people you run into do. As a 3-percenter, you don't complain when things don't go your way. You learn from the situation and move forward. As a 3-percenter, you realize that every opportunity to quit is either a chance to identify with the 97-percenters, or to set yourself apart. As a 3-percenter, you have to love challenging yourself to do more. As a 3-percenter, you've got to be able to roll with the punches. You have to be able to adapt to situations that would break others. You have to operate at all times from the position of "I can and will do this, and I will keep doing it UNTIL I am successful." You have to be able to sacrifice some things in the now in order to have the lifestyle and the things you want in the future. You have to be open to new ideas and ways of being. You can't be too attached to yourself the way you are, if it's not getting you what you want.

All of these behaviors are ways of being that come with new ways of thinking. Be willing to think differently about your fears, life's challenges, other people and what they do, and especially about yourself and what you believe.....and things will never be the same again!

Be flexible to necessary changes, but see them as detours not deterrents.

The Bonus Secret: The 3 V's of Victory: Value, Vicinity & Visuals

In listening to, dissecting, reframing, practicing, testing, evaluating and implementing the advice of million-dollar entrepreneurs, I've discovered certain techniques they use to grow their companies beyond the limits others tend to encounter. There are many tips and techniques that will be effective in growing your record label into the realms of wealth you aspire to. Here are three:

1. If you wish to grow your business, you must be keenly aware of the value you bring to the world. It's not enough simply to sell something. When dealing with potential clients, distributors, A&R reps from the major labels, and even the artists you sign, you must be able to recognize, express and put into terms they can relate to, why doing business with you is a win situation for them. This is the VALUE in the three V's.

2. When fostering relationships that will be important for your long term success, get in the vicinity of the people who matter. There's a unique synergy and benefits that result when people are in each other's physical space. When making deals face-to-fact, it's harder for people to say no. It's easier to build rapport and trust. And, through body language, eye contact, and the exchange of "energy" you can communicate on levels that aren't possible in emails, over the phone, or in letters sent by mail. This is especially critical when nurturing relationships in the music industry where so much hinges on "who you know" and what they think about you. This is VICINITY in the three V's. Finally,

3. When communicating the value in the vicinity of your potential clients, customers, and partners, bring something they can see and touch that represents you, the value you represent and/or your company. This can be a product prototype, a marketing piece like a flier, poster, promotional CD, a write up in a major magazine, a slide presentation that captures your proposal, a media kit, or even a free t-shirt. But, whatever you do, bring something that shows you mean business, and that you can produce results. This is the VISUAL in the three V's.

And that, my friend, is how you become great and build a great record label!

Oh yes, and you need some good music and effective promotion, too! But that's a whole different chapter altogether!

<u>SUMMARY of Chapter 2: *" PREPARATION: What Game are YOU Playing?"*</u>

• Why do you want to start a record label? Have the answer to this question clearly defined before you play the game.

• The most important preparation that you should do is the personal preparation that all those must do who aspire to be great and then do great things First decide which game you want to play. Are you playing an Ego Game or an Economic Game. The two are not mutually exclusive. Determine your goals, your standards, your ethics, your "will" and "will not" lists, and the standard of ethics to which you'll hold yourself BEFORE you begin this journey. Decide if you want to play an Ego Game or an Economic Game, or a combination of the two. Regardless of which you choose, never compromise your ethics, or violate your will and will not list as you build your business. Your concept of self is all you really have in any game. When challenged, ask yourself, "Is this decision consistent with my original non-negotiables? Will it raise or lower my opinion of myself in my heart of hearts? Having this sort of inner dialogue can help you avoid the trap that so many people fall into.

• You'll be required to assume many roles and titles as you build and grow your record label. Assess your strengths and weaknesses and take steps to harness the former, and compensate for the latter. Incorporate others whose weaknesses you complement, and whose strengths complement your weaknesses. Among the things you will need to do is gather information and become a "problem solver", or as we prefer to say, a challenge conqueror. Don't be afraid to call strangers, approach larger organizations, and make full use of the vast potential of the internet in order to get your questions answered, and to get your goals achieved. With the advent of the Internet, a little patience, and a few dollars invested, there is absolutely NO REASON why ANY question you need answered, or task you need accomplished should go unaddressed.

• Your success in this business will depend upon how well you understand the rules of the game. There are many practices and terminology that are considered standard. Understanding some of the basics, like how a record label makes money, how the money is apportioned to an artist who goes gold, what Publishing rights and income are, comprise just some of the knowledge you'll need in order to succeed.

• Work ON your business rather than simply IN it. Follow Michael Gerber's advice in the *E-myth Revisited.*

• Devote yourself to discovering who you are, who you need to be, and who you are becoming, and be open to changing your perceptions (in the direction of your better self) as you encounter new challenges.

• Determine what success will look like for you. Set your goals and create a task list, and a milestone road map for their attainment. Decide what success will look like for you. It is an intensely personal experience, different for everyone, but vitally important that you envision it clearly before you begin. Even as a record label owner, there's an element of your success that has nothing to do with the music industry, its practices, history and future. Greater than 50%--some would say as much as 99% of your success starting your own label and releasing your music influenced by how you think, the questions you ask, and your ability to keep moving forward despite the obstacles. Therefore, commit to personal growth. Ask the right questions. Keep moving forward. That's how you become great!

RESOURCES for Chapter 2--*What Game are YOU Playing?*
(BOOKS, AUDIO PROGRAMS, MAGAZINES, ORGANIZATIONS & WEBSITES)

½ *For help choosing which game to play; Ego or Economics? Ethics or Everything Goes?*
  - *One Cup at a Time: The Starbucks Story* by Susan Jeffers (sticking to ethics in your game)
  - Martha Stewart by Christopher Byron
  - *Johnnie Cochran: A Lawyer's Life* by Johnnie Cochran

½ *For adopting the right mindset for the game*
  - *Feel The Fear And Do It Anyway* by Susan Jeffers
  - *As a Man Thinketh* by James Allen
  - *The Psychology of Achievement* by Brian Tracy
  - *Lessons In Success Volume 1: The Silent Performer* by Walt Goodridge
  - *The Tao of Wow* by Walt F.J. Goodridge (What would a Wow Master Do?)
  - *The Game of Life and How to Play It* by Florence Shimm
  - *Creative Visualization* by Shakti Gawain
  - *WishCraft: How to Get What You Really Want* by Barbara Sher
  - Nightingale-Conant Corporation, IL; (800)323-3938; www.nightingale-conant.com

½ *For images and inspiration of the world you desire*
  - *Visioning: Ten Steps to Designing the Life of Your Dreams* by Lucia Capacchione, Ph.D., A.T.R.
  - Robb Report For the Luxury Lifestyle Magazine; www.robbreport.com;

½ *The Right Questions To Ask*
  - Why do I want to start a record label?
  - What are the talents and skills I have that will aid in my success?
  - What weaknesses will I need to address in order to be successful?
  - What are my 20 frequently asked questions about starting and operating a record label?
  - What do successful people know that I need to learn?
  - How did Russell, Puffy, Damon Dash and Master P succeed?

½ *Suggestion*
  - Read the stories of people whom you admire for pursuing their passions. Their stories will have the common element of the triumph over adversity and will inspire you to greatness. People like Michael Jordan, Oprah Winfrey, Tony Robbins, Sylvester Stallone, Ray Croc, or even local heroes profiled in newspapers, magazines or online exist as examples of the courage you need to create the world of your desires.

CHAPTER 3:
"Running a Record Label"

Today is a very special day. It's your first day of business. Your mission running your record label is quite simple. Whether your company is a "me, myself and I" operation run on the weekends and in your spare time, or if it's a fully funded and financed operation with staff, a real budget, investors and advisory board, everything that you and your team should be doing on a daily basis should fall into one or more of the ten steps of the game plan. So, for starters, let's review the game plan.

<table>
<tr><td>

The day to day activities of your label must focus on these 10 steps.

</td><td>

The Game Plan

½   **Monitor your operations**
½   **Find, sign and develop talented artists**
½   **Create your product**
½   **Market, Promote & Advertise it**
½   **Sell to stores, distributors and to the public**
½   **Maximize additional streams of income**
½   **Recoup your expenses**
½   **Pay the players**
½   **Make a profit.**
½   **Grow your business**

</td></tr>
</table>

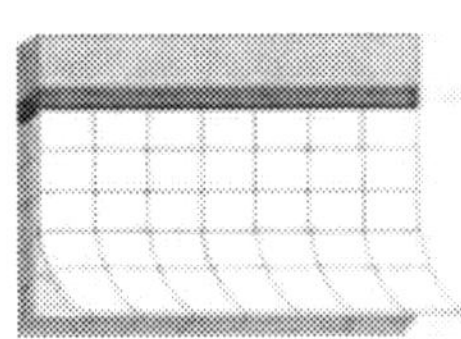

A Week In the Life of a Hip Hop Label
BRINGING THE RECORD LABEL GAME PLAN TO LIFE

I've been told that this section was the most valuable to those who read the preview edition of this book. It is designed to prepare for the details of running a record label, especially if, as will probably be the case initially, you're running the label by yourself from out of your home. This in-dept exploration of the Record Label Game Plan forms the basis of the next several chapters.

On Any Given Day, as you...

▶ Monitor your operations,

you or someone on your team will be incorporating your company, keeping track of tax filing deadlines, registering company with search engines, filling orders to customers, stores and to the public, organizing the office, watching expenses; striking deals with the landlord, scouting and hiring interns to do certain tasks; approving costs of various expenses; writing checks or giving credit card numbers to pay for all of this, and thinking, "How can we be more efficient at what we're doing?"

▶ Find, sign and develop talented artists,

you or someone on your team will be listening to demo tapes; going to recording studios to network with producers and other artists; attending music industry events in search of talent; calling, traveling to, meeting with and assessing the array of talent that you'll come in contact with; attending photo shoots to give input on current artist image; visit websites, chatrooms, bulletin boards on the internet to scout talent; listening to tapes in your car or during your commute; dealing with lawyers and artist's legal representative on details of contract; sending out rejection letters; taking calls from artists and managers; paying for all of this, and asking, "How can we really sell this artist?"

▶ Create your product,

you or someone on your team will be working with artists to complete masters, calling suppliers to price manufacturing costs and to negotiate a good deal; approving CD insert design, working with photographers, approving pictures to be used on CD, posters, t-shirts, etc.; listening to a master recording to approve it for final manufacturing; driving to pick up the finished product; planning future releases; paying for studio time, photography, printing and duplication, and wondering, "How can we create a product that sells on the strength of the music, as well as visually, through our marketing efforts, and by word of mouth?"

▶ Market, Promote & Advertise it,

you or someone on your team will be writing a press release, deciding on the angle or hook with which to publicize your artist; calling newspapers, magazines, radio stations, stores, distributors to promote it; waiting for return calls; designing an ad for a trade magazine; negotiating advertising cost with a magazine salesperson;

▶ Sell to stores, distributors and to the public,

you or someone on your team will be preparing sales materials for stores, calling new distributors; calling new stores; designing and launching website; opening envelopes with checks from stores, distributors and the public; preparing orders for shipping; calling UPS or USPS for pickup; dropping off orders at post office or other shipping location; monitoring how many people visited the website; reading emails from fans and using them to determine what to sell next; working with web designer on creating your site.

▶ **Maximize additional streams of income,**
you or someone on your team will be calling ASCAP, BMI or SESAC to register; compiling a list of alternate streams; negotiating with merchandising companies; contact movie studios to offer tracks; reading trade journals like Billboard to see what other types of deals are being struck; contacting advertisers and ad agencies to offer tracks; sending media kits to companies for potential sponsorship and advertising or to consider endorsements;

▶ **Recoup your expenses,**
you or someone on your team will be adjusting the financial records to account for expenses related to individual projects; providing artists and all parties concerned with a statement itemizing income received and what it's "recouping."

▶ **Pay the players,**
you or someone on your team will be wiring money to an artist's account; writing a check to be given to artist, producer, suppliers, street teams, PR person, staff, creditors, etc.

▶ **Make a profit,**
you or someone on your team will be making sure all allowable deductions are being claimed on taxes; taking advantage of volume discounts in purchasing supplies; finding ways of deferring taxable income; selling more products with low overhead;

▶ **Grow your business,**
you or someone on your team will be adding new products to your catalog; setting new sales goals; selling to new countries; focusing on getting signed to a major.

SUMMARY of Chapter 3: *"Running A Record Label"*

½ *Main Points*
- Running your record label essentially means focusing on the 10 Point Record Label Game Plan.

- Become familiar with the titles and responsibilities of the roles and positions within your company. It helps to have a job description attached to each position.

- There's no such thing as an average day, but every day should be spent engaged in some activity that pushes you, your business, your company, your artist and your product towards your goals.

½ *The Right Questions To Ask*
- Is there an existing record label at which I can intern to gain experience?
- How can I operate more efficiently?
- How can I find talented artists?
- Is this a product that can stand on its own and attract attention visually?

RESOURCES for Chapter 3: *"Running A Record Label"*
BOOKS, AUDIO PROGRAMS, MAGAZINES, ORGANIZATIONS & WEBSITES

½ *For additional perspectives on releasing your music*
- *How to Make And Sell Your Own Recording* by Diane Rappaport

½ *For information from a UK perspective*
- http://www.cops.co.uk is a UK-based manufacturer. Their site also features their version of the Hip Hop Answerman: Auntie Bobbie, who answers questions about the industry from a British perspective.

CHAPTER 4:
"The Industry"

Remember the Game Plan

To be successful playing the game, we must be familiar with how others are playing it. Let's talk a bit about the Music Industry.

▶ Monitor your OPERATIONS
Find, sign and develop talented ARTISTS
Create your PRODUCT on CD or other media
MARKET, Promote & Advertise it…
SELL IT to stores, distributors and to the public
Maximize additional streams of INCOME
RECOUP your expenses
PAY the players
Make a PROFIT.
GROW your business

MINDCHECK

There's Enough! Always Remember "Bollywood"

As you read this section, you should develop a sense for just how much money and opportunity the music industry generates. There are millions of dollars being spent every day by eager consumers. Many entrepreneurs, however, believe that success in business means grabbing it from people who are already successful. They, as well as our society perpetuate the belief that in order to win, someone has to lose. True, the average consumer doesn't have an infinite amount of money. But, here's why you should never worry about sufficiency. Remember, as you enter the industry, any industry, you make it bigger. You bring additional value that wasn't there before. You'll bring choices of music that didn't exist. Therefore, your very presence in this industry will result in new customers and additional money being spent. Therefore, you never have to worry that there won't be enough for you, or that in order for you to win, that someone has to lose. Think abundance. Remember, there's enough for everyone!

Whenever I think that people won't spend additional money for what I bring to the market, I always remember a fact I heard about life in India. Even though for many average people, life in India represents hardships, insufficiency, deprivation, inflation, and a low standard of living, one of the most prosperous and financially thriving industries is the Indian film Industry. With over 800 new releases each year, "BollyWood" (a word which is a conflation of "Bombay" and "Hollywood" and which many South Asian filmmakers have taken exception to citing it implies that theirs is a cheap imitation of Hollywood's) allows Indians to spend more on entertainment and movie-going especially, per capita, than in many western nations! And you think there's not enough wealth for you???

Music Industry Overview

Here are some statistics designed to give you a clear picture of what's going in the music industry:
[Source: http://www.riaa.com/PR_story.cfm?id=512]

Worldwide Music Industry Sales (Incl US) $40 Billion

Domestic Music Industry sales (i.e. US only) : $13.7 Billion (2001 year-end figure)

Major Labels' Market Share for 2000 84%

Individual Labels' market share for 2000 Universal Music Group (28%)
BMG Entertainment (19.4%)
Sony Music (15.4%),
Warner Music Group (13.5%)
EMI (8.7%).

Gold and Platinum SoundScan Stats 202 albums sold 500,000 units or more. (Gold)
88 album releases sold at least 1 million units (Platinum)

Internet Sales For 2000, 1.6% of total album sales came via the Web

The top 10-selling albums of 2000 were

'N Sync's "No Strings Attached" (9.9 million),
Eminem's "The Marshall Mathers LP" (7.9 million),
Britney Spears' "Oops! ... I Did It Again" (7.89 million),
Creed's "Human Clay" (6.58 million),
Santana's "Supernatural" (5.85 million),
the Beatles' "Beatles 1" (5 million),
Nelly's "Country Grammar" (5 million),
Backstreet Boys' "Black & Blue" (4.2 million),
Dr. Dre's "Dr. Dre 2001" (4 million) and
Destiny's Child's "Writing's on the Wall" (3.8 million).

% of music consumers who list Rap/Hip
Hop as their favorite genre 29%

Sales Breakdown by Genre (2001 figures)

Genre	Percentage
Rock Sales	24.0% (i.e. 24% of all records sold were in the Rock category)
Pop	12.1%
Rap/Hip Hop	11.2%
R&B/Urban	10.6%
Country	10.5%
Jazz	3.4%
Classical	3.2%

Sales by Format (Singles and Cassettes)

Full-length cassettes decreased in popularity, dropping from 4.9 percent of the market in 2000 to 3.4 percent in 2001. Music singles continued to decrease as they did in 2000. Of those surveyed, only 2.4 percent of music purchased were music singles in 2001, whereas just two years earlier 5.4 percent were singles.

Sales by Age

Age Purchases in 2001 showed that music is enjoyed at any age. There was a very small change among music consumers of all ages from 2000 to 2001. Rather than growing, music purchasing among consumers between the ages of 15 and 30 remained flat. Since 1990, the 45-and-older segment has steadily increased its proportion of the marketplace, continuing to be strong in 2001 at 23.7 percent.

Sales by Gender

Women now account for 51 percent of music purchasers in 2001,

according to the Recording Industry Association of America's (RIAA) 2001 Consumer Profile, an annual demographic survey of 3,153 music consumers in the United States.

Hip Hop By Comparison

Worldwide sales	$40 Billion
US Sales	$13 Billion
Rap Sales	$1 Billion

Note: According to the Recording Industry Association of America (RIAA), young white audiences purchase 66% of rap music. As I said in "How to Use This Book", "every statistic represents a trend you can spot and capitalize on."

What's Standard In The Industry?
(aka: "Why you need to do it yourself!")

As record label, you'll be forging relationships with virtually every other entity and individual concern within the industry. You'll be entering the field in a game that's been going on for many decades now. As a result, there are many standard practices, trends, beliefs and terms that you should be familiar with. There are many good books that cover the range of standard practices in the industry. My goal is not to repeat them here. There's enough value that I can offer without repeating them here. Remember, this is a how to book. relationships with the artist and his/her team. Here, then, is an overview of the monies typically received, spent, accrued within the music industry. Here's some valuable information on how income is divided up between label, artist, and everyone else.

[2000 statistic from the Recording Industry Association of America]

What An Artist Gets Paid On A "Gold" Record
("Simply shocking!")

	$480,000	500,000 units sold at a royalty rate of $0.96 per unit
1.	-$100,000	recoupable stuff (NOT the advance)
2.	= $380,000	New Subtotal
3.	− $190,000 (placed in reserves)	Still sounds OK? Watch... Now, half of the $380,000 stays "in reserve" (accounting for returned items from retail stores) for 2 to 4 years depending on the length specified in the recording contract.
4.	= $190,000	New Subtotal
5.	− $70,000 (advance; recording costs)	Next, the $70,000 advance is actually subtracted from $190,000 (the other $190,000 is in reserves for 2 years).
6.	= $120,000	New Subtotal
7.	- $62,000 (manager)	Now, there's also the artist's manager, who is entitled to 20% of all of the entertainment income which would be 20% of $310,000, or $62,000. Remember, the artist is the last to get paid, so even the manager gets paid before the artist.
8.	**= $58,000**	New Subtotal (What's left for the 3-member group to split)
9.	(divided by 3) **=$19,000 Each**	What each member of the 3-member group receives.

So the artists actually receive $19,333 each for their gold album, and in two years when the reserves are liquidated, IF they've recouped, they will each receive another $63,000.

IF they've recouped. Guess who keeps track of all of this accounting? The label. Most contracts are "cross-collateralized," which means if the artist does not recoup on the first album, the money will be paid back out of the second album. Also, if the money is not recouped on the second album, repayment can come out of the "in reserve" funds from the first album, if the funds have not already been liquidated.

Even after the reserves are paid, each artist only actually made 50 cents per unit based on this example. The label made about $2.68 per unit. This example also doesn't include any additional production costs for an outside producer to come in and do a re-mix, and you know how often that happens.

So each artist in this group has received a total of about $82,000. After legal expenses and costs of new clothing to wear on stage while touring, etc, each artist has probably made a total of $75,000 before paying taxes (which the artist is responsible for-- remember Kool Moe Dee?). Let's look at the time line now. Let's assume the artists had no jobs when they started this. They spent 4 months putting their demo tape together and getting the tracks just right. They spent another 6 months to a year getting to know who all of the players are in the rap music industry and shopping their demo tape. After signing to a label, it took another 8 months to make an album and to get through all of the label's bureaucracy. When the first single dropped, the group went into promotion mode and traveled all over promoting the single at radio, retail, concerts, and publications. This was another six months. The record label decided to push three singles off the album so it was another year before they got back into the studio to make album number two. This scenario has been a total of 36 months. Each member of the group made $75,000 for a three year investment of time, which averages out to $25,000 per year. In corporate America, that works out to be $12 per hour (before taxes).

And the artist doesn't actually get paid until the record label recoups the $500,000 they gave the artist as an advance. Therefore, "the artist" doesn't actually get their $1.51 on the first 326,797 CDs sold.

From-ARTISTS DON'T MAKE MONEY FROM RECORD DEALS By Wendy Day from Rap Coalition

Now, if you're the label, then the above scenario isn't so bad. You want your artists to go "Gold" because you stand to reap the rewards of your as well as their hard work. If, on the other hand, you're the artist, then the above picture might not appear so rosy! $19,000 in my pocket after generating close to eight and a half-million dollars in retail sales! (500,000 x $17 retail price=$8,500,000)

What EXACTLY is "Publishing"??????
The Ultimate "Publishing" explanation

How to Learn

The best way to learn something is to teach it. After you've read the following, call up a friend and attempt to explain it to them so they understand AND can explain it back to you. It is in explaining concepts to others that we learn best. If you REALLY understand the concept of publishing, you must be able to answer their questions to THEIR satisfaction! If you have ANY questions, visit the www.hiphopbiz.com website, or, if you're reading this 10 years from the date of publication, find me on whatever the latest mode of communication is in our world, and I'll explain it even further to you! – Walt F.J. Goodridge

Perhaps the most confusing topic in the music industry is the concept of "publishing." Technically, when someone says "publishing" they may be referring to publishing RIGHTS and/or publishing INCOME. The two are related in that whoever owns the publishing RIGHTS will be earning the publishing INCOME. In our Ultimate Publishing Explanation, however, I'll make sure that I explain things in such a way that there's no longer any confusion about this extremely important subject.

This section is by no means intended as a comprehensive , thorough explanation of the entire range of details concerning publishing. It is, however, intended to explain things in such a way that you understand the underlying concepts that drive industry, and might clarify WHY things are structured the way they are from both the artist and label perspective. With this knowledge, you'll be better equipped to protect yourself as an artist, or to secure your viability and success as a record label owner.

So let's take this idea by idea, and remember what I said in the very first "Mindcheck" about not going past a word you don't understand!

Idea 1. Ownership

When you create a piece of musical work which we'll call a work or a composition, you AUTOMATICALLY own something called the "Publishing RIGHTS." Remember, this composition is YOURS! You made it, you created it, you own ALL the rights! Period. No one can take these rights away from you without your consent. And, you don't have to beg, borrow or buy these rights from ANYONE in order to exercise them and make money from them. When you create a piece of musical work, YOU are the original "publisher," so you own all the Publishing Rights. Got it? Good. But you haven't really published it, yet, so that's going to be your next step if you want to get it out there and make money with it.

Idea 2. Publishing Defined

"to publish" The act of disseminating intellectual and other material to its intended audience.

In other words, your composition is considered "published" when it is made available to the public, or some specific audience. You can publish your work in the form(s) of a record, in the soundtrack for a film, as background music for a television program, as music for a commercial, or maybe a within the soundtrack of a video game.

Idea 3. Anyone can be a publisher

In the same way that you automatically became the original publisher just by creating the work, ANYONE can be a publisher.

Record labels can be publishers. Artists can be publishers. People set up separate companies for the express purpose of "publishing" other people's work. A publishing company, therefore, has the job

Idea 4. The Ownership Exchange!

You may well be asking, "So if the original creator owns all the rights, how is that so many talented artists and creators end up bankrupt after being in the music industry?".

ANSWER: Making money in the music industry is based on an "Ownership Exchange"

Think of it this way. You just baked a pie. This pie is all yours! It's a delicious pie that you want to take with you on a journey across the country to sell at a state fair. So you start your journey on foot. Along the way, you meet someone who offers to drive you part of the way. But, in exchange, she asks for some of your pie (she noticed how delicious it smelled). You agree, cut her a slice of the pie, and she takes you part of the way. After a while, you may part company, wave goodbye, and continue on your journey. Your driving partner now has a piece of your pie that she can eat or sell. You have less of your original pie, but you're a little further ahead in your journey than if you hadn't sacrificed that piece. You'll make a little less money at the fair, since you now have less to sell, but you should still do ok.

Soon, you meet a number of other individuals who, intrigued by the appeal of your pie, offer to do other such favors for you. One offers to drive you further. Another offers to protect your pie in case it rain. Still others even offer to sell it at other fairs promising that they can get you better prices. All seem like great offers, and at each meeting, you cut a slice of the pie in exchange for the help these people provide.

Or, things may have gone differently if the first person you met had said, "I'll take you ALL THE WAY across the country, as long as you split any money you make along the way with me when you get to the fair. You might simply have met

Choose wisely because, if you're not careful, you may end up giving away more than is in your best interest, and end up at the fair flat broke, and with no pie to sell!

When you sign an agreement with a record label, a publishing company, an agent, a producer, etc., in some way you are GIVING AWAY a piece of the pie—more accurately, its money earning potential--IN EXCHANGE FOR their help in getting it out to the public in ways that generate money.   When money is made, they'll be entitled to a percentage based on the percentage of ownership that you've given them.

Your "pie" is the total publishing rights that you have as original publisher. What you sign away are various percentages which entitle your new "part owners" to share in the income generated.

To anticipate and answer a question you may have at this point: YES, you can publish your work yourself. However, in making the decision of whether or not to self-publish, many artists realize two things about the industry. 1. Publishing is and can be a very time-consuming enterprise that would take time and energy away from the artist's creative pursuits, and 2. Labels and publishing companies already have the financial resources, contacts, networks, staff, distribution channels and relationships in place to make publishing easier and pretty much more lucrative than most new artists could on their own.

Idea 5. Publishing Income!

So, let's say that you've signed an agreement with a record label. The money that's generated as a result of the different ways they publish your work is called publishing income. The share that you'll be entitled to (they've got more leverage, so they've put themselves in the position to monitor and distribute the income they make for you) per the same agreement are called publishing royalties.

There are four types of publishing royalties based on the ways that a song is exploited: performance royalties, mechanical royalties, synchronization fees, and print royalties (although sheet music is rare for rap music).

performance royalties: you can get paid when your song is performed on the radio, in a club, at an event, or other public venue.
Who writes the checks: PERFORMANCE RIGHTS ORGANIZATIONS

mechanical royalties: you can get paid when your song is published "mechanically." The term comes from the days when music recordings were sold as piano rolls which mechanically triggered a player piano, now represent royalties due to songwriters and their publishers for each copy of a record sold.
Who writes the checks: RECORD LABEL

Synchronization fees: you can get paid for the use of a song in a motion picture. This includes the right to distribute the film to network, local, syndicated, pay-per-view, pay, satellite, cable, and subscription television stations; the right to show the film in motion picture theaters in the United States; and the right to include the song as part of in-context trailers, previews, and advertisements of the motion picture
Who writes the checks: MOTION PICTURE PRODUCTION COMPANY OR PERFORMANCE RIGHTS ORGANIZATION

print royalties: you can earn money from the sale of sheet music of your songs.
(although sheet music is rare for rap music).
Who writes the checks: THE PUBLISHING COMPANY

As an independent record label, or as an artist/label you may find yourself negotiating and arranging deals and fees in any number of these areas. However, to maintain our focus, let's spend a little time on the Record Label's mechanical royalties.

[Excerpt from **Songwriters & Publishers Beware: The Controlled Composition Clause**
By, Wallace Collins, Esq. From rapcoalition.org
However, for a simplified example of how it works, lets assume a typical clause which might say that the songwriter/artist will receive 3/4 of the minimum statutory mechanical rate payable on a maximum of 10 songs per LP.

The mechanical royalty on the artist's entire LP (based on the label contract the artist signed) has a cap of 52 cents (3/4 rate x 10 songs) so that, even if the songwriter/artist writes 12 songs for its own album, the artist's publishing which should be worth about 83 cents an album at the full rate is only allocated 52 cents under this clause.

1. To further illustrate, assume the 12 song album has 6 songs written by the artist and 6 songs from outside publishers. The outside publishers are not subject to the artist's 3/4 rate so the 6 outside songs get the full rate and are entitled to a total of about 41 cents. Since the mechanical royalty on the entire LP for the artist has a contractual cap of 52 cents, the recording artist's publisher is limited to applying the remaining 11 cents to the artist's 6 songs, so that the artist's publishing is worth less than 2 cents per song.

2. To take it another step further, imagine a case where 8 of the 12 songs on the LP were from outside publishers. The outside publishers would be entitled to about 55 cents in mechanical royalties. Since the artist's contractual cap is 52 cents, then for Each LP sold the songwriter/record artist would actually owe its record company 3 cents which would be deducted out of its recording royalties. In addition, the artist's own 4 songs receive no mechanical royalties at all.

Translation:

1. In other words, as far as the record label is concerned, regardless of who legally owns the publishing rights, they are only required to pay out a TOTAL of 52 cents as "mechanical publishing income." Since they already paid out 41 cents to the outside publishers, --and these may also include people from whom the artist has "sampled." –they are only required to pay out another 11 cents. This 11 cents is what the artist has to make due with, regardless of how many songs he/she has actually written for the album.
2. And, if they pay out more than the 52 cents stated in the contract--because the artist has used (or sampled) too many outside publishers—then the artist must reimburse the label for the extra costs.

Remember the Game Plan

½	Monitor your OPERATIONS
½	Find, sign and develop talented ARTISTS
½	Create your PRODUCT on CD or other media
½	MARKET, Promote & Advertise it…
½	SELL IT to stores, distributors and to the public
½	**Maximize additional streams of INCOME**
½	RECOUP your expenses
½	PAY the players
½	Make a PROFIT
½	GROW your business

Publishing income, mechanicals, soundtrack licensing will create additional streams of income for your label.   ---------------½

Where's the Profit for the Label?

With all the information we've just acquired, we can now answer the question that's been on your mind ever since you started reading: How do I make my money as a record label? First let's take a look at how a typical major label makes its money: In this example, we'll explore what would happen for a new artist whose debut release sells 200,000 copies. First, let's review the game plan:

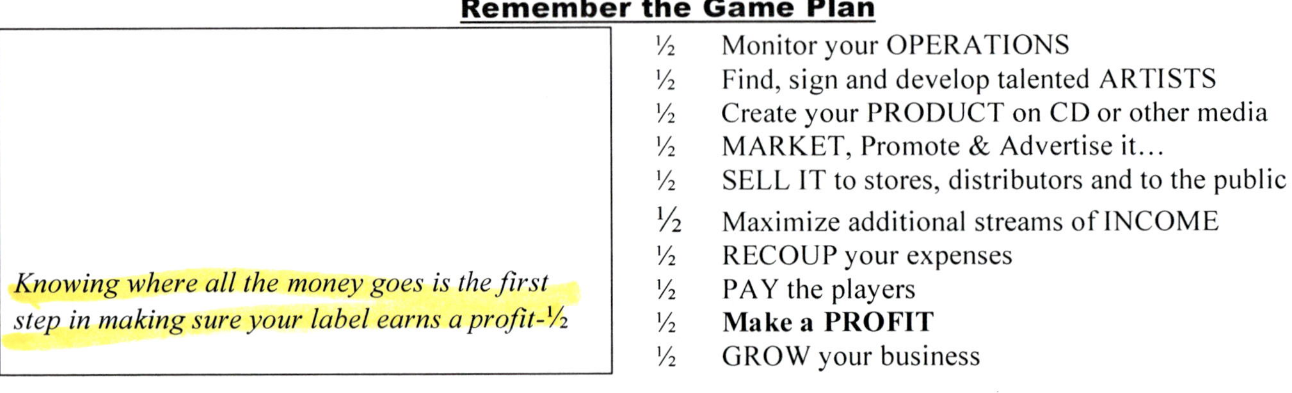

Remember the Game Plan

½	Monitor your OPERATIONS
½	Find, sign and develop talented ARTISTS
½	Create your PRODUCT on CD or other media
½	MARKET, Promote & Advertise it…
½	SELL IT to stores, distributors and to the public
½	Maximize additional streams of INCOME
½	RECOUP your expenses
½	PAY the players
½	**Make a PROFIT**
½	GROW your business

Signing advance

"Rap acts are routinely signed for half the $300,000 advance that the average new white alternative band can expect for their first album. Traditionally the performer gets an 8 to 12 percent royalty on the retail price of his record and the option to re-negotiate."--*From Newsweek July 18, 1994*

The following is adapted from-ARTISTS DON'T MAKE MONEY FROM RECORD DEALS By, Wendy Day from Rap Coalition (www.rapcoalition.org)

Record Deal Royalty Rate

We're going to assume that there are 3 artists in the group, and that they split everything equally. We're also going to assume that they produce their own tracks themselves.

ROYALTY RATE: 12%
Suggested retail list price (cassettes) $10.98
less 15% packaging deduction (usually 20%) =$ 9.33
Artist gets paid on 85% of records sold ("free goods") =$7.93

So the artists' 12% is equal to about 96 cents per record sold. In most deals, the producer's 3% comes out of that 12%. But for the sake of brevity, we'll assume in this example that the group produced the whole album themselves, buying no tracks from outside producers, which is rare.

Let's assume that the group is a hit and their record goes Gold (although it is rare that a first record blows up like this). Let's also assume they were a priority at their record label and that their label understood exactly how to market them. So they went Gold, selling 500,000 units according to SoundScan (and due to the inaccuracies in SoundScan tracking at the rap retail level, 500,000 scanned probably means more like 600,000 actually sold).

GOLD RECORD = 500,000 units sold x $ .96 = $480,000. Looks like a nice chunk of loot, huh? Watch this. Now the label recoups what they've spent: independent promotion, 1/2 the video cost, some tour support, all those limo rides, all those out of town trips for the artist and their friends, etc . And the artist doesn't actually get paid until the record label recoups the $500,000 they gave the artist as an advance. Therefore, "the artist" doesn't actually get their $1.51 on the first 326,797 CDs sold.

Break-Even Point

If the "average" rap record costs $1,000,000 to create, market, and promote (and I could argue that this figure is low, but it's the average figure Craig Kallman, President of Atlantic Records gave me), then just to break even a label must sell 123,000 records.

Percentage for managers/accountant/lawyer

Everyone gets their cut first: the label, the manager (15%- 20% of all of the artist's entertainment income), the lawyer (by the hour or 5%-10% of the deal), the accountant (by the hour or 5% of all income), and, of course, the IRS (28% to 50% depending on the tax bracket).

So the artists' 12% is equal to about 96 cents per record sold. In most deals, the producer's 3% comes out of that 12%, but for the sake of brevity, in this example the group produced the whole album, buying no tracks from outside producers, which is rare.

Business manager

Never agree to pay a business manager more than 5% no matter how much money he says he can make you or save you.

Talent agent

A standard fee for a talent agent is 10%, but it may go as high as 20%.

So, where DOES the money go??

So, even though you probably won't be dealing in $200,000 advances right away, we'll use this as a nice round figure as our standard budget. So, let's say we, as the label, advance the artist $200,000.

Of that 200,000 advanced to "the artist"
$30,000 (15%) goes to the manager
$5,000 (2.5%) goes to the lawyer for negotiating the deal
$10,000 (20%, though it varies) goes to the Producer as a fee, which leaves
$155,000 to actually make the record and cover the artist's living expenses (assuming no other income)

Now, once the record is actually released and selling, for every CD sold, of a typical $17.00 retail cost that's made, 12% goes to "the artist"

Of the 12% that goes to "the artist"
3% goes to the producer ($0.51 cents)
9% goes to "the artist" (that's $1.51)
88% goes to "the label" (this must cover our label expenses and result in a profit)

Now, let's say we're ready to do an accounting of the profit we made from our venture. Let's assume that we sell 200,000 albums. Here, then are the record company's expenses:
· Recording and recoupable marketing costs: $300,000 (including the advance)
· Mechanicals: $120,000
· Non-recoupable marketing costs: $600,000
· Manufacturing and Distribution: $330,000
· Total label expenses: $1,350,000

So, what would the label make on the sale of these 200,000 albums? Retailers pay around $10 an album, which amounts to a gross revenue for the label on those 200,000 CDs of $2 million. No one knows exactly how much distribution and manufacturing costs. The big companies all have large overheads to provide these functions, often creating separate divisions to handle them. The record company presidents run their divisions with internal charges for manufacturing and distribution that add up to around $2.65 a unit. There's obviously profit built into that but the per-unit amount varies, depending on the amount of overall record-group volume as well as unpredictable outside events such as retail bankruptcies. As a rule of thumb, I was always told to assume about $1.00 a unit profit on these combined functions. For the purpose of this exercise I'm assuming a "real" cost of $1.65 per unit for combined manufacturing and distribution.

This leaves $650,000 in profit, right? Not necessarily. Out of that comes all of the salaries of the people who work at the record company. These include the people who do the color separations for CD covers, who create Web sites for artists, and who make hundreds of calls to radio stations, journalists, and retailers. Struggling divisions spend more, but a healthy U.S. record company with a decent catalog allots around 20 percent of their gross revenues to overhead, or, in this instance, $400,000.

That still leaves the label with a profit of $250,000, right? Yes, and the middle-level artist has reason to gripe, but not without coming to terms with a fundamental fact: big record companies weren't established to enable artists to sell 200,000 copies. Big record companies need big sales. Even the most astute A&R people are wrong two-thirds of the time. On average, even at a successful company the cost of promoting and marketing a label's "misses" eats up most of the profits, from not only the mid-level successes but even the gold-plus hits. Executives at major labels, then, are usually disappointed by sales of 200,000.

A major record company's profits come from the Shania Twains of the world, the very artists who have the least to complain about. Remember the $600,000 allocated to marketing on 200,000 albums, this represents 30 percent of the total revenue. On an album that goes on to sell millions, the share of income spent on advertising and promotion drops to 10 percent, leaving an extra $2 an album profit for the label.

The Future of the Industry: MP3, The Internet and You
("Where's it all going?")

In case you've been out of the loop for a while, here is a quick overview to bring you up to speed on what's been going on in the industry.

• The Internet has wrought massive changes to the Music Industry

• It has enabled artists to establish and nurture direct links to their fans via email, websites.

• MP3s are digital audio files that allow music to be played online, via the web and in non-traditional formats.

• MP3 and Internet communication allow fans from all over the world to share music to a degree never before possible.

• This new consumer listening model threatens the business model of record labels who would like to charge customers a purchase price for products with music.

The debate that now arises and about which there is much division, disagreement, but also delight (depending on where you stand), is whether the Internet and MP3 are helping or hurting the music industry. Who is benefiting from the technology? Are they benefiting at someone else's expense? Are artists ultimately losing money and income due to the new technology? Is the overall sale of music as a commodity increasing or decreasing as a result of the widespread availability and access to MP3? Is there an alternate business model that can be created that will keep everybody happy?

Does MP3 affect the artist's livelihood? I know of many artists who are now more financially successful as a result of the new technology. I can only speculate as to the actual effects on artists who claim to be hurt by the new world order. Labels who make their money from the sale of vinyl, cassettes and CDs will undoubtedly feel their livelihood is threatened by a format over which they have no control, and for which no clear boundaries and standards have been established. A better question to ask (remembering our earlier advice), is "How can we use the new technology to improve our financial situation.

As far as the effect of the technology on consumer spending: Trust your own experience as a music consumer. The question is simple: Has the new technology increased or decreased your purchases of music? Has the Internet/MP3 exposed you to new artists? Has it allowed you to keep more money in your pocket? Have you been able to bootleg rather than buy? Whether the answer is yes or no, you can be sure you're not alone.

On the other hand, has MP3 exposed you to new artists? Has it allowed you to be exposed to artists whom you wouldn't have known of otherwise? Did you still go out and buy an artist's CD even though you may have it on your computer's hard drive? Again, whether the answer is yes or no, you can be sure you're not alone. There are others like you who are going to be spending about the same, or more as they always did. Your mission is to use the technology to affect those consumers' buying habits in your favor.

My best advice is this: Stay on top of the latest developments and don't wait to be on the trailing edge of the adopters. If there IS going to be a new business model that compensates the artist, while satisfying the customer's now expanded appetite and palate, then you, as an independent label should make sure you're aware of it and using it before the masses.

We're still in a market-driven, demand-based economy. For those of us in capitalistic societies, the nature of trade, competition, marketing and the exchange of money for goods and services—the basic formula of capitalism—isn't changing anytime soon. In addition, the concept of music as such a good or service has been around for quite some time. Given that, though possible, it's unlikely that those two factors are going to simply collapse any time soon. Therefore, knowing that we can't stop the tide of change and evolution of technology, the right question is, "Given this. Now What?"

<u>SUMMARY of Chapter 4: *"The Industry"*</u>

- There's enough money for everyone to benefit. Your very arrival in the industry brings new value, new music and creates new possibilities for you and everyone else, consumer as well as creator.

- The Music industry is a $40 Billion industry worldwide and a $13 Billion industry in the United States. At $1 Billion, Rap accounts for 11% of this total.

- Understanding standard music industry practices like royalty rates, publishing, and how much an artist typically makes on a "gold" record will equip you with an understanding of how to really change the game for your benefit.

- While internet-enabled file sharing of MP3s is undoubtedly changing consumer buying habits in some way, the overall effect is still undetermined, and predictions of the industry's demise have been greatly exaggerated. Keep in mind that the greatest outcry will usually come from those with the most to lose as a result of the new technology. The savvy independent label, with less overhead costs, may continue to do quite well in this new era provided it stays ahead of the latest trends and finds ways to move WITH the flow rather than against it.

- A good philosophy to have when you encounter challenges on your journey is to accept them as given, and focus your energies on dealing with the present reality rather than the past circumstances. Here is a sample of an Inspiration (my own rap, perhaps?) that underscores this point.

Given That It Is

Given that things right now in fact
are how they seem to be
how then should you respond
instead of saying woe is me?

Given that things around you
didn't quite work out as you planned
how best to turn these cards you're dealt
into a winning hand?

It's all in the response
so, you can focus on the flaws
or simply use events
to help you find your life's great cause

No answers come by saying
"My life's worse than hers or his..."
You find them when you start by saying
"Given that it is..."

RESOURCES for Chapter 4: *"The Industry"*
(BOOKS, AUDIO PROGRAMS, MAGAZINES, ORGANIZATIONS & WEBSITES)

For understanding the Music Industry Game
- *This Business of Music* by M. William Krasilovsky
- *Fight the Power* by Chuck D
- *Hit Men by Frederic Dannen*
- *Confessions of a Record Producer* by Moses Avalon

ORGANIZATIONS & WEBSITES (Music Industry)
- Recording Industry Association of America (www.riaa.org)
- Rap Coalition (www.rapcoalition.org)
- Billboard Magazine website
- Music Business Solutions (mbsolutions.com)

CHAPTER 5:
"A Business Startup Primer for ANY Business"

Now that we've prepared ourselves for the game by understanding ourselves, our expectations and the nature of the game, let's start with the first step in the Game Plan, and set up our operations.

▶ **Monitor your OPERATIONS**
Find, sign and develop talented ARTISTS
Create your PRODUCT on CD or other media
MARKET, Promote & Advertise it…
SELL IT to stores, distributors and to the public
Maximize additional streams of INCOME
RECOUP your expenses
PAY the players
Make a PROFIT.
GROW your business

In Part 1 of this section, we'll explore
1. Business Startup
2. Choosing the right structure
3. Basic Business Operational requirements, and finally
4. Internet Business—the new frontier.

In Part 2, we'll get into more specific detail and cover the business concepts that relate specifically to running a record label.
1. Daily Label Operations
2. Creating Your Products and Tools

Starting A Business

If you want to be taken seriously, you have to be organized, professional and committed. It helps also if you're intelligent, well-spoken and pleasing to look at, but these aren't pre-requisites since this is America. Anyone with a good idea and a way to sell it can make it. However, you have to have a clear and realistic idea of what you're doing, and why you're doing it. If you think of yourself as a guy or girl with a good record that, with one phone call, will magically put you in the same league as Ice Cube or Latifah, then close this manual, put it back in the envelope, send it to me, and I'll send your money back. To get on the same level as Ice or Latifah, or entrepreneurs like Russell or Luke, you have to think big! Think Control! Think office space! Think secretary! Think calls from all over the world for your record! Think Source Awards! Think checks from BMI or ASCAP! Think personal freedom! Think independence! If all of this sounds appealing. You need to start a company.

Just How Easy It Is To Start A Company

To make my point on just how easy it is to start a company, I'll take you step by step on how I started a Sole Proprietorship in New York State. Don't worry if you aren't familiar with some of the forms and offices mentioned, they will all be explained later. Also, when you start your own company, you'll find that some of the specifics may be slightly different in your state. I'll explain how to find out what the differences are.

December 11

I decided to start a company.   Spent the day thinking of a name.
In a flash of inspiration, it came to me! I tried it out on a few friends and got a good response.

December 12

Possessing some artistic talent, I designed a logo. (I know not everyone can do this. You may want to spend some extra money and have someone devise one for you.) I did a cut and paste job, and with the aid of a copying machine and lettering from a magazine, came up with a letterhead. Used a copying machine to reduce the logo 50% and pasted that on a #10 envelope. Took both letterhead and envelope to a printer, chose a color and texture paper and paid my money.

(By the way, you can't use "Inc." in your company name unless you're incorporated. It's illegal.)

December 13

I went to the local post office and put my name on the waiting list for a P.O. Box. Depending on the area,
you may not have any wait at all. (The annual fee at that time was $34). I decided to use a Post Office Box,
since my home address didn't really look professional enough. Another option is to use a mail center with an impressive street address.

I walked into the local IRS office (the same day) and asked for Form SS-4. I filled it out, photocopied it (remember to keep copies of all forms and applications that you complete) and mailed it out the same day. The SS-4 is an application for an ID# for the business. I could have used my social security number, since I was an individual with no employees, but, you never know.....

December 14

I got form X-201 NYS Certificate of Conducting Business Under an Assumed Name for Individual (also known as a "DBA" (for "Doing Business As") from a stationery store and filled it out in triplicate. I took the forms to a notary public at a bank, and signed them in front of him and had it notarized. For this form I
needed a physical address (no post office boxes), so I used my home address since only the bank, and the county clerk's office would know about it. I then went to the local County Clerk's Office to see if anyone else was using the name I chose.   No one was, so I proceeded with my plans.

December 15

Having a legitimate sounding company name and an address, I could now do some groundwork. I could have done this at any time, but it's good to start getting the name of the company out as soon as possible.
- → Phoned the Uniform Code Council in Dayton, OH (513-435-3870) and requested an application.
- → Phoned BMI (212-586-2000), (or ASCAP-212-621-6000) and requested a publisher application.
- → Phoned the Copyright office in Washington (202 707-9100) and requested an information kit.
- → Phoned the Trademark Office in Washington (703-557-INFO) and requested an information kit.
- → Phoned RIAA (Recording Industry Association of America-202-775-0101)   and requested a membership application.

December 21
➔ Registered the company with the County Clerk's office. (Total cost at the time: $33.00)

At the county clerk's office, I received two of the three copies of the DBA form (now validated). One was to be displayed in the place of business, the other was for my bank. Bank? That's right, at some point in the future, I would need to write checks and have checks written to me: I needed a bank account! In order to open a business account under the company name, I would have to show the DBA form I had filed earlier. (Your business will have a bit more credibility if you can write and receive checks in the company's name, but you can choose not to take this step right away.)

December 24
I took the DBA form to a local bank with a few hundred dollars and opened a checking account. I ordered some nice checks (had my logo put on them for an extra charge) and got some temporary checks right on the spot so I could start spending in the name of my record company. Your bank may want to do a background check on you before the account is finally approved.

December 27
Once the Uniform Code Council's UPC application arrived, I was a few days closer to being official. I paid the $300 application fee (a bit high, but don't even think about taking your record to a distributor without a bar code) and in a few days I had my company code. You'll find that once you get in the business, you'll get more information than you anticipated on how to make everything work for you. Read everything, start a filing system and again, save all the forms.
Completed and mailed BMI forms. You must register your song so you can get paid from radio play.
Completed and mailed Trademark forms. This step is optional; I felt I had a very unique logo and company name that I wanted to protect.
And that's it! I was ready! I had a name, an image, an address, a bank account, an industry code, and a federal identity. I was in business! *STARTING YOUR OWN COMPANY IS ONE OF THE EASIEST THINGS TO DO IN AMERICA!!!!*

The Process

In truth, you're IN business from the moment you say you are. However, for the purpose of being a legitimately recognized entity, there are usually several steps you need to take;

- Choose a business structure.
- Announce your intention. Some states require that you publish an announcement in a newspaper.
- File necessary papers and pay fees as required for your chosen structure.
- Get appropriate licenses, permits, insurance as necessary.
- Set up a bank account.

In order to be legitimate, your business must be a registered under a legally recognized structure. There are several possible forms your business can take: **Hopefully you'll leave this chapter with a specific answer to the question: "Which structure is best for my record label?"**

Types of Business Structures

In order to be a legitimate, your business must be registered with the government as a legally recognized entity. There are several possible structures for your company:
- $ Sole Proprietorship
- $ Corporation
- $ Subchapter "S" Corporation
- $ Non-profit Corporation
- $ Professional Corporation
- $ Foreign Corporation
- $ Foreign Non-Profit Corporation
- $ General Partnership
- $ Limited Liability Company (LLC)
- $ Limited Liability Partnership (LLP)
- $ Foreign Limited Liability Company (LLC)
- $ Foreign Limited Liability Partnership

With few exceptions, every single business, operation, or other money-making venture, even not-for-profit organizations fall into one of these categories. Each form has its advantages and disadvantages which may make it appropriate for certain types of businesses and not others. To make this easier, here's the format we'll be following. For each structure, we'll explain what it is, explore the advantages, disadvantages, how to start/file, what fees are involved. We'll wrap things up with a chart comparing all your options.

Sole Proprietorship

If you are going into this alone, you may want to consider starting a Sole Proprietorship. As the name implies, this means YOU are the company. You can still have employees, of course, but the company itself is owned entirely by you. You alone have the power of the checkbook. While this control
is appealing to many, it also means some other things you should be aware of. As a Sole Proprietor, the courts and the government don't differentiate between you and your company. In other words, if for some reason, someone decides to sue your business and wins, or if you rack up a sizable debt and the company fails, or if you owe taxes on the business, you, the individual, will ultimately be responsible for it. Your assets, that is, anything you own, including your personal savings, may be used to repay the debt. This is the reality of America. Don't let this discourage you, though. There are between 13 and 14 million small businesses in the United States, and a good 75% of them are Sole Proprietorships. This fact alone must mean that there is something inherently appealing in this form.   I highly recommend it as it gives the least hassle to get up and running and, if you set realistic goals, plan your strategy, and do things the right way, you can avoid the legal and tax headaches mentioned above.

Form to file: "DBA"/Certificate of Doing Business Under an Assumed Name or similarly titled form
you'll need about 3 forms; one for the county, one for your bank, and one for your place of business. Additional copies will be required if your state requires any special permits.)
Where to file: County Clerk's Office/County Courthouse
Fees: Filing fee (anywhere from $0 to $50,depending on the state)
Certification fee (varies widely per state);

NOTE: Some states also require you to announce the formation of your new business in the local press.

Partnership

If you and some friends are going into this, you might want to consider forming a Partnership. A partnership is the relationship between two or more persons who join together to carry on a trade or business. The main reason people form partnerships is to increase the money, labor and skills available to the business. In a General Partnership (the most common form), the partners share control, profit, as well as liability for debt. In the Limited Partnership, there are some partners who invest money or property in return for a cut of the profit, but their control is limited and their liability, as well, is limited to the amount of their investment (Limited partners are sometimes referred to as "silent" partners). In determining how profits are split, or how control will be shared, the partners are free to come to any arrangement they choose without government restrictions. It is similar to a Sole Proprietorship in that the persons involved are generally still considered individuals as far as the government and tax law are concerned. This structure also involves minimal paperwork to get started. In fact, in some states, the individuals involved don't even need a written agreement among them to be considered in a partnership. We recommend, however, always having something in writing. The drawbacks to a partnership are more personal than legal. Conflicts of egos, miscommunication, incompatibility of management and operational styles are among the main issues cited as problems by entrepreneurs involved in partnerships. Liability should also be a concern for anyone considering a partnership. You should be aware that legally, any decision, agreement or deal made by one member of a partnership is binding on the other members as well, even if the other members were not consulted or present when the decision was made. So, for example, regardless of the reasons for it, both you and your partner would be held legally responsible for paying for the 10,000 records your partner ordered (acting on his/her own initiative) the Friday you were out of town

Form to file: Certificate of Conducting Business as Partners (check business stationery store)
Where to file: County Clerk's Office/County Courthouse
Fees: *Filing fee* Anywhere from $0 to $50, depending on the state.
   Certification fee Usually less than $10 per form; you'll need about 3 forms; one each for the county, your bank, and your place of business. Additional copies will be required if your state requires any special permits.

Limited Liability Company (LLC)

The Limited Liability Corporation or LLC is the newest form of business entity. Owners of an LLC are referred to as active or non-active "members." Active members are taxed like general partners whereas non-active members are taxed like limited partners, but all members enjoy limited liability and may report profits or losses on their personal tax returns. What makes the LLC attractive to many entrepreneurs is that it combines the best features of a corporation and a partnership. Briefly, the members have limited liability like a corporation while income and losses are passed through to the individual members like in a partnership. The LLC itself is not a taxable entity like a corporation is.

Although an LLC sounds a lot like an S-corporation (Both LLC and an S-corporation avoid double taxation by allowing the pass through of income to the owners (or members) and they both provide for limited liability), the LLC does have some additional flexibility that may be important for some businesses.

Advantages of an LLC
- Limited liability for all members, unlike a general partner.
- No taxation as an entity, no double taxation as in a corporation.
- May have more than one class of stock, profits and losses need not be distributed in proportion of ownership, unlike a S-corporation..
- No limit to the number of members, unlike an S corporation.

Disadvantages of an LLC
- Fairly complex to setup properly & each state is slightly different so careful research is required.
- No "continuity of life" like a regular corporation. The LLC dissolves if one of the members dies or leaves. Formal agreements can solve this.

Important bits of information concerning LLCs

A business that intends issuing stock incentives to employees or selling shares public should consider incorporating instead of LLC. A few states, (Texas, California)impose annual fees or taxes on LLCs. As of Oct 1998, in California, the District of Columbia, Massachusetts, New Jersey and Tennessee, an LLC must have at least two owners. Most other states allow LLCs to be formed with as few as 1 person.

Forms to File: You can establish an LLC by filing a document called Articles of Organization with your state's corporate filing office (often the Secretary of State or Commissioner of Corporations).

The decision of which form of business to use will depend on a number of factors: the particular financial situations of the individuals involved, tax and legal requirements of the business, record keeping, the need for and number of employees, and other unique circumstances. Also, since each state will have its own set of filing and tax requirements for each form of business, these must be considered as well when deciding which is best for you. After my own personal experience with The Service Corps of Retired Executives (SCORE), I strongly recommend finding the office nearest you and establishing a relationship with an adviser now. Having someone who can guide you through the right questions you should be asking can save you major heartaches in the future.

The LLC is not a corporation, but it offers many of the same advantages. Many small business owners and entrepreneurs prefer LLC's because they combine the limited liability protection of a corporation with the "pass through"" taxation of a sole proprietorship or partnership.

LLC's have additional advantages over corporations:

LLC's allow greater flexibility in management and business organization.

LLC's do not have the ownership restrictions of S Corp, making them ideal for foreign investors.

LLC's accomplish these aims without the IRS' restrictions of an S Corporation.

LLC's are now available in all 50 states and Washington, D.C. If you have other questions regarding LLC's, be sure to speak with a qualified legal and/or financial advisor.

There are only 4 reasons why a corporation is more advisable than an LLC.

1. Your business needs the ability to issue stock or stock options to attract key employees or investors.

2. Your business is so profitable that you can save significant income tax dollars by keeping some profits in the corporation each year. This strategy is called "income splitting" because profits are essentially split between the individual owners and the corporation itself. (See Cut Taxes With Corporate Income Splitting.)

3. You own a family business and you want to begin making gifts of ownership to your family as part of your financial or estate plan or to plan for the next generation of owners. With a corporation you can easily make gifts of shares in your company without necessarily giving up management control and, if it's done correctly, without paying gift tax.

4. Others insist that you incorporate your business. For example, if you are an independent contractor, companies you want to work for may ask you to incorporate before they will sign contracts for your services. This is because if you form a corporation, the IRS is more likely to view you as an independent contractor than an employee -- a less-risky proposition for those who want to hire you.

How to Form an LLC

It's more work than forming a partnership and easier than creating a corporation -- and it may be the best thing you can do for your business. By now, you're probably familiar with the advantages of running your business as an LLC: limited liability protection and a simpler method of paying taxes than that imposed on corporations. (To learn more about these benefits, read LLC Basics.) This article focuses on the steps you will take to make your LLC a legal reality. Essentially, you must:

1. Choose an available business name that complies with your state's LLC rules.
2. File formal paperwork, ("articles of organization"), pay filing fee (from $40 to $900 dependent on state).
3. Create an LLC operating agreement, which sets out the rights and responsibilities of the LLC members.
4. Publish a notice of your intent to form an LLC (required in only a few states).
5. Obtain licenses and permits that may be required for your business.

Choosing a Name for Your LLC

The name of your LLC must comply with the rules of your state's LLC division. (Typically, this office is combined with the corporations division, and is part of the Department or Secretary of State's office.) While requirements differ from state to state, generally: the name cannot be the same as the name of another LLC on file with the LLC office the name must end with an LLC designator, such as "Limited Liability Company" or "Limited Company," or an abbreviation of one of these phrases ("LLC," "L.L.C." or "Ltd. Liability Co."), and the name cannot include certain words prohibited by the state, such as Bank, Insurance, Corporation or City (states differ widely on prohibited terms).

Your state's LLC office can tell you how to check if your proposed name is available for your use. Often, for a small fee, you can reserve your LLC name for a short period of time until you file your articles of organization. Besides following your state's LLC naming rules, you must make sure your name won't violate another company's trademark. For information on trademark law and general advice on picking a successful business name, see Choosing a Business Name.

Once you've found a legal and available name, you don't usually need to register it with your state; when you file your articles of organization your business name will be automatically registered.

Filing Articles of Organization

After deciding on a name, you must now prepare and file "articles of organization" with your state's LLC filing office. While most states use the term "articles of organization" to refer to the basic document creating an LLC, some states (including Delaware, Mississippi, New Hampshire, New Jersey and Washington) use the term "certificate of formation." Two other states (Massachusetts and Pennsylvania) call the document a "certificate of organization."

One disadvantage of forming an LLC instead of a partnership or a sole proprietorship is that you'll have to pay a filing fee when you submit your articles of organization. In most states, the fees are modest -- typically around $100. In a few others, they take a bigger bite: consider California ($70, plus an $800 annual tax), Illinois ($400) and Massachusetts ($500).

Articles of organization are short, simple documents. In fact, you can usually prepare your own in just a few minutes by filling in the blanks and checking the boxes on a form provided by your state's filing office.

Typically, you must provide only your LLC's name, its address and sometimes the names of all of the owners -- called members. You will probably also be required to list the name and address of a person --usually one of the LLC members -- who will act as your LLC's "registered agent," or "agent for service of process." Your agent is the person who will receive legal papers in any future lawsuit involving your LLC. Generally, all of the LLC owners may prepare and sign the articles, or they can appoint just one person to do so.

Creating an LLC Operating Agreement

Even though operating agreements need not be filed with the LLC filing office and are rarely required by state law, it is essential that you create one. In an LLC operating agreement, you set out rules for the ownership and operation of the business (much like a partnership agreement or corporate bylaws). A typical operating agreement includes:

- the members' percentage interests in the business
- the members' rights and responsibilities
- the members' voting power
- how profits and losses will be allocated
- how the LLC will be managed
- rules for holding meetings and taking votes, and
- "buy-sell" provisions, which establish rules for what happens if a member wants to sell his interest, dies or becomes disabled.

The decision of which form of business to use will depend on a number of factors: the particular financial situations of the individuals involved, tax and legal requirements of the business, record keeping, the need for and number of employees, and other special circumstances. Also, since each state will have its own set of filing and tax requirements for each form of business, these must be considered as well when deciding which is best for you. My general advice for the individual is to start off initially as a sole proprietorship. Since the incorporation process can take as little as a few days, you can modify the status of your business at any time in the future, as your company grows.

Corporations

Of the three forms of business, the corporation involves the most paperwork, "legalese", and is the most regulated by the government through state and federal laws. A corporation is formed after an individual or group of individuals applies to the state for a charter. The corporation, which the state approves into existence, has its own identity. It needs to file its own taxes, and have its own bank account. Income and losses are taxed to the corporation. Any income generated by the corporation for the stockholders is also taxed. In other words, if the company makes $100, and your share is $50, the government would tax the $100 at the corporate rate, and then tax your $50 at the individual rate. This "double taxation" is one of the more annoying drawbacks to the corporation. One advantage to the corporation is that the government does recognize it as being separate from the individuals who run it. That means your personal assets usually cannot be touched in the event of legal or financial action against the company.

NOTE: Since the original publication of this book in 1992, I've learned a lot, seen a lot change, and now advocate the forming of a corporation more strongly now than before. Robert Kiyosaki's series of Rich Dad books give detailed explanations of why it's wiser to incorporate. Yes, it's a bit more costly. Yes, there's more paperwork involved. Yes, the initial tax requirement might seem higher since you may have to be estimated taxes every quarter. BUT, the bottom line is, if you really are serious about playing the game with the "pros", you can't afford to present yourself as an amateur. I've always advised that you can always start as a Sole-Proprietor and then form your corporation later. That's still something you can choose to do. However, in this edition of *Change The Game*, which I intend to serve as a guideline for true success from now into the next several years, I now stress going with a corporation as early as possible.

Here are a few of the benefits of setting up a corporation.

Reduces Personal Liability

Incorporating helps separate your personal identity from that of your business. Sole proprietors and partners are subject to unlimited personal liability for business debt or law suits against their company. Creditors of the sole proprietorship or partnership can bring suit against the owners of the business and can move to seize the owners' homes, cars, savings or other personal assets. Once incorporated, the shareholders of a corporation have only the money they put into the company to lose, and usually no more.

Adds Credibility

A corporate structure communicates permanence, credibility and stature. Even if you are the only stockholder or employee, your incorporated business may be perceived as a much larger and more credible company. Seeing ",inc." or "corp." at the end of your business name can send a powerful message to your customers, suppliers, and associates about your commitment to the ongoing success of your venture.

Provides Tax Advantages – Deductible Employee Benefits

Incorporating usually provides tax-deductible benefits for you and your employees. Even if you are the only shareholder and employee of your business, benefits such as health insurance, life insurance, travel and entertainment expenses may now be deductible. Best of all, corporations usually provide an increased tax shelter for qualified pensions plans or retirement plans (e.g. 401K's).

Allows Easier Access to Capital Funding

Capital can be more easily raised with a corporation through the sale of stock. With sole proprietorships and partnerships, investors are much harder to attract because of the personal liability. Investors are more likely to purchase shares in a corporation where there usually is a separation between personal and business assets. Also, some banks prefer to lend money to corporations.

Creates an Enduring Structure

A corporation is the most enduring legal business structure. Corporations may continue on regardless of what happens to its individual directors, officers, managers or shareholders. If a sole proprietor or partner dies, the business may automatically end or it may become involved in various legal entanglements. Corporations can have unlimited life, extending beyond the illness or death of the owners.

Allows Easier Transfer of Ownership

Ownership of a corporation may be transferred, without substantially disrupting operations or the need for complex legal documentation, through the sale of stock.

Provides Anonymity

Corporations can offer anonymity to its owners. For example, if you want to open an independent small business of any kind and do not want your involvement to be public knowledge, your best choice may be to incorporate. If you open as a sole proprietorship, it is hard to hide the fact that you are the owner. And as a partnership, you will most likely be required to register your name and the names of your partners with the state and/or county officials in which you are doing business.

Offers Centralized Management

With a corporation's centralized management, all decisions are made by your board of directors. Your shareholders cannot unilaterally bind your company by their acts simply because of their investment. With partnerships, each individual general partner may make binding agreements on behalf of the business that may result in serious financial difficulty to you or the partnership as a whole.

Types of Corporations: a closer look

Paperwork Involved

Corporations must comply with statutory rules that unincorporated businesses, such as limited liability companies (LLCs), partnerships and sole proprietorships, don't have to bother with. For instance, corporations must observe corporate formalities such as holding (and taking minutes of) annual shareholder and director meetings and documenting important directors' decisions. Also, corporations must file and pay taxes on a separate corporate tax return and must set up a double-entry bookkeeping system to record business transactions, complete with daily journals and a general ledger.

- $ General Corporation ("C" Corporation)
- $ Close Corporation
- $ Non-profit Corporation
- $ Professional Corporation
- $ Foreign Corporation
- $ Foreign Non-Profit Corporation
- $ Subchapter "S" Corporation

General or "C" Corporation

A general corporation, also known as a "C" corporation, is the most common corporate structure. A general corporation may have an unlimited number of stockholders. Consequently, it is usually chosen by those companies planning to have more than 30 stockholders or large public stock offerings. Since a corporation is a separate legal entity, a stockholder's personal liability is usually limited to the amount of investment in the corporation and no more.

Close Corporation

A close corporation is most appropriate for the individual starting a company alone or with a small number of people. There are a few significant differences between a general corporation and a close corporation. A close corporation limits stockholders to a maximum of 30. In addition, many close corporation statutes require that the directors of a close corporation must first offer the shares to existing stockholders before selling to new stockholders. Not all states recognize close corporations.

Non-profit Corporation

A nonprofit corporation is a corporation formed for purposes other than generating a profit and in which no part of the organization's income is distributed to its directors or officers. A nonprofit corporation can be a church or church association, school, charity, medical provider, legal aid society, volunteer services organization, professional association, research institute, museum, or in some cases a sports association. Nonprofit corporations must apply for tax-exempt status at both the federal and state level.

Professional Corporation (PC)

A professional corporation is a corporation engaged in providing professional services. The corporations formed by Architects , attorneys-at-Law, Public Accountants, Physicians, Dentists, Optometrists, Osteopaths, Chiropractors, Registered Nurses, Veterinarians, Podiatrists, Practicing Psychologists, Occupational Therapists, Engineers and Land surveyors, Landscape Architects, Certified Clinical Social Workers, Geologists & Foresters are usually considered PCs.

Foreign Corporation

Although there are two definitions, typical usage refers to definition 2.

Definition 1 : A corporation which was incorporated under the laws of a foreign country; also called an alien corporation.

Definition 2: A corporation doing business in a state other than the one in which it is incorporated; here also called out-of-state corporation; opposite of domestic corporation.

Foreign Non-Profit Corporation

A foreign non-profit corporation is one that is incorporated under laws other than the laws of this state. A foreign corporation is required to obtain a Certificate of Authority if it is "transacting business" or "conducting affairs" in this state.

Subchapter S Corporation

A Subchapter S Corporation is a general corporation that has elected a special tax status with the IRS after the corporation has been formed. Subchapter S corporations are most appropriate for small business owners and entrepreneurs who prefer to be taxed as if they were still sole proprietors or partners. When a general corporation makes a profit, it pays a federal corporate income tax on the profit.

If the company also declares a dividend, the stockholders must report the dividend as personal income and pay more taxes. S Corporations avoid this "double taxation" (once at the corporate level and again at the personal level) because all income or loss is reported only once on the personal tax returns of the stockholders. For many small businesses, the S Corporation offers the best of both worlds, combining the tax advantages of a sole proprietorship or partnership with the limited liability and enduring life of a corporate structure.

The S-Corporation (formerly called Sub-Chapter S Corporation) is a unique form of the corporation. The main advantage of the S-corporation is that income and losses are taxed through individual shareholders. This may be advantageous for new businesses owners who would benefit from the low individual tax rates, corporate rates are higher, during the early life of the company when profits are usually low (or negative)! Though you can do it yourself, it is advisable to have a lawyer handle the incorporation process. For an average cost of from $100 to $400 (includes filing fee and lawyer's fee) it's worth being sure it's done right.

How to File as a Subchapter S Corporation

- Form a general or close corporation in the state of your choice.
- Obtain the formal consent of the corporation's stockholders and note this consent in your minutes.
- Complete Form 2553, Election by a Small Business Corporation

Forms to File: Certificate of Incorporation. Each state has its own form.
Federal Form 2553--Election by a Small Business Corporation.
Each state will have its own S Corp form requirements as well.

Fees: Filing fees, minimum taxes, and other requirements vary widely by state. If you choose to do it yourself, your local bookstore should have books under the general title of "How to Start a Corporation in (Your State)". Your State Department of Taxation or Comptroller's Department or State Revenue Department may also have information booklets.

Restrictions:
- To elect S Corporation status, your corporation must meet specific guidelines. All stockholders must be citizens or permanent residents of the United States. The maximum number of stockholders for an S Corporation is 75. If an S Corporation is held by an "electing small business trust," then all beneficiaries of the trust must be individuals, estates or charitable organizations. Interests in the trust cannot be purchased. S Corporations may only issue one class of stock. No more than 25 percent of the gross corporate income may be derived from passive income. Not all domestic general business corporations are eligible for S Corporation Status.

Exclusions:
- a financial institution that is a bank
- an insurance company taxed under Subchapter L
- a Domestic International Sales Corporation (DISC)
- certain affiliated groups of corporations
- For more detailed information about these changes and other aspects regarding S
- corporation status, contact your accountant, attorney or local IRS office.

How To Form A Corporation

There are several steps required to legally create a corporation. The first is filing a short document called "articles of incorporation" with the corporations division of your state government. (Some states refer to this organizational document as a "certificate of incorporation," "articles of organization," a "certificate of formation" or a "charter.") To file this document, you'll have to pay a filing fee of $100 or so. Articles of incorporation contain:

- ➜ the name of your corporation
- ➜ the corporation's address
- ➜ a "registered agent" (the person to be contacted by any member of the public who needs to speak to
- ➜ someone about the corporation), and in some states,
- ➜ the names of the corporation's directors.

When forming your corporation, you must also create "corporate bylaws," a longer document that sets out the rules that govern your corporation, including necessary decision-making procedures and voting rights. Finally, before you start doing business, you must hold an initial meeting of your board of directors to take care of some formalities, and you need to issue shares of stock to the initial owners (shareholders).

Steps For Starting A Corporation In New York State

Following is a summary of the major steps you need to set up a corporation in New York State. It's much easier than you think! The specifics of each step have been omitted in the interest of space. If you are in NY, CA, TX, or FL, I recommend purchasing the Nolo Press Self Help Law book "How to Form a [state] Corporation."

Preliminary Step. The first place to start is a stationery store that carries legal forms (The Blumberg line of legal forms is the most popular). There, you can purchase a corporate kit ($50-$100) which includes most of the forms mentioned below that you'll need to complete and/or file. The forms not included in the corporate kit can be purchased directly from the stationer. Use a typewriter to complete all forms! Professionalism is one of the reasons you would pay a lawyer to do this for you.

Step 1. Choose a corporate name (Certain restrictions apply). Contact Dept. of State and request a name search ($5) to make sure no one else has registered the name. You may also wish to check phone book listings, The Federal Trademark Register (at your library), the county clerk's office, and industry directories to make sure the name you want is not being used by someone else.

Step 2. Complete and file Certificate of Incorporation. Mail to Department of State along with appropriate fees, ($125 + $0.05 per share tax), backing sheet (a sheet with corporate name and person submitting certificate), and a cover letter.

Step 3. File Stock Registration Certificate. (No filing fee required, but the form must be notarized) The purpose is to notify the Tax Commission of the existence of your corporation. This is necessary because every time stock is transferred a small tax is required to be paid to the Commission.

Step 4. Set up your Corporate Records Book. This is simply where you keep all your corporate papers (Certificate of Incorporation, Stock Registration Certificate, Bylaws, Statement of Incorporators, Minutes of Meetings, stock certificates, etc). Many people will just get a three-ring binder to accomplish this.

Step 5. Get a corporate seal. (about $40) You've probably seen Notary Publics use a similar type of embossed seal. Your corporate seal serves the similar purpose of authorizing certain formal documents like leases, stock certificates, mortgages and loan documents as being valid acts of the corporation.

Step 6. Order stock certificates. Your legal stationer can get custom-made ones for you, or you can use the generic ones included in your corporate kit. These are given to your shareholders in return for their monetary investment in your company.

Step 7. Prepare Bylaws. The Bylaws are the rules for the management and operation of the corporation. Once again there are standard forms with a few blank spaces for you to fill in specific information about your corporation. These are also in your corporate kit.

Step 8. Prepare Statement of Incorporators. This step is a formality that's required before the corporation can legally begin to operate. The person(s) who signed the Certificate of Incorporation are required to officially adopt the bylaws and elect the directors who are going to manage the corporation. The statement is simply a signed letter stating just that. Of course if you are the only member of the board, getting the required signatures is quite easy!

Step 9. Prepare and sign minutes of first meeting. This may seem a tedious formality, but if you're going to do this, do it right! There are certain items which must be resolved at a first meeting. So, again, there's not much to do since there are generic "minutes of first meeting" forms with blank spaces to be filled in.

Step 10. Issue shares of stock. The number of shares to be issued and the price per stock were determined at the first meeting. There are federal and state securities laws which govern how stock can be issued. Contact the Securities Exchange Commission (SEC) to have them send you a package.

The preceding was a summary of the major steps involved. You will need to have the particular corporate kit for your state and some instructions in order to do everything correctly. As you see, none of these steps requires any great outlay of money nor any knowledge that you can't find in the instructions. On the other hand, there are differences within each state, so sometimes it might be worth going to a lawyer.

[There are many companies that will incorporate your company for fees ranging from $49 to thousands. Visit the www.hiphopbiz.com site to see who our current partners are.]

Business Structure Comparison Chart

Sole Proprietorship	Simple and inexpensive to create and operate Owner reports profit or loss on his or her personal tax return	Owner personally liable for business debts
General Partnership	Simple and inexpensive to create and operate Owners (partners) report their share of profit or loss on their personal tax returns	Owners (partners) personally liable for business debts
Limited Partnership	Limited partners have limited personal liability for business debts as long as they don't participate in management. General partners can raise cash without involving outside investors in management of business	General partners personally liable for business debts More expensive to create than general partnership Suitable mainly for companies that invest in real estate
Regular Corporation (Also available: Professional Corporation and non-profit corporation)	Owners have limited personal liability for business debts Fringe benefits can be deducted as business expense Owners can split corporate profit among owners and corporation paying lower overall tax rate	More expensive to create than partnership or sole proprietorship Paperwork can seem burdensome to some owners Separate taxable entity
S Corporation	Owners have limited personal liability for business debts Owners report their share of corporate profit or loss on their personal tax returns Owners can use corporate loss to offset income from other sources	More expensive to create than partnership or sole proprietorship More paperwork than for a limited liability company which offers similar advantages Income must be allocated to owners according to their ownership interests Fringe benefits limited for owners who own more than 2% of shares
Limited Liability Company (LLC) (also Professional LLC in which Members must all belong to the same profession) Also LLP (Limited Liability Partnerships)	Owners have limited personal liability for business debts even if they participate in management. Profit and loss can be allocated differently than ownership interests IRS rules now allow LLCs to choose between being taxed as partnership or corporation	More expensive to create than partnership or sole proprietorship. State laws for creating LLCs may not reflect latest federal tax changes

So, which structure should you choose?

For the record: Here's my FINAL Answer!

I'll gladly go on record as saying that I believe your choice will be between an LLC and a Corporation. Again, I say this because of the tax benefits provided. The game that the rich play is in how to separate themselves from their money. In other words, the average person feels more secure with everything in their name. The rich, to avoid liability, seek to have nothing in their personal name, but everything at their direct disposal as an asset or perk of doing business. Think about that.

The major advantage to having a corporation is that you can legally benefit from many "perks of doing business" without having the financial accountability an tax burden of having these perks in your own name.

So, for the record, I'm advocating LLC or Corporation as your choice of business structure. And, unless a new entity comes along before I revise this book, that's my story and I'm sticking with it!

LLC and Partnership are really "pass through" concepts. In other words, they are simply structures through which the money passes through on its way to you. And, as a result, you pay taxes.

Corporation is the only entity which and which has its own taxing structure. The benefit of having a separate taxing structure is that you can do things to fall in the lowest tax brackets in both of your tax obligations. In other words, say you're making a ton of money. So much that you cringe when you compute how much tax you'll have to pay. Well, if you owned a corporation, you could deduct the costs of various perks and benefits and expenses that you get the benefit of, while deducting them as business expenses. So the corporation pays less taxes because it had expenses that lowered its taxable income. And you get the benefit of these perks without having to purchase them yourself out of a salary.

A good resource to learn more about the benefits of corporations is the *Rich Dad Series* of books by Robert Kiyosaki.

Other Considerations

Every business has different needs that vary by state and municipality. Here is a typical list of some of the things you may need in order to get started .

Licenses and Permits

Depending on the type of business, the type of product or service you offer, or the part of town you set up shop, you may need to get a local business license, federal import license, county license, state license, or federal license. Licenses are an indication that you have the authorization, expertise, or zoning approval for a given jurisdiction.

The issuing agency for a given license varies by state. You may need to contact the county clerk's office, city hall, the county registrar, or the recorder's office. If in doubt, contact the local Small Business Administration (SBA) office in your area. They'll put you in touch with the right agency where you can get information on the required certifications for your business as well as the appropriate fees.

Permits, on the other hand, are an indication that you have complied with certain local and state laws affecting safety, appearance or the right to collect sales tax. Again, a call or trip to your state government office, or the local SBA can steer you in the right direction.

Resale Certificate

As a business, you do not pay sales tax on the purchase of goods and services which will be resold, or which will be used up in creating a product or service for resale. For example, if you buy lumber to make chairs to be sold to the public, you would not be required to pay taxes on the purchase of the lumber. Whatever your passion, your payments to your printing company, supplier, manufacturer or other individuals or businesses (vendors) involved in your trade will generally be exempt from sales taxes. To qualify for this exemption from paying sales taxes (on purchases for resale only), you need to be authorized to do so by your state. You will need to apply for a Sales Tax Vendor ID/Certificate of Authority with your state department of taxation. You will be given a sales tax vendor ID number (in most cases, you will be able to use the EIN which you received after filling out form SS-4).

When making purchases on behalf of your company, inform the vendor that you have a resale certificate. You'll need to provide them with a completed copy of a certificate. (The state or your local stationery store can supply you with this form. Be sure to make extra copies). Generally, this form must be completed each time a purchase is made. If you anticipate dealing on a regular basis with a particular vendor, you should request that she or he keep a completed form on file for your company. The completed form, which will now be considered a "Blanket Certificate", will cover any future purchases you make from this vendor, and eliminate the need to fill out a new form each time you make a purchase.

Sales tax is charged on purchases at the retail level. That is, at the point where it is offered for retail sale to the consumer. Your status as a vendor will also authorize you to collect sales tax on retail sales--that is, sales directly to the public. You are collecting taxes on behalf of the state, and are therefore required to hand over what you've collected at (usually) quarterly intervals. The necessary forms, coupons or deposit slips will be provided to you by your state agency at the time you apply for your Vendor ID.

Insurance

While some experts advise strongly in favor of insurance, others ignore it altogether. The reasoning in favor of insurance is that, as a business, because you will come in contact with customers, suppliers and employees who, for any reason might file a claim against you for negligence, bodily injury, product liability, worker's compensation, or because your property may get stolen or damaged, that you must prepare and protect yourself for that possibility by taking out an insurance policy.

Ultimately, this decision will be influenced by the type of business you operate, the likelihood of such need, industry trends and practices, your comfort level of risk, and the cost of insurance relative to your budget. Contact the Small Business Administration (SBA), the Insurance Information Institute and The Service Corps of Retired Executives (SCORE) for advice and information.

Your EIN

You'll need an EIN (Federal Employer Identification number) if you are a sole proprietor and you pay wages to one or more employees, or if your business is a partnership or a corporation. If you are a sole proprietorship with no employees, you can usually use your own social security number as your business identification number. In this case, the tax department of your state will assign a special account number for state tax returns and business records. I recommend getting an EIN in anticipation of your first employee, as well as to establish a separate identity for your company.

To get an EIN, file federal Form SS-4 (Application for Employer Identification Number) with the IRS. On the back of the form are instructions for receiving your EIN over the phone if you need it fast.

Your Resale Certificate

The sales tax charged on purchases is usually done at the retail level. That is, at the point where it is offered for retail sale to the consumer. Consequently, those who deal and trade at the wholesale level (which now includes you) do not pay sales tax on the purchase of goods and services which will be resold, or which will be used up in creating product for resale. Payments to your supplier, printing company, photographer, and other individuals or businesses involved in your trade will generally be exempt from sales tax.

To get this exemption from paying sales taxes (only on business purchases) you need to be authorized to do so by your state. You'll need to apply for a State Sales Tax Vendor ID/Certificate of Authority with your state department of taxation. You will be given a sales tax vendor ID number (in most cases you will be able to use your Federal Tax ID, which you received after filling out form SS-4) which identifies you as a manufacturer/wholesaler.

When making purchases on behalf of your company, inform the vendor that you have a resale Certificate. (The state will supply you with the form; make copies) Generally, this form must be completed each time a purchase is made. If you anticipate dealing on a continual basis with a particular vendor, you should request that she or he keep a completed form on file for your company. The form, which will now be considered a "Blanket Certificate", will cover any future purchases and eliminate the need to fill out a new form each time you deal with that vendor.

Your status as a vendor, will also authorize you to collect sales tax on retail sales. That is, sales directly to the public. This may not apply to you right now since most of your business will probably be on the wholesale level with your distributors and "one stops."

NOTE: The resale certificate is intended to cover legitimate business-related purchases only.
A sample of a New York State Resale Certificate is provided in Appendix A.

Financing Your Business

If possible, you should start your business without getting into debt. Most people start their business using their own money and often use their present source of employment to provide the necessary funding.

Some passions, on the other hand, may require start-up cash that's greater than what you currently have on that hand. For example, you may need large sums of money to buy equipment, purchase inventory, get patents, etc. In figuring out how to raise money to jump-start your business, there are essentially two ways to get it.

1. Debt Financing.

As the name implies, with debt financing, you are financing your passion by going into debt. Someone lends you the money that you need. You are required to pay back this loan with interest. The interest rate that you pay on the loan will vary depending on who gives you the money. The vast majority of small businesses that need more money than they have available use debt financing.

2. Equity Financing.

With equity financing, you are financing your passion by giving away a piece of the future income of your business. The person or organization that provides you with the money becomes an investor who then has "equity" or a piece of the company "equivalent" to how much they invested. Equity investments involve a certain amount of risk on the part of the investor. Investors make their money if the business is profitable, but lose their money if the business fails. The downside for you is that you are giving up a certain degree of ownership of your company.

Here is a list of possible sources and methods you can use to get money, or it's equivalent, to finance your business.

Non-debt Sources
1. YOU. You are your own best "lender". If you have the savings, this approach can be quick and easy. Entrepreneurs have started billion-dollar companies with as little as $0 invested.

2. BARTERING. You need money to pay for supplies, starting inventory, advertising, etc. But what if you could get those goods and services directly in return for providing some service or product you already have? Bartering allows you to trade your goods and services for those of other companies. Contact the International Reciprocal Trade Association in Chicago, IL, at (312)461-0236, or online at www.irta.org for more information.

3. GRANTS. Many foundations provide funding in the form of grants. The "Foundation Directory" can provide a list of foundations that may have an interest in your specific business idea. The Foundation Center may be reached at (212) 620-4230, or online at www.fdncenter.org. You may also wish to contact the National Endowment for the Arts at (202) 682-5400, or online at www.arts.endow.gov for information on their programs. Another little-known fact is that the US Department of Agriculture, in addition to sponsoring over two dozen money-lending programs, encourages growth in rural areas, with an Industrial Loan Program which provides funds for businesses in towns of less than 50,000 people. Contact the USDA at www.usda.gov.

4. VENDOR FINANCING. If your business is one that relies heavily on certain vendors, it may be possible to obtain financing through the vendor. After all, they want you to use their product or service and therefore have an interest in helping you be successful. Contact the SBA or SCORE for guidance.

5. FACTORING. If you are owed money by customers, there are finance companies, banks and individuals, known as factors, who will purchase the right to collect these debts. Say you have an invoice for $2,000 owed

to you by Carrie Customer. ABC factor may purchase this invoice for say, 85% of it's value. You receive $1700 that you can use right away for your business, and Carrie now owes ABC factor the $2,000. ABC factor now has the responsibility of collecting the $2,000 from Carrie.

You can also factor purchase orders. If you receive an order from a large store, chain or other buyer, the purchase order represents a promise to pay which can be sold to ABC factor. You get money up front to use to purchase inventory or manufacture the product. Again, the disadvantage is that you get a percentage of the total amount of the purchase order. Look in your local yellow pages, or online search engines under "factors", or call the SBA, SCORE, your bank, or The Commercial Finance Association (NY), at (212)594-3490, or online www.cfa.com for more information.

6. PRE-SELLING. You may wish to consider pre-selling your product as a means of generating capital by taking orders in advance from friends, family, advertisers, etc. Offer a "pre-publication/release/launch discount" as an incentive. (*ie. Pre-order NOW and save 10%!*)

Debt Sources

7. RETIREMENT PLANS. Some retirement plans (401K for example) allow you to borrow against vested benefits. Generally, up to 50% may be borrowed as long as this is less than $50,000. If you quit your employment, the loan must be repaid immediately. If you don't pay, the amount borrowed is treated as an "early distribution" and is taxable.

8. LIFE INSURANCE. Some types of life insurance policies, namely "whole life" and "universal", have cash value which can be borrowed at very low interest rates. You are not obligated to pay this money back but if you don't, your policy payout is reduced by the amount borrowed.

9. HOME EQUITY LOAN. Interest rates for this kind of loan are generally quite low and the interest is fully deductible for the first $100,000 borrowed. Keep in mind that you are placing your home on the line as collateral with this method of financing.

10. THE SMALL BUSINESS ADMINISTRATION (SBA). The SBA does NOT generally loan money directly but rather guarantees a loan (normally up to 90% of the loan amount). They, in effect, become your co-signer on the loan. This can make it a lot easier to obtain a bank loan since the bank's risk is lowered considerably. The exception is that the SBA does provide direct loans to certain groups including disabled veterans and handicapped individuals. In general, the SBA will not offer any assistance until you have been turned down for a loan by a commercial bank. Most loans guaranteed through the SBA are between $25,000 and $750,000. However, there is a "microloan" program for amounts from a few hundred dollars up to $25,000. Another loan program, SBALowDoc, under which an entrepreneur can borrow up to $150,000 is a popular new option with a streamlined loan-application process. Find your local SBA office on the agency's Web site at www.sba.gov, or call the Answer Desk at 800-822-5722.

11. SMALL BUSINESS INVESTMENT COMPANIES (SBICs) The SBIC program was formed by the Small Business Administration (SBA) in 1958 to help small businesses and entrepreneurs secure financing. SBICs are typically formed by a group of people experienced in venture capital financing who have at least $5 million in capital they want to invest. They pool their money together, and apply to the SBA for an SBIC license. SBICs can use the money to offer loans or buy equity in companies they feel strongly about.

12. FRIENDS and RELATIVES. If they believe in you and your idea, friends and relatives are sometimes willing to fund you. Choose this route with care and execute a formal loan document stating loan terms (interest, terms of repayment). Be advised, however, that many friends have been lost and many relatives alienated because of a small business failure.

13. BANKS and CREDIT UNIONS. Many banks and credit unions will loan money for starting a small business. Check with your own first and then with the local chamber of commerce for alternate possibilities. This approach will require that you present a formal business plan to the bank showing justification for the amount you are borrowing.

14. STATE. Some states have small business financing authorities that issue tax-exempt development bonds that can be used to finance land, buildings and equipment for manufacturing businesses. Check with your local government office for details.

15. CREDIT CARDS. Despite stories of credit-card funded start-ups which have gone on to million-dollar success, the best advice is to use this option as a last resort. Credit card interest rates are excessively high.

Equity sources

There are several sources you can use if you're in need of amounts ranging in the hundreds of thousands to millions. America's Business Funding Directory (ABFD), is a directory for venture-capital funding. They have a searchable database of more than 15,000 potential lenders and investors. Keep in mind that many venture capitalists are usually interested in experienced small businesses in high-growth areas like technology that can provide potentially big returns.

Angels, as these investors are called, look for a clearly identifiable niche with a large market potential, a competitive advantage and, ideally, a product or process that can be protected with a patent. Angels are investing in the people behind the business, and therefore look for people who are passionate about what they do. Angels often expect to cash out after five to seven years. And although they know they probably won't earn much, if anything, along the way, they eventually expect an annualized rate of return of 20% to 40%, perhaps through a buyout of their shares or a sale of the business.

Remember that many of these loan ideas will require you to sign a personal guarantee. This means that regardless of what structure your business is operating under, and regardless of what happens to your business, you are personally liable for the repayment of the loan amount. Think carefully before signing.

<u>**SUMMARY for Chapter 4: *"Business Startup"***</u>

- If you want to be taken seriously, and if you really intend to reach the personal and financial goals you've set for yourself, then you need to start a business. 75% of the Gross National Product GNP is generated by the efforts of small business. Therefore, the government has made it relatively easy to set up a business.

- In choosing the type of business structure that is right for you, you can choose a Sole-Proprietorship, Partnership, Corporation or Limited Liability Corporation. Each has its pros and cons and the best one may depend on certain factors that are unique to your situation. There are many benefits of choosing a corporation that may be wise to consider. Author Robert Kiyosaki's *Rich Dad* series of books and products explain these and give advice that will help you.

- You may also need licenses, permits, a resale certificate and insurance when you start your own business. Every country and state has its own set of guidelines.

- Your business plan can be used to raise capital for your business venture, and can help you to structure and set goals for your business.

- There are many ways that you can generate capital for launching your business.

RESOURCES for Chapter 4: *"Business Startup"*
BOOKS, AUDIO PROGRAMS, MAGAZINES, ORGANIZATIONS & WEBSITES

☐ **For business start-up, naming**
- *Form Your Own Limited Liability Company* by Attorney Anthony Mancuso
- *Legal Guide for Starting & Running a Small Business*, by Attorney Fred S. Steingold
- *Small Business Legal Guide* by Robert Friedman
- *Trademark--How to Name a Business or Product* by Kate McGrath and Stephen Elias /Sarah Shena
- *Naming for Power: Creating Successful Names For The Business World* by Naseem Javed
- *The Small Business Start-Up Guide* by Robert Sullivan
- *The Gold Book of Venture Capital Firms* by Kennedy Information; www.kennedyinfo.com
- *Roget's College Thesaurus* for coming up with names for your business
- A good dictionary

☐ **Audiotapes**
- *Multiple Streams of Income* by Robert G. Allen   (visit www.nightingale-conant.com)

☐ **Magazines**
- Home Office Computing; $19.97/year; (800)288-7812
- BarterNews; $40/year; (714)495-6529

☐ **Organizations**
- Small Business Administration (SBA) call information for local chapter
- Small Business Administration Answer Desk; (800)827-5722
- Service Corps of Retired Executives; ask local SBA for information
- National Association of Women Business Owners; DC; (301)608-2500;   NY; (212) 779-7504
- National Federation of Independent Business; TN; (800)634-2669
- National Business Incubation Association (NBIA); OH; (740)593-4331; www.nbia.org
- Retail Council or similar retail member organization in your state.
- International Franchise Association; DC; (202)628-8000
- US Department of Commerce; NY; (212)264-0635
- Register of Copyrights Library Of Congress, DC; (202)707-5959
- US Patent &Trademark Office; Washington DC; (703)557-INFO;(703)308-9000; www.uspto.gov
- The Society of American Inventors (SAI); (800)USA-IDEA; www..inventorshelp.com
- International Trademark Association; NY; (212)768-9887
- Home Office Association of America; (800)809-4622; www.hoaa.com
- National Association of Home-Based Businesses (NAHBB); (410)363-3698; www.ameribiz.com
- International Reciprocal Trade Association (IRTA); IL; (312)461-0236
- National Association of Trade Exchanges; OH; (503)684-6105
- Manufacturers Agents National Association (MANA); CA; (714)859-4040
- National Business Incubation Association; 20 East Circle Dr., Suite 190, Athens, OH 45701
- International Venture Capital Institute, P.O. Box 1333, Stamford, CT 06904; letters preferred
- International Licensing Industry Merchandisers' Assoc; NY,(212)244-1944; www.licensing.org
- Insurance Information Institute; NY; (212)669-9200; www.iii.org
- Society of Risk Management Consultants; NY; (212)572-6246

☐ ***Miscellaneous***
- The SBA Financing Kit; ask your local SBA chapter about it.
- Internet Matching Services (to connect you to angel investors)
- ACE-Net (An SBA Program); http://ace-net.sr.unh.edu/pub
- Garage.com; CA; service@garage.com (contact by email preferred)
- Capital Network, TX; (512)305-0831; www.thecapitalnetwork.com
- Colorado Capital Alliance; CO; (303)499-9646; www.angelcapital.org
- JumpStart Investments; http://www.angelmoney.com
- Capital Connection; AZ; (602)837-9590; www.capital-connection.com
- BBB   (Better Business Bureau)
- SBA   (Small Business Association)
- EDIC   (Economic Development Information Center)
- NFIB   (National Federation of Independent Businesses)
- SBDC   (Small Business Development Centers)
- SCORE (Service Corps of Retired Executives)
- NAU Small Business Institute

☐ ***Software for creating business plans and naming your company***
- Business Resource Software, Inc.; (800)423-1228 Fax: (512)251-4401;   www.brs-inc.com;
- The NameStormers, TX; (512)267-1814; www.namestormers.com

☐ ***The Right Questions to Ask***
- What specific names can I come up with that might make my product or business stand out?
- What specific things will I acquire in order to help me run my business?
- Who do I know whom I could recruit for my business?
- What specific sources of money do I have to launch my business?
- What suppliers/manufacturers will I contact to create my product/invention.
- What are the specific questions I have for my SCORE adviser?

CHAPTER 6
"Basic Business Concepts and Tools"

Remember the Game Plan

We're still in the operational stages of the game. Let's learn some more about how we'll run the day to day operations of our record label.

▶ Monitor your OPERATIONS
Find, sign and develop talented ARTISTS
Create your PRODUCT on CD or other media
MARKET, Promote & Advertise it…
SELL IT to stores, distributors and to the public
Maximize additional streams of INCOME
RECOUP your expenses
PAY the players
Make a PROFIT.
GROW your business

Concepts and Tools

Now that you've set up your company, there are certain basic concepts and tools you'll need at your disposal in order to function efficiently. In this section, we'll be discussing

- The Team
- The Business Plan
- The Organizational Chart
- Copyrights, Patents & Trademarks
- Recording Industry Contracts, Clearances & Agreements

You also need to master the concepts of;
- Markup
- Break Even Point
- Profit Margins

You also need to use the following tools to diagnose the health and direction of your business;
- Profit & Loss Statement
- Cash Flow Statement

Finally, in order to successfully grow and sell your business, you must understand;
- How to streamline, delegate responsibilities & manage others in a team.
- How to compute your company's value.

Assemble Your Team

In assembling your team, create a list of the departments/divisions/subsidiaries you anticipate needing in your company. Some key departments to include are Sales, Production, Marketing, Publicity, Research, Customer Service, Legal and Internet. Some positions you may want to include are secretary, web designer, sales manager, research assistant, accountant, business manager and legal advisor.

Even though at this moment, you might be the one filling all those positions, the purpose of going into business is not to work 10 times harder than you did when you had one job. The goal is to create freedom for yourself by delegating those tasks to others. Ask yourself who you would hire for your board of directors. Look back on the Relationship List you compiled back in Chapter 3. Enter the individual's name, their title and who they report to. This is a good way to visualize your company, its structure, and growth, and it will also help you when you're putting together your business plan.

A Quick And Easy Business Plan

What You'll Need

Your business plan will be needed to secure financing and loans for your venture. The business plan also serves the equally important role of organizing your thoughts about your business. Used correctly, a good business plan can help you to structure, set goals, and project into the future to anticipate needs you may have and that you can start planning for in advance. Here are the major sections of the typical business plan along with the specific questions each should address:

Executive Summary

What's your company mission? How is your business structured? Where is it located? How long have you been in business? Who are the people running the business and what are their qualifications?

Business Description

What exactly does your business do? What is your product or service? How is it sold? What job positions will you need filled to get this done? How and where does the business operate? How is it going to be managed?

Marketing Plan

Who are you selling to? Who is your audience? How do you plan to market your product to your audience? What are your pricing, distribution, advertising and customer service policies? What do you know about the industry you are getting into? Who is your competition? What sets you apart from them?

Operation and Management

How will you recruit, qualify, hire, train, manage, evaluate, compensate, delegate, reward, promote and terminate your full/part-time employees, consultants in your business?

Financial Plan

How much money do you anticipate making in the next 12 months? The next 2 years? The next 5 years? What's your personal financial history? What do your balance sheet, profit & loss statement and cash flow analysis reveal about your business? (Samples of these statements are in the next chapter) How do you plan to budget any money invested in your company? What returns on investment do you project for someone who invests in your company? This is, perhaps, the most important part of your business plan. Potential investors are most interested in how much they need to invest, and how much they will earn in return.

Other Information

What's your long-range plan for the business? How do you plan to transfer ownership of the business in the future? Has the sale of your business been planned for?

The business plan is a tool for running your business. And just like any other tool, if it's not doing the job you intend it to, you need a different tool. In other words, you need to update and revise your business plan, just as you would sharpen, or oil or maintain any other tool you use repeatedly. Over the course of time, it may change and provide the basis for contingency plans for running your business when customer preferences, technology, the economy or foreign and domestic policy affect your business.

The Organization Chart

Exercise: create an organization chart for your business

A powerful exercise you can do is to create an organizational chart for your business(es). Create a structure for the departments/divisions/subsidiaries you anticipate needing in your company. Some key departments to include are Sales, Production, Marketing, Publicity, Research, Customer Service, Legal and Internet. Some positions you may want to include are secretary, web designer, sales manager, research assistant, accountant, business manager and legal advisor.

Even though at this moment, you might be the one filling all those positions, the purpose of going into business is not to work 10 times harder as you did when you had one job. The goal is to create freedom for yourself by delegating those tasks to others. Ask yourself who you would hire for your board of directors. Look back on the Relationship List you compiled back in chapter 3. Enter the individual's name, his/her title and who they report to. This is a good way to visualize your company, it's structure, and growth, and it will also help you when you're putting together your business plan.

There are many different ways to organize your company. The structure below is just one of many. For example, you may choose to have all the directors in the Sales & Marketing Department be Vice Presidents of their respective departments and report to you directly rather than report to a VP of Sales and Marketing as in the example below. Feel free to experiment until you find a structure that works best for you.

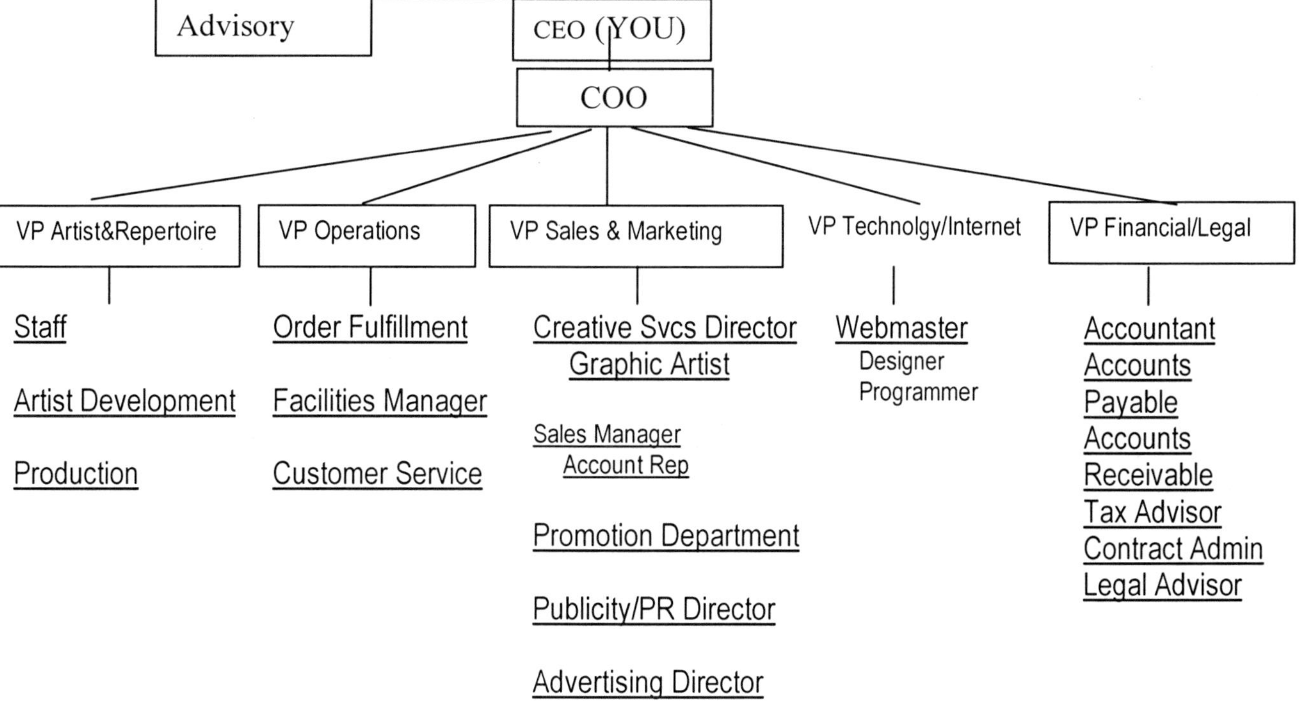

Excerpt from a Record Label Business Plan

Following is a description of the key roles and responsibilities of LightSabre Records' Vice Presidents, and daily operations. At the onset of this venture, each vice president will be responsible for all the functions within his or her particular label. While engaged in these activities, each VP will be responsible for the creation of an operations manual that will define the goals, procedures and standards associated with each position. As sales revenues increase, and we are able to hire necessary staff, these tasks will be delegated to new hires as required. As all three labels will be operating from a single location, staff will be shared among labels in order to minimize expenses.

Marketing/Sales Department

Goal: To sell the company's products to wholesalers, retailers and directly to the public.

Responsibilities: Develop sales campaigns, set discount policy, take and fulfill product orders, oversee sales activities.

Staff: National sales team; senior executives; salespersons, order-fulfillment team. The Marketing/Sales department works closely with Creative Services in the creation and proper use of marketing/sales support materials.

Artist Development

Goal: To oversee the career growth of signed artists.

Responsibilities: Coordinate, schedule and oversee all aspects of a current release, including packaging, advertising, tours, publicity, promotion and sales activities.

Staff: Product Managers, support staff. Product Managers work closely with every other department within the label and report directly to the President.

Publicity Department

Goal: Create press and media exposure and attention for the artist and his or her releases

Responsibilities: Work with artist and label to establish artist image, create media releases, contact press, schedule interviews. PR staff must work closely with Product Managers in order to effect the seamless marketing of artist according to product release schedules.

Promotion Department

Goal: To gain the greatest possible exposure of the release through radio and video airplay.

Responsibilities: Establish relationships with gatekeepers, mail/deliver promotional copies of products to appropriate radio/video outlets, follow-up with mailings, faxes, email and phone calls to encourage airplay, monitor play lists. Promotion staff must work closely with Marketing/Sales department to ensure that availability of product within retail outlets coincides with promotional efforts. In other words, the public must be able to find the product in the stores once it is heard on radio and seen on television.

Artist Relations Department

Goal: To provide support and services to our signed artists.

Responsibilities: Contract negotiation, artist management if necessary, tour support.

Artist & Repertoire (A&R)

Goals: To maximize the salability of the products we sell.

Responsibilities: Scouting for talent, locating songs, providing creative input, scouting for producers, planning product budgets, reviewing tracks, recommending singles, overseeing mastering and manufacturing.

Production Administration

Goal: To manage the clerical aspects related to the creation and manufacture of product.
Responsibilities: Monitoring budgets, studio bills, and other production-related expenses, creating reports of expenditures; managing copyright, trademark, sampling issues related to each release.

Creative Services

Goal: To create support materials for marketing campaigns
Responsibilities: develop marketing concepts, create graphic art, design posters, banners, window displays and other point-of-purchase items.

3 Tips For Organizing Your Business

It took me years of running my business in a state of chaos before the benefit of having an organization chart really hit home for me on a practical level. Here are three strategies I've implemented based on really understanding the Org Chart.

1. I now organize my office based on the departments in the org chart

Now, instead of filing and fitting items where they are in easy reach, or simply where there's space to fit, these items are now located in the section of my home office devoted to the department that they belong. So now, in much the same way that an actual office or suite would have to be organized, I have an order fulfillment center, separate from the mailroom, distinct from the product development work area, each with their own filing/holding area for the papers, supplies and equipment they require to function efficiently. So, if I have a piece of paper that requires filing or placement, I ask, which department needs this paper? Is this a Sales & Marketing, an Operations, Finance/Legal or something for the Tech Division?

2. I now organize the computer files on my desktop according to my org chart

The same structure Sales& Marketing, Operations, Finance & Legal, and Technology/Internet is also reflected in the files on my computer desktop. Just as the org chart has different departments reporting to it, each sub-department has its own folder within each major division. Now, therefore, instead of the 50 files I previously had scattered across the screen, I now have the following FOUR folders.

SALES & MRKTG

OPERATIONS

FINANCE & LEGAL

TECH/INTERNET

Within each folder are the sub-folders relating to each department and then each position. For example, in the "Operations" folder, there's a folder for "Senior Project Development Manager". Within that folder is another folder for specific Project manager positions and their assigned tasks.

I can't begin to tell you how much easier it's made the day to day operation of my business. When I made the handoff to a new webmaster, I simply copied the contents of the appropriate file onto a disk and handed it to him along with his job description, terms and conditions and a welcome letter! I used, a tool something I call the "Turning Professional" Operations Manual, available in the Appendix.

4. I delegate responsibilities, create task lists, search for interns, and devote my time to projects based on the org chart divisions of my company.

Mondays are devoted to the Product Development Division, Tuesdays are for Sales & Marketing, etc. can't begin to express the tremendous benefits my epiphany has resulted in. Doing business with the org chart template

½keeps my office neat; reduces clutter

½helps organize my thinking, as well as

½streamlines operations

½creates a standard structure

½ allows for the smooth transition of responsibility

½makes expanding the company manageable

And, if you do things correctly right from the beginning, you'll have less backtracking, reorganizing, (what I call "chaos management")months from now when the hectic, urgent, immediate, time consuming, time sensitive, deadline driven demands and tasks start piling up.

Protecting Your Assets And Ideas: More Tools

Even though we know, metaphysically speaking, your passion idea is yours, and cannot be taken way from you, there are other souls on the planet who've chosen to forget how things work, and who may attempt to turn *your* passion for music into *their* profit by infringing upon your ideas. Patents, trademarks and copyrights exist as a way of protecting your creations, ideas and business interests.

Patents

If following your passion results in an invention, a patent will help to protect that invention within the marketplace. A patent is a right granted by the government. It gives the patent holder the exclusive right to exclude others from making, using, selling, or importing a particular invention, product or process for a period of twenty years from the filing date. According to the actual terminology of the patent law, a patent it is granted to an individual who "invents or discovers any new and useful process, machine, [method of] manufacture, or composition of matter, or any new and useful improvement thereof..."

Because of the different fees involved (filing fees, maintenance fees, resubmission fees), as well as the legal costs, a patent application can cost thousands of dollars. The process may take several months or even years due to required searches, as well as the actual approval process. And various types of drawings, models, exhibits, specimens are required to complete your application. Contact the US Patent and Trademark office at 2900 Crystal Drive, 4B10, Arlington VA, 22202; 703-308-900, or online at www.uspto.gov.

Trademarks

Trademarks and Service Marks protect the words, names, symbols or devices that embody your company, your reputation, or what you offer your customers. These can be logos, characters, designs, slogans or particular unique ways of writing. These images--or marks--are the symbols under which you trade (do business) or provide service, and with which the public has come to associate your particular brand of quality, expertise, price, or whatever your Unique Selling Point (USP) is. Trademark rights may be used to prevent others from using a confusingly similar mark, but not to prevent others from making the same goods or from selling the same goods or services under a clearly different mark. So, the Coca-Cola trademark prevents other from using that name, but doesn't prevent Pepsi from selling cola as well.

The registration process for trademarks as well as general information concerning trademarks is described in a pamphlet entitled *"Basic Facts about Trademarks"*. As of January 10th, 2000, the basic filing fee is $325. There are also fees of varying amounts for renewals, extensions, cancellations and oppositions. Contact the US Patent and Trademark office at 2900 Crystal Drive, 4B10, Arlington VA, 22202; 703-308-900, or online at www.uspto.gov for details.

Copyright

Copyright is a form of protection provided to the authors of "original works of authorship." If your passion involves the creation of literary, dramatic, musical, artistic, and certain other intellectual works, both published and unpublished, then a copyright can help you protect your creations. The 1976 Copyright Act generally gives the owner of copyright the exclusive right to reproduce (copy) the copyrighted work, to prepare derivative works, to distribute copies or phonorecords of the copyrighted work, to perform the copyrighted work publicly, or to display the copyrighted work publicly.

The copyright protects the form of expression rather than the subject matter of the writing. For example, a description of a machine could be copyrighted, but this would only prevent others from copying the description; it would not prevent others from writing a description of their own or from making and using the machine. Your greeting cards, brochures, poems, novels, posters, lyrics, can all be copyrighted.

Contact the U.S. Copyright Office Library of Congress, 101 Independence Ave., S.E., Washington DC 20559-6000 Public Information Office: (202) 707-3000; Forms Hotline: (202) 707-9100 or online at http://lcweb.loc.gov/copyright, for more details.

NOTE: Keep in mind that your rights of ownership exist from the moment you create your product. Often, these rights are enforceable, even without the patent, trademark and copyright, if you can show prior use in some valid way. The patent, trademark and copyright are simply legal ways for you to enforce these rights. They prove that by virtue of the filing dates and dates of first use, that you got there first.

The Costs of Doing Business

Record Label Expenses

Here is an overview of typical expense categories based on interviews with label owners. To run your business on a day-to-day basis, you'll likely spend money on the items in the table below. This is by no means a comprehensive list.

Artist & Repertoire	Operations	Sales & Marketing	Technology	Finance/Legal
Travel	Salaries and wages	Design	Computer System	Incorporation
Conference fees	Utilities	Printing	Domain registration	Contract review
Transportation	Office expense	Mastering	Web hosting	Consulting
Auto Expenses	Postage	Pressing/Duplication		
Tolls	Telephone	Freight/Shipping		
Studio Time	Utilities	Advertising		
Photography	Rent	Video Production		
		Promotion		

Some Other Suggestions For A Smooth Operation

There are a few more things you might want to get a hold of to make your business life a little easier.

1. Computer with printer (If you're not that familiar with computers, start now!)
    a) Word Processing Software
    b) Database Software
2. Fax Machine. There are some on the market now that are combination answering/fax machine.
3. Long Distance Carrier with good rates (As a member of certain trade organizations, for example, you can get discounts on specific ones if you set up a business line. Remember, however that business lines are more expensive)
4. Map of the U.S. and a map of the world.
5. Rubber stamp with your company name and address.
6. Record Mailers (even if you don't plan to do mass mailings yourself.)
7. Padded envelopes (9X12 is a convenient and versatile size.)
8. Mailing labels compatible with your printer.
9. Express delivery company account. (UPS, Federal Express, or other such company)
10. Filing Cabinet (The cardboard ones are just as good and much cheaper).

You may not have to get all of these things right away. You can pick them up as the need arises and when you have a better idea of what quantity or size to purchase. At the very least however, do some research to find a place with good prices so that when you do need them, you know where to go so you're not scrambling around at the last minute.

A Chapter on Cheap
"Cut Costs, Get it FREE, Get THEM to pay YOU!
Money-Saving, Profit-Extracting Secrets

There are only two ways to make a profit in business. You can sell more, or you can spend less. The best strategy is to do a lot of both. Once you realize that fluctuations of just 5 to 10% in gross sales can cause a business to go into bankruptcy, you'll recognize the importance of cutting costs wherever you can. A small increase in the cost of your supplies, manufacturing, even postage costs, for instance, can have a detrimental effect on your bottom line. Profit margins are what keep your company going and growing. Don't underestimate the power of those small percentages. In a recent year, Boeing Aircraft Manufacturers had a profit of 1 Billion dollars. Admittedly, 1 Billion dollars is a lot of money. But, in terms of percentages, that's ONLY 1.7% of total sales of 57 Billion. Get a hold of any year-end report of companies you have stock in and you'll see that their profit is usually anywhere from 1 -10% of total sales. Seen in this light, it makes even more sense to cut costs as much as possible. When I first started my mail order company, I was unaware of this little fact of business accounting, and carelessly tossed away my profit by doing things like not charging for shipping, sending correspondences by overnight delivery, and other no-nos. To save you the heartache of going through what I did, here is a list of ways to cut costs in 17 major expense categories.

Not every business has expenses in every category, but I'm sure you'll find a few tips that will save you hundreds, even thousands each year! First, however, let's explore some key concepts and principles.

The 7 Immutable Laws of Cheap & The Hierarchy of Holding On to Your Money

Being cheap can be taught! Once you understand how the world of business works, you'll never be taken advantage of and pay full price again! Here's how I view the world so that I never pay full price.

Here are 7 principles that govern business that will help you seek out the best deals.

1. Competition. "There's Always Someone Cheaper. There's Even Someone Free."
2. The Art of Barter
3. Buying in Bulk.
4. Mixing and Matching
5. Out of State? Out of Sight! aka "Paper is Cheaper in Canada, so buy your fish by the sea!"
6. You Can Get a Better Deal by Asking
7. The Hierarchy of Holding On to Your Money

1.   Competition. *"There's Always Someone Cheaper. There's Even Someone Free."*

The basic underlying principle of capitalism is that the next guy is always trying to get more customers by charging less than the next guy! As a result, there's always someone selling it cheaper. And, in this day and age, there's usually someone giving it away free. Many products that others are selling at a price, are being given away free by someone else as an enticement, premium, incentive. In addition, there's always someone whose overhead is less, whose got inventory to move, who got a good deal on a wholesale price that they're passing on to you, or has some other circumstance or situation that can result in a better price for you. Knowing this, you should always be on the lookout for new deals!

2. The Art of Barter

Even though, "cash is king", it's also equally true that trade is just as powerful a means of getting what you want without parting with cash. Join barter organizations like Intagio.com or do a search for "barter" at your favorite search engine.

3. Buy Bulk. Pay Less.

Companies that purchase in large quantities are able take advantage of discounts. That's why it's often cheaper to buy your supplies at office supply superstores. Take advantage of purchasing larger quantities of often-used supplies, and ask for a discount when you do!

4. Mix and Match

Don't feel obligated to fulfill all your needs at one supplier. You can often save a bundle by, for example, getting your merchant services processing through one company, but the actual terminal from a different supplier.

5. Out of State? Out of Sight! *"Paper is Cheaper in Canada, so Buy Your Fish by the Sea!"*

It often seems so natural to do business with companies in your geographical area, that it often goes unnoticed that companies in other states and even other countries can provide the same product or service at better prices. Many factors affect the price of a particular product. Labor costs, storage, shipping, trucking and delivery charges will often boost the price of a particular commodity in a given region. However, companies doing business in states and countries with lower labor costs, and with little to no need for shipping their raw materials or finished products to the point of manufacture, or sale, can charge less for the final product. That's why book printing in paper-producing states and certain states close to Canada, (Michigan, Minnesota, Wisconsin, Montana, North Dakota and South Dakota) is cheaper. So, remember: "paper is cheaper in Canada, so buy fish by the sea!"

6. You Can Get a Better Deal Just by Asking

Yes, it's true. It's even truer if you're dealing with the owner of the company, or a representative who gets paid on commission, and who would rather make a slightly lower commission than lose the sale entirely.

7. The Hierarchy of Holding on to your Money

Before shelling out your hard-earned cash, there are several options (including some mentioned above) that you can explore which might be able to get you your desired product or service free! We call them "The Hierarchy of Cheap". Let's say there's a new product, service that interests you, you might contact the agent, supplier, manufacturer, publisher, etc. and

A. Request a review/evaluation copy (This works well if you're the head of an organization with enough members who might be interested in future purchases.) We, at the Passion Profit Company receive many of the books in our library as review copies given to use based on the promise of our doing an online review, or making them available for sale to our subscribers.
B. Ask for a quantity discount that gets you yours for free. (Offer to bring them 3 new customers in exchange for one free copy).
C. Ask about barter options. If you find the "no pay" options, don't work, then
D. First shop out of state or internationally for cheaper options. Then, based on your research,
E. Ask them to beat a competitor's price (another discount tactic)
F. Simply ask for a discount: Yes, sometimes all you have to do is ask! And finally,
G. Ask for older versions, editions and models which may now be available as excess inventory.

With these new skills, perspectives, mindset and practices, you're now ready to hunt for and eliminate the secret "profit stealers" that exist in most business. These are the often overlooked expense categories that slowly deplete your cash reserves, stifle your cash flow, and eat away your profits.

The 17 Secret "Profit Stealers" of your business

The following are tips you can use to cut corners and reduce costs in several major expense categories. When you add them all up, you can see that there are really a lot more than 17!

Secret 1—Shipping/Mailing Costs

A major cost for many small businesses and mail order companies. The savings in this section can add up to thousands annually!

Use Priority Mail Flat Rate—This is a little-known feature of the United States Postal Service that there's a "Flate Rate" Envelope that you can use to send items through the mail (2-3 day delivery). As long as what you're sending can fit inside the flexible cardboard 9x12 envelope (some clerks insist it must fit securely without any additional taping on your part, but you might get a lenient clerk), you'll only be charged the 2lb rate, which, at the time of this printing, is $3.85. I've sent books of up to 4 lbs in this way, and saved as much as $6.00! (see comparison below)

Global Priority Flat Rate—Similarly, for $9.00, you can send items to many countries. You can calculate postage on the www.usps.com website before making the trek to the post office.

Printed Matter and Media Mail—If you're sending "books (at least eight pages), film, printed music, printed test materials, sound recordings, play scripts, printed educational charts, loose-leaf pages and binders consisting of medical information, and computer-readable media" to customers, (up to 70 lbs) you can also consider using the USPS "media mail" option. The advertised shipping time is between 3-7 days, but I've found that items I've shipped reach just as quickly as first class mail. The savings can be as much as 50%.For example, a 3lb package (a book, say) that you're sending from New York to California. Here's what it would cost, and what you'd save based on sending it Regular Priority Mail.

Comparison

Regular Priority	$8.85	
Priority Mail Flat Rate:	$3.85	(save $5.00)
Bounded Printed Matter:	$3.07	(save $5.78)
Media Mail	$2.26	(save $6.59!)

Other Tips:

- Email instead of faxing.
- Presort your mail if you mail to large lists. Contact US Postal Service (USPS) for details.
- Remove bad addresses from your mailing list (USPS offers address verification services as well).
- Investigate and use co-op mailing programs.
- Purchase stamps online (www.stamps.com, www.estamp.com or www.pcstamps.com)
- Don't send overnight unless absolutely necessary.
- Cut back on unnecessary packaging items. (Priority envelopes are free)
- Eliminate envelopes. Trifold your letters, and seal with address labels.
- Charge your customers for shipping.
- Have packages to be shipped to customers picked up (all the major carriers offer this service for a one-time fee per pickup).

Secret 2—Communications Costs

Cell Phone Service—Despite the technology safety issues, there are great plans and services for those who don't mind exposing their brains to the electromagnetic waves these phones produce.

Find a Plan—Many companies are now offering "Flat Rate Plans" which include unlimited Local as well as Long Distance calls. At the time of this writing, you can get plans as low as $29.95 per month. If a per-minute plan is best for you, check out www.lowermybills.com for an instant comparison of available plans in your area. (current rates are as low as $0./04 /minute) According to the site, the average American consumer could save up to $400 annually simply by choosing a different plan!

Don't use Operator Assistance ("411 Information")—Yes, it's convenient. But, every time you call the operator for information, it can cost you as much as several dollars, for a single number!! Try www.5551212.com, www.anywho.com, or any of the many directory services at any of the major portals like Yahoo.com. Also check out www.melissadata.com/lookups/

Other Tips

- Get the lowest long distance rates. At the time of this writing, companies are offering 5 cents/minute. Look for single-second, or actual time billing. Some websites are even offering free calling capability using your personal computer and a microphone. (Visit www.vonage.com)
- If you're on a calling plan that has better rates at night, do your "broadcast faxing" during the night hours.
- Get only the basic necessary services on your phone line (call waiting; 3 way calling).
- Use the Internet's 411.com instead of the phone company's 411.
- Use (800)555-1212 first to determine if a business you're calling has a toll-free number.

- Ask your local phone company about their unlimited calling plans.
- Review your bills every month. You'd be surprised how many mistakes might be on your phone bill.
- Consider the pros and cons of using an 800 number for your business. Is it really necessary? If you use an 800 number, ask about blocking incoming calls from within your state or immediate calling area.
- **Free Teleconferencing is available at--** www.Mrconference.com
- Consider an Order Taking Center to handle incoming calls and catalog requests. (Use out of town companies in states "where the reps have low stress, and the overhead is less.")

Secret 3—Web Hosting and Things Internet
- Don't pay more than $7.99/year for Domain Name Registration. Use www.PowerPipe.com
- Find a Flat Rate Web Hosting Service; Use www.PassionProfit.com's hosting service ($49/year!)
- Buy, don't lease Shopping Cart for your website

Secret 4—Merchant Processing Fees
- When becoming a Credit Card Merchant, purchase, don't lease, your equipment; Check ebay, or do a search engine search for "merchant processing terminals" and shop around for deals. Most companies that offer processing hope to make more money by selling, or leasing you the terminals at exorbitant prices.

Secret 5—Printing & Design Costs
- For Free Business Cards, Use VistaPrint.com (you pay only for shipping and have a range of templates)
- Print your own checks; Visit www.shareware.com for free check writing software
- Logos; Visit www.gotlogos.com
- Try out a Print on Demand Service for your book/catalog printing; Try www. expressmedia.com. The advantage: small runs; quick turnaround;

Secret 6—Reduce Banking/ATM Fees
- Shop around for the lowest fees. Maintenance, overdraft and deposit fees add up.
- Order your checks by mail from independent printers.
- Find "0 fee" Credit Cards/Low interest Credit Cards; Visit www.lowermybills.com for comparisons of
- various credit card offers.
- ATM Fees. Don't use ATMs for withdrawing money from your account. If offered in your area, consider asking for "cashback" when you make purchases at the Supermarket, Post Office and many pharmacies. Yes, there's often a small fee associated, but it's usually much less (say 25 cents) than the increasingly larger ATM fees (often as much as $3.00!) incurred every time you use an ATM.
- Credit/Debit Card Purchases. If you use your credit/debit card for purchases, you may be paying more in fees than you realize. A credit card purchase is usually free, while a debit card purchase has a fee associated. If you're debit card as a Visa/Mastercard logo, it means you can use it as a credit card. You're usually given the option at the time of checkout. Check your bank statement to see what charges apply.

Secret 7—Save on Office Supplies
- Buy "house brands".
- Compare prices between major outlets like Staples, Office Depot, Office Max, Quill, as well as the dozens of other online companies to find the best prices.
- Use the Internet to compare different supplier prices.

- Cut back on magazine subscriptions. Use the local library.
- Buy office supplies in bulk; If you use paper in your copier or printer, you can save as much as 30% by purchasing cases rather than single reams (500 sheet packs)
- Use reconditioned laser cartridges instead of new (visit www.fifonline.com).
- Barter when possible.
- Consider auctioned, second hand or previously owned equipment. Check *ebay* first.
- Use Shareware programs downloadable for free from the Internet (try www.shareware.com) You can get programs for invoicing, scheduling, mailing list management, spreadsheets, expense tracking…
- Laminate daily work sheets so you can reuse them by writing with erasable markers.
- Before shopping, find coupons first online; www.couponclub.com, www.edealfinder.com, Try Bartering for your supplies – Join Intagio.com.
- Shop at Used Computers/Computer Trade Shows.

Secret 8—Legal & Accountant Fees

- Consider arbitration, mediation and/or alternative dispute resolution (ADR) instead of costly litigation.
- Contact the local Better Business Bureau for these and other low cost legal alternatives.
- Check local listings for the Lawyer Referral Service nearest you. You can often get low cost (sometimes the first session is free) advice from lawyers who specialize in your specific area of interest.

Secret 9—Staff, Salaries & Wages and Payroll costs

- "Rent" your employees rather than hiring them full time.
- Offer workers the option of working from home to cut down on your costs.
- Utilize free resources before hiring consultants (contact SBA or local SCORE office).
- Use independent sales reps to sell your product or service.
- Pay employees every two weeks, or even monthly, to save on payroll costs.
- Use debit cards to pay employees
- Consider using lower-cost interns, college students, family members, friends, and investigate work exchange programs which the program sponsors pay the salaries of the student participants

Secret 10—Consulting & Experts

- While there's no substitute for experienced, seasoned help, there are many online sources of experts in their field that can offer some valuable insights and "out the box" thinking. Visit www.ExpertCentral.com, www.About.com, www.Ask.com.
- Check with the SBA's Service Corps of Retired Executives (SCORE) for absolutely free business advice from those who've been in the trenches.

Secret 11—Reduce Staff, Salaries & Wages and Payroll costs

- Remember the 80-20 Rule: 80% of your income is usually through the sale of 20% of your products. Keep a careful eye on which products are moving and cut back on slow sellers.
- Barcoding products aid inventory tracking and helps businesses run more efficiently.

Secret 12—Collecting Debt

- Charge interest on monies owed to you.
- Fax letters and invoices in addition to mailing them to debtors.
- Offer discounts for early payment; 1% - 3% for paying within 10 days.

Secret 13—Travel Expenses
- Sign up for "e-saver" email lists through which major carriers advertise low-cost last-minute fares.
- Sign up for a courier service (try Int'l Association of Air Couriers at www.courier.org).
- NEVER EVER use the phone in a hotel room.
- Ask for it. Sometimes all you have to do is ask for a lower rate, or if there are any specials going on when making reservations and you might get it.
- Sign up for "EZ-Pass" type discount if you do a lot of driving through tolls this can save you hours

Secret 14--Printing
- Print brochures in quantities that take advantage of price breaks.
- Streamline forms, receipts, invoices etc. Make them smaller if possible to save paper.
- Print rather than photocopy. Sometimes going to a printing company can be less expensive than going to the corner copy center.
- Consider "two color" rather than "full color" for fliers, brochures and posters.

Secret 15--Marketing (Advertising, Publicity, Promotion)
- Don't spend more than you need to. Smaller classified ads often do better than bigger display ads.
- Never pay a magazine or newspaper the rate card rate. Remember, they still need to print the paper or magazine even if all the spaces aren't sold. Therefore, magazine and newspaper publishers would rather get something than nothing.
- If a newspaper or magazine ad isn't working, drop it.
- Websites have become more important than brochures. It may not be necessary to spend a lot on brochures that people may never see. Your business may require both, but assess their relative effectiveness before committing to either.

Secret 16--Events
- Don't overdo it. If you stage seminars as part of your passion, remember that people attend seminars for the information. They won't mind spending to get their own food. Fancy catering is often unnecessary.
- Research how well other vendors fared before investing in a trade show, expo or convention booth.

Bonus Secret 17—Operations, Time & Energy & Miscellaneous
Save time. Since time is money, anything you can do to streamline your operations to be as efficient as possible, will increase productivity, cut waste and increase profits.
- Set your preferences/frequently used options/home screen/defaults so that you can access them quickly.
- Designate certain days ONLY for certain tasks. For example, in our business, we ship out orders on Mondays, Wednesdays and Fridays only. Especially if you have a small staff, you'd be surprised just how much time this frees up!
- Organize your office space by department and function., not by convenience.
- Run your business from your home and save with the many tax advantages the IRS allows.
- Search for industry, demographic info at www.melissadata.com/lookups/
- Negotiate! Many costs, including advertising, supplies, legal fees and even rent can be negotiated.
- Use the Internet. These days, just about any information you need is now available online. Everything from rates, advice, contact information, prices, demographic info, grammar, spell check, weather, time and more are now available. So click, don't call. (Check out www.RefDesk.com)

CONCEPTS

Markup

Markup is what you do to your costs in order to arrive at a selling price. For example, let's say you spent $2.50 per unit to make a CD and then added $5.00 to arrive at a selling price of $7.50. Your mark up, therefore was $5.00. Keep in mind, however, that this $5 represents much less than it first appears. **Don't assume that just because you added $5 to cost of the item, that you're actually making $5 profit every time one of them sells.** That 5 dollars now has to cover all your fixed costs like rent, office equipment and salaries, as well as your variable costs like telephone and advertising.

The chart which follows is not intended to substitute for a detailed cost and break-even analysis for your business. It is an estimation of the figures involved in generating income for your company. The first column lists the various music formats. The second column lists the actual manufacturing cost per unit. The third column lists what you would typically sell each for to your distributor. Finally, column 4 gives the gross profit per unit sold (column 2 minus column 3). Manufacturing costs include pressing/duplication costs and jackets/inserts as described earlier. These manufacturing costs are those associated with smaller runs (in the 500 to 2000 unit range). As your run quantity increases, you can start to realize greater unit profits.

Singles (Per Unit)

Format	Manufacturing Cost	Wholesale Price	Gross Unit Profit
Cassingles (<10 min)	0.65	1.30	0.65
12"	0.85 to 1.10	2.50	1.40 to $1.65
Maxi-cass	0.70 to 1.00	2.50	1.50 to 1.80
CD Singles	1.35	3.50	2.15
EP's	0.70 to 1.00	3.50	2.50 to 2.80

Albums (Per Unit)

Format	Manufacturing Cost	Wholesale Price	Gross Unit Profit
LP's	0.85 to 1.10	4.50	3.40 to 3.65
Cassettes	0.90 to 1.15	4.50	3.35 to 3.60
CD's	1.35	6.75	5.40

Videos (Per Unit)

Format	Manufacturing Cost	Wholesale Price	Gross Unit Profit
VHS	2.00 to 3.00	5.00	2.00 to 3.40

Keep in mind that your record will be marked up at least twice before it reaches the consumer. With markups like that, you might be thinking right about now, that if you distributed your own records you could rake in a higher profit. You might even be tempted to cut out the middlemen altogether and deal directly with the consumer to further maximize your profits. An enterprising thought executed in fine entrepreneurial style. However, there are a few problems with it--the least of which, for right now, might be the lack of an adequate staff, warehouse space, business reputation, and product demand to justify the venture. A few words of advice: decide once whether you want to be a record company, a distributor, a management company or whatever, then focus on that one goal and let other people make their living doing what they do best. There's enough to go around and satisfy everyone.

Markup is not profit. Markups are simply added to the money that's going out. What's more important is what's left over after expenses. For that we need to discuss margins.

Profit Margins

What do you think of when you hear the word *margin*? If you're like most people, you think of setting the margins in a word processing document, or you think of the margins of a book--the clear space that's not used up that you can jot notes to yourself while reading. Well, just like the margins of a book, your Profit Margin is how much is left over, or "not used up" in every dollar of sales you earn. When you make your first sale, a portion of that dollar represents the cost to you of making or acquiring the product you sold. In other words, if the CD you're selling for $7.50 cost you $2 to make or purchase, then the (gross) profit margin is $5.00 As a percentage of sales it is 5.00/7.50 or 66%. But that's not your "real" profit. It's called "gross" profit margin because you haven't subtracted other expenses and determined what actually ends up in your "net." It's called a margin because somewhere inside that amount is where your actual, final, net profit is going to be. When someone says that their gross profit margin is 66%, they're saying that for every dollar they make, 66% of it is what's left over to pay the expenses AND provide a net profit.

Break-Even Point

The next concept is the break-even point. As the name implies, this is the point where your business is finally going to start making a profit. It happens after all your variable and fixed costs have been met.

Assuming you already know the price of your product, a Breakeven Analysis requires you to:
1. Determine the Variable Cost Ratio,
2. Determine the Fixed Costs, then
3. Determine the Breakeven points.

1) Variable Cost Ratio

First, you need to determine your variable costs. For instance, in our example, let's say you buy your CDs in batches of 1000. You determine that for each batch of 1000 CDs, you incur the following costs:
-- for CDs $ 2500 (1000@$2.5 each)
-- shipping at $ 100.00 per shipment of 1000
-- insurance $50.00 per shipment of 1000

All these variable costs total: 2500 + 100 + 50 = $ 2650.00 for 1000 CDs

Next, you set the price for 1 CD at $ 7.50. That's $ 7,500.00 for 100 CDs
Therefore, for 1000 CDs
Your variable cost per batch is $2,650
with a selling price per batch of $7,500

The variable cost ratio is:
= Variable Cost / Selling Price
= $2,650 / $7,500
= 35.3% (or 0.353) [every time you sell a CD, 35% of the income is covering variable costs. These costs, therefore, will keep going up as you sell more hats.]

2) Fixed Costs

Next, determine the amount of your fixed costs per year. Let's say, for this ideal scenario, that rent is your only fixed cost and is $700/month. That's $8400 for the year. Therefore, with a fixed cost of $8400 per year, and a variable cost ratio of 35.3%, (0.353) and a selling price of $7,500 per batch, your breakeven point is as follows.

3) Breakeven Point.
(Breakeven Dollar Sales)
= Fixed Costs / (1 - Variable Cost Ratio)
= $8,400.00 / (1 - .353)
= $ 8,400.00 /(.647)
= $ 12,982 of sales must be achieved for turning a profit.

 (Breakeven Unit Sales)
= Breakeven Sales / Selling Price
= $ 12,982 / $ 10.00
= 1,298 CDs must be sold to make a profit.

In other words, you can see you'd have to sell 1298 CDs for your business to break even. The concept of the break-even analysis is very powerful. You can play around with the numbers to create the specific scenario you desire. For example, to make a profit earlier than 1850 hats, you can increase your selling price, or you can reduce your variable costs, or you can reduce your unit cost by printing up more CDs.

These three concepts of profit margin, markup and break-even ratio are important to making your record label profitable. Practice doing various break-even analyses using different price combinations.

Money Flow Tools

The next several pages of this chapter provides the tools you need in order to understand where your money is going, how to monitor income and expenses, and how to keep track of your profit. If you've followed the discussion up to now, you're more than ready to tackle the next section. If not, then read through it anyway with the goal of just getting through it, even if you don't fully understand every concept or figure. As you get more involved in your business, all the terms and procedures as well as the importance of each tool will become more apparent, and understandable. These three tools are usually also a required part of your business plan. They are the balance sheet, income statement and cash flow analysis.

Balance Sheet
The balance sheet is a diagnosis of the health of your business *at any given moment*. Because it represents what your business owns, and what is owed to you, what's on a balance sheet can change from day to day. I like to think of it in this way: any given moment, my business, like my body and other areas of my life need to be balanced in order to be considered healthy. I'm balancing what I own with what I owe, what's left over is called "net worth."

Income Statement (also known as Profit and Loss Statement)
The income statement, on the other hand, shows what was made and what was spent in your business over an *extended period of time* (typically a tax year).

Cash Flow Analysis
The cash flow analysis shows the flow of money into and out of your business. For income, it shows when money came into your business, and where it came from. For expenses, it shows when the money was spent and what it was spent on. Because there are columns for "estimated" as well as "actual" income and expenses, broken up into periods of time (4 periods in the example which follows), it can help determine when certain expenses will fall due, and when certain monies can be expected to help you pay them. This is a great tool to help you run your business more effectively and less stressfully. On the following pages are samples of each business tool, followed by explanations of the terms contained in each.

Balance Sheet Template   For: Year Ended December 31, 20____

ASSETS

CURRENT ASSETS
      Cash on hand and in bank
      Marketable securities
      Accounts receivable (less allowance for bad debts)
      Merchandise inventory
      Supplies Inventory
        Total current Assets   ________

FIXED ASSETS
      Office Machinery and equipment (less depreciation)
      Furniture
      Improvements on property
        Total fixed assets   +   ________

TOTAL ASSETS (Current Assets + Fixed Assets)   =   ________

LIABILITIES AND NET WORTH

CURRENT LIABILITIES
      Accounts payable
      Notes payable within year
      Accrued taxes
        Total current liabilities   ________

LONG-TERM LIABILITIES
      Notes payable
      Total long-term liabilities   +   ________

TOTAL LIABILITIES
 (Current Liabilities + Long Term Liabilities)   =   ________

NET WORTH (OWNER'S EQUITY)
(Total Assets - Total Liabilities)   ________

Balance Sheet Explanation Of Terms

CURRENT ASSETS are the resources of value that you use every day to conduct business and generate wealth. It includes cash, merchandise, supplies, stationery, boxes, etc.

Cash on hand includes EVERY form of money that you have on hand. That includes actual paper bills, coins, checks/money orders not yet deposited, petty cash in a jar behind the counter, money in your safe, etc.

Marketable securities includes the market value (what they are currently trading at) of all business-owned stocks, mutual funds, and other securities that can be converted into cash.

Accounts receivable (or simply "Receivables") is the money that your customers owe you that they haven't paid yet. Since some people may never pay you, deduct a small percentage (1-10%) from this figure to reflect that fact. In other words, you are taking a 10% allowance for bad debts because in the real world, if you are owed $1,000, by the time all money owed to you is paid, you may only receive $900.

Merchandise Inventory, as the name implies, is the value of the products you keep on hand to fill customer orders. You may base it on the cost you incurred to acquire/create these products, or you can use the current market value of the goods, whichever is less.

Supplies Inventory is the value of boxes, letterheads, staples, paper clips, paper, and all the various supplies you keep on hand to run your business.

Fixed assets are the more permanent possessions the company has. Include the value of furniture, office equipment, machinery, trucks, servers, the building and land on which the business sits (if owned) . Depreciation is the gradual loss of value of your fixed assets. So, for example, if you bought your copier two years ago for $1,000 and it depreciates 10% each year, then after the first year, it's only worth $900, the second year it's worth $810 and so on. IRS Publication 534 gives information on how to figure out a realistic depreciation schedule.

Leaseholder Improvements is the money spent by the tenant on improvements to the building or space leased for the business.

Liabilities means all the money you owe. It includes everything from bank loans, money owed to suppliers, customers, employees, magazines or newspapers, and taxes you owe.

Current liabilities are those monies owed which you'll need to pay back in the next 12 months.

Accounts payable are the monies owed to suppliers and individuals from whom you buy on credit.

Long-Term liabilities is money your business owes that you must repay in the future, beyond the next twelve months

Net Worth is simply assets minus liabilities. This is also called Owner's Equity.

Profit And Loss Statement (aka Income Statement)

The P&L Statement, as the name implies, is a report of your income expenses, and profit (or loss) for a given period. You should compute a P&L for your business operations at regular intervals in order to keep track of the money you are making, and how much you are spending. Understanding the concept behind the P&L statement will help you to run your business more efficiently, and to complete your tax returns at the end of the year. 4For any period of time, you should be aware of:

1. How much income was generated by your company through the sale of your product or goods.
2. How much money was spent in creating the product.(called "cost of goods sold")
3. How much money was spent to market the product and run the company.
4. After subtracting items 2 and 3 from item 1, how much was left over--as profit.

As you look over your profit and loss statement during the course of the year, you will develop a feel where most of your money is and should be going, which areas need to be cut back, and how these adjustments affect your bottom line

Sample Profit And Loss Statement
FOR FIRST QUARTER

NET SALES.. $ 25,000

LESS COST OF GOODS SOLD
     Opening inventory, January 1........................ 0
     Design.. 100
     Photography... 200
     Printing.. 3,500
     Mastering... 350
     Pressing/Duplication..................................... 7,000
     Freight/Shipping... 200
     TOTAL COST OF GOODS SOLD........................... $ 11,350

GROSS MARGIN... $ 13,650

LESS OPERATING EXPENSES
     Salaries and wages....................................... 0
     Utilities... 200
     Office expense... 200
     Postage.. 400
     Advertising.. 800
     Video Production.. 5,000
     Promotion.. 1,000
     Legal... 100
     Travel/Conferences...................................... 0
     Telephone.. 300
     Rent.. 1,500
     Miscellaneous.. 300
     TOTAL OPERATING EXPENSE............................. $ 9,800

NET PROFIT... $ 3,850

Income Statement (Profit And Loss) Explanation Of Terms

Gross Sales is the total amount of income taken in by your business.

Net Sales is the above amount minus any amounts refunded to customers, any amounts not received because of discounts given to customers, employees, or any other losses.

Cost of Goods Sold is the answer to the question "How much did you spend to create those items that were sold during the year?" To compute that, determine
start   cost of what you started with,
+   cost of what you added during the year
+   cost of getting those items to you (can't forget the shipping/freight charges!)
=   cost of all the merchandise you had on hand during the year, then subtract
--   cost of what you have left at the end of the year

So for example, if you started with 10 hats, then bought/created 90 during the year and ended up with 15 at the end of the year, you actually sold 85 hats. Those 85 hats were the "goods sold." But, in order to have those hats to sell, you had to buy/create 90, plus have them shipped to you.

Gross Margin is an important number in business. This represents what you really have to work with to turn your passion into net profit. After you figure out how much it cost to buy/create the products you're selling, and subtract that from what you actually made in sales, the gross margin, or gross profit, as it's sometimes called, must be large enough to pay all your operating expenses with enough left over to yield a healthy profit.

Operating Expenses are all the costs incurred in running your business. Every business has a different set of operating expenses to work with.

Operating Profit is computed by subtracting the operating expenses from the Gross Margin. This is the amount of profit from actually running the business. But wait, we're not done yet! We still have to pay taxes, but before we do that, we have to factor in...

Other income is money the business may have generated from sources other than the sale of products. This can include interest on savings accounts, royalties, licensing income, mailing list rental, etc.

Total Income (and profit) before income tax is precisely that.

Provision for income tax. Even though you may not have actually paid taxes, you should subtract the amount you expect to pay (see IRS tax tables online at www.irs.gov, or in form 1040 instructions) before calling the above figure your profit.

Net Profit is your "bottom line" (hence its position on the P&L Statement). This is how much after-tax profit your business has earned

Cash Flow Statement

"Like a flowing river to which more water is added and some is taken out." That's a handy image I use to explain what cash flow is.

DEFINITION
CASH FLOW: "The flow of cash you're swimming in"
Cash flow is a combination of
1. what is ALREADY THERE flowing in the river
2. What is added IN
3. Minus what is taken out

FORMULA:
Cash on hand + Cash brought in - Cash paid/taken out = "CASH FLOW"
Say, for example, you have $50 on hand. Someone gives you an additional $50, and you give someone else $30. Your cash flow is $50 + $50 - $30 = $70. In other words, what is "flowing" through your business at that moment is your on-hand cash of $50 plus a gain of $20. Your business cash flow is an important gauge of how your business is doing.

Monthly Cash Flow Statement Template

During your first year in business, you should complete one for each month.

	Est	Actual	Est	Actual	Est	Actual	Est	Actual	Est	Actual	Est	Actual	
1. CASH ON HAND (Beginning of month)													1.
2. CASH RECEIPTS **(a) Cash Sales** **(b) Collections** **(c) Loans/other cash in**													2. (a) (b) (c)
3. TOTAL CASH RECEIPTS													3.
4. TOT CASH AVAILABLE													4.
5. CASH PAID OUT													5.
Purchases (Merchandise)													
Gross Wages													
Payroll Expenses													
Outside Services													
Supplies (Office)													
Repairs and Maintenance													
Commissions & Fees													
Advertising													
Travel Meals/Entertainmt													
Legal and Professional Svc													
Rent													
Utilities													
Taxes													
Loan Payment (Interest)													
Other _____________													
Other_____________													
Other_____________													
Miscellaneous													
SUBTOTAL													
Purchases													
Loan Payment (Principal)													
Startup costs													
For Owner's Personal Use													
6.TOTAL CASH PAID OUT													6.
7. NET CASH FLOW (end of month)													7.

Cash Flow Analysis Explanation Of Terms

Line 1   **Cash on Hand-** The total money available as readily usable cash

Line 2   **Cash Receipts** are cash that is received in the form of
                a. Cash sales
                b. Collections from customers who owe you money
                c. Loans, gifts or other investments into the business

Line 3   **Total Cash Receipts** (Lines 2a + 2b + 2c) is the sum of all the
                cash coming in from line 2.

Line 4   **Total Cash Available** is the sum of all cash on hand
                and cash receipts. (Lines 1 + 3)

Line 5   **Cash Paid Out** This category includes all business expenses.

Line 6   **Total Cash Paid Out** is the sum of all the itemized expenses in
                line section 5

Line 7   **Cash Flow**, therefore is Total Cash Available minus Total Cash
                Paid out (lines 4 - Line 6)

***

Taxes

Accounting And Taxes

In a later chapter, we'll explore in greater detail the nuts and bolts of actually completing your taxes. For now, however, let's just taxes.

Partner with the Government

The U.S. government wants to make money. The way they make money is through taxes. The more money you make, the more taxes they charge you. At the same time, they want to keep the economy going. Annually, small businesses account for the creation of at least 30% of all the new jobs in the US. Anyone who launches a business in America is rewarded for keeping the economy going. You are rewarded by tax breaks. The government knows that it takes a while for a new company to get off the ground, so for the first three or so years of a new business, you're allowed to claim a loss (if it really is a loss, that is) and get a refund or credit for the money you've invested. The government has to put a limit on the time period, since anyone can just keep starting phony businesses, spend a lot of money and claim refunds for the rest of their lives. With this frame of mind, you can eliminate a lot of the fear of starting up a business and seeing all of your hard earned money going into it. Take advantage of the tax laws to channel money back into your business.

The next statement could be the key to your future. It could be the key to your family's future, the future of your assets, your estate, your future royalties, your company, your car, your bank account and everything that you are striving for. The advice is simple, and well within your abilities to do. Here it is: **KEEP GOOD RECORDS!** One more time, in case you missed it: **KEEP GOOD RECORDS!**

ANY time you spend ANY amount of money, ASK FOR A RECEIPT. If you pay by check, your cancelled check will be your receipt. The receipts and any proof of expenditure are your main line of defense in the event of a tax audit. They do happen, and as long as you've kept good, clear, honest records, you'll have nothing to worry about. Get into the habit of asking for receipts. Once you get it, get into the habit of writing what the receipt is for on the back. It doesn't take much time. Trust me, the time you try to save now, you'll spend going crazy trying to remember at tax time, or during a tax audit! When you get home try to log the information right away. If you don't have a computer, or if you intend to have someone do your taxes, store the receipt in a large envelope labeled for that MONTH. Make sure you open a new envelope for each month. Your accountant, tax preparer, or even you as you become more familiar with the tax requirements, will be grateful for this bit of foresight when tax time comes. The categories in the next chapter help you in organizing you record label expenses for tax time, and in keeping track of where your money is going:

If you utilize some type of database program, you'll be able to access and organize your information in a wide number of ways: by date, by type, by selection number and so on. This way of record keeping is merely a suggestion. You should find a method which works best for you. Whichever method you choose, the goal should be the same: access, clarity, accuracy and flexibility. If you have partners, or a small staff, delegate this task to the most organize person. If that happens to be you, then do it! With those business basics out of the way, the next section will explore areas which are unique to the daily operation of your record label. Now that some of the formalities and generalities of your business are in place, it's time to focus on more of the specifics of what your company is all about--making and selling music!

Document Everything!

You should keep track of everything related to your business. Create a file to record how, why, when and in what order you do the things you do. Keep records of who your suppliers are, key contacts, copies of local and national media coverage, your first sale, your millionth customer, even how you answer the phones. This information may come in handy if you ever write a book on how to start and operate your particular type of business. And it will help you to put together an operations manual--which you should do anyway--should you need to train new employees or sell your business.

In an upcoming chapter, you'll learn how all this information and documentation will help make doing your taxes a breeze!

A Handy Accounting Reminder

Keep this as a reminder of how often to complete the key business analyses

Tool	Purpose	Frequency	Key Terms/Formula
Balance Sheet	Snapshot of "Net Worth" ie Health of Business at any single moment	1ST **of MONTH** As often as desired, but I do once at beginning and once at end of month to chart my progress. **END of MONTH**	Assets − Liabilities = net worth What I own minus what I owe
Cash Flow	What I have to left over $1 + $1 -$0.50 FLOW IS $1.50	**ONCE A /MONTH**	Cash available to me to do business for the month minus what I spent to run the company = cash flow OR, thought of another way: the flow "in" combined with the flow "out" A dollar came in, fifty cents went out. That adds up to $1.50 total flow
Profit & Loss *or "income" Statement*		**END OF YEAR** Usually needed for end-of-year taxes	Income − Expenses = Profit/Loss What I earned minus what I spent

<u>SUMMARY</u> for Chapter 6: *"Basic Business Concepts & Tools"*

½ *Key Points*

- Retail and wholesale costs are pretty standard within the industry; meaning you don't have the flexibility of setting your own prices. The market, the demand, the cost to you, and the perceived value of your product or service has pretty much already been established in the industry. However, you should master the concepts of profit margins, markup, break-even analysis to better understand where the profit in your venture exists.

- It's important to be organized, to protect your assets, to understand the importance of contracts to your business success, and to be able to wield key business concepts appropriately.

- Use the organizational chart to add structure and efficiency to your business. Used correctly, it can help you conceive of and operate your business in ways that ultimately make you more money! When deciding who will fill the positions in your "org chart", experts suggest choosing based on personality. Ask yourself, "Who do I want reporting to me?" What talents, skills, mindsets do I want my core team to exemplify? "Whom do I want to make money with?" "Who energizes me and is both productive as well as fun to work with on projects?"

- Growing your company is a function of how well you manage people and processes. Use the mantra, "Delegate, Automate, or Eliminate" to help you in streamlining your business operations to be more effective.

- Your business will fail or succeed based on your grasp and effective manipulation of such concepts as markup, break-even, profit margin, profit and loss and cash flow. Make it your business to understand them well. This is a task that may be delegated, but first must be understood thoroughly.

- Cutting costs and saving money is a vital component of succeeding in business. There are numerous principles and practices that can help you maximize profits by minimizing expenses.

½ *The Right Questions*

- How can I learn more about how to run my business?
- Whom can I approach to mentor me in running my business?
- How did Puffy, Master P, Russell, and other Hip Hop Entrepreneurs learn their business skills?

BOOKS, AUDIO PROGRAMS, MAGAZINES, ORGANIZATIONS & WEBSITES

½ *For managing fast growth*
- *Mastering the Rockefeller Habits* by Verne Harnish; www.gazelles.com

½ *For mastering business concepts*
- *Musicians Business & Legal Guide* by Mark Halloran

½ *For managing your team*
- *The One Minute Manager* by Kenneth Blanchard

½ *For attracting and managing wealth*
- *The One-Minute Millionaire* by Mark Victor Hansen; Robert G. Allen

½ *Magazines (Available on newsstands or at your local library)*
- Inc. Magazine
- Entrepreneur Magazine
- Business 2.0

Chapter 7:
"Launching Your Label on the Internet"

Remember the Game Plan

Another important aspect of your operations is your web presence.

▶ **Monitor your OPERATIONS**
Find, sign and develop talented ARTISTS
Create your PRODUCT on CD or other media
MARKET, Promote & Advertise it...
SELL IT to stores, distributors and to the public
Maximize additional streams of INCOME
RECOUP your expenses
PAY the players
Make a PROFIT.
GROW your business

Making Money with Your Online Presence

This is a "how to" manual. So rather than waste time teaching you the history of the internet and the benefit of having a website, I'm going to assume you are either familiar with, already know, don't care, and are already convinced of the value of the internet and the need to have a web presence. That being the case, I'm going to offer you a process in the form of an FAQ and a checklist for getting up and running.

Your mission is to establish an internet presence on which people purchase copies of your products, t-shirts, merchandise, tickets to events, memberships in fan clubs, and anything else you're selling. Look at your online business as a virtual storefront and a place for people to congregate, not simply as a brochure. Your website is a place, not a thing. The more reasons people have for getting to know more about your artists, your site and what you have to offer, the more loyalty they develop and the more sales you'll eventually have. Here then are some tips to keep in mind when planning, creating and growing your record label's website:

*   make the experience of visiting your site an informative and enjoyable one
*   develop a sense of community (use chat rooms, bulletin boards, distribution lists)
*   give people a reason to return to your site (update your content occasionally; contests, etc.)
*   collect demographic information (your visitors' identity, likes and dislikes)
*   commerce-enable your site (make it possible for customers to purchase online)
*   keep in touch with customers with occasional emails from your artists or label staff
*   provide a place for visitors to listen to your artists' music
*   link with other Hip Hop sites
*   register with search engines
*   remind your artists to mention the site whenever performing, or whenever interviewed

Frequently Asked Questions About Setting Up A Web Presence:

Why do people abandon their shopping carts?

Here is some good information to have that will help you focus on the essential elements to increase sales.

41% The Web page was too slow
20% The Web page looked unprofessional
16% The site didn't take credit cards
14% Couldn't find the check out area
12% Couldn't find a return policy

Source: Esearch; from a survey of 1000 consumers

What can I do to increase my online sales?

Duplicate the winners. Check out what sites like Amazon.com, Dell and other music sites that you KNOW FOR SURE are making money, and see how they design their pages, as well as how they structure their checkout and ordering process. Notice where they place their guarantee statements, privacy statements, pictures, white space. Remember, sometimes the simplest thing like where you place your "click here to order" link, may have an effect on your sales. So pay attention and follow the leaders.

Any tips for choosing a domain name?

Make sure you own your label name, your artist's name and any other catch phrase, album title, or single title by which the public may come to identify you. Also, avoid ambiguity or confusion. Avoid words that may be misspelled. If your ideal .com does not exist, choose something else. Avoid going for a .net Tip: sometimes, names become available when the current owner fails to renew their ownership for the next year. Avoid letters that may not be heard clearly over the phone or when performing in front of a crowd. (is it "f" as in "frank" or "s" as in "sam" did she say "d" as in "david" or "t" as in tom?"

Can I have more than one domain name?

YES. You can always have more than one domain name "pointing" to the same site. For example, both my www.hiphopentrepreneur.com, and my www.hiphopbiz.com domain names take you to the same site. Having different domain names allows you to experiment to discover which one is easier for people to remember and which one may lend itself to unique marketing ideas.

If I have more than one domain name should I set up multiple pages?

That's not necessary, based on the answer to the previous question. However, if each page has a different content and different key word meta tags, it might prove helpful in securing multiple placement in search engines.

What if someone owns the domain name I want?

Find another one. If you brainstorm long enough, you can come up with something that suits you perfectly. But, here's a tip: just because someone currently owns your desire domain name, doesn't mean you can't have it soon. If someone owns your domain name, but hasn't put up a site yet, they may not really have plans to. Consequently, they may let their ownership lapse by not renewing their ownership with the registrar. When you check on the ownership using networksolutions.com's "WhoIs" Database, make note of the "record expires" date. It it's scheduled to expire in a few weeks or months, you might get lucky and be able to grab it if they don't renew But, whatever you do, DO NOT, I repeat, DO NOT notify the current owner that you're interested in the domain name, unless you DESPERATELY, REALLY want it and are willing to pay them for it now that they know it now has value to you!

Should I purchase email names off the Internet?

ABSOLUTELY NOT. Unless it's an "opt-in" list where the names of the list belong to people who've specifically requested to be on the list. Otherwise, you'll make many enemies, and may even have your website shut down for sending unsolicited email. (a crime known as "spamming")

Should I get a "toll free" number to make ordering easier for my customers?

These days, since long distance charges are as low as 4.9 cents/minute, offering a toll free number for your customers to reach you is not as much of an enticement as it once was. However, since it IS so cheap, you may wish to invest in one. It'll probably result in a few extra calls.

What things should I include on my site's order form and brochures?

Website info on upper section (with picture) and lower section (with order form)
Phone number on upper and lower sections
Visa/MC/Amex/Discover logo
The words "Order Now"
Where to send payment and how to make payable
Shipping and handling information
Sales Tax information
Order form should request
Name, Address, City, State, Zip, Email Address, Telephone, quantity desired

What's the community concept you refer to?

In Webonomics, Evan Shwartz talks about the new paradigm for selling on the net. Key in this equation is the ability to create a sense of community among your visitors....

What other ways can I keep people coming back to my site?

A) Make your site a portal of information. It encourages your visitors to return and stay. Hotsheet.com is one example of a one-page portal.

B) Add games to your site. You can get some here: www.uproar.co.uk or at www.pogo.com/affiliates.

C) Make your site interactive with a guest book, forum, tell-a-friend link, webring, customizable news, contests, polls, e-card, and free for all links. Bizland.com allows you to sign up for an account and place the code on your site.

D) Provide links to freebies, get-paid-to-surf sites, contests, incentives, jokes, quotes, mp3, and gnutella.

How often should I communicate with my mailing list?

I find once per week to be an acceptable frequency. Once every two weeks may also be good. Unless you have a daily news like and entertainment column, or a horoscope feature that people want to read each day, you might be wise to keep it to no more than once per week.

✔ A Web Label Launching Checklist

The process of launching your online business is perhaps the easiest thing you will ever do. The challenge, of course, lies in how to make it profitable. But, first things first. Let's go through the process of actually creating an online presence for your record label and your artists.

PHASE 1 – Understanding The Psychology of Internet Selling

☐ Get the Ultimate Web Promotion Guide at www.passionprofit.com and start announcing your site.

½ Read *Turn Your Passion Into Profit* by Walt Goodridge   Read the chapter on Internet Basics

½ Read *The Musician's Internet* by Peter Spellman

½ Read *Webonomics* by Evan Schwartz for ideas and tips on how to think differently about web selling

½ Read *IdeaVirus* by Seth Godin; download free at www.ideavirus.com This will help you come up with some unique marketing ideas to create a powerful word-of-mouth campaign

½ Read *The E-Myth* Revisited by Michael Gerber

½ Start collecting email addresses

PHASE 2 - Administrative Stuff

½ Contact Local Bank for details to set up business account; You'll need this when you

½ Decide on & search for domain name; Use PowerPipe.com

½ Complete/Submit SS-4; See sample of completed form on page 184

½ Set up business checking account

½ Rent PO Box or Mailboxes Etc. box to receive mail orders

½ The following are optional
    (Optional) Set up a Portable 800 Number through any long distance carrier
    (Optional) Establish a Dedicated fax/internet line
    (Optional) Use a Call Answering service
    (Optional) Retain an Order Fulfillment Company to actually ship the orders
    (Optional) Set up UPS or other business shipping account

PHASE 3 – Establish your online identity

☐ Set up an email account and Internet access.

☐ Visit www.passionprofit.com or any other domain name registrar to see if your URL is available

☐ Set up hosting for the domain. (We do that, too! Visit www.passionprofit.com)

☐ Visit other artists' sites to get a feel for what yours might look like

☐ Design your site. Remember to include
- music files
- artist bio
- appearances
- products/merchandise page
- news and event announcements
- links to other related sites
- contact information
- online media kit
- include information on shipping charges
- add po box or physical address for customers who wish to mail checks
- add fax number for customers who wish to fax orders
- add guarantee and privacy information

☐ Upload your site

½ Download Netscape/Internet Explorer (IE) Browser, Microsoft Outlook or find some means that allows you to send out emails to your mailing list as "yourname@yourdomainname.com" as in walt@hiphopbiz.com. This adds a level of professionalism to your email correspondence.

½ Create the following email accounts
[yourname]@yourdomain.com
orders@yourdomain.com
info@yourdomain.com
email@yourdomain.com
events@yourdomain.com
news@yourdomain.com
advertise@yourdomain.com

½ Set up Merchant Account to be able to process your customers' credit cards
The Passion Profit Company (www.passionprofit.com) provides merchant services.
Get your terminal/printer for offline sales.
Here's what you should expect to pay for these typical terminals
Verifone Tranz 330 (t) new:$359 refurbished:$299
Verifone Tranz 460 (t/p) new:$495 refurbished: $395
Verifone Omni 3200 (t/p) new:$495
Nurit 3010 Wireless new:$1095
t=terminal
t/p=terminal and printer

½ Set up an "internet gateway account" which allows for real-time credit card processing through your website; Processing Software new:$99-$295

PHASE 4 – - Promoting Your Site

☐ Start collecting email addresses

½Read the Chapter on Momentum Marketing

½ List your site with Google.com and other search engines

½Find similar community sites to swap links with

½ Prepare for these daily tasks
- -Check & respond to email
- -Charge customer credit cards
- -Prepare and fill orders
- -Send out brochures
- -Update site as necessary

½ Prepare for these weekly tasks
- -Communicate with your subscribers
- -Swap ads with other webmasters

½ Expose your artists on other websites

In addition to launching your own website, here are additional sites on which you can make your music available to the public. Register your artists, label and music on the following sites
- MP3.com
- CDBaby.com
- AudioGalaxy.com
- UBL.com (Ultimate Band List)
- Undergroundhiphop.com

½ Announce your artists on these sites
- Manhunt.com
- EURWeb.com
- BET.com

Using the search term: "underground hip hop", find other sites to link with, register on, and sign up to expose your artists.

<u>SUMMARY</u> of Chapter 7: *"Launching Your Label on The Internet"*

½ *Main Points*

- The Internet represents a whole new frontier for doing business. If you are not doing business online, you are losing business, and will soon be out of business! Familiarize yourself with this new world and get up to speed as quickly as possible. Understand the vocabulary, what it means, how it applies to the selling of music online.

- The Web Launching Checklist provides direct guidance for getting up and running.

½ *The Right Questions*

- What do I want my website to accomplish?
- What do I want visitors to actually do once they come to my site?
- How are people hearing about and finding me online?
- What specific things can I do to make my site easier to notice?
- What specific things can I do to make my site easier to navigate?
- What other high profile and high traffic sites can I exchange links with?
- Who has a mailing list to which I can suggest making an endorsed offer?
- What other sites have a face, feel, flow & features that I wish to emulate?

½ For understanding website design
- *Teach Yourself HTML in a Week* by Laura Lemay

▶ For understanding Internet marketing
- *Multiple Streams of Internet Income* by Robert G. Allen
- *The Idea Virus* by Seth Godin
- *Webonomics* by Evan Schwartz
- *Clicking Through* by Jonathan I Ezor

½ For understanding the Music Industry Game on the Internet
- *The Musician's Internet* by Peter Spellman

½ Websites
- Google.com's ADWORDS advertising program is great for searchable products and services.
- Google.com's ADSENSE program is a great way to generate income through your site.

"Let the games begin!"
--source unknown

PART 2

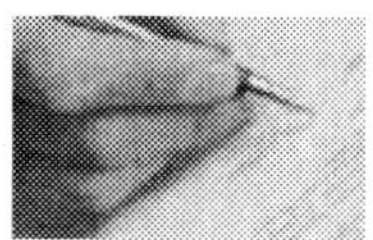

CHAPTER 8:
"Find, Sign and Develop Talented Artists"
Remember the Game Plan

The next step in the game plan is finding, signing and developing talented artists.

Monitor your OPERATIONS
► Find, sign and develop talented ARTISTS
Create your PRODUCT on CD or other media
MARKET, Promote & Advertise it...
SELL IT to stores, distributors and to the public
Maximize additional streams of INCOME
RECOUP your expenses
PAY the players
Make a PROFIT.
GROW your business

Where to Find Them

Since the success of the artist/label relationship is based partly on trust, most independent labels find their talent from within their immediate circles of contacts.

If you have benefit of funding or have achieved a certain amount of clout within your market, and are in search of talent, consider recording studios, music industry events, seminars and workshops & clubs. You might also advertise in the classified section of industry magazines.

The Internet has now created a whole new set of options for scouting for talent: chat rooms, message boards, email distribution lists are a few of the places to look in this new global community in which to network and get talent. You can also scout sites that feature other indie labels around the world. See the Chapter 6 Internet checklist for sites which feature other independent artists.

What Questions To Ask:

When considering signing an artist, there are certain specific questions you should ask.
• Does this artist have the level of commitment necessary to succeed?
• Does this artist really understand the music industry?
• Can this person work well with others?
• Are they open to creative input from other sources?
• Is this artist of legal age to enter into a contract?
• Do I [like, respect, trust, enjoy working with] this person?
• Do I [like, respect, trust, enjoy working with] this person's management, lawyers, et al?
• Do the artist's image, lyrics and overall presence fit with that of my label?
• Is this a mature, self-starting, self-aware individual who takes responsibility for his/her actions?

Once you Find Them

Your mission is to your artists in your company's vision. This is especially important if your company is rather small. Depending on the size and budget of your company, you may not have the luxury of offering your artists an advance. In this scenario, you may consider offering them a greater share of future profits, ownership of the company, or some other incentive to justify them

THE RECORD LABEL CONTRACT

As the head of an independent label, the relationship between you and your artists will be of critical importance in determining the future of your company. That relationship will be fueled by your commitment to your artist(s) and their commitment to you and to their careers. It will be driven by the expectations that both of you have for each other. And finally, it will be guided by something concrete, something realistic, and something defined and understood by each. That something will be your contract.

On the pages that follow, is a sample of a recording contract. While the language may at times be a bit tricky to follow, you'd be well advised to read it over and over from a record label owner's perspective. A thorough understanding of the intricacies of a standard label might be the single most important knowledge you can develop to really change the game!

EXCLUSIVE RECORDING AGREEMENT

THIS Agreement is made this ___________ day of __________ in the year _______ by and between Mindblowin Entertainment, Inc., a Florida corporation, whose address is (hereinafter"Company") and _________________________________, professionally known as _______________________ (hereinafter individually or collectively referred to as "Artist"): whose address is:____

Reference is made to Exhibits A, B and C attached hereto and the terms of which are incorporated herein.

WHEREAS Artist is a professional entertainer and recording artist known as "________________;"

WHEREAS, Company is in the business of producing Master Recordings, or causing such Master Recordings to be produced, and Company is also in the business of manufacturing, distributing and selling records, or causing their manufacture, distribution and sale through third parties; and

WHEREAS, Artist wishes to cause Company to record Master Recordings embodying Artist's performances and to exploit these Master Recordings if Company is able to do so; and Company is willing to undertake to do so, subject to the terms and conditions as follows:

NOW THEREFORE, in Consideration of the promises and warranties, representations and agreements herein contained, the parties hereby agree as follows:

1. TERM: (a) The Term of this Agreement shall consist of an Initial Period ("Initial Contract Period") commencing on the date set forth above and ending on the date seven (7) months following the Initial Release in the United States of the Album Delivered in complete satisfaction of Artist's "Recording Commitment" for the Initial Contract Period, but in no event later than the date twelve (12) months following Company's receipt of Notice of Delivery of all Recordings constituting Artist's "Recording Commitment" for the Initial Contract Period. The Term may be extended by Company's exercise of one or more of the options granted to Company below (unless extended or suspended as provided herein).

(b) Artist hereby irrevocably grants to Company five (5) separate consecutive options to extend the Term for a "Second", "Third", "Fourth", "Fifth" and "Sixth" additional Contract Period(s) (sometimes, hereinafter, referred to as "Option Period(s)") on the same terms and conditions applicable to the Initial Contract Period except as otherwise expressly provided in this Agreement. Each Option Period shall be exercised automatically by Company unless Company shall give Artist written notice to the contrary prior to the date that the then current Contract Period would otherwise expire. The Option Period concerned shall begin immediately after the end of the current Contract Period and shall continue until the date seven (7) months following the Initial Release in the United States of the

Album(s) Delivered in complete satisfaction of Artist's Recording Commitment for that Option Period but in no event later than the date twelve (12) months following Company's receipt of Notice of Delivery of all Recordings constituting the Recording Commitment for that Option Period. In the event that Company has assigned this Agreement in whole or in part to any entity and Company elects not to exercise an option to extend the term of this Agreement, Artist agrees that Artist will promptly notify such assignee entity of the same. Each such notice shall be in writing and shall be sent by courier or other personal delivery or by registered or certified mail to the address listed above or to such address as Artist notifies Company of in writing.

(c) The aggregate of the Initial Contract Period together with Option Periods, if any, for which rights are exercised by Company in accordance with subparagraph (b) above, and any extensions and suspensions thereof, shall be referred to herein as the "Term".

2. SERVICES:
(a) During the Term of this Agreement, Artist shall furnish, exclusively to Company, Artist's services as a recording artist for the purpose of making Master Recordings, throughout the universe, and as otherwise set forth herein, and Artist shall not render services as a recording artist for any other entity whatsoever. For the purposes hereof "services as a recording artist" shall mean and include, but shall not be limited to, the rendering of performances as a vocalist, musician and/or narrator fixed by any method, mode or device, whether now known or hereinafter developed, regardless of whether such method, mode or device is capable of fixing sound alone or sound fixed together with visual images.

(b) Artist will make himself available to render the services customarily performed by first class professional recording artists, on an exclusive basis to Company, at recording sessions scheduled at times and places designated by the Company. Upon Company's request Artist shall perform services hereunder, which shall include but not be limited to, performing, rehearsing, and editing of tape recordings for the purpose of obtaining a commercially and technically satisfactory Master Recording in the sole discretion of Company.

(c) Artist's obligations hereunder shall include furnishing the services of the producers of those Master Recording(s), and Artist shall be solely responsible for engaging and paying them. (Producers whom Artist or Company engage for production services on Master Recording(s) recorded pursuant to this agreement is sometimes referred to in this Agreement by the term "Producers".)

(d) If Company, instead, engages producers for any of those Master Recordings, or if the producers of any such Master Recordings are employees of Company or render their services under contract to Company, the following terms shall apply:

(i) Artist's royalty account and the production budget for the recording project concerned shall be charged with a Recording Cost item of the production fee for the producers.

(ii) Artist's royalty under paragraph 9 on Records made from those Master Recording(s) shall be reduced by the amount of the royalty payable to producers on Albums under paragraph 9, adjusted in proportion to the other royalty rates and royalty adjustments provided for in the other provisions of paragraphs 9 and 10. Artist hereby directs Company to deduct, from any and all monies payable or becoming payable to Artist, the royalties that Company is obligated to pay such producers in respect of Record(s) derived from Master Recording(s) produced by such producers.
Company Artist

3. RECORDING COMMITMENT.
(a)
(i) During the Initial Contract Period, Artist will perform for the recording of Master
Recordings and Company will record such Master Recordings, to comprise not fewer than thirteen (13) but not more than twenty six (26) songs, except as otherwise set forth herein, if requested by Company and, at Company's election, other versions embodying the same Composition(s).

(ii) During each Contract Period following the Initial Contract Period, Artist will perform for the recording of Master Recordings, and Company will record such Master Recordings, to comprise not fewer than thirteen (13) but not more than twenty six (26) songs, except as otherwise set forth herein, if requested by Company and, at Company's election, other versions embodying the same Composition(s).

(iii) The Master Recordings referred to in subparagraphs (i) and (ii) immediately above, as may be applicable, are sometimes referred to herein as the "Minimum Recording Commitment". The Minimum Recording Commitment for each Contract Period will be fulfilled within the first three (3) months of the Contract Period concerned.

(iv) Nothing contained herein shall be construed so as to require Company to release any Master Recording pursuant to this Agreement. However, if Company does not release any Master Recordings (on a national level) within eighteen (18) months after delivery by Artist, Artist may terminate this agreement and purchase the master Recordings at their actual cost.

(v) During each Contract Period, including the Initial Period, Company shall have the right to require that Artist render services and perform for the recording of additional Master Recordings (the "Additional Recordings"). Company's option for Additional Recordings shall be for the number of Master Recordings or sides designated by Company, in increments determined by Company. Nothing contained herein shall be construed so as to require Company to release the Additional Recordings. The Minimum Recording Commitment for any Contract Period taken together with the Additional Recordings requested by Company for that Contract Period shall be referred to as the "Recording Commitment" or "Artist's Recording Commitment" for that Contract Period.

(vi) At Company's request, Artist shall perform for the recording of dub mixes, Maxi Single mixes, re-edits, Single edits, and other variations of the Compositions embodied on any Master, and such additional recording(s) will not be applied in reduction of Artist's Recording Commitment hereunder.

(b) Each time Company notifies Artist to record Master Recordings hereunder, Artist will complete such performances for the requested Master Recordings within Twenty (20) days following Company's notice to Artist that Company requires same m respect of Master Recordings to compromise a Single or Maxi-Single, and within ninety (90) days of such notice if Company requires Artist's services in respect of Master Recordings to comprise an LP. Whenever Artist is recording hereunder, Artist shall follow all requests and instructions of Company or its designees and representatives.

(c) Artist will not perform for (nor will Artist consent to or permit the use by any Person other than Company of Artist's name or likeness for) or in connection with the recording or exploitation of any Phonograph Record embodying any Composition recorded by Artist under this Agreement prior to the later of either five (5) years subsequent to the date of delivery to Company hereunder of the last Master embodying that Composition or two (2) years subsequent to the expiration or termination of the Term of this Agreement, or any subsequent agreement between Artist and any Person relating to Artist's recording services for Company, provided that the term of such subsequent agreement commences no later than three (3) months after the Term hereof terminates. Artist's agreement(s) with an individual producer hereunder shall restrict said producer from producing the Composition on another Master for any Person other than Company for at least two (2) years from the date of Delivery to Company of such Master. Artist shall provide Company of such agreement, in writing, prior to recording of said Master(s)

4. RECORDING PROCEDURE:

(a) In connection with Master Recordings to be made hereunder, the following matters shall be selected or designated by Company: (1) the producer(s); (2) the arrangers, musicians, background vocalists, copyists, contractors, engineers, and other technical personnel; (3) the studio where the recording is to take place; (4) the scheduling and booking of all studio time; (5) the dates of the recording; (6) the recording budget therefore; (7) material to be recorded; (8) the number of Compositions to be recorded; (9) the number of Compositions to be contained on all records hereunder; (10) the Compositions to be contained on all Phonograph Records hereunder; (11) all artwork used in advertising materials, promotional materials, record sleeves, and record jackets; and (12) all other elements to be utilized or embodied in recording activity conducted hereunder and/or to promote the records derived from the Masters. Artist shall be consulted with regard to the above matters but the decision of the Company shall control.

(b) Each time Company notifies Artist that it requires Artist to record Master Recordings hereunder, Artist will make himself available to commence recording in accordance with Company's instructions. Company's notices shall be issued reasonably in advance of the scheduled recording session.

(c) Each Master Recording made hereunder shall be subject to Company's approval as commercially and technically satisfactory for the manufacture and sale of records. Artist agrees to re-record each Composition until Company is satisfied, in its sole discretion, that a Master has been produced, which is commercially and technically satisfactory for the manufacture and sale of records. In the event that Company is not able to obtain clearances for the samples used on a Master at a reasonable rate in Company's sole discretion, the Master shall be determined to be unsatisfactory. Artist shall not be deemed to have completed his services in respect to any Master until Company has acknowledged in writing that a Master has been so produced. In the event that any Master delivered by Artist is deemed unsatisfactory by Company, Company shall notify Artist within sixty (60) days thereafter of its rejection of said recorded Master and Artist shall have thirty (30) days to deliver a replacement Master.

(d) No Master Recording made hereunder fixing the performance shall apply in reduction of the Recording Commitment to Company if it is a "Live Performance", if it is a Composition previously recorded by Artist, or if it embodies a Composition which Artist is legally prohibited from recording. In the event Company requests or accepts as part of the Recording Commitment a Multiple Record Set, same shall be deemed to be a number of Masters sufficient to comprise only one (1) LP for the purposes of the Recording Commitment hereunder. Company's or a Distribution Company's release of the "best of" LP, "greatest hits" LP, soundtrack LP, cast albums, or "live" LP, and the Master Recordings embodied thereon, shall not apply in reduction of Artist's Recording Commitment hereunder.

(e) Any Master Recordings made hereunder which are not recorded m all respects m accordance with the terms and provisions hereof shall not, unless Company otherwise consents in writing, count as Master Recordings, nor shall they apply toward the fulfillment of the applicable Recording Commitment hereunder. Furthermore, in the event that any payments shall be made with respect to non-complying Master Recordings made hereunder and such non-compliance is a result of the act or omission on Artist's part which constitutes a breach of a material term or provision of this Agreement, then Artist shall, upon Company's demand, promptly reimburse Company for any such payments. If Artist should fail to so reimburse Company for any such payments, Company, in addition to all of Company's other remedies in such event, shall have the right to deduct such sums from any monies thereafter becoming payable under this Agreement or to treat such sums as an Advance to Artist.

(f) If Company requires or requests that Artist render services as a producer of any Master Recordings made hereunder, then Artist shall render such services and Artist shall not receive or be entitled to any additional royalty or compensation for production services.

(g) Artist shall not make any use of so called "samples" or "sampled material" in the Master Recordings hereunder without the previous express written approval of Company. Artist hereby agrees to notify, Company, in writing prior to recording, of the title, artist(s), label, author(s), and publisher(s) of the recording Artist intends to use and shall supply Company with a copy of a release of said recording with its cover art and liner notes.

(h) Artist shall timely supply Company with all of the information Company needs in order: (1) to make payments due or required in connection with Recordings hereunder; (2) to comply with any and all other obligations Company may have in connection with the making of Recordings hereunder; and (3) to release Records derived from such Recordings. Artist shall be solely responsible for and shall pay any penalties incurred for late payment caused by Artist's delay in submitting union contract forms, report forms or invoices, or other documents.

(i) Artist's submission of Recordings to Company shall constitute Artist's representation that Artist has obtained all necessary licenses, approvals, consents and permissions.

(j) The Master Recordings shall be produced in accordance and otherwise comply with the rules and regulations of the American Federation of Television and Radio Artists and all other unions having, jurisdiction, including without limitation paragraph 31 of the 1990-1993 AFTRA Code of Fair Practice for Phonograph Recordings (or the comparable provision of any successor agreement). All Persons rendering services in connection with the Master Recordings shall fully comply with the provisions of the Immigration Reform Control Act of 1986. Artist is or will become and will remain, to the extent necessary to enable the performance, of this Agreement, a member in good standing of all labor unions or guilds in which membership may be lawfully required for the performance of each Artist's services under the applicable Artist Agreement.

(k) Company shall be permitted to reject any Master Recording if such Master Recording, as determined in the sole opinion of Company, shall (i) be objectionable on the basis of obscenity or violence, (ii) constitute a potential defamation or libel of, or violate any personal, property or other right of, any Person or (iii) constitute a potential violation of any law or governmental regulation. if Company rejects any Master Recording pursuant to this subparagraph (k), then such Master Recording shall not count as a Master Recording Delivered to the Company in fulfillment of the Recording Commitment pursuant to Paragraph 3.

5. RECOUPABLE AND REIMBURSABLE ADVANCES AND COSTS:
All costs and advances paid by Company in connection with the Master Recordings made hereunder shall constitute Advances to Artist recoupable from Artist's royalties unless otherwise expressly agreed in writing by an authorized officer of Company and no royalties shall be payable to Artist until said Advances are recouped from Artist's royalties. Such costs and advances include but are not limited to the following:
Company Artist

(a) All amounts paid by Company or caused to be paid by Company as Recording Costs, in connection with the Master Recordings made hereunder including but not limited to recording costs, musicians, producers, payment to any unions, all studio tape, editing, mixing, mastering and engineering costs; and all other costs and expenses incurred in producing the Master Recording hereunder which are then customarily recognized as Recording Costs in the record industry.

(b) All amounts equal to all of Company's direct and indirect expenses actually incurred by Company for the Master(s), including but not limited to: (i) advertising, marketing and promotional expenses; (ii) commissions and/or royalties payable to third parties, and (iii) all payments made on behalf of Artist prior to the rendition of the statement.

(c) All costs paid or incurred by Company in connection with the production of, and/or the acquisition of rights in, audiovisual works embodying the Artist's performances shall constitute Advances subject to subparagraph 11(c) below.

(d) In the event that Company has to pay for the use of any Sampled Material in the Master Recordings hereunder, all costs, including but not limited to, sample clearance fees, Company's legal fees, and third party legal fees, shall be considered advances to the Artist and no royalties shall be payable to Artist until said advances are recouped from Artist's royalties.

(e) All costs paid or incurred by Company with respect to any trademark search, or
registration in connection with any name or sobriquet now or hereafter used or proposed to be used by the Artist under this Agreement, shall constitute Advances. hereunder shall restrict said producer from producing the Composition on another Master for any Person other than Company for at least two (2) years from the date of Delivery to Company of such Master. Artist shall provide Company with a copy of such agreement, in writing, prior to the recording of said Master(s).

(f) All monies paid by Company to Artist during the Term, other than royalties paid pursuant to paragraphs 9 and 12, shall constitute Advances unless otherwise expressly agreed in writing by an authorized officer of Company. Each payment (except such royalties) made by Company during the Term to another Person on behalf of Artist shall also constitute an Advance if it is made with the consent of Artist, Wit is required by law, or if it is made by Company to satisfy an obligation incurred by Artist in connection with the subject matter of this Agreement.

(g) Notwithstanding anything to the contrary contained herein, any costs or expenditures which are payable by Artist or chargeable against Artist's royalties and which are applicable to any Joint Recordings shall be computed by apportionment as provided in paragraph 9(f)(viii).

6. RIGHTS IN RECORDINGS:
(a) Each Master Recording which embodies Artist's performances and which is made by Artist during the term of this Agreement, from the Inception of Recording and whether or not intended as a Master Recording, shall, for the purposes of the United States Copyright Law, be considered a "work for hire" for Company or it's assignees and designees. If any such Master Recording is determined not to be a work made for hire, it will be deemed transferred to Company by Artist in perpetuity throughout the universe. All such Master Recordings and all Masters and records manufactured from them, together with the performances embodied on them, shall be the sole property of Company, it's assignees and designees in perpetuity throughout the universe, free from whatever claim whatsoever by Artist, Entity, or by anyone deriving rights from Artist; and Company shall have the exclusive right to copyright those Master Recordings in its name as the author and owner of them and secure any and all renewals and extensions of such Copyrights throughout the universe. Artist will execute and deliver to Company such instruments of transfer and other documents regarding the rights of Company in the Master Recordings as Company may reasonably request to carry out the purposes of this Agreement and Company may sign such documents in Artist's name and make appropriate disposition of them.

(b) Without limiting the generality of the foregoing, Company shall have the exclusive unlimited worldwide right, but not the obligation, to: (1) manufacture, or grant others the right to manufacture, recordings and Video-Records from the Master Recordings produced hereunder by any means, including but not limited to Albums, Singles, Cassettes, Compact Discs, Digital Audio Tape or Digital/Internet Methodology; (2) to perform, advertise, import, export, sell, lease, rent, synchronize, license, distribute, or otherwise exploit said property, in any manner of media now known or hereafter invented, including the public performance thereof in any medium, (3) to use in On-line Multimedia Production and place on interactive computer-based presentations, including but not limited to the Internet and World-Wide Web; (4) to obtain copyrights and renewals thereof in sound recordings; (5) to transfer or otherwise deal in the same under any trademarks, trade names and labels, and to authorize others to do so or to refrain from doing so; and (6) to edit, adapt, add, delete from, alter, mix and remix the Master Recordings to conform to technological or commercial requirements in various formats now or hereafter known or developed, or to eliminate material which might subject Company to any legal action, without any payment other than as provided herein; or Company and its affiliates and licensees may, at their election, delay or refrain from doing any one or more of the foregoing.

(c) Solely for the purposes of any applicable copyright law, all persons rendering services in connection with the recording of such Master Recordings, including Artist, shall be deemed "employees for hire". Company shall have the right to edit and re-edit, couple and re-couple the Master Recordings that are subject matter of this Agreement with Master Recordings embodying the performance of other Artists.

(d) Artist recognizes that the sale of records is speculative and agrees that the judgment of Company, a Distribution Company, and Company's licensees with respect to any matter affecting the sale, distribution, presentation or exploitation of records derived from the Master Recordings made hereunder and any other derivatives thereof shall be binding and conclusive upon Artist.

(e) Artist shall execute and deliver promptly to Company any instruments of transfer and other documents, including the Exhibits attached hereto, which Company may reasonably request to carry out the purposes and effects contemplated by this Agreement. Artist hereby irrevocably appoints Company as Artist's agent and attorney-in-fact to sign any such documents in Artist's name and to make appropriate disposition of them consistent with this Agreement and irrevocably authorizes Company to proceed, whether in Company's name or Artist's name, with any appropriate action necessary to enforce Company's rights hereunder (including, without limitation, all rights of exclusivity).

7. RIGHTS IN MUSICAL COMPOSITIONS:
As to any Composition wholly or partially written or controlled directly or indirectly by Artist which is recorded and released pursuant to the provisions hereof (hereinafter referred to as "Controlled Composition(s)"), Artist agrees to assign to Company or Company's Publishing Affiliate, One Hundred (100%) percent of Artist's interest in the copyright of the Controlled Composition, as well as the sole and exclusive right to administer and protect such interest in the Controlled Composition throughout the world, for the frill life of the copyright including any extensions and renewals thereof Company or Company's Publishing Affiliate, will account to Artist, and pay Artist according to the provisions of the songwriter-publisher contract attached hereto as Exhibit "B".

8. NAME AND LIKENESS:
(a) Company and any Assignees and Licensee of Company each shall have the perpetual right without any liability to any person, and may grant to others the right to reproduce, print, publish and disseminate in any medium, Artist's name, portraits, pictures and likenesses or biographical material concerning Artist, as news or information, or for the purposes of trade, or for advertising purposes in connection with Master Recordings produced hereunder (including without limitation, all professional, group, and other assumed or fictitious names now or hereafter used by Artist) and other commercial and/or trade uses. During the Term of this Agreement, Artist shall not authorize any person other than Company to use Artist's name or likeness (or any professional, group, and other assumed or fictitious names now or hereafter used by Artist) in connection with the advertising or sale of (i) Master Recordings or derivatives thereof made during the Term, or (ii) blank tape or tape recording equipment. Company, and any applicable Assignee, shall have the right to refer to Artist as their "Exclusive Recording Artist" and Artist shall use Artist's best efforts to be similarly billed.
(b) Artist shall use a service mark (the "Mark") for the rendering of all entertainment services during the Term of which Company has approved in writing. Such Mark is and will be Artist's sole and exclusive property and Artist warrants and represents that Artist owns all rights in and to the Mark throughout the world and that there

are, and will be, no competing claims with respect to Artist's right to use that Mark in all areas of the entertainment industry. Artist shall not alter the service mark under which Artist renders professional services as a performer and recording artist without Company's prior written consent.

(c) Artist hereby grants to Company the exclusive right during the Term hereof and throughout the Territory to use and/or sublicense to others the use of Artist's name(s) (both real and professional), logotype, likeness and facsimile signature for merchandising and commercial purposes (whether or not such merchandising and commercial purposes are related to the manufacture and sale of records) in connection with the advertising, promotion, and sale of T-shirts and other apparel, posters, stickers, novelties and other articles of merchandise through any means or media, provided that such items embody only artwork. and/or graphics (whether or not including the Mark and the Mark logo) embodied on the cover and packaging artwork and promotional material prepared for use by Company. Upon Company's request, Artist shall execute a license agreement in addition to this Agreement to evidence the grant of rights in the preceding sentence, which license agreement shall contain standard terms and provisions used in the licensing of name and likeness rights for merchandising purposes, though the failure on Artist's part to do so shall not diminish Company's rights with respect to the merchandising of aforesaid properties. If Artist fails to do so Artist hereby irrevocably appoints an officer of Company as Artist's agent and attorney-in-fact for the purpose of executing such documents.

(d) Company agrees to credit Artist's royalty account fifty (500/o) percent of the net income actually received in hand by Company (as opposed to Company's licensees, agents or other representatives) from the exploitation of the rights granted hereunder by virtue of subparagraph (c) immediately above. For the purposes hereof "net income" shall mean the gross income actually received by Company which is derived directly and solely from the sale of any of the articles referred to in subparagraph (c) above, following the deduction of all direct and indirect expenses actually incurred by Company relative thereto, including, but not limited to: (i) cost of manufacturing, pressing and design, (ii) advertising and promotional expenses; (iii) costs of packaging, shipping, storing, postage and insurance; (iv) costs of collection; (v) commissions and/or royalties payable to third parties; and (vi) any other costs incurred in the manufacturing and exploitation of such merchandise.

9. ROYALTIES:
(a) Conditioned upon the full and faithful performance of all of the terms and conditions hereof and in consideration of: (1) Artist's services hereunder; (2) the copyright ownership as provided herein; (3) Company's right to exploit the products recorded by Artist and owned by Company as provided herein; (4) Company's right to use Artist's name and likeness as provided herein; and (5) Artist's representations and warranties contained herein, Company shall accrue to Artist's account the following royalties for the sale of Phonograph Records derived from Master Recordings hereunder calculated on the Retail List Price of Records (less governmental taxes and duties, and all other deductions set forth herein) in the country of sale (except in the country of manufacture if Company is paid on such basis) and Company may, from time to time, at our election, base the percentages either upon the retail list price in the country of manufacture, or the country of sale all of against which shall be charged all Advances, recoupable expenses, and other permissible offsets hereunder, as follows:

(b)
(i) A royalty of__________ percent (__%) percent of the Retail List Price of such Albums for Net Sales thereof sold in the United States and Puerto Rico derived from the Master Recordings hereunder.
(ii) In the event any Album of the Recording Commitment shall have Net Sales in the US in excess of 500,000 units, but less than 1,000,000 units, Company shall pay an additional royalty of one (1%) percent, but only with respect to those Net Sales in excess of 500,000, but less than 1,000,000 units of that particular Album.

(iii) In the event any Album of the Recording Commitment shall have Net Sales in the US in excess of 1,000,000 units, Company shall pay an additional royalty of one (1%) percent, but only with respect to those Net Sales in excess of 1,000,000 units of that particular Album.

(c) The base royalty provided for in paragraph 9(b) above shall be payable, only with respect to Master Recordings completely produced by Artist. In the event that Artist does not completely produce a Master Recording hereunder and Company agrees to pay a royalty to a third party to produce or co-produce such Master Recording, then the royalty payable to such third party shall be deducted from the royalty payable to Artist hereunder up to a maximum of one-half of the otherwise applicable royalty for records of the types referred to in subparagraphs 9(b) above, and otherwise computed in the same manner as Artist's royalties are computed hereunder.

(d) Company shall credit to Artist's royalty account for Singles embodying any Master Recordings made hereunder a royalty computed at a rate of one quarter (1/4) of the otherwise applicable rate for records sold within the territory and for EP (extended play) formats a royalty computed at a rate of one-third (1/3) of the otherwise applicable rate for records sold within the territory.

(e) Company will not pay Artist royalties on the sale of vinyl records and any costs incurred by Company in the manufacturing of said vinyl records shall be deemed a promotional expense which is an Advance to Artist and recoupable by Company.

(f) The following, however, shall apply with respect to the computation of royalties:

(i) With respect to each particular type Record (e.g., Singles Record, EP, LP) sold outside the United States (including Records exported to third parties outside the United States and for which Company is paid by such third parties on a royalty-inclusive basis), royalties shall be at one-half (1/2) the rate applicable under subparagraph 9(b) above to the first unit of each such particular type of Record sold. Such royalties shall be computed in the same national currency as Company is accounted to, at the rate of exchange in effect at the time of payment to Company for such Records, and shall not accrue until payment for the Record sales to which such royalties are attributable has been received by Company in the US.

(ii) (A) With respect to Records sold through a Record club (including, without limitation, a Record club affiliated with Company), or through a sales operation of the type commonly known as "TV/key outlet merchandising" wherein Company is a licensor, and with respect to Masters licensed by Company to others for their distribution of Records in the United States (other than Records as described in subparagraph 9(f)(ii)(B) below), the royalty shall be a fraction of fifty (50%) percent of all royalties received by Company in the United States from its licensees arising out of the foregoing sales or other distribution or Records embodying Masters recorded hereunder, after deduction of all applicable copyright, union, legal fees, or other third party payments. The fraction ("Artist's Fraction") referred to in the immediately preceding sentence shall have a numerator equal to the Basic Rate and a denominator equal to the aggregate of the Basic Rate and the royalty rates accruable to any other royalty participants other than Artist ("Other Participants").

(B) With respect to Records manufactured by or for Company and sold to or through a direct-to consumer mail-fulfillment sales operation other than a Record club and with respect to Records manufactured by or for Company and sold through TV/key outlet merchandising wherein Company is not a licensor, royalties shall be at one-half(V2) the applicable royalty rate and the royalty base shall be the actual selling price (less Container Deductions and any taxes) to the consumer.

(C) With respect to Masters embodied on any soundtrack or compilation Record released by Company, royalties paid to Artist shall be on a most favored nations basis with any other Company artist whose master recordings may be embodied on such soundtrack or compilation Record, provided that the royalty actually paid to Artist shall, in no event, be less than one-half (1/2) the rate otherwise payable to Artist hereunder with respect to any such Record.

(iii) With respect to sales hereunder of Audiophile Records the royalty rate hereunder shall be deemed to be seventy-five (75%) percent of the applicable royalty rate.

(iv) (A) With respect to Records sold in the United States on a Mid-price line, royalties shall be at two-thirds (2/3) the applicable royalty rate.

(B) With respect to Records sold in the United States on a Budget line, royalties shall be at one-half (1/2) the applicable royalty rate.

(C) With Respect to Records sold outside the United States on a "price line" or "list category" which is lower than Company's Top Line on the country or territory (as applicable) in which such Records are sold, royalties shall be reduced in the same proportion that such actual "price line" or "list category" bears to Company Top Line in the country or territory (as applicable) in which such Records are sold.

(v) With respect to Multiple LP Albums, and with respect to Records sold to any government or its subdivisions, departments or agencies, or to military exchanges, or to educational institutions or libraries, royalties' shall be at one-half (1/2) the applicable royalty rate.

(vi) With respect to Records sold to a commercial purchaser for use as a premium promotional item, sale incentive or for a similar purpose ("premium Record(s)"), royalties shall be at one-half (1/2) the applicable royalty rate and the royalty base shall be Company's actual selling price of such Record (less Packaging Deductions and taxes).

(vii) With respect to Records sold embodying Masters recorded hereunder coupled with masters not recorded hereunder ("Coupled Record(s)"), royalties shall be at that proportion of the applicable royalty rate which the number of such Masters recorded hereunder and included on such Coupled Record bears to the total number of Masters comprising such Coupled Record.

(viii) If Artist performs hereunder jointly with any artist(s) with respect to whom Company is obligated to accrue royalties regarding sales of Records bearing such joint performances ("Joint Recording(s)"), then royalties for Records sold which embody such joint performances shall be computed by multiplying the otherwise applicable royalty rate and recording costs by a fraction, the numerator of which shall be one (1); and the denominator of which shall be the sum of one (1) and the total number of such other artists whose performances are embodied thereon.

(ix) If Company receives income from the use of Masters hereunder in synchronization with motion picture or television soundtracks or in Videograms (as hereinafter defined) thereof, or if Company licenses the use of any Master hereunder on a flat fee or cent-rate basis, or if Artist's royalties are expressed herein as a percentage of Company's Net Royalty Receipts, Company shall accrue an additional royalty hereunder of Artist's Fraction of fifty (50%) percent of the net amount of such income so received by Company. For purposes of this subparagraph, "net amount" shall mean payment received by Company in connection with the subject matter hereof, less duplication costs and less Company's out-of-pocket costs and any amounts, which Company is obligated to pay to third parties (such as, without limitation, mechanical copyright payments, AFM and other union find payments).

(x) No royalties whatsoever shall accrue hereunder with respect to (A) Records distributed to any person primarily for purposes of promotion or critique, (B) Records sold as "scrap" or "surplus", which terms shall mean excess inventory of a particular Record which is listed in the Company catalog and sold at one-third (1/3) or less of Company's then current sub-distributor price, (C) Records cut out of Company catalog and sold as discontinued merchandise, (D) Records furnished on a no-charge basis or sold by Company or any Distributor for less than fifty (50%) percent of Company's or Distributor's Wholesale price to distributors to disc jockeys, publishers, Company's or its licensees', or Distributor's employees, motion picture companies radio and television stations and other customary recipients of free, discounted, or promotional Records and

(E) sampler Records.

(g) Notwithstanding anything to the contrary contained herein:

(i) If in respect of any exploitation of any Masters by any licensee of Company the royalty provided in this paragraph 9 (inclusive of royalties payable to producers or any other third parties) shall exceed one-quarter (1/4) of the net royalty which Company shall receive or which is credited to Company's account then the corresponding royalty under this paragraph 9 (including royalties payable to producers and any other third parties) shall be proportionately reduced so that the sum thereof shall equal one-quarter (1/4) of such net royalty.

(ii) Artist shall not be entitled to receive any portion of any amounts received by Company as advances in connection with any license or other agreement relating to the exploitation of any of Company's rights under this Agreement, it being understood that royalties shall be payable to Artist hereunder as actually earned and received by Company or credited to Company's account against advances already received by Company.

(iii) Royalties with respect to the sale of Records by a Distributor or licensee shall be computed and paid upon the same basis as Company is paid and shall be subject to all of the same limitations and exclusions as are Company's royalties with respect to various categories and methods of sale and the computation thereof (including, without limitation, reserve provisions, "free goods" exclusions, discounts and other deductions, reductions and pro- rations); provided that the foregoing provisions shall not operate to increase the amount of royalties which would otherwise be payable hereunder.

(iv) Royalties, advances, and other sums payable pursuant to this Agreement shall be inclusive of any and all royalties, advances, and other sums payable to producer(s), Artist, and any other Person(s) or entities rendering performances or providing services or granting rights or otherwise entitled to payment in connection with Masters or any other items required to be Delivered pursuant to this Agreement.

(v) No royalty shall be due Artist on any record sold hereunder until such time as Company is finally paid or received a credit for such sale.

(vi) For the purpose of computing royalties there shall be a Packaging Deduction from the Retail List Price (or other applicable price, if any, upon which Royalties are calculated) of Phonograph Records hereunder, thereof for EPs or other Records sold in non-audiophile form packaged in Company's standard "singlefold" jackets without any special elements (such as, but not limited to, inserts or attachments); fifteen (15%) percent thereof for all other extended play records in non-audiophile form; and twenty (20%) percent thereof for reel-to-reel tapes, cartridges, cassettes or other record in non-audiophile form; and twenty five (25%) percent thereof for so-called "compact discs", digital audio tape, and other audiophile records.

(h) If at any time during the Term hereof (i) Company enters into an agreement with a third party record distribution company (the "Distribution Company") pursuant to which records embodying Your performances are to be manufactured and sold in the United States (a "Distribution Agreement") by such third party and (ii) the terms of the Distribution Agreement require the Company deliver to the Distribution Company rights relating to or derived from You which are different from those contained in this Agreement, then such different terms in the Distribution Agreement shall nevertheless be deemed a part of this Agreement during the Term of the Distribution Agreement even if the result is that obligations imposed upon You differ from this Agreement. Such Distribution Agreement may not, however, impose terms less favorable to you than those offered by this Agreement. It is the intention of the parties to:

(i) During the Term of the Distribution Agreement, You shall be required to perform for company such that Company has available to it all rights, benefits and privileges relating to or derived from You to enable Company to comply with all terms of the Distribution Agreement.

(ii) If there is an inconsistency between the requirements of the Distribution Agreement and this Agreement relating to Your undertaking obligations, covenants and duties, the requirements of the Distribution Agreement shall govern during its term; and,

(iii) When no such inconsistency exists, undertakings, obligations, covenants and duties imposed upon you, directly or indirectly, by the Distribution Agreement shall be considered as supplement to rights benefits and privileges granted to Company in this Agreement.

(i) If Company shall' enter into a Distribution Agreement:

(i) The Term of this Agreement shall be deemed to be identical in length to the term of the Distribution Agreement. In no event shall the Term hereof expire or terminate prior to the expiration of the Distribution Agreement between Company and the Distribution Company. If the Distribution Company shall exercise an option to extend the term of the Distribution Agreement or to suspend the term thereof, the Term hereof shall automatically be deemed suspended or extended for an equal period of time.

(ii) If the term of the Distribution Agreement shall expire or be terminated, the Term hereof shall nevertheless continue for an additional period of six (6) months during which the Company shall have the exclusive right to secure a new Distribution Agreement (a "Successor Distribution Agreement"). If Company shall enter into a Successor Distribution Agreement, then the Term hereof shall continue for a period of time identical to the complete term of the Successor Distribution Agreement and shall end on the same day as the Successor Distribution Agreement. In no event shall the term hereof expire or terminate prior to the expiration of the Successor Distribution Agreement. If the Successor Distribution Company shall exercise an option to extend the term of the Successor Distribution Agreement or to suspend the term thereof, the Term hereof shall automatically be deemed suspended or extended for an equal period of time.

(j) Company shall be entitled to recoup Advances and monies owed for expenses incurred hereunder from Artist's Royalties payable under this or any other agreement between Company and/or its affiliates and Artist.

10. ROYALTY ACCOUNTING.
(a) On or before September 30th for the period ending on the preceding June 30th, and on or before March 31st for the period ending on the preceding December 31st, or such other accounting periods as Company may in general adopt (the "accounting period(s)"), but in no case less frequently than semi-annually, Company shall send to Artist a statement setting forth in detail, the computation of royalties and any other sums due, the number of records sold from each Album during the applicable accounting period, the royalty rate, the royalties earned for each Album, and the aggregate royalties due. Concurrently with the rendition of each statement,

Company shall pay Artist all royalties shown to be due by such statement in United States Dollars. All payments shall be sent Registered or Certified mail, return receipt requested, postage prepaid, to the address first listed above. All such royalty statements shall be binding upon Artist unless written notification of objection is received by Company within one (1) year from the date rendered, or should have been rendered, stating in detail the basis of such objection. Company will treat any sale or exploitation by a third party licensee or other entity, which renders accountings and payment to Company thereof as a sale, or exploitation made during the same six-month period in which Company receives an accounting and payment or credit for such sale. Company shall have the right to withhold from royalties payable to Artist a reasonable reserve for returns and other credits, however, Company's newly established reserve for any accounting period shall not exceed one quarter (1/4) of the amounts shown to be due for only that accounting period and shall be liquidated within four (4) accounting periods following that for which such reserve was established. Concurrently with the rendition of each statement, Company shall pay Artist all royalties shown to be due by such statement, after deducting all Advances and recoupable costs incurred by Company for all products created during the Term of this Agreement. Company shall deduct all direct and indirect expenses actually incurred by Company relative thereto, including, but not limited to: (i) advertising, marketing and promotional expenses; (ii) commissions and/or royalties payable to third parties; and (iii) all payments made on behalf of Artist prior to the rendition of the statement. Notwithstanding anything to the contrary herein contained, Company shall not be required to render an accounting to Artist or pay royalties to Artist for any accounting period in which Royalties are payable to Artist are less than fifty ($50.00) dollars. If Company shall make an overpayment of Royalties to Artist; Artist shall repay such overpayment to Company on demand. If Artist fails to do so, then in addition to any and all of Company's other rights in such instance, Company shall have the right to deduct such sums from any other sums due to Artist under this Agreement (including monies payable to Artist as a result of Artist's merchandising, publishing and/or songwriter interests).

(b) In the event Company shall not receive payment in United States Dollars due to governmental regulations or elects to accept payment in a foreign currency, Company or its designee shall deposit to the credit of the Artist (and at the expense of Artist) in such foreign currency m a depository selected by Company the portion of any payments due to Artist thereof promptly. Deposit as previously mentioned shall fulfill Company's obligations under this Agreement as to the record sales to which such royalty payments are applicable.

(c) Artist shall have the right to audit the books and the records of Company, no more than once annually, upon at least thirty-(30)-days written notice with respect to all matters hereunder. Audits shall be performed during business hours at company's offices by a certified public accountant at Artist's sole cost and expense.

(d) Artist shall provide to Company, or shall cause to be provided to Company, a true copy of any preliminary and final audit reports issued by the certified public accountant engaged by Artist to examine Company's books and records if Artist is claiming additional sums are due to Artist. Any examination conducted hereunder, and any reports in respect thereof; shall be conducted and/or provided, as may be applicable, in a reasonably expeditious manner.

(e) Artist acknowledges that Company's books and records contain confidential trade information. Artist warrants and represents that neither Artist nor Artist's representatives will communicate to others or use on behalf of any other Person any other facts or information obtained as a result of any examination.

(f) Unless notice shall have been given to Company as provided herein, Artist shall be foreclosed from maintaining any action, claim, or proceeding against Company in any forum or tribunal with respect to any statement or accounting rendered hereunder unless such action, claim, or proceeding is commenced against Company in a court of competent jurisdiction within one (1) year after Artist's receipt of such statement or accounting. Unless notice shall have been given to Company as provided hereof; each royalty statement rendered shall be final, conclusive and binding on Artist and shall constitute an account stated.

(g) If Artist commences a suit on any controversy or claim concerning royalty accountings rendered to Artist under this Agreement, the scope of the proceeding will be limited to the determination of the amount of the royalties due for the accounting periods concerned, and the court will have no authority to consider any other issues or award any relief except the recovery of any royalties found owing.

Artist's recovery of any such royalties will be the sole remedy available to Artist by reason of any claim related to Company's royalty accountings. Without limiting the generality of the preceding sentence, Artist will not have any right to seek termination of this Agreement or avoid the performance of Artist's obligation under it by any reason of any such claim and waives trial by jury.

11. AUDIO-VISUAL WORKS:
(a) In the event Company elects to produce audio-visual programs ("Video(s)") embodying Artist's performances, Artist shall appear on dates and at places designated by Company for the filming. taping, or other fixation thereof Artist shall perform services with respect thereto as Company deems desirable in a timely, professional and first class manner. Artist acknowledges that the production of a Video involves matters of judgment with respect to art and taste, and Company's judgment with respect to all creative and technical matters relating thereto shall be final. The provisions of Paragraphs 4(a) and 4(b) shall be equally applicable to the production of Videos hereunder.

(b) (i) Each Video produced during the Term of this Agreement, as between Artist and Company, shall be owned by Company (including the worldwide copyrights therein and thereto and all extensions and renewals thereof) to the same extent as Company's rights in Master Recordings made hereunder.
(ii) Company shall have the unlimited right to manufacture Video-Records of the Video and to perform, advertise, import, export, sell, lease, rent, synchronize, license, distribute, or otherwise exploit said Video-Records under any trademarks, trade names and labels; to exploit the Video by any means now or hereafter known or developed; or to refrain from any such exploitation, throughout the world.

(c) Company agrees to pay or cause to be paid all costs actually incurred in the production of Videos made at Company's request hereunder provided that Company has approved of such costs in writing. All sums, if any, paid by Company or caused to be paid by Company in connection with each Video shall be an Advance against and recoupable by Company out of all royalties becoming due under this Agreement:
(i) from Artist's royalties in respect to the exploitation of the Masters, fifty (500/o) percent of such expenditures.
(ii) from Artist's royalties in respect of the commercial exploitation of such Video or film, any portions of such expenditures not otherwise recouped pursuant to subparagraph (A) above. Sums treated in accordance with the foregoing shall include, but shall not be limited to all expenses incurred in connection with the preparation, production, and manufacturing of the Video and the conversion of the Video to Video Master Recordings that are made to serve as prototypes for the duplication of the Video on Video-Records, all out-of-pocket costs incurred or caused to be incurred by Company in connection with all steps in the production and manufacturing of the Video and the processes leading to and including the production and manufacturing of such Video-Records (including, but not limited to costs for rights, artists including Artist, personnel, facilities, materials, services, use of equipment, packaging costs and the cost of making and delivering duplicate copies of such Video Masters), and all sums that Company in its sole discretion deems necessary or advisable to pay or causes to be paid in connection with the production and manufacturing of Videos and the exploitation of Company's Rights therein in order to clear rights or to make any contractual payments that are or may become due on the part of Company or any other person, firm or corporation by virtue of the exploitation of Company's rights therein, if such payment is made in respect of rights, which should have been provided to Company from or through Artist without charge, then such amount shall be an Advance. No payment pursuant to this subparagraph(c) shall constitute a waiver of any of Artist's express or implied warranties or representations.

(d) Company shall have the right to use and allow others to use each Video for advertising and promotional purposes with no payment to Artist. As used herein, "advertising and promotional purposes" shall mean all uses for which Company receives no monetary consideration from licensees in excess of a reasonable amount of legal fees, administration cost or similar type payments and as reimbursement for transaction costs incurred by Company in connection with such uses, such as tape, duplication costs, shipping, handling and insurance costs.

(e) (i) If Company grants to a third party the right to exploit Videos, Company shall credit to Artist's royalty account fifty (50%) percent of Company's exploitation of the Videos subject to this Agreement. For the purposes hereof, "Video Net Receipts" shall mean monies earned and received in hand by Company in respect of the exploitation of the Videos less any out-of-pocket production and manufacturing expenses, copyright, union and other third party payments, taxes and adjustments borne by Company, or caused to be borne by Company, in connection with such exploitation and collection and receipt by Company of such monies.

(ii) If Company engages m the manufacture and sale of Videogram Records embodying Videos made hereunder, Company shall pay to Artist the following royalty on Net Sales of Videogram Records:
(A) Fifty (500/o) percent of the Retail List Price of such Videogram Records for Videogram Records distributed in the United States; and
(B) Twenty Five (25%) percent of the Retail List Price of such Videogram Records for Videogram Records distributed outside the United States; and

(iii) For the purposes hereof, a videogram record manufactured by Company shall include only Videogram Records manufactured by Company for its own account and does not include Videogram Records manufactured for the account of anyone else, even though they maybe manufactured under rights derived from Company or distributed by Company.

(iv) With respect to audio-visual material made hereunder coupled with other audiovisual material not made hereunder, royalties payable to Artist shall be computed by multiplying the royalties otherwise applicable by a fraction, the numerator of which is the amount of playing time on the audio-visual device and the denominator of which shall be the total playing time of all such audio-visual material.

(f) In all other respects (e.g. - the times for accounting statements to be rendered, and warranties and representations made by Artist), Video Masters and Videos shall be governed by the same terms and conditions contained herein as are applicable to Master Recordings.

12. LICENSES FOR MUSICAL COMPOSITIONS:
(a) (i) Artist hereby grants to Company an irrevocable license under copyright to reproduce all Controlled Compositions, as defined herein, on Phonograph Records, to distribute them worldwide, and to assign such rights to third parties.

(ii) For such license, Company will pay Mechanical Royalties, on the basis of Net Sales, at a rate equal to seventy-five (75%) percent of the minimum compulsory license rate applicable to the use of musical compositions on Phonograph Records under the United States copyright law at the time of the commencement of the recording of the Master concerned but in no event later than the last date for timely delivery of such Master (the "Controlled Rate").

(iii) Without limiting the above, it is agreed that the maximum copyright royalty which Company shall be required to pay in respect of a Record embodying Master Recordings recorded hereunder (inclusive of payments with respect to non-Controlled Composition(s)) shall be equal to the number of Compositions on such Record times the Controlled Rate provided, however, that in no event shall the aforesaid maximum copyright royalty exceed an overall limit of:

(A) ten (10) times the Controlled Rate for an LP;
(B) two (2) times the Controlled Rate for Singles Record; and
(C) four (4) times the Controlled Rate for an EP.

(b) Mechanical Royalties shall not be payable with respect to:
(i) Records otherwise not royalty bearing under Paragraph 9 herein;

(ii) any work which is non-musical, including without limitation spoken work Compositions (e.g. comedic Material);

(iii) any more than one use of the same Composition(s), including different versions of the same Composition(s), sometimes referred to as "remixed" versions, on a particular Record;

(iv) any Controlled Composition(s) of less than two (2) minutes duration; and

(v) any Controlled Composition(s) which are in the public domain or are arrangements of compositions in the public domain except that if such arrangement is accredited by ASCAP or BMII, then the Mechanical Royalty otherwise payable hereunder will be apportioned in the same ratio used by ASCAP or BML in determining the credits for public performance of the work, provided that Artist furnish Company with satisfactory evidence of that ratio. Notwithstanding the foregoing, if on any date any Composition becomes property of the public domain in any territory, no mechanical royalties whatsoever shall become payable in connection with Records hereunder manufactured, distributed, sold or otherwise exploited in such territory on and after said date insofar as such Composition is concerned.

(c) Without limiting Company's rights, if for any reason Company is required to pay any mechanical royalties in excess of limits specified herein, Company shall have the right to offset such payments against all Royalties payable to Artist hereunder.

(d) Artist hereby grants Company the right to reprint the lyrics of Compositions on the jackets, sleeves or other packaging of Records derived from Masters hereunder free of charge.
(e) Any assignment or other disposition of the rights in any Controlled Composition shall be specifically made subject to Company's rights hereunder.

(f) Artist's execution hereof shall include, but not be limited to, execution as an officer(s) and/or authorized signatory(ies) agreeing to the issuance of the licenses in this Agreement on behalf of any music publishing company which is the publisher of Controlled Compositions.

(g) Notwithstanding anything to the contrary contained herein, with respect to Records hereunder distributed pursuant to a Distribution Agreement, if the mechanical license provisions for Controlled Compositions contained in such Distribution Agreement differ from the foregoing provisions, the applicable provisions hereof shall be deemed amended to conform to such Distribution Agreement; provided that the foregoing provisions of this subparagraph (g) shall not operate to increase the amount of mechanical royalties which would otherwise be payable hereunder.

(h) Artist hereby agrees that all Controlled Compositions shall be available for licensing by Company and Company's licensees, for reproduction and distribution in each applicable country outside the US through the author's society or other licensing and collecting body generally responsible for such activities in the country concerned.

(i) Company or its affiliated publishing company shall account to Artist for Mechanical Royalties on Controlled Compositions on the same terms of Paragraph 10 herein and in accordance with the provisions of Exhibit "B".

(j) Artist also grants to Company an irrevocable license, under copyright, to reproduce each Controlled Composition in motion pictures and other audiovisual works ("Pictures") and to distribute and to perform those pictures throughout the world for the purpose of marketing Phonograph Records, and to authorize others to do so.

13. WARRANTIES; REPRESENTATIONS; RESTRICTIONS; INDEMNITIES:
(a) Artist represents and warrants that:
(i) Artist has the right and power to enter into and fully perform this Agreement and that Artist is under no disability, restriction or prohibition with respect to his right to execute this Agreement and fully perform its terms and conditions.

(ii) Company shall not be required to make any payments of any nature for, or in connection with, the acquisition, exercise or exploitation of rights by Company pursuant to this Agreement except as specifically provided in this Agreement.

(iii) No Materials, as hereinafter defined, or any use thereof; will violate any law or infringe upon or violate the rights of any Person. "Materials," as used in this provision, means: (1) all the Master Recordings made under this Agreement, (2) all "Controlled Compositions" which are compositions wholly or partially written, owned, or controlled by Artist, the producer, or any Person in which Artist or producer has a direct or indirect interest, (3) each name used by Artist and producer in connection with Recordings made hereunder, and (4) all other musical, dramatic, artistic and literary materials, ideas, and other intellectual properties, furnished or selected by Artist or the producer and contained in or used in connection with any Recordings made hereunder or the packaging, sale, distribution, advertising, publicizing, or other exploitation thereof

(iv) No person other than Company has the right to use any existing Master Recordings of the Artist's or producer's performances for making, promoting, or marketing Records.
(b) During the Term of this Agreement: (i) Artist will not enter into any agreement, which would interfere with the full and prompt performance of Artist's obligations hereunder;

(ii) No person other than Company will be authorized to use any existing Recordings of the Artist's for making, promoting, or marketing records;

(iii) Artist will not perform or render any services, as a performing artist, for the purpose of making, promoting, or marketing Recordings or Records for any person except Company.

(c) Artist also agrees to indemnify Company and to hold harmless from and against any damages, costs, expenses, liabilities, or fees (including reasonable attorney's fees and costs) incurred by the Company in any claim, suit, or proceeding instituted against Company and/or Artist in which any assertion is made which is inconsistent with any warranty, representation or covenant made by Artist hereunder. Pending final judgment or settlement, Company may withhold all sums otherwise payable to Artist hereunder in an amount consistent with such potential liabilities.

14. REMEDIES:
(a) Artist agrees that because his services as a professional Artist are unique and cannot be adequately compensated for in damages, Company shall be entitled to injunctive relief, in addition to damages, to enforce the provisions of this Agreement.

(b) If at any time, Artist fails (except solely for Company's refusal without cause to allow Artist to perform) to timely fulfill Artist's obligations herein within the reasonable schedules set forth from time to time by Company, then without limiting Company's rights, the term of the current Contract Period shall be automatically extended and Company shall have the right to suspend Company's obligation to Artist hereunder (including, without limitations, Company's obligation to make payments to Artist hereunder) for the period of the default.

(c) If this Agreement is terminated by either Company or Artist for good cause, Company's sole obligation to Artist shall be to account for and pay royalties to Artist for Albums produced prior to termination.

(d) If, because of act of God, inevitable accident, fire, war, lockout, strike or other labor dispute, riot or civil commotion, act of public enemy, oil embargo or shortage, enactment, rule, order or act of any government of governmental instrumentality (whether federal, state, local or foreign), failure of technical facilities, illness or incapacity of any performer, producer, or Artist, or other cause of a similar or different nature not reasonably within Company's control, and if Company is materially hampered in either the recording, manufacture, distribution or sale of Records, or Company's normal business operations become commercially impractical, then, without limiting Company's rights, Company shall have the option by giving Artist notice to suspend the Term for the duration of any such contingency plus such additional time as is necessary so that Company shall have no less than sixty (60) days or more than ninety (90) days alter the cessation of such contingency in which to exercise its option, if any; for the next following Contract Period.

15. PUBLICITY:
Artist shall make himself available from time to time at Company's request and expense and upon reasonable notice of not less than five (5) days, to appear for publicity sessions, including but not limited to: photographs, posters, cover art, interviews, appearances, autograph signings, and to perform other promotional functions during the Term hereof

16. ASSIGNMENT:
(a) Company may assign its rights under this Agreement, in whole or in part. In the event that this Agreement is or shall become subject to assignment, the assignee shall have the right to exercise, implement or enforce any rights granted to Company hereunder on Company's behalf

(b) Artist may not assign this Agreement, in whole or in part.

(c) In the event Company assigns this Agreement to another entity, whether or not said entity is owned in whole or in part by Company, Artist hereby agrees to execute such further documents, if any, as reasonably required by Company or Assignee to ensure the rights granted under such assignment.

17. CREDIT: It is expressly agreed that Artist shall receive credit on the outside jacket and on the record label, as well as, wherever else appropriate. The agreed upon credit will extend to all releases of the recorded material, including but not limited to cassettes, compact discs, singles, EPs, and full length albums. In the event that the music from any recording produced hereunder, is used for release in a motion picture or on television or other video or film productions, Artist shall receive appropriate screen credit as well as other credit on any and all jackets, labels, and packages stating: Performed by

18. LIFE INSURANCE: Artist acknowledges that Company has an insurable interest in the life of Artist, and therefore Artist agrees that should Company, at Company's expense, elect to secure a life insurance policy on Artist with Company as beneficiary, Artist will assist Company in obtaining such a policy, including submitting to a physical examination.

19. INDEPENDENT CONTRACTOR: This Agreement does not and shall not be construed to create a partnership or joint venture between the parties hereto, it being specifically understood and agreed that Artist is an independent contractor.

20. NOTICES:
(a) As a condition precedent to any assertion by Company or Artist that the other is in default in performing any obligation contained herein, the Party alleging the default which it is claimed that the other is in default and of the specific obligations which it is claimed have been breached and said other Party shall be allowed a period of sixty (60) days after receipt of such written notice within which to cure such breach or default. The Parties agree that no breach of any obligation shall be deemed to be incurable during such sixty (60) day period.

(b) Except as otherwise specifically provided herein, all notices hereunder shall be in writing and shall be given by registered or certified mail, or return receipt requested, at the respective addresses hereinabove set forth, or such other address or addresses as may be designated by either Party. A copy of any notice to Company shall also be sent to John F. Bradley, Esq. 1215 East Broward Blvd. Suite #200, Ft. Lauderdale, Florida 33301. Such notices shall be deemed given when mailed, except a notice of change of address shall be effective only from the date of its receipt. In the event that this Agreement is or shall become subject to assignment, a copy of all notices given by Artist to Company shall be sent to the assignee and the assignee shall have the right to cure each default on behalf of Company.

21. JURISDICTION: This Agreement shall be deemed made in and shall be construed in accordance with the laws of the State of Florida. Any action or suit pertaining to, or arising out of this Agreement shall be determined by a court or tribunal exclusively in Broward County, Florida, except that it is agreed that Company may institute a suit or action for a provisional remedy such as an injunction in any court having jurisdiction in any country of the world.

22. ENTIRE AGREEMENT: This Agreement may not be modified orally and shall not be binding until it is signed by both Parties hereto. A waiver by either Party of any term or condition of this Agreement in any instance shall not be deemed or construed as a waiver of such term or condition for the future, or of any subsequent breach thereof All remedies, rights, undertakings, obligations, an agreements contained in this Agreement shall be cumulative and none of them shall be in limitation of any other remedy, right, undertaking, obligation or agreement of either Party. If any part of this Agreement shall be determined to be invalid or unenforceable by a court of competent jurisdiction, or by any other legally
Company Artist

constituted body having the jurisdiction to make such determination, the remainder of this Agreement shall remain in full force and effect. No ambiguity in any provision in this Agreement shall be construed against Company by reason of the fact it was drafted by Company or its counsel.

23. ARTIST ACKNOWLEDGES THAT HE/SHE HAS BEEN ADVISED TO SEEK INDEPENDENT LEGAL COUNSEL OF HIS/HER CHOICE WITH RESPECT TO HIS/HER UNDERSTANDING OF THE TERMS, PROVISIONS AND OBLIGATIONS HEREINABOVE AND DOING SO EITHER SATISFIED WITH SAID REPRESENTATION OR ARTIST HAS KNOWINGLY AND VOLUNTARILY WAIVED ARTIST'S RIGHT TO SUCH LEGAL COUNSEL AND DESIRES TO ENTER INTO THIS AGREEMENT WITHOUT THE BENEFIT OF INDEPENDENT LEGAL REPRESENTATION. ARTIST COVENANTS AND AGREES THAT HE/SHE FULLY UNDERSTANDS THIS AGREEMENT AND WILL BE BOUND BY SAID CONTRACT.

IN WITNESS WHEREOF the parties hereto have entered into this Agreement the day and year first above written.

COMPANY   ARTIST
Mindblowin Entertainment, Inc.
_______________________________   _______________________________
                                           p/k/a _______________________
_______________________________   S/S#_______________________
By: p/k/a   Date of Birth_______________
As:_______________________________   Phone Number_______________
S/S#_______________________

*p/k/a = professionally known as

Contract Exhibit "A"

DEFINITIONS

(a) "Master Recording" - every recording of sound, whether or not coupled with a visual image, by any method and on any substance or material, whether now or hereafter known, which is used or useful in the recording, production and/or manufacture of records or Video-Records. A "Master" or "Master Recording" shall be a Master Recording made hereunder embodying Artist's performance which has been recorded and delivered .to Company in all respects in accordance with the terms hereof and which applies in reduction of the then current Recording Commitment.

(i) Unless otherwise agreed to by Company, a Master Recording shall consist of a continuous performance of a particular arrangement or version of a Composition and shall be not less than two and one-quarter (2 1/4) minutes in playing time. If any record includes Master Recordings of more than one (1) arrangement or version of any Composition, all of those recording will be deemed to constitute one (1) side or one (1) Master for the purpose of Artist's Recording Commitment.

(ii) An Audio-visual Master Recording made hereunder, though sometimes referred to in this Agreement as a "Master Recording" shall not apply in reduction of a Recording Commitment hereunder.

(b) "Inception Of Recording" - the first recording of performances or other sounds with a view to the eventual fixation of a Master Recording. The term "Master Recordings from the inception of recording" includes, without limitation all rehearsal recordings, "outtakes", and other preliminary or alternate versions of sound recordings, which are created during the production of Master Recording, made under this Agreement.

(c) "Records" and "Phonograph Records" - all forms of reproductions, now or hereafter known, manufactured or distributed primarily for home use, school use, jukebox use, or use in means of transportation, including records of sound alone but excluding Video-Records.

(d) "Net Sales" - Eighty Five (8 5%) percent of gross sales for which Company receives payment and which are not returned or for which an exchange is not made; however, if any third party pays or credits Company upon a lesser amount of Net Sales, then for Records or Video-Records sold by that licensee such lesser percentage shall be applicable.

(e) "Advance" - Any pre-payments or payments, other than royalties, paid to Artist or third parties on Artist's behalf, including but not limited to payments for Recording Costs, producers, etc. Company shall have the right to recoup from any and all royalties payable to Artist pursuant to this Agreement.

(f) "Net Royalty Receipts" - the gross royalty actually placed into Company's control (as distinguished from Company's agents, licensees and representatives) in the United States in respect of only Master Recordings made hereunder, less an amount equal to any monies required to be paid by Company in respect of such sales or other exploitations of the Master Recordings made hereunder in the form of contributions to the American Federations of Musicians Special Payments Trust Fund or the Music Company Artist
Performance Trust Fund or any similar fund, costs of collection, taxes withheld, fees paid to Company's representatives directly attributed to such net royalties or net royalty receipts, such other deductions as are permitted elsewhere in this Agreement, and direct and reasonable out-of-pocket expenses incurred by Company in connection with the particular transactions concerned and, in respect of income earned by Videos produced hereunder, amounts payable to the copyright proprietor(s) or their designee(s) of the Compositions embodied in the Master Recordings which are the subject of or which are included in such Videos.

(g) "Composition" - a single musical composition, irrespective of length, including but not limited to all spoken words, bridging passages and medleys.

(h) "Controlled Composition" - a Composition wholly or partly written, owned or controlled by Artist or any Person to whom Artist is related or who is employed by Artist or in whose business affairs Artist has a direct or indirect interest.

(i) "Album" or "LP" - one (1) or more 12-Inch 33 1/3 r.p.m. records, or its equivalent, having at least thirty-five (35) minutes or less of playing time on each side.

(j) "Single" - a 7-inch, 45 r.p.m. record, or its equivalent, having approximately five minutes or less of playing time on each side.

(k) "Maxi-Single" - a record of not less than twelve (12) inches in diameter, or its equivalent, and having not less than five (5) minutes in playing time, sold in a single package.

(l) "EP" - means a Record with five (5) or more Sides and a playing time of more than twenty-five (25) minutes and less than thirty-five (35) minutes. In computing the amount of playing time or number of Sides of any EP hereunder, if any Master or any Composition contained in any Master is included thereon more than once, only the first usage of such Master shall be included in such computation.

(m) "Container Deduction" - means twenty-five (25%) percent (except twenty (20%) percent for Records in conventional analog cassette form and fifteen (15%) percent for Records in vinyl disc form of either the "wholesale price", or other applicable base royalty price of such Record, whichever is the applicable price in computing the royalty on such Record.

(n) "Delivery" and "Deliver" - with respect to Masters to be Delivered hereunder the thorough and complete performance by Artist of all of Artist's obligations hereunder with respect to such Masters, and the approval by Company of such Masters and shall include delivery to Company's offices at the address written above or such other address as Company shall specify in writing, of all consents, approvals, licenses, clearances, out-takes, copy information, credits, all information as required by Exhibit "C" and other material required by Company and/or its Distributor to release Records embodying such Master Recordings and to manufacture album covers and other packaging therefore.
Company Artist

(o) "Distribution Agreement" - an agreement between Company and Distributor, regardless of whether termed a master assignment agreement, master purchase agreement, production agreement, exclusive recording agreement, joint venture agreement, pressing and distribution agreement, label distributor agreement or otherwise, pursuant to which Company grants to such Distributor the right to manufacture and/or distribute records derived from the Masters in the United States (or the United States and other countries of the world).

(p) "Distributor" - shall mean a record company or other entity, regardless of whether the entity is wholly or partly owned by Company, which has the right to manufacture and/or distribute Records derived from the Masters recorded hereunder.

(q) "Video" - an audio-visual work produced during the Term embodying a Master of one (1) or more Compositions in synchronization with a visual rendition of Artist performances and/or other performances and/or images.

(r) "Video-Record" - a video-cassette, video-disc, or functionally similar technology, whether now or hereafter known, capable of emitting aural and visual signals simultaneously and intended for use in the home with electronic or mechanical playback equipment.

(s) "Videogram" - a material object, including without limitation, tape, disc or film embodying a video or a compilation, collective work or derivative work which embodies a video together with other video(s) and/or other work(s) intended for home use, including without limitation, video cassettes and video discs.

(t) "Licensee" - the term Licensee shall include, without limitation, subsidiaries, wholly or partly owned, and other divisions of Company or its licensee(s).

(u) "Mid-Priced Line" - a record, whether or not previously released, having a royalty calculation price hereunder which is at least twenty (200/o) percent lower, but not more than thirty-six (36%) percent lower, than the royalty calculation price which Company computes royalties for top line records in the same configuration.

(v) "Multiple Record Set" - an Album containing two (2) or more 12-Inch 33 1/3 r.p.m. records packaged as a single unit, or the equivalent.

(w) "Recording Costs" - all amounts representing direct expenses paid or incurred by Company in connection with the pre-production, production and post-production of Master Recordings made hereunder which are customarily considered "Recording Costs" in the record industry. Recording Costs include, without limitation, all costs advances and fees incurred for travel, lodging, immigration clearances, all producers, engineers, other technical and creative personnel, and others reasonably necessary for the production process (including Company's executives), all rehearsal and equipment rental expenses, cartage, and to all entities providing goods and services for the Masters recorded hereunder, personnel or otherwise, the costs of mastering and remixing, the costs of lacquer, copper and other equivalent masters, and amounts paid to collective bargaining organizations, pension and welfare fluids based on wages, and other amounts paid by Company in connection with the recording and delivery of Master Recordings made hereunder.

(x) "Audiophile Records" - records (other than Video-Records and not including compact discs) marketed in specially priced catalogue series by reason of their superior sound quality or other distinctive technical or artistic characteristics. All records made for digital playback including compact disc are audiophile records.
Company Artist

Contract Exhibit "B"

Delivery Requirement Checklist

The following is a checklist for compliance with the Delivery requirements in the Exclusive Recording Agreement. This checklist must be completed for each and every Master Recording.

1. Performers
(a) A list of all persons performing on the record (whether or not signed to another label); and
(b) An executed side-person agreement for each person (copy attached).

2. Producers:
(a) A list of the producers; and
(b) A written agreement with each producer, with provisions for the producer's compliance with the recording agreement (including the controlled composition clause).

3. Samples used in Recordings:
(a) A separate labeled cassette of entire song recorded embodying the sampled song;
(b) A completed sample information form (copy attached), including for each sample the name of the original song, artist, record company, writers, publishers, length of sample in seconds and beats, description (e.g. drums, horn, guitar, etc.), description of where sample appears in original song and where and how used in Artist's song;
(c) A separate labeled cassette of the original song from which the sample is taken; and
(d) A separate labeled cassette containing just the sound sample used.
The above sample materials must be Delivered before any final mixes are completed.

4. Publishing:
(a) A list of all writers and publishers, showing their percentage shares; and
(b) for songs, which are not, controlled compositions, written confirmation that a satisfactory mechanical copyright license will be issued.

5. Lyrics: Lyric sheets must be Delivered before the final mixes are completed. Different
versions may be needed to make songs acceptable to radio and video outlets an/or create an edited version of the album, which can be sold to those accounts that refuse to carry stickered product (which can be a very significant number of sales). If done as part of the original recording process, these versions sound better and cost less.

6. Credits:
(a) agreed upon sequence list for album;
(b) running times; and
(c) names of persons who did mixes.

7. Tapes:
(a) original multi-track two-inch master tapes; and (b) two-track stereo mixed masters.

Understanding some of the terms and concepts of the contract

The label/artist contract represents the basis of your relationship with your artist. It details what each party can expect from the other. With few exceptions, all unhappiness and conflict in life-- from divorce to wars to business failures-- are the result of unrealistic expectations. It would be very unrealistic to expect from an independent the same things that a major label is capable of. Grand expectations of "overnight stardom" (which doesn't exist, even at the majors) lead to disappointment and can sour an otherwise good relationship. The realities of limited finances, limited staff and limited influence (at the beginning) within the industry make the game slightly different for an independent.

The artist should be aware that signing with an independent label is very different from signing with a major. Each has its advantages and drawbacks. One obvious drawback is the smaller budget an independent will typically have to lavish upon an artist's career. At the same time, there are advantages. The independent will usually be able to devote much more quality time and energy in the promotion of the artist's music. Independents can take more chances, respond quicker to demands and trends in the industry, and be in a better position to notice those demands and trends. The artist will usually receive much more personal attention than would be possible at a major.

It may not always be desirable to be with a major label especially as a new artist with no track record. With bigger budgets come bigger expectations. It follows that the more a label invests in an artist, the more they expect to make back. Keep in mind that while sales of 20,000 at an independent label might be enough to pay the bills, pay the artist and be reason for a celebration, the same figures at a major would surely have that company reevaluate their renewal option, and quite possibly be grounds for dropping an artist.

The contract is a standard part of business. It should not be looked upon as indicating a lack of trust between business associates. It is necessary for smooth operation, as a written record of the many agreements and compromises that occur in the negotiation process, as a reference, as well as for protection.

The following terms represent some key ideas within the label/artist relationship and should be clearly detailed and set forth within the contract as well as through discussion. The explanations and common practices given for each illustrate current industry standards. Remember, however, that you and your artists can agree to alter, modify, or totally disregard the suggestions as long as what you do agree upon is set forth in writing, understood, and signed by all parties concerned. For the most part, any agreement that two or more consenting adults agree upon and sign is legally binding and enforceable under the law. A copy of a sample contract that you can use as the basis for your own company is provided in Appendix A.

Terms and Options

An independent label will usually want to sign an artist to a one-year initial term with a certain number of additional one-year options. During this time, it will be specified how many singles and albums are expected from the artist. At the end of the first term, the label has the right to "exercise its option" for an additional year. Submitting a letter to the artist notifying him or her that their contract is being picked up for another year will usually do that. Usually, the only way that the artist can get out of the contract is if the label has failed to deliver (that is, "breached the contract") on whatever promises were written into the contract. Some artists may insist that the option be valid for renewal only if the label sells a certain number of records. The label will usually not want this written into the contract since it is difficult to predict just how well an act (especially a new act) will do.

Advances

As the name implies, an advance is a sum of money paid by the label to the artist in advance of the release of the project whether single or album. This money is intended for the artist's pocket, and is usually separate from any other monies which may be paid in advance for the purpose of producing and recording. Both of these, however, may be included in the total budget for the project and paid to the artist in one lump sum.

While major labels are known for hefty advances which can reach into the millions of dollars, a small independent label, may give an artist no advance at all. Or, they may give anywhere from $500 to $2000 for a single, or $1000 to $5000 for an album. An independent will usually pay the advance (if any) upon delivery of the completed project by the artist. When income from sales (and sometimes publishing royalties, too) start coming in, the artist generally won't see any of it until the advance, as well as any other advance payments, are recouped by the label.

Royalties

The average royalty rate paid by independent labels is about 5% to 8% of the U.S. RETAIL price for singles, and 10% to 12% for albums. While most literature will explain royalties in this way, we suggest using a more tangible figure based on WHOLESALE price, since this is what you will be dealing with in your business relationship with your distributors. Using the average figure given above, and with the figures we provide in this manual, we arrive at a royalty rate of about 10% to 16% of wholesale price for singles and 18% to 25% for albums. In other words, for every $2.50 you receive from your distributor for each single sold (and after all expenses are recouped) the artist will get about 25 cents to 40 cents.

Remember, this royalty rate is based on the typical situation where the label fronts all of the expenses relating to the production, recording, manufacturing and release of the record. In the case of many small independent labels, however, the artist may be an equal partner in the company, contributing financially to every aspect of his/her record. As such, the artist should be entitled to substantially more of the income from sales. In this case, we suggest a fair split of the profits from sales based upon how much of the expenses each party contributes. In either case, company expenses should be recouped first to ensure the future of the business

Even after you (as the label) have recouped all expenses and you begin to pay the artist his or her royalties, you typically will not pay 100% of all royalties earned. In your dealings with your distributor you might recall that unsold items might not get returned to your distributor until several weeks even months after you've been paid by your distributor. For this reason, and your own business survival, you'll probably want to pay a percentage (typically about 70%) of the money owed to the artist just in case.

Grant of Rights

Entire volumes have been written on the intricacies of the copyright law and the protection granted to the artist. The terms copyright, publishing right, mechanical right, synchronization right, etc., are often very confusing to many even veterans of the music industry. Hopefully the following won't add to the confusion.

The COPYRIGHT to a piece of musical work are those rights that the artist usually has as a result of being the creator of the work. The term literally means the "right to copy", and includes the exclusive rights to make and publish copies of the copyrighted work, to make other versions of the work, and with certain limitations, to make recordings of the work and to perform the work in public.

Once the artist signs into a legal agreement with a label over his creations, he will have to part with some of these rights so that everyone can get paid for their part in getting the creations exposed, marketed and sold. The creator (that is, the artist) gives a part of the following rights away:

The PUBLISHING rights are those rights to reproduce, distribute and sell copies or phonorecords of the work. A work is considered "published" once it is made available for sale to the public whether in written form (sheet music) or recorded form (record, tape, CD). Publishing income includes the performance royalties (which includes performances of the work by other artists) mechanical license fees, and income from the sale of sheet music. There are Publishing Companies whose sole job is the exploitation of a musical work by any means necessary to generate publishing income, and many writers/artists will grant a percentage of publishing rights to these companies for that purpose.

However, in the course of promoting a record, many record companies end up doing exactly what these publishing companies do. Many record companies will even have an affiliated "publishing company".   As a result, it is almost standard practice these days that a record company will ask for and get a percentage of the publishing rights from the artist. The typical agreement calls for a 50-50 split of the Publishing rights. The artist is not obligated to grant publishing rights to the label. He may opt to use any publishing company even his own while still signing an agreement with the label.

The MECHANICAL license is the right to reproduce the music by mechanical means, including tapes and records and CD's and is given by the artist/writer to the publishing company or label. The label is supposed to pay a licensing fee to the holder of the mechanical rights.   If the artist has given publishing rights to a publishing company, then the label will have to deal with the publishing company, and make mechanical royalty payments to that publishing company. The standard mechanical license fee is 5 cents per composition (song) for each record sold OR 95 cents per minute, whichever is greater.

The SYNCHRONIZATION license is the right to synchronize or reproduce the music on television or motion picture soundtracks. A typical synchronization license fee is $150. The movie production company (Spike's 40 Acres and a Mule Filmworks, for example) will pay this fee to the holder(s) of the publishing rights. Each 50% publishing right holder would receive $75.

Indemnification

indemnify v.   1. to protect against loss or damage 2. to compensate for loss

This section of the contract is intended for the protection of the label. In those cases where a legal suit is filed against the artist for breach of contract (if for example the artist was signed to another label previously), copyright infringement (if some other artist is claiming that a song you have released was written by him and not by the artist you signed), or any other claim, it puts the financial burden of fighting the claim on the artist. With all the confusion and greed surrounding the sampling issue in Rap, it may be wise to expand this to include cases arising from the use of samples. As a further suggestion, you may wish to require that the artist be responsible for securing any necessary permission from both the copyright holder(s) writers/artists and publishing rights holder(s) writer/publishing company or label for any sample used in a recording before you allow it to be released. If you are the artist, the same advice applies: it is better to be safe than sorry!

Audit Privileges

For those entrepreneurs who are launching their labels promoting someone else's music, and/or whose artists aren't involved in the day to day business decisions to know what's happening with their record. They will probably want access to your accounting records and sales information for their own security. This right is a standard within the industry under the heading of audit rights. That is, the artist has the right to audit the record company books generally once a year. However, the record company will usually provide royalty statements to the artist every six months.

The Producer/Artist/Label Relationship

What does a producer really do?

Producers are those individuals who lend their musical talents to the final musical outcome of a record. There are many such producers—I call them hitmakers--whose musical talent and ear for what makes a hit, is undisputed within the industry is often sought out by artists, new and established to help "produce" their songs. The artist may have the lyrics and the basics of the track already developed, or just the lyrics. She may then take it to a Producer who is often counted on to add that special "feel" or "sound" that can make the difference between a hit and a miss. Some producers may have an identifiable style to their production, or may have the ability to create a sound tailor-made to the artist's image and style.

Things to Know When Hiring a Producer

While many Rap acts tend to produce their own music, there will be situations where the services of an outside producer are desired to complete a project (single or album). In these cases, the label will usually expect the artist to negotiate a separate deal with the producer. In this way, the label will pay all royalties to the artist, who will in turn be responsible for paying the producer. All other payments, including the advance will be between artist and producer. It is also common that the label will find a producer for the artist and negotiate with the producer directly for the production fee and advance.

The production fee as well as the advance will usually be recoupable costs. That is, they will be deductible from the artist royalties.

On average, a producer's royalty rate will be between 2.5% and 5% depending on the status of the producer. Here again, this percentage is based on RETAIL price. This works out to about 5% to 10% of WHOLESALE price. If the producer has produced only one track on a ten-track album, his royalty rate will be one-tenth of the total production royalty listed about. The advance may range from several hundred dollars to several thousand dollars per track again, depending on how famous the producer is. It is usually paid in two installments: half when the recording starts, and the other half when the recording is complete.

Before the producer has been hired, the producer should submit a budget to the artist and the label of how much it will cost to complete the final product. If, during the course of producing the work, the budget is exceeded, additional costs may be deducted from the advance still owed the producer, or deducted from the producer royalty.

BONUS: A Sampling Overview

One of the newest and most controversial issues to develop within the music industry during the past several years is the issue of sampling. Sampling is the inclusion of pre-existing compositions, musical or otherwise, in the creation of new recordings. We can credit the development of the issue, and all its legal ramifications, to the unique creativity of Rap producers who made the practice a necessary component in their creative process. Legal precedents by a judicial system unfamiliar with the cultural significance of the process have made it almost taboo to sample. Record companies are being ridiculously cautious about releasing music which contain samples. To avoid the hassles and possible lawsuits altogether, many artists are opting to recreate familiar sounds from old recordings rather than use the original.

Your First Step

Your first step in acquiring a sample license should be to contact the record company which released the recording you wish to sample. That company will usually have a lawyer, or a licensing department to guide you through the necessary process. It would be wise to get a lawyer on your side as well. Because of the big business opportunity that the sampling issue has provided, there are many entertainment lawyers who now offer sample clearances as part of their services. There are now also companies built solely around the process of obtaining clearances. Simply tell them what record(s) you are considering sampling, and they'll do the rest.

Types Of Sample Licenses

In order to sample an artist's music, mechanical rights as well as publishing rights to the sampled sound recording must be obtained. The mechanical rights may be obtained in one of two types of agreements: A Master-recording license or a Lump Sum Buyout Agreement.

Master-recording License

In a master recording sample license, the owner of the original master (usually the record company) grants the necessary rights in exchange for royalties based on units sold. For example, a typical sample agreement might involve paying the owner of the master a royalty of 1 or 2 cents for every copy of the record sold. The original agreement between the record company (from which the sample is being sought), and the original artist will determine that artist's share of the royalties. The rights granted include the mechanical rights (the rights to manufacture records which include the sampled music), synchronization rights (the rights to use the sample within videos or other audiovisual media).

Lump-Sum Buyout Agreement

In a Lump sum Buyout Agreement, the party seeking use of the sample pays to the owner of the master recording, a one-time payment for the right to use the master recording for any and all purposes. To avoid involved accounting and auditing obligations, and just in case the new recording becomes a million-seller, many producers and labels prefer the buyout agreement rather than the master recording license.

Publishing Agreement

When the original recording was first released, the original record company negotiated for publishing rights to the music. You, as a label seeking, in effect to re-release the music, must also negotiate publishing rights with the original publisher. You have three options for the type of agreement you can enter into with the original record company (or publishing company).

Co-Publishing

In this agreement, both you and the original publisher will own a percentage of the new composition. You would then pay royalties to the original publisher based on this percentage.

Buyout

In this agreement, similarly to the buyout agreement for the mechanical rights, you would pay a one-time fee in order to secure all publishing rights to the new recording.

Income share

In this agreement, as the name implies, both parties agree to simply share in any income the record generates. In this scenario, you, as the label will not own any part of the recording.

<u>SUMMARY</u> of Chapter 8: *"Find, Sign and Develop Talented Artists"*

½ *Main Points*

- Since the success of the artist/label relationship is based partly on trust, most independent labels find their talent from within their immediate circles of contacts.

- If you have benefit of funding or have achieved a certain amount of clout within your market, and are in search of talent, consider recording studios, music industry events, seminars and workshops & clubs. You might also advertise in the classified section of industry magazines.

- The Internet has now created a whole new set of options for scouting for talent: chat rooms, message boards, email distribution lists are a few of the places to look in this new global community in which to network and get talent. You can also scout sites that feature other indie labels around the world.

- Thoroughly read and understand the record label contract. It represents the wealth of your company, and forms the basis of your relationship with your artists. The contract, combined with the exhibits, provide a very important understanding of how your business is supposed to work.

½ *The Right Questions To Ask:*

- Does this artist have the level of commitment necessary to succeed?
- Does this artist really understand the music industry?
- Can this person work well with others?
- Are they open to creative input from other sources?
- Is this artist of legal age to enter into a contract?
- Do I [like, respect, trust, enjoy working with] this person?
- Do I [like, respect, trust, enjoy working with] this person's management, lawyers, et al?
- Do the artist's image, lyrics and overall presence fit with that of my label?
- Is this a mature, self-starting, self-aware individual who takes responsibility for his/her actions?
- What aspects of this contract do I need to have explained?
- What aspects of this contract do I wish to change?
- Are the terms and conditions in this contract applicable to my situation as a small label?

<u>**RESORCES** for Chapter 8:</u>*"Find, Sign & Develop Talented Artists"*
BOOKS, AUDIO PROGRAMS, MAGAZINES, ORGANIZATIONS & WEBSITES

½ *For finding more online places to scout talent*
- The Musician's Internet by Peter Spellman

½ *Websites to find talent*
- CDBaby.com
- Our own HipHopBiz.com

½ *Where to find free Contract samples online*
- http://www.musicianassist.com/archive/contract/files/member.htm
- another sample contract has been provided in the appendix

½ *Where to find Contracts online at a price*
- http://www.musiclegalforms.com

Chapter 9:
"How to Create Your Product"
Remember the Game Plan

<table>
<tr>
<td>

The next step in the game plan is creating your product.

</td>
<td>

Monitor your OPERATIONS
Find, sign and develop talented ARTISTS
½ Create your PRODUCT on CD or other media
MARKET, Promote & Advertise it...
SELL IT to stores, distributors and to the public
Maximize additional streams of INCOME
RECOUP your expenses
PAY the players
Make a PROFIT.
GROW your business

</td>
</tr>
</table>

Finding Suppliers

The efficiency of your company's operation will depend directly upon the efficiency of your suppliers: the photographer (if you use one), the designer/graphic artist (again, if you use one), the printing company that prints your jackets and inserts and the mastering/pressing plant or broker that presses your records. Your job is to find the best ones for your money. Many of these companies will also be members of trade organizations (NAIRD or NAARM, for example--see "Associations to Join", Section Four), which will make it easier for you to find one--try a cold call! The classified section of your favorite music magazine will also have some listings. Also try the Yellow Pages, or the directory from any music convention you may have attended recently. Unlike radio stations and video shows whose "customer" base lies only within their broadcast area, you can live in New York, for example, and use a supplier in California. (Shipping costs may make this an impractical option in certain situations). These companies usually advertise heavily and are looking for you just as eagerly as you are looking for them. It means more business for them, so they try to make it as easy as possible for you to find them. I recommend using suppliers within a fairly close distance to your home or place of business. In this way, if an emergency comes up on a Friday afternoon, and you have to get that test press before the weekend, you may have the option of messenger delivery or of picking it up yourself. This may not be possible if you live far away from a major city (so if you do, make sure you don't have any emergencies!)

When you do find a supplier, remember: cheapest isn't always best. It may take a few hard lessons for you to learn the difference between low prices as a result of competition, and low prices as a result of inferior quality. Ask for samples of work before you start using any supplier, and ask around within your circle of contacts for recommendations. Everyone in the music business knows of a supplier or two, and has a horror story or two about a supplier's reputation.

(A fairly comprehensive list of suppliers is published by Billboard Publications. It is called the International Buyer's Guide, and has listings of suppliers within each state as well as overseas, encompassing every area of the music business: printers, tape duplicators, pressing plants, etc.)

Manufacturing A Record, Cassette Or CD

Your UPC Code (Barcode)

As within practically every other industry, computerization and barcode technology have revolutionized the ret ail side of the business. Grocery stores, book publishing, even the health industry have all adopted some form of the barcode in the identification, tracking, and sale of product. The music industry has taken the step as well. The barcode has been so incorporated into the industry that it is now unthinkable to release a record without it. Almost every distributor will insist on it, before handling any product. To get a barcode for your product, you must be a member of the Uniform Code Council based in Ohio (513-435-3870). The one-time membership fee is $300.

Within a week of becoming a member, you will receive a barrage of mail from barcode companies across the country. You'll have no trouble finding a company to take care of your barcode needs.

Some companies will even offer to produce your first barcode free of charge! The average cost per code, which is usually produced in film form to be incorporated into the artwork of your 12" label, or jacket/insert, is about $20. Another option available to you for producing the code is your own computer, if you have one. There is software available which can produce the barcode. The drawbacks to this are the price (about $200) and the fact that you'll probably need a laser printer to make a readable code. If you choose this option, you still need to be a Uniform Code Council (UCC) member in order to get a code number registered and assigned to your company.

If your product is already in its final form, you can have barcode stickers made which you or your pressing plant (for a small charge) will stick onto the record jacket or cassette. Again, you'll still need to apply for UCC membership before you can have this done.

Your Selection Number

Every piece of product your company puts out must have a selection number. This is an identifying code associated with the product and should be tied in to the UPC code. For example, if the name of your company is Tyrone Anderson Records , the selection number of your first single release might be TARS001. The second single would be TARS002, and so on. Remember, each product should have a different selection number. Even if it's the same song, but just in a different format, your selection number, and your barcode, will have to identify it as such. The same release on cassette might be TARC001, and on CD it might be TARCD001. You might want to play the image game by choosing your code to give the impression that your single is one in a string of many previous releases. TACD6701, for example might be more desirable. The "67" might have no more significance than being the year you were born. Whatever you choose, make sure you plan for growth and leave room for flexibility. Remember, you should be thinking in terms of LP's, EP's, even videos! The selection number should be printed and visible on each separate component of your product: Jackets, inserts, stickers, booklets and posters. The reasons for this standard are many. The printer who will print your 12" jackets, or cassette inserts, has hundreds of other jobs that all look the same to him and he has to keep track of them all. The pressing plant that manufactures and packages the record, cassette or CD, must be able to identify which jacket goes with which record, or which sticker goes with which jacket. I'm sure you wouldn't want to receive your shipment of professionally shrink wrapped records, with someone else's LP inside! Your distributor, as well, may only communicate in terms of selection numbers with his or her store accounts. Keep this in mind also, when you do any advertising of your record. You'll want to include the selection number somewhere in the ad copy. Storeowners who see your ad will know to look for it, so that they can order from their distributor.

Choosing your format

Vinyl is still alive and well within Rap Music. DJ's, both on radio and at the club, still require the 12" record to perform their unique art of crowd-pleasing. Rap music buyers still require that their music be available on vinyl for their own parties and on cassette, for portability. While CD sales have definitely outpaced vinyl, you'll probably still need to do a vinyl pressing to generate a street buzz for your music. The few vinyl that you do press can go a long way to increasing exposure for your music. While the industry at large has been moving away from vinyl production for reasons of economy and technology, those within Rap circles have cited this trend as detrimental to traditional Rap and Dance music promotion.

The particular region of the country you happen to be in will also be a determining factor in the percentage demand of each configuration and consequently, the amount you press. As one moves from east to west across the US, vinyl becomes more and more extinct on the retail and radio scenes. Also, if your release is a single, you will probably opt to do an initial run of vinyl and cassette only, since it might be economically impractical to incur the expense of CD single production before generating a significant demand for your record. Listen to the distributors and the stores in the particular regions you are targeting.

After you've come from the recording studio and have your final mix on D.A.T. (Digital Audio Tape) or 2-track/1/4" tape, you have two options to get your music on wax.

1. You can go to different companies to get each of the steps done, or

2. You can take it to a one-stop company or broker who will take care of all of it for you.

A broker is nothing but a middleperson between you and a large pressing plant. Since the broker handles pressing and duplication for a number of labels and generates a lot of business for the plant, he can usually get a discount which can get passed on to you. Also, because of the volume of business which the broker generates, she may have as much clout as a major label would (that can mean quicker turnaround for you job). Choosing option 2 can save a lot of running around. Some one stop companies will just quote one price for a package deal which includes all of the steps. Use the figures on pages 28- 30 to decide whether you're really getting a good deal. Prices may vary by region. On the next few pages are the steps involved in manufacturing a 12" vinyl record, cassette, or CD.

The Product Package Development Process

Photography

You are going to need photographs of your artist to use as Promo shots (8X10 black & white) as well as for adorning the packages. You can take the pictures yourself or hire a professional to do it. Keep in mind, however, that this picture will often be the first (and maybe the only) chance you'll get to make an impression on people within the industry and the buying public. If you decide to go all the way with color jacket/insert production, video, etc, I recommend that you make the foundation of all this future effort as strong as possible. Do it professionally from step one, and save yourself the headache of having to re-shoot pictures at a later, more hectic time. A good photographer might charge a few hundred dollars for a package session. A typical package deal would involve a set number of rolls of film, developing, and a set number of prints. If the photographer is open to it, you might want to incorporate both the Promo shots as well as the album/12" cover shots into the same session. Some photographers will want additional money if they know you'll be using the shots for the jacket as well. Others don't care. Another standard practice is that the photographer will hold ownership and rights to the negatives. In this way, he assures himself of future income should you need prints of other poses. Again, other photographers don't care, and will even part with the negatives for an extra charge. Shop around.

Before the artist steps in front of the camera, everyone involved should have a general idea of what sort of "image" he or she will be going for. Ultimately, the best results will come from capturing what is natural and real about the artist. You as a marketing executive, however, must see more. You have the unique challenge of marrying art with business. The creativity of the rapper/musician, the creativity of the photographer, and your desire to produce packaging that sells, all must find a happy medium in the finished product.

12" Jacket & Cassette/CD Insert Production

Keep in mind as you read, that some people prefer not to get too deeply involved with the intricacies of the design process. Their main concern is the finished product--who cares how it's done? This is an understandable position, especially for those individuals who might be too busy getting other things done, or those who have a lot of money. I recommend, however, knowing as much as one can about how and where your money gets spent. Especially if you're looking to cut corners, you need to know where those corners are!

The "corners" you'll be able to cut will be found in the three stages of your jacket/insert production: 1) design, 2) color separation/film, and 3) printing.

Design

Before your jacket can be printed, it first must be designed. The design cost is actually quite flexible. It could range from a few cents if you do it yourself, to in the thousands if you get a professional to do it. It involves choosing the right picture, deciding on the layout of the jacket, the text, the colors and overall image. It is an art unto itself involving utilizing theories of composition, balance, color for maximum effect. The industry recognizes the art and creativity involved and even has annual awards for Album Art. While you may not really care at this point whether the final design of your record gets the award for outstanding Rap album/single cover of 1993, good design is something you must be aware of. Many of the one stop brokers offer design of your jacket for an additional cost, or as part of a package. Make sure that you make a detailed list, in advance, of all the information that needs to appear on the jacket before you start, or before you give the job to a graphic artist. These include THE BARCODE, SELECTION # (usually on the spine), track title/time, artist credit, producer credit (on each song), recording studios, performing rights organization info (BMI/ASCAP), lyrics, special thanks to moms and families, company name and address and logo, photographer credit, association membership information, fan mail address. Go to your local record store, and make a mental note of how the other companies do it, and where everything usually goes. The printing company or graphic artist you choose will also inform you what's customary and what's esthetically "correct".

The end product of the design stage is called the "mechanical" or "camera-ready art". This is an actual size flat master of the design that will be used to make the jacket. It can be anything from a clean "cut-and-paste" layout to a computer-generated job.   There are strict size guidelines one must stick to in order to get the most professional looking product. The mechanical (there will be a separate mechanical for the cassette insert as well as for the CD insert) along with a color key (which is an indication of the specific colors you wish each element in the final product to be), and the "chrome" (the slide you chose from the photo session), may all be taken to the printer who will usually offer color separation services (that's the next step).

In your job as Art Director, you will be capturing the image of the artist as well as the image of your company.   Even after the life of the release, the product will still represent you as part of your catalog, and should be something that you are proud of. Try to develop an eye for what works and what doesn't. This advice becomes more important if you do the design yourself and don't have the guidance of professionals.   Visit stores; check out the pictures and the designs. You'll be competing with bigger budgets and more experience, but this doesn't mean you have to sacrifice quality and effect.

Color Separation/Film

A basic knowledge of the separation process is necessary in order to facilitate getting the exact colors one wants for all the text and logo elements of your design. This is part of the training that most graphic artists go through. If you do it yourself, your printer will be happy to show you catalogs of available colors. If you decide to go with the full color look, your jacket/insert will be printed using what's known as a Four Color (4-C) Process (ask your printer about other money-saving options and how to get the color "look" without using the full 4-C process.)

The four "primary" colors in the printing world are black, magenta (near red), yellow, and cyan (near blue). Every possible color you can imagine is created using varying combinations and percentages of these four. When your 12" jacket is printed, it is actually passed through the press four times (if you're using a four color process). On each pass, the printing "plates" add a specific amount of each color at the appropriate places to make the finished product. From the color separation process comes what is known as Plate-Ready Film, which is one piece of film for each color, used to create the printing plates. Don't forget, you'll need to have your barcodes (one for each configuration) before the actual printing process occurs. The barcode should be provided in the form of a "film negative" and provided to the printer for "stripping" into the Plate Ready film. The separation and plate-ready film processes are usually considered and quoted as one item.

These are the basics of the jacket/insert production process.   Your printer may have specific requirements for camera-ready art and provide other options that you need to be aware of. The elements of the CD package, for example, come in a wide range of options from 2-panel to 8-panel cards, CD booklets with anywhere from 8 to 20 pages. Request a brochure/kit and familiarize yourself with all of the options to decide which is right for you and your budget.

Printing

In printing, as with most quantity orders, the more you press, the less the unit cost.   Don't go overboard, however, since you can't "un-print" the jackets once they are done. Since the printing process usually takes 7-10 days, it would be wise to print just what you need initially (though it will cost a bit more per jacket), rather than have 10,000 jackets paid for and sitting in a warehouse gathering dust.

Product Manufacturing Costs

Some typical costs for all the steps described are provided below.

12" or Album Jacket Production

    One time costs
        UPC Code $ 20
        Design/Camera Ready Art $****
        Color Separation/film $ 750
        TOTAL $ 770 (plus design)   plus

    Printing   approx $350 per 1000 ($0.35 ea)

Cassette Insert Production (J-Card)

    One time costs
        UPC Code $ 20
        Design/Camera Ready Art $****
        Color Separation/film $ 200
        TOTAL $ 220 (plus design)   plus

    Printing   approx $40 per 1000 ($0.04 ea)

CD/DVD Insert Production

    One time costs
        UPC Code $ 20
        Design $ ****
        Color Separation/film $ 250
        TOTAL $ 270 (plus design)   plus

    Printing   approx $140 to $190 per 1000
                                          ($0.14 to $0.19ea)

note: CD insert prices are for a 2-panel card (front and back) and include (as will most quotes from your printer) a Tray Card for the back of the CD jewel box.

Posters (4-color, 18 X24)

    One-time costs
        Design $ ***
        Color Separation/film $ 450
        TOTAL $ 450 (plus design)   plus
    Printing $500 per thousand ($0.50)ea

Note: total one-time costs as well as printing costs for posters can be cut in half by going with 2 colors
    instead of 4. **** Indicates the flexibility of the design stage.

Pressing And Duplication Costs

Getting your music into its final form on vinyl, cassette, or CD is the next step. Regardless of the format, the concept remains the same: conversion of your finished music into a physical form from which mass production can be done. For vinyl it's the "stamper"; for cassettes, it's the "running master", and for CD's it's the "glass master". With new developments in technology, the specifics of this process are ever-changing. With the advent of the digital age, it has become more possible to significantly reduce the loss of quality and distortion normally inherent to the process. Below are the steps and typical costs associated with production. The names of each step may vary slightly from company to company but describe essentially the same process.

12" Production

	One-time costs		
	Digital Setup	$ 50+	(needed if your master is on D.A.T.)
	Mastering	$350+	
	Reference Acetate/Lacquer	$200+	(recommended to test the sound quality)
	Metal Mother/Stamper	$480+	
	*Labels	$ 75+	
	Tests	$ 30+	
	TOTAL	$1185	plus
Unit cost		from $ 0.85 to $ 1.10 each	

12" Labels are sometimes printed separately and shipped to the pressing plant. This option has become outmoded, since most pressing plants offer label printing as part of a package.

Cassette Production

	One-time costs		
	Running Master	$ 75+	
	Plate for Cass. Printing	$ 50+	
	Tests	$ 25+	
	TOTAL	$ 150+ plus	
Unit cost		from $0.65 to $0.85 each	

CD Production

	One-time costs	
	1630 Tape	$475+
	Glass Master	$300+
	Label Film/for CD	$125+
	TOTAL	$900 plus
Unit cost		from $1.35 to $1.75

Note: $300+ indicates that the actual cost could be a bit more or a bit less than $300.

Don't let these numbers deter you. You are running a company now. One of the additional advantages of doing business with other companies is the "payment term."

Your First Pressing

Your first pressing should include enough records and tapes to begin your initial promotion campaign as well as to satisfy any early demand. Before you jump into this one, decide whether your campaign will be a regional or national one. "Going national" will be more expensive and may be a bit riskier. If your financial resources are a bit stretched, you'll probably be able to do a better job going regional.   (Better to do a small job well, than a big job poorly.)

In arriving at the amount to press, you will need enough for the following people/companies:

Distributors-   to target certain radio stations and key retailers. Also for the initial order. your distributor will tell you how many of each format she needs.

Record pools- for club play as well as mix show play on radio stations.
Most pools are primarily geared toward dance music. Call the pools you wish to target, and ask what their rap requirements are. In many cases it will be less than the total number of DJ's in the pool. Before requesting service, pool director will first request a review copy or two to determine just how well your record fits into the formats of the clubs the DJ's spin for.

Radio stations- caution: you might be duplicating some of your distributor's efforts here. If you can afford to, you might decide that it's wise to "back up" their efforts.

Retail outlets- (see caution above)

Magazines-   to get press coverage and reviews. The editors and reviewers will most likely request cassettes or CD's.

Other -   Promoters, clubs, booking agents, movie producers, newspapers, video programs, etc.

Most pressing plants require an initial minimum pressing of 1000 units. There are always special packages being offered, however, if this number is out of your range. Five hundred units is usually as low as you want to press, since the less you press, the more you pay per unit.

Other Product Costs
Products you sell may also include t-shirts and other clothing, baseball caps, mugs, posters, and other merchandising items.

Making A Video

The New Playing Field

You must have some visual means of selling your music. Videos have fast become a must for any serious artist promotion campaign. If you want to compete, you should start making arrangements to do one. The purpose of having a video is to sustain interest and generate more sales of your record.

The Video Production Process

Following is an overview of the steps involved in the production of a video. The format for the project we will describe is 16MM film. If you've already hooked up with a Producer or Production company, they'll usually take care of all of these steps. It pays, however, to know what's going on with your money.

Pre-Production

Even before you start filming, the *final* mixed version of the song must be complete. When your video is complete and edited, your master copy will probably be on 1" Video Tape. Other names you'll hear for tape types for your master are "Betacomponent", "D1" or "D2". Your director may have a particular format he or she prefers to work with. However, your budget should ultimately be the deciding factor.

The finished and mixed song will usually be dubbed onto:

1. The 1" Video Tape that will become the Master, and
2. Several 1/4" reels, which will be used for playback during the filming.

Both of these will be dubbed along with a TIMECODE (sometimes referred to as a Simpte Timecode.) A timecode is a number code which will identify every single fraction of a second of your song, and frame of your video. It's a digital code that's imposed directly onto the same tape that the music is on. Generally all post production tapes have an additional track reserved specifically for this purpose. This "center" or "address" track is where the timecode will be laid. I suggest that both the 1" and 1/4" dubs be handled by the same company or individual and at the same time to avoid any chance of mismatched or out-of-synch time code. This can be a disaster when it comes time for the final edit.

A typical time code as it may be displayed might look something like this: **02:33:43:16.** It indicates a scene which is on Master tape #2 and which begins at a point 33 minutes, 43 and 16/100 of a second into the tape.

Filming

Before filming, you, as the label, your director and the artist should spend some time planning each scene, its content and location. Once the camera and equipment are rented, you won't have any time to waste. Your time for rehearsals is way before the meter starts running on the equipment. The day of the shoot should run according to a schedule worked out and planned beforehand. If you plan on shooting outdoors, you should go scouting locations and making note of what time of day you'll be using them.

A word about permits and shooting outdoors. Some cities require that the local government be advised of your shooting schedule. The production company will usually be responsible for securing the necessary permits from the appropriate local government agency. While some directors and production houses working on small budgets sometimes prefer to avoid it, the process of getting the OK from the appropriate office isn't a complicated or involved process, and should be encouraged. It pays to do things the right way. There's no sense planning for weeks only to have police officer ruin the day of the shoot by insisting on seeing a permit. The permit, which should be photocopied and placed in the windshield of any vehicle associated with the shoot may also spare you some headache from overzealous traffic inspectors.

During the actual filming, the music is played through a playback machine, which is a portable reel to reel player (sometimes referred to as a NAGRA) which reads timecode, and which is hooked up to a slate. The purpose of the slate, which you've seen in movies being snapped just prior to shooting a scene, is more related to what happens after the actual filming. During the editing process, the director will match the timecode on the screen to the timecode on the music track to get the two "in synch", that is, perfectly synchronized. In that way, the scene is placed precisely where it needs to be in relation to the music on the track.

The Crew

A film crew can range from 4 or 5 people to a small army. A "No-Frills" production may have

*Director *Director of Photography (camera operator) *Assistant DP (assistant camera operator) *Playback machine operator *Slate Operator *Gaffer (puts lights up, takes lightmeter readings) while the bigger productions may have in addition to the above, more Gaffers Choreographers	Hair Stylists Wardrobe Consultants Makeup Artist Traffic detail Security

More elaborate film techniques, locations, etc can make this read like the credits of a major motion picture.

Post Production

This is where most of the money gets spent in the completion of a video. Post production simply refers to the steps and procedures one must do post (i.e. after) the actual filming.

Developing

Developing your film will cost anywhere from $0.10 to $0.15 per foot of film, with color film being a cent or two more expensive than black and white. There will sometimes be a "prep/cleaning" charge of anywhere from $0.01 to $0.03 per foot.

Film To Tape Transfer

As the name implies, this is the process whereby the images on film are transferred onto 1" tape or some other standard. The timecode is transferred as well, but is not visible. In the video biz this is referred to as an "address" time code.

Off-Line Editing

This is where your video is first pieced together. The producer/director/editor may work with 3/4" tape copies (dubs) of the originals. These dubs will most likely have the timecodes visible in a corner of the image to make editing easier.   In the video biz this is called a "window" dub and has what is called a "visual" time code. Working with the 3/4"dubs, your producer/director/editor chooses the best scenes and cuts and pastes them in the best order.. This is where the creative process of creating your video is the most critical. Good scenes shot during the filming can lose their power if put together poorly. Good editing can transform an okay scene into one which packs a lot of energy and builds excitement. The director's eye for what works and what doesn't is the art that you're paying for.   This is the also the stage where your own suggestions and wish lists should be made known.   There are Off-Line Editing studios which may charge anywhere from $75 upwards per hour.

On-Line Editing

This is it. Once you walk out of the on-line editing session, you'll have in hand what is called the "edited master" of your music video. There are several techniques by which the on-line editing process may be accomplished. Since your director knew exactly which scenes (by virtue of the timecode) were to be used in the final video, he/she may have input all the timecodes associated with each scene onto a computer disk. Armed with the disk and the master tapes (from the film to tape transfer) and the 1" master created in step one, the process could be completely automated, with a computer reading the timecode from the disk, locating the appropriate scenes on the master tapes and dubbing them onto the 1" master in synch with the appropriate part of the soundtrack. The other way is to have the engineer manually input the code for each scene. In this manner, each scene can be fine tuned to make sure everything is in time with the music. This is where the big bucks get spent (unless you're friends with the engineer). Expect to pay in the $150-$250 per hour range. Expect also that it might take 3,4, or 5 or even 10 hours to get a 4 minute video perfect, in synch, and with any effects you might want.

At the on-line, you may want to make a few dub masters of the music video. The dub master is a working copy of the video from which multiple copies will be made. This is the copy that you'll give out to the duplication houses when you are making (for example) the 50 copies you need to send out to the magazines. NEVER give out your edited master. It should be kept in your vault, safe, mattress, or wherever you keep your irreplaceable valuables. You may want an extra 1" master, a 3/4" dub master, and perhaps a VHS dub master. You may want to have these made at the on-line studio so as to take advantage of their quality facilities. Don't do any more than is absolutely necessary, however, and don't be tempted to make copies there for the artist, or her mom, or his girlfriend.   Find a specialty duplicating house to do that. To make a VHS copy of your video at the on-line studio for instance, might cost you $7 for the tape, and $15-$20 for the actual duplication, compared to $1.60 for the tape and $1.50 for the duplication at a duplicating company.

Video Alternatives

If the traditional video is out of your range, there are other options.   With the increased access to camcorders and Hi-8 video cameras, you can produce a visual means of exposing your artist and music without incurring the expense of a film production.

Performances offer yet another alternative. If you've managed to get a performance for the act, either you, the promoter or club owner may have the means to videotape or film the event. He or she may be willing to part with a tape of the evening's performance (or just your act's performance).   It may not have the professional editing and fast moving excitement of a music video, but it will serve its purpose of providing a "visual aid" for the full appreciation of your artist.

The alternatives are only as limited as your own imagination. One artist I know took the bold step of creating a video collage of still photographs featuring pictures of everything from his childhood, graduation, performances and candid shots from daily life. It worked, and got him the desired attention.

Video production, like every other aspect of the industry, has been affected by technology. According to several video show hosts, Hi Definition Video is where the industry is heading, and many producers are already requesting artist videos in the mini-DV format. Such cameras can be purchased for under $2,000 or rented for considerable less. Editing, including special effects as well as all aspects of sound and image synchronization, can now be done on a desktop computer using readily available software.

The Total Cost of Shooting Your Video

The final cost could vary greatly depending on who you get to help you do your video. There are many aspiring filmmakers who are looking to break into the business doing music videos. There are many young directors, just out of film school who can do an excellent job of creating your video at a great savings to you. It is not uncommon for a new director to forego getting paid to do a video just to have the chance to start building his/her "reel, a video resumé. In this case, you would be responsible for the film, rentals, editing, and the basic necessities. However, you wouldn't be paying producer fees. If you're lucky enough to get someone with a lot of connections, or who is still in film school or just recently graduated, it can be to your benefit financially as well. Your director, being more familiar with this side of the business, may know of inexpensive film equipment/supply stores, or other filmmakers who may have their own equipment. Something else you should be aware of is the student discount. Many companies sell film and rent equipment to student filmmakers at discount prices. Offline and Online studios may have student rates you might also be able to take advantage of. All you or your director would need to do is present a valid student ID. I've mentioned the route above to illustrate the sort of approach and thinking you should take not just in making your video, but also in every aspect of running your business. Many business owners get so accustomed to operating and interacting at a certain level, and at certain cost that they neglect to explore some of the more creative, equally valid and accessible means of getting the job done.

Despite the seemingly high expenses already quoted, the final cost of your video is completely within your control. So, how much does a video cost? Only you can answer that question for yourself!

Paying for It All

Payment Terms

In getting your product manufactured, you will usually be able to avail yourself of any service or product with anywhere from 0 to 50% in advance. You'll then be sent an invoice for the total amount or balance some time after the job is completed (in some cases, you'll have to pay the balance upon completion). On the invoice, there will usually be a notice of terms, something like "TERMS: Net 30 days", which means you now have 30 days in which to pay the balance (or make some arrangement with the vendor). This is particularly helpful if you are financing your new company from paycheck to paycheck of your current "suit and tie" job. The specific term agreements will vary with each company. Some offer 60 days, others won't release a job until you've paid for everything.

If you would rather not put yourself in debt, you might choose to cut costs altogether, rather than defer them. Consider going with a plain white jacket, or a black and white picture, if you must, on the inserts and jackets. Your ingenuity, creativity, and who you know, will go a long way to save you money. Shopping around and negotiating can also cut your bills down. Some companies will give you a discount to get your business for the first time, rather than lose it to another business offering a lower price.

Managing DEBT

Getting the capital to run your business effectively is going to be one of your primary concerns. There are many publications which offer advice on how to acquire capital. The options fall into four main categories:
Self (personal savings, credit cards)
Friends and Family
Financial Institutions
Investors

You've probably already committed your own bank account to the venture you are undertaking. Some of you may have family and friends who are silent partners in your venture. Others may have been able to secure a bank loan. Still others of you may have been able to convince investors of the strength of your releases, and the strength of your company. Whichever means you choose, the responsibility of repaying the loan from friends, family or the bank, or pleasing your investors will ultimately be yours. Part of this responsibility will involve knowing how to manage the money you may have access to.

Sometimes it may actually be more of a curse than a blessing to have access to money.   This is especially true if you don't have a sound plan on how to use it. Trust me, once you have money, you tend to spend money. Once you spend money when it's around, you tend to wish you hadn't, when it's gone. Not having the immediate financial resources to do a particular job may actually force you to exercise your creativity in getting things done. A person who wants a video done, and who has $10,000 to spend on it, will spend the $10,000 and get a video. Another person who also wants a video done, but who has no money to spend, through dedication, commitment, favors and a lot of ingenuity, can get a video of similar quality done, without spending $10,000, because he has no other choice.

To control your debt, it helps to work within a budget. Even if you're running your business from paycheck to paycheck from your current job. You'll find that you can easily spend your entire paycheck weeks before it actually arrives. Now a budget is only effective if you stick to it. However, just the act of writing down all of the financial requirements of releasing and promoting your record helps you to keep the entire picture in focus, and reminds you why you need to keep the spending in check. It will make no sense to spend all of your money getting a great looking package together and not have a cent to mail any records out.   With the information provided within this book, and your own research, you will be able to devise a list of everything that needs to get done, how much it costs, and how much you can afford to devote to it. Done at this stage, the funds you will allocate to a particular item will tend to be a little more in line with what you can actually afford. The budget you create (while it may still be unrealistic), will provide more of an incentive to stick to it, especially if approached from a "what do I have to spend right now" frame of mind. In other words, try not to do your spending based on how much money you hope to have next month. This "future spending" is a very dangerous habit to develop. Invariably, you'll end up future spending $100 on something today, then forgetting, and spending it again tomorrow on something else. What you end up with next month is two bills totaling $200 and only $100 in your pocket.

The entrepreneur must take risks, must act boldly, and sometimes must jump into uncharted territory without fear. This sort of behavior can also be very expensive.   My best advice to you to stay out of an unnecessary amount of debt, is to do all of these things, but do it with a "Plan B" in your back pocket. You should always have a second plan of action in case your original doesn't work out. A good "Plan B" is to make sure that your ability to pay off the debt is not being based on the "future sales" of your record. Your "Plan B" must include recovering relatively quickly from a "Plan A" that didn't work out exactly as planned. In other words, don't spend so much that if you don't realize a profit the first time around, you'll be out of commission for the next 10 years paying it all back!

<u>SUMMARY</u> of Chapter 9: *"Create Your Product"*

▶ *Main Points:*

- New technology makes it even easier to launch your label. Advancements in printing, CD replication, and Internet distribution reduce the cost of going from concept to product right from your own home-based office/record label!

- Stay on top of industry trends as they relate to CD, vinyl and cassette purchases.

- Work with your distributor in determining what formats and quantities will be needed for promotion

- While a promotion tool, your video may also be a product. Advancements in technology are making it easier to create high quality videos at lower cost.

▶ *The Right Questions to Ask:*

- In what formats and in what quantities should I manufacture this release?
- Can I get this manufactured cheaper somewhere else?
- What's the turnaround time? Can I get finished product in a timely manner?
- Is the quality adequate?

<u>**RESOURCES** for **Chapter 9:** *"Create Your Product"*</u>
BOOKS, AUDIO PROGRAMS, MAGAZINES, ORGANIZATIONS & WEBSITES

▶ *For understanding the production/manufacturing process*
- Diskmaker's Production Guide/Catalog

▶ *For a selection of suppliers*
- HipHopBiz.com's *Hip Hop Entrepreneur Lists of Exposure Supplement*

▶ *Magazines featuring ads from various suppliers*
- Source Magazine
- XXL
- Billboard

Chapter 10
"How to Promote, Market and Advertise Cheaply and Effectively"

<u>**Remember the Game Plan**</u>

Now it's time to tell the world about it!

Monitor your OPERATIONS
Find, sign and develop talented ARTISTS
Create your PRODUCT on CD or other media
½ MARKET, Promote & Advertise it…
   SELL IT to stores, distributors and to the public
   Maximize additional streams of INCOME
   RECOUP your expenses
   PAY the players
   Make a PROFIT.
   GROW your business

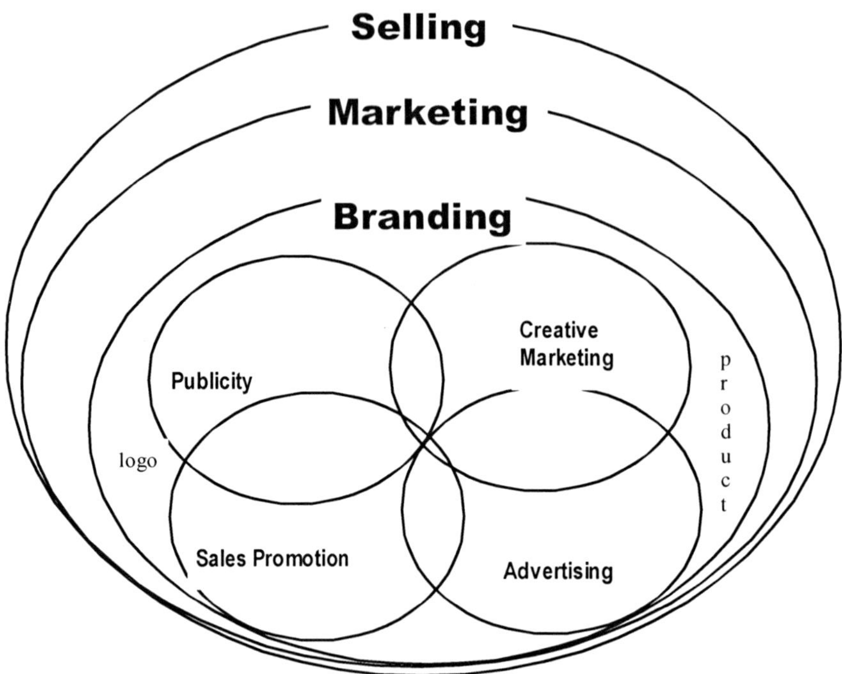

Selling is the name of the game

In the game of succeeding at your hip hop record label, selling is the name of the game! Many people are often confused by the terminology that marketing people toss around when explaining how to make money in business. Here is my take on the big picture. As illustrated above, the terms involved are:

½ Selling
½ Marketing
½ Branding
½ Promotion
½ Publicity
½ Advertising

- **Selling** is what you want to do; it's your ultimate goal
- **Marketing** is how you do it (i.e. Promotion, Publicity and Advertising are forms or techniques of marketing which help you to sell more); There's overlap among all forms of marketing. Some advertising looks like publicity; some advertising might be called creative marketing, etc.
- **Branding** is what you will accomplish in the process; Branding happens whether you focus on it or not. If it's done effectively and consciously, you'll create a strong brand identity and sell more. If not done effectively, then your sales will suffer because of a poorly perceived brand.
- **Promotion** is the marketing of your product to the people who sell your product. It includes sending samples, putting on sales, creating and positioning point-of-purchase displays, anything that gets your product better positioned in the places it will sell.

- **Publicity** is the free coverage you get in newspapers, magazines, radio programs, video shows and television. If you, your unique story, your product, or some other aspect of your passion is of newsworthy interest to the world, you have the chance of being interviewed, reviewed or exposed to the readers, viewers or listeners of particular programs. Publicity is the best form of marketing because: 1. It's free, and 2. Third-party validation (what others say about you) is more powerful than what you say about yourself. The task of gaining publicity is called Public Relations, or PR for short.
- **Advertising** does just about the same thing publicity and promotion are intended to do with one difference: Advertising costs money. You may need to advertise in magazines, newspapers, on websites, television, radio or billboards to sell your passion.

Regardless of the terminology you use, the bottom line becomes a single, simple question: "What will I say and do to get people to purchase my product or service?" The solutions you develop to answer that question are what form the strategy of any marketing, promotion, publicity or advertising campaign you launch. Here are some tips on the right mindset required to master the art of selling.

THE ART OF SELLING

Successful selling requires a certain attitude to overcome the many challenges you will encounter. These 10 mindsets and 20 methods can help you in any venture you undertake.

Mindsets

1. Always have a plan B!

NEVER, ever let any ONE person be the only key to your success. As I always say to people who get discouraged by rejection, "no one person has the key to EVERY door that leads to success." Just because one distributor won't carry your product doesn't mean you're doomed. Just because the most powerful newspaper in the country doesn't write a story about your novel, doesn't mean it'll never be read, UNLESS you believe it. There is ALWAYS a way to get things done. When you make your plans, think positively and expect success, but always ask yourself, "what will I do if this plan doesn't work? What's my Plan B?" Even if it means selling your product yourself on the Internet, or out of the back of a van, there's a way. Find a way, even if it means having someone else talk to the same distributor about your product. Plan B Thinking" means that no one will ever stand in the way of your success. As Bob Marley said, "When one door is closed, another is open!"

2. Think: Do For Self

When I set my business goals, my basic mindset to achieve it is "How will I use my talents and skills to get this done?" I've met too many people whose basic thought pattern is "Who can I get to let me in the door." I've always been more of an independent achiever. As a result, I've always acted as if everything was up to me. Now that doesn't mean you don't rely on others to a certain degree (see #1), but it means you approach success as something you claim and take for yourself, not something that someone else gives to you. No one wants to distribute your product? Great! Then do it yourself! Can't find someone to represent you? Then represent yourself! Can't find a publisher to sign you? Then publish it yourself! Get the right information, become your own expert, and make your own path to success!

3. Every Challenge or Situation Has a "Right" Answer

Perhaps it's because of my math and engineering background that I always act under the assumption that everything has a right answer. I design brochures knowing that there is one perfect arrangement of words and pictures that will sell the most products. My mission and yours is to find that right way!

4. Never Accept the First Answer As Final

Whenever I call a company for some information, or to get something accomplished that may be outside of their normal scope of activities, I have a certain rule that I always follow. If I don't get the answer I'm looking for, or the respect I expect, or a speedy response, I always call back and ask the same question to another salesperson or representative. First, I politely thank the first person for their help, wait a few minutes, or until lunch time, or the next day and call back. There have been many times that a "no" has turned into a "yes", or an "I don't know" has become a "here's the answer you're looking for", or a "she's not here" has become a "hold on, I'll get her." That's simply because not everyone is operating with all the information. The person you first speak to might be a new hire, a person from another department who just happened to answer the phone, or simply a misinformed employee. In any company of greater than 10 people, the law of averages predicts that if you simply call back in a few minutes, you can get a new person who might be better able to help you. Now, if it's a small company, and you're sure you'll get the same person again, ask for a different department, the supervisor, or perhaps call with a different question which might lead you to different person with the authority to grant your request.

5. It's Not Necessary to Have Everything In Place Before You Start Selling.

As we learned in the chapter on prioritizing your brainstorming tasks, you can sometimes jump directly to sales activities even before you have a product to sell. For many entrepreneurs, this is a way of creating structure in the form of a deadline that keeps them working to get the product out. Don't try this one if you don't like that sort of pressure.

6. If You Put a Price Tag On It, People Will Buy It

This doesn't mean you should sell junk, or that people will buy garbage. What it does mean is that everything has value to someone else. Just think of garage sales, auctions and flea markets.

7. You Can Make Money Doing Just About ANYTHING

I truly believe this. The idea is reinforced every time I read another story about an entrepreneur who sells a new invention, or an off-the-wall service that's making a millionaire out of it's originator. I only have to recall the fact that I, too, bought a "pet rock" when I was a child.

8. If You Can Sell ONE, You Can Sell A MILLION

Sure, that one sale could be a fluke. But, if you've been able to sell your product to someone other than your mother or your best friend, it's a good sign. If two people buy it, you might have a winner on your hands. You've passed the first test. Most people ask, "Can it sell?" The right question is "What can I say or do to create value in the minds of others to make it sell?" The Slinky, a popular toy for years, was simply a spring from a machine. Value was created for it as a toy, and the rest is the stuff of entrepreneurial legend.

9. There's Enough For Everyone

When it comes to money, customers, ideas, happiness and even love, many people believe that there's just not enough to go around. They operate from an assumption of scarce resources. Now the world may not really need another book on investing in the stock market, but every person has his own unique way of doing things, so therefore every person has his own unique audience. As many McDonald's restaurants as there are in the world, there always seems to be enough hungry people to support another one, sometimes right on opposite sides of the same street. In matters of money, there is, in fact, enough wealth for everyone. Some people will choose different levels of wealth for themselves. But that's not an indication of scarcity, it's just a fact.

10. Ten percent (10%) Innovation is All You Need To Be Considered Innovative

This bit of marketing wisdom, that I've never forgotten, is probably based on how the human mind perceives differences. It's simply a reminder that it doesn't take much to stand out from the crowd. However, if you set out to make your product or service 100% different, then you'll be way ahead of the pack.

Methods

Effective marketing is nothing more than communicating an idea from within the right mindset. In order to have the right mindset, you need to know who you're speaking to, what they want to hear, and you have to know the words to use to say it to them. Here then, are 20 secrets which can help you sell effectively. They can be used in creating brochures, producing radio and television ads, and in practically any form of contact you have with your potential customers.

1. Follow the Leaders

Duplication is often a powerful key to success. Notice what it is about other companies' ads that grab your attention. Notice which ads are consistently run in magazines and determine the successful ones.

2. Image Is Everything

People often use some strange criteria to determine whether to do business with you. Have you ever decided NOT to buy something at a store because you didn't like the store owner? Or have you decided NOT to buy something from a catalog because you couldn't hold the item in your hands first? It's been shown that people often weigh boxes of merchandise in their hands in an attempt to determine if they're getting their money's worth? In the absence of dealing with you personally, or of being able to touch a product, consumers rely on the image that you project. If you're creating a video, a book, a doll, or whatever, you'd better make sure that your product and it's packaging looks as professional as others out there. Details matter, take a look at how and where other successful companies place the fine print, logos, wording, copyright notices, trademarks, barcodes etc. and then see "Method #1"!

3. Build Relationships

At some point in your journey, you're going to need the assistance of others. Whether it's getting a newspaper editor to write a story on you, or getting a distributor or store owner to carry your product, other people's help will be vital. It's said that "who you know" is important. What's equally important is "who knows you" and "who LIKES you." According to *How to Win Friends and Influence People* by Dale Carnegie "people will do things for you if they like you." What you need to know, therefore, are the techniques for getting people to think favorably about who you are and what you're doing. It's necessary for you to cultivate relationships that are not just about "getting", but about mutual benefit and long term interaction.

4. Use Power Words

According to researchers at Yale University, here are some of the most powerful words in the English Language. When possible, you'll want to incorporate them into the words you use when marketing to your audience.

Discover	Proven	Health	New
Easy	Results	Save	Secret
Guarantee	Safety	You	Power
Love	Money	Free	Tested

5. Give People What They Need

People need to feel special. Feelings and emotions are what drive consumer spending. If your product can provide your customer with any of the following, you'll be well on your way to success. People want the feelings associated with: love, power, sex appeal, control, security, importance, excitement, hope, appreciation, improved competence. To provide them with these feelings, you need to stress the benefits your product or service provides, NOT the features. A feature is what something is. A benefit is what it does. *"Our book has information"*, is a feature. *"It saves you time"* is a benefit.

6. People Will Pay For It

One of the worst mistakes you can make in business is to underestimate the buying power of your customer. You'll learn, if you haven't already, that people will pay for what they want and need. A statistic that has always stuck in my mind comes from India, which is known to be one of the poorest nations per capita. Did you know that people in India, who supposedly have little money, spend more on the movie industry than any other? Going to the movies provides an escape that people in that country somehow find the means to afford!

7. Offer a Money-Back Guarantee

Some new businesses worry that they'll lose money by offering a money-back guarantee. Trust me, if you're product is good, only a small percentage of people will ever take you up on it. However, you build a world of trust simply by having those words prominently displayed on your product or brochure.

8. Include Pictures

Pictures sell products. People like to see what they're buying. Whether on the Internet, in brochures, in magazines or on radio & television, pictures sell products. If you're selling a service, then have pictures of people in your ads, or include pictures of something you want people to associate with your service. Hint: adding color to brochures, packaging and ads sell even more.

9. Make It Easy

Make it easy for customers to find you, reach you and buy from you. Depending on your business and product, the following suggestions may not all apply to you:
1. Get an 800 number
2. Establish "merchant status" (so customers can order by credit card)
3. Display your address and order information prominently on all items
4. Set up a website
5. Get listed in trade journals, directories, 800 directory, search engines etc.

10. Keep It Simple

Speak in clear simple language that an eighth-grader can understand. Don't use acronyms unless you explain them. Don't use slang or colloquialisms unless you know your audience quite well. Think about how someone new to this society would interpret the following if the explanations in parentheses were not there. "I called someone at the IRS (Internal Revenue Service), who told me to call the SBA (Small Business Administration) ASAP (as soon as possible) to get a DBA form ("Doing Business As") to start my IT (Information Technology) company." No one is ever offended by simplicity.

11. Repeat the Desired Action

No matter how clear you think it is to your audience that what you're selling is a book, for example, tell them, in no uncertain terms EXACTLY what you want them to do. *"Order this great book now!", "Send $39.50 today and...", or "Use your credit card to order today."*

12. Use the power of the Postscript

Studies have shown that people reading a sales letter almost always read the postscript. People who ARE interested, but who don't have time to read the full letter, will scan the headline then the postscript. In fact, people who DON'T want to read a sales letter almost always look at the postscript before they throw it out. With that in mind, a postscript should include your entire sales pitch in a single sentence or two. Tip: Sometimes putting the P.S. in a different color will draw even more attention to it. For example:

13. Offer Something Free

Offering something free is a very powerful incentive that moves people to action. Make sure it's something useful or somehow related to the main product or service. See postscript example above.

14. Do The Two-Step

No, it's not a dance. The "two-step" is a process through which you take your potential customers to improve the chances of making a sale. Let's say that you're selling a book and you place a small ad in a magazine, which asks them to take **step one**: call and request a free brochure or sales letter. The sales letter they receive then asks them to take **step two**: place an order.

The two-step is powerful because it allows you to make initial contact with those who are interested in your offer with no risk on their part. And it then allows you to repeat your message to qualified prospects in more detail thereby improving the chances of making the sale.

15. Up-sell, Up-sell, Up-sell

In many business transactions, follow-up is the key to success. Up-selling is following up with an existing customer in order to sell an additional item. For many businesses repeat customers can represent a sizable portion of income. And as we learned from Chapter 1, selling many items to the same customers is key to success in the new paradigm of business. Someone who buys from you once is more likely to buy from you again. And it costs much less to sell to an existing customer than it does to find a new one. For best results, follow up within 30 days after the initial sale.

16. Include a Return Label

Here's a little tip that builds trust and warm fuzzy feelings between you and your customer. If you're offering money-back guarantee, or if you offer a product that's sold by size, like clothing or shoes, you may want to include a return label to make it easier for your customer to return the item to you should they need to.

17. Get Referrals

Word of mouth advertising is very powerful. A happy customer is your best advertiser. If people like doing business with you, they will refer others. I once launched a referral campaign that rewarded people who referred others to my business with a 10% commission on whatever that new customer purchased!

18. Stay Current

Staying up-to-date with your market, your industry and your product is key to selling more things to ever-increasing groups of people. If you are not changing with the times, the times are passing you by.

19. Be Honest and Respectful

I'll also add that you should be nice, smile, greet people, treat others the way they want to be treated, remember peoples' names, and birthdays, deliver what you promise and be honest in all your dealings.

20. Put People First

People don't care how much you know, until they know how much you care. Make customer service an important part of your business and treat your customers, as well as suppliers and employees well. Do whatever it takes to make a good impression with everyone who does business with you. Sometimes it means refunding the money of an angry customer, even if he or she is in the wrong. Sometimes it means shipping out a product overnight at your expense even though it means you make no money on the sale. One unhappy customer can do more to damage your reputation than ten happy customers will do to improve it.

Selling Basics

1.   Why to call,
2.   Who to call,
3.   When to call,
4.   Where to call,
5.   How often to call, and
6.   What to say when you call!

If you've never worked at a radio station, or a record store, published a magazine, or produced a video program, you may never know just what happens behind their doors on a daily basis and just how critical it is to your success that you do call. Working in any one of these companies is probably more hectic than you can imagine. Remember, every day these people have: shows to edit and produce, orders to make, inventories to take, customers to sell to, deadlines to meet, clients to solicit, advertisers to please, interviews to conduct, charts to compile, and the list does go on. You are calling because the record or tape you sent that just arrived in the day's mail could easily find itself at the bottom of a very big pile of other people's stuff even before anyone has had a chance to check it out.

Who You Are Calling

Luckily, you are a little further ahead here. Section Two has a few hundred answers to that question. You can't always know ahead of time what the chain of command is at any office you call.
At a radio station, it's usually the music director. For commercial stations with mix-shows, the individual DJ of a mix show usually has the say as to what he mixes. At the retail level, it may be the owner for smaller stores, or the buyer in the Rap Department for bigger ones. Whether you are trying to get radio, retail, video, or press coverage, keep in mind that that the final decision isn't always one person's. If you can't get through directly to the person you need to, be just as persuasive and pleasant to the person who you do get through to. Sometimes secretaries and assistants have as much influence in the final decision as the top player.

When To Call

One of the first things you'll learn in developing your technique is when to call. Most businesses in the industry have certain days designated to receive "reporter calls" and "music calls". For many radio stations, the Music Director won't even take calls having anything do with music. There will usually be a secretary or assistant screening calls first to find out the nature of the calls.
Whatever you do, don't break the rules on this one. When you first call the stations find out what day is dedicated to taking calls and meeting with labels and promotion companies so that you don't start out on a bad note.

Where To Call

The best practice is to contact your decision maker during business hours and only at their place of business. Don't ever call them at home without their permission. However, some people work out of their homes, and getting calls there isn't a problem. Some of the mix show DJ's, for example, may even prefer that you reach them or send records to them at home since they don't keep office hours and are usually at the station only for a few minutes before and after their shows. Use your best judgment. Sometimes that extra assertiveness can make the difference. Other times it can kill any chance you might ever have.

How Often To Call

Your best judgment is called for here as well. Since most radio stations and video shows will only set aside one or two days for receiving music calls, it would seem that the minimum number of times you should be interacting with them is that once or twice per week. If you feel that isn't enough opportunity to let a music director know just how exciting your new release is, you might try leaving messages on those days when he/she doesn't take music calls; you might try faxing a flier or press release, writing a letter or doing anything else you can think of to get noticed.

What to say when you call

The sky is the limit. As you start out promoting your record, few people will know about it or you. You'll want to introduce yourself and the music as professionally as possible. Much of this may have been done already through the press kit, any cover letter you may have sent, and of course, the music itself. You should inquire if they've had a chance to listen to the music. This is just a formality, since you should still have your plan of attack rehearsed to let them know what's going on with your record. Whether they have or they haven't listened should not affect what you have to tell them. If the record is doing well in the clubs, let them know. If it's getting airplay in other markets, tell them that as well. If you're getting magazine coverage or whatever, now is the time to "hype" your record. The excitement that they feel they're missing out on, may be enough to get them to "put the needle to the record".

From Their Point Of View

Keep in mind that the decision makers at every stop along the way are only human. They are caught up in their own life goals and dreams, just as much as you are in yours. They will act in a way that is governed by what they want to accomplish in this industry: whether it's creating a number one rated radio station, a top rated weekly radio show, or whatever is real to them. You are each fulfilling roles in this game called music exposure, so don't take it personally. None of these industry professionals is trying to help or harm your label, be patient until you find the moment when what you are promoting becomes exactly what they were looking for. If it's quality music, that moment will come.

Promotion, The Art

Your strength and effectiveness as a promotion person, will rest as much on who you are, as what you are promoting. The relationships you develop today, form the basis for better response in the future. Be prepared, however, for the negative as well. You'll run into the honest as well as the dishonest. You'll meet people from whom you'll get the distinct impression that somehow all of your talk and charm and persistence won't be enough to get the job done. Don't let this discourage you. There are enough out there who you'll be able to reach and win over because of your commitment and (hopefully) the strength of your music.

Promotion, just like any job or art requires a skill or talent that improves by doing. Each day that you continue the promotion of your music, your skill in getting the job done will improve. The technique you want to develop is one that encourages others to think that they are missing out on something big by not playing or stocking your record.

Remember, your success is measured by your accomplishments. A favorable response to your record is as much an accomplishment as high sales figures. Each accomplishment can and should be used as a stepping stone to get to the next level. Keep track of ALL of your accomplishments. Write them down, include them in your press kit and use them with each new record you send out, or with each new follow-up call. Be professional and remember that presentation counts.

Creative Selling

Now that you are promoting your own music, act or record label your main concern at all times should be getting exposure for your product. This is the only way to ensure the survival of your label. Hopefully, this manual has provided some guidance in how to play the game and has challenged you to create and develop as many effective new plays as possible for your play book. As mentioned, creativity and adaptability are trademarks of the successful promotion campaign and the successful entrepreneur. Train your mind to look for opportunities in everything your eyes see and ears hear. Don't be satisfied with the traditional or conventional. Break new ground. Rap has been hailed as the voice of young America capturing the feeling and emotion of today's youth. Corporate America has acknowledged this as well. They are incorporating Rap in everything from movies to game shows.

When and where you hear Jazz, R&B , Rock, European Classical, or another rappers' music, ask yourself: why not my Rap? The possibilities are endless: commercials, television shows, newspapers, magazines. A good publicity campaign may be able to achieve some of these while the record is current, but don't think it all has to stop after radio has had enough of your record. Promotion should be viewed as an ongoing process that can continue even after the life of your current release. Even if you perceive your record as "dead" in one region, there are always new areas open to you. It's safe to say that not each and every one in America heard your record while it was being initially promoted. There will always be new ears and minds to reach. Keep in mind also that many sleeping records have been revived and brought to national attention by a single radio or club DJ or inclusion in a movie soundtrack.

If you've taken the time to create a professional image with your release, you can benefit from that alone even after radio has moved on. The record is now part of your growing catalog, and should still be used to your benefit.

The particular subject matter of your record or the image or beliefs of the artist may also warrant continued media attention. Magazines which don't ordinarily cater to Rap or even music, for that matter, might be willing to dedicate space to covering you if you happen to be addressing an issue which might concern their readers. It's not inconceivable that a women's magazine, doing a piece on teenage pregnancy in general, or the depiction of women in the media or in the music industry might want to mention your lyrics if they have something positive to say about the issue. An education magazine doing a story on teaching through music might want to talk to you if you happen to be an "artist with a message". Many newspapers have Music Sections which feature local musicians, or Business Sections which might highlight local entrepreneurs. As more people realize the power of Rap Music in speaking to and reaching today's youth, the opportunities for exposing your music will increase. Creative marketing means always looking for new angles and untried ways of exposing your music. The new Rap game rewards the bold and innovative!

Since selling is the name of the game, let's start with an overview of selling including the who, what, where, when and why of it all. Below are 30 different methods, channels, media as well as a few unique ideas for successful selling.

- **Personal Sales** Better known as the "trunk of the car" method, this has been the starting point of many successful journeys. You should always have samples of your product, or brochures with you at all times.

- **Warm Market Referrals** Your immediate "warm market"--your circle of friends, family and acquaintances--can be a great sales team. Offer them a monetary incentive and give them commissions whenever they refer a new customer to you.

- **Word of Mouth Marketing** In his book, *Rules for Revolutionaries*, Guy Kawasaki recounts how Apple Computers grew as a result of the passionate loyalty of Macintosh users. The Macintosh, or Mac, was an early alternative to the personal computer that was favored by artsy types. Converts became "disciples" and spread the word far and wide to their friends. It was the best, and cheapest marketing campaign Apple could have hoped for. Sales of the Mac grew phenomenally. Network Marketing has used this concept for years. The best salespeople for a product are often satisfied, converted customers. Word of Mouth marketing gives customers an incentive for telling others about your product. In Apple's case, the reward was simply being able to belong to a unique community of users.

- WARNING: Many new entrepreneurs naively rely on word-of-mouth alone to get the word out. There are only two conditions under which you should rely on word-of-mouth exclusively to build your business. 1. If you're selling your product via network marketing AND have a compensation plan or some incentive that makes it worthwhile. 2. Your product is so global in it's appeal, and life-changing in it's effect that the standard of living of everyone is enhanced by using it. (Cures for cancer, the perfect mousetrap, and replacements for the telephone fall into this category). But be careful, for even Viagra (male potency booster) needed to be advertised. Perhaps the men who used it were not too eager to boast to their friends via word-of-mouth.

- **Door to Door** Though this is not the preferred method to make sales, it might be effective in some instances and for some products. However, if you're allergic to having doors slammed in your face, then you might NOT want to make this your primary method of getting customers.

- **Sidewalk Selling** If you have a new product that needs to be demonstrated, then you may want to set up your display on the sidewalk, in the local mall, or in a shopping center inside or just outside a store where your product can be purchased. If you've got boundless energy, enthusiasm and an engaging personality, this method can work to get you some sales and may be effective in starting a word-of-mouth campaign.

- **The Party Plan** Also called "the Tupperware way" in honor of the in-home events that independent representatives use to sell this company's products, you may also have a sales party in your home to kick off your venture.

- **Cold-Calling (Telemarketing)** Another method with a high "rejection ratio", telemarketing involves calling complete strangers and giving your sales pitch to them.

- **Mailing Lists (Direct Mail)** You can purchase addresses that have been sorted by occupation, age, race, religion, etc. to whom you can send a direct mail brochure or sales letter. (See yellow pages or search engines under "mailing lists")

- **CO-OP Mailings** To reduce the often high cost of creating, printing, stuffing and mailing brochures to thousands of people, there are companies and organizations that offer you the chance to be part of a mailing with other vendors like you. Merchant member organizations, Retail Councils and Barter organizations can direct you to these programs.

- **Email Lists** You can purchase the email addresses of people who might be interested in your product or service. It's considered a cyber faux-pas to send unsolicited email. "Spamming", as it is called, can make you many online enemies, and can even get your website, or email account shut down. To prevent this, use a service that offers "opt-in" lists. These are lists in which the people on the list have "opted in", or chosen to be on them and may have requested to receive emails from companies like yours offering certain types of products.

- **Get Celebrity Endorsements** Just as powerful as word of mouth marketing is the concept of celebrity endorsements. What people say about your product has power. What people with power people say about your product is even more powerful. But what do you do if you can't afford millions of dollars to pay Michael Jordan to say good things about your product? Don't despair. You may be able to get some indirect endorsements simply by sending samples of your product to famous people. If they like it, these people may become passionate endorsers simply by being seen in or using your creations or they may end up unofficially endorsing it out of sincere appreciation of what it does for them. Sales of my books got a boost and continue to be influenced by rapper Chuck D's public endorsements of them. He does it out of a sincere desire to help others by sharing the information in the books. (He also told me he was glad the book existed, so he wouldn't have to continually answer all the questions that I had now conveniently answered!)

    You can also act as your own celebrity if you first establish yourself as an expert. Write and offer articles about your passion to local and national papers and magazines. Place your bio and contact information at the end of each article. These will serve as indirect advertising for you and your business.

What Medium Sells

- **Classifieds** Despite their size, classifieds are one of the best ways to get customers. Millions of people in search of specific objects or services for sale, scour these fine-print ads every day. For this reason, they often out-produce big ads which may get lost in a newspaper or magazine. Classifieds should be short and should move people to action to call a number for a brochure or to speak to a sales person. The best medium to place a classified is in a magazine or newsletter that caters to the particular niche you sell to. If your product has mass appeal, then newspaper ads might do well also. Late-night infomercial king Don Lapre sells a great package with information and tips on using newspaper classifieds to sell a product. (Visit Don at www.makingmoney.com)

- **Online Classifieds**   Because of the sheer number of websites out there and the tremendous volume of listings, online classified ads are not as effective as print classifieds. Services that automatically match customer inquiries with vendor offerings, on the other hand, do better.

- **Online Auction** If your passion is antiques, collectibles, movies, books or the latest toy craze, posting your product on an online auction site can get you a truckload of customers. While there are now dozens of online auctions, www.Ebay.com remains the leader.

- **Directories** Getting listed in industry directories is a wise way of letting people know you exist. People who are just getting into a particular field, or those doing research often use directories extensively. If, for example, you sell a product for boat owners, then getting your business listed in, say a National Directory Boating Industry Dealers & Manufacturers wouldn't hurt. Trade organizations are a good place to start to discover what directories exist. In most cases listings are usually free.

- **Catalogs** Getting featured in catalogs is another way to sell your product. For comprehensive lists of the more than 12,000 catalogs published today check out www.catalogs2go.com, www.catalogsite.com, www.buyersindex.com or www.catalogsusa.com and search for those which cater to your market. As more people make their purchases online, getting featured in the online editions of popular mail order catalogs will also be a good way to gain exposure.

When To Sell

- **Holidays** Since people make emotional buying decisions, specific holidays like Mothers day, Fathers day and Valentines day, when emotions are running high, are excellent times to push your passion. Many flower shops do over 50% of the year's business just on Valentines day!

- **Theme Days, Months, Years and Centuries** The year of the child. Black History Month. Secretaries Day. These theme periods all present the perfect opportunity to create a tie-in to your passion. If you have a passion for animals, you may want to follow the Chinese calendar to find out which animal is featured this year. And by the way, I've heard that this is the "Century of the Entrepreneur", so if your passion appeals to people just like you who are pursuing their passion, then you have a 100 years of prime marketing time to make sales!

- **Seasons** If your passion is linked to a particular season, you may want to focus your marketing efforts, or the launch of your venture to capitalize on that time of year. The key is to realize that in many cases, marketing needs to start several months, or maybe years in advance in order to be in place for a particular time. For example, if you wanted an ad to appear in a magazine for the winter months, you'd need to make those arrangements in August or September.

Where To Sell

- **Craft Fairs, Street Events, Flea Markets** If your passion involves selling something that people need to see up close, or touch and feel before they purchase, then the outdoor or indoor flea market/crafts fair setting might do well for you.

- **Conventions, Expos and Trade Shows** If your passion appeals to specific groups of people who gather on a regular basis, then renting a booth, or taking out an ad in the event directory of a convention, expo or trade show might bring you a host of customers.

- **Sidewalks, Malls, Stores, Libraries, Subway Stations, Bus Stops, Gas Stations** In other words, just about any place where people congregate or pass through presents an opportunity to get the word out about your passion.

- **Sell to Stores**   Chains, discount stores, supermarkets and department stores usually have buyers located on the premises or at a company headquarters who make the decisions on what stock to carry. Sometimes, however, they may prefer to deal with distributors rather than with new companies like yours. Call the stores you're interested in and ask if they deal with small businesses like yours, or if they prefer to deal with distributors.

- **Sell to Distributors**   Depending on your product, it may be necessary to sell to distributors in order to get it placed in the retail outlets it needs to be in.

- **Sell to Government**   Local and federal governments offer a great resource for selling products. If the government decides that they need a copy of your book, or invention in the hands of every government employee, you'll have found a lucrative source of sales. There are also many federal programs specifically designed to benefit small, minority, and woman-owned businesses. (Ask the SBA about government programs.)

- **Sell to Large Corporations**   Corporations may use various products as premiums, incentives, giveaways and gifts. You can offer a customized version of your product just for a company to sell or give to their employees.

- **Sell to Special Interest Organizations**   There are many organizations which might be interested in using your product in their fund-raising efforts, or that may request that your service be provided at gatherings. Visit your library for a copy of the *Encyclopedia of Associations*, and also *National Trade and Professional Associations.*

- **Sell to School Systems, Library systems & the Military**   These large institutions represent tremendous opportunities for sales. A passion which caters to teachers, librarians, students or armed forces personnel and which can be purchased in bulk can pay your rent for months to come! Some are notoriously slow in paying, but may be well worth the wait.

- **Get Creative**   There are as many creative ways to sell your product or service as there are products and services. Do you have a passion for running? Is there some product or service that practically every marathon runner, or their families could use? Where can you find a lot of marathon runners all in one place? Hmmm. That's a tough one! Have you considered advertising in or on newspaper inserts, matchbooks, grocery store bags, inserts in books, milk cartons, paper restaurant placemats, the sides of buildings, the backs of commuter passes or tickets, bumper stickers, supermarket bulletin boards, in-flight magazines, store receipts, campus student centers or t-shirts?

MORE WAYS TO PROMOTE

Conferences And Seminars

Many business friendships have been started across telephone lines and have progressed for years without the individuals ever actually meeting. The many conferences, conventions and seminars within the music industry   provide the opportunity to finally meet many of the individuals you will be interacting with. As well, you'll have the chance do some concentrated face to face networking, hyping and selling of your record. Many of the larger conferences have showcasing where (usually up and coming) artists get to perform. You may use the opportunity as well to do some targeting of industry people by including a sample of your product in an attendee pack usually issued to every registrant of the conference. It includes important conference information and directories plus advertising and giveaways from other companies. You need to set this up with the conference organizers well in advance of the actual conference.

Giveaways--The Power Of Freeness

In a society where freeness is the most pursued non-existing commodity around, you can generate favor towards your product by supplying it to the public. In fact the President of one of the world's most successful Rap Labels suggested the giveaway technique to me as a surefire means of generating response and testing the waters with a new release. Obviously, for a small label, the catch-22 in this approach   is that if they had the money to press 5000 copies of the record just to give away, they would be much better off financially and wouldn't need to. Conferences, as mentioned previously, as well as concerts, offer good opportunities to test the freeness theory.

The Endorsed Offer

One particularly powerful way to market yourself to new customers is something called an endorsed offer. Quite simply, an endorsed offer is an offer of a product or service made to a list of subscribers, prospects by the owner of the list. It's based on the finding that you are more likely to respond to an offer of third party goods and services if the offer comes from someone you trust. Whereas a generic offer might be expected to create a response of 1-3%, endorsed offers have been known to generate responses of up to 33%!

Find someone with a list, and suggest the following. Tell them you're willing to split the profits of a joint venture, if they'd be willing to recommend your product to their subscribers.

Here's a sample of a letter that the owner of a list could send to their mailing list of subscribers or customers. It's the actual letter I suggested to one of our strategic partners.

Sample of an Endorsed Offer

To all BizJump clients and friends,

> *SPECIAL: 20% off all PassionProfit® Products and Services on ANY of their 5 websites!*

We here at BizJump are always looking for new products and services to share with you to help jump-start and grow your business. As we form new alliances, we come across exciting companies with great offers like this one that we'll share with you. It's our way of thanking you for your support, and to encourage you to keep striving to grow your business.

We've recently partnered with The Passion Profit Company Inc., an innovative 10 year old company which helps people "find, develop and profit from their passions." Their website, www.PassionProfit.com, website features a unique collection of books, business plans, audio programs on cassette and CD, coaching, merchant services, website hosting, marketing consulting and more with the purpose of helping your business grow and prosper. President and founder Walt Goodridge has been featured in Entrepreneur, Wall Street Journal,Time and other media.

Walt has himself been interviewed nationally, has appeared across the country, and at the Learning Annex promoting his book (Turn Your Passion Into Profit) and sharing the unique Passion Profit philosophy he's used to help thousands "profitize" their talents, hobbies and passions. We feel confident recommending this innovator in what's becoming an increasingly voiced desire to find more personal fulfillment and satisfaction beyond the financial reward of owning a business.

At our request, Walt, has agreed to offer a 20% discount to all BizJump mailing list members who visit and purchase anything on his family of websites (currently 6 and counting) within the next 90 days. The discount applies to any purchase you make this year. So, whether you purchase an actual business plan from PassionProfit.com now, or an earth-conscious t-shirt from earthforall.org later ,or sign up for coaching and website hosting 6 months from now, the discount will apply every time (Tip: You can sign up now for some services like coaching, and start the clock anytime in the future)

This is OUR special way of saying thank you to our valued members. Since almost everyone will have a need for one or more of these products at some time during the course of business, we feel this is a great way of saying thank you!

ClintonB
Principal

P.S. All you have to do is enter coupon code "bizjump001" when you place your order, and you'll automatically receive 20% off any product or service

The PassionProfit family of sites includes:
PassionProfit.com | ArtofWow.com | SponsorshipDollars.com | HipHopEntrepreneur.com |
PoetsNiche | NicheMarket.com, with more added all the time

You can strike similar deals with other labels, online magazines and e-zine list owners.

SELLING TO GET PUBLICITY—Target, Tools & Techniques

Target: Magazines, Newspapers, Websites, E-zines
Tools:
1. Music (CD, cassette, MP3)
2. Video in correct format
3. Media Kit, (also known as Press Kit) including: Promo picture of the artist/group; Press Release; Bio of the artist/group; Sample of music (record, cassette or CD); Magazine write-ups/testimonials if any; Video, if any; Any other relevant information, posters, buttons, anything to impress!

Sample Press Release

FOR IMMEDIATE RELEASE   **Interviews Contact: (718)464-3754**

Tricky Returns With New Album "Vulnerable" On June 17th, 2003   Words: Carleen Donovan
New York, NY - April 22, 2003 - In what is being hailed as the best album of his career, British-born musical chameleon Tricky is set to release his seventh album Vulnerable on June 17, 2003. Recorded in Los Angeles, Tricky has returned with an inspirational thirteen song collection that reverberates with emotional intensity and echoes artistic rebirth. Vulnerable is being released on Tricky's Brown Punk Records imprint via his new exclusive worldwide (ex-UK and Europe) deal with Sanctuary Records, a division of the Sanctuary Records Group.

"I called this album Vulnerable because it's my most honest and open record," said Tricky. "On this album I've stopped hiding and I'm allowing people to see different sides of the real me. Vulnerable is me breaking free and being myself again."

With new vocal muse, Italian chanteuse Costanza Francavilla, the songs on Vulnerable are textured soundscapes of jaunting beats, stirring guitars and gorgeous voices that resonate with Tricky's unique fusion of the rock, electronica, and hip hop genres. The result is an extraordinary album that finds Tricky at his very best. From the wildly inventive dub-sonic sound of "Stay" to the haunting grooves of "Hollow," and off-kilter beats of the album's first single, "Antimatter," Tricky has again created an album that defies easy categorization.
Said Tricky, "I might not be the most talented, but I am the only artist around now with their own sound."
An unparalleled visionary, Tricky s influence can be seen and felt everywhere in music today. As the founding father of trip hop, Tricky has destroyed artistic barriers due to his unequivocal combination of artistry and style. Through his acclaimed solo albums and collaborations he has altered the sounds of pop, electronic and hip-hop music as we know today and is a celebrated figure amongst his artistic peers and fans alike. On Vulnerable, he once again constructs an exhilarating musical world unlike any other through his voice and adventurous manipulation of sound.

A true renaissance man, Tricky shot the photography and co-designed the packaging for Vulnerable, which in turn has led to the first museum exhibition of his digital photography at Palais de Tokyo in Paris. The month long exhibition premiers April 29th at a special reception and will also feature the first viewing of the "Antimatter" video, which was directed by Stephane Sednaoui. This is the fourth collaboration between Sednaoui and Tricky.

In addition, the Vulnerable album is an enhanced CD which includes an interview, three guerilla style cinema films, conceived and co-directed by Tricky, and the "Antimatter" video.Tricky embarks on a six week European tour, The 13 Tour, on June 13th in Vicenza, Italy. He will then be returning to the US to produce Costanza's first solo album for his Brown Punk Records label. His North American tour is scheduled to begin in the early fall.

###

Promoting To Magazines

Magazines appeal to a unique combination of the public's wants: visual stimulation, satisfaction of curiosity, and entertainment. Keep these three things in mind when you compile the artist bio and press kit, and you'll have addressed half the job of promotion and getting coverage.

The editor, while looking through your press kit, will be asking him/herself: Do my readers want to know about this?   Your press kit should have been compiled and written to answer this question.   The press kit will be the first and most critical introduction to your artist and your company that the magazine editor sees. Make it work for you. If you don't remember everything you learned in English class about effective writing and rules of grammar, get someone who does. What you say, and how you say it will be key in generating an interest which could translate into valuable magazine coverage.

Remember:

Your artist's unique and different physical appearance can get coverage.(visual stimulation)

Who your artist is and what their all about (if it's interesting) can get coverage. (curiosity)

Your artist's music/performances can get coverage.(entertainment)

One major point you should be aware of when seeking magazine exposure is Lead Time.   The magazine that you picked up at the newsstand today was probably written about 3 to 4 months ago. Magazine editors must have a sufficient amount of lead or preparation time, because of all the time needed to compile and edit the articles, secure advertising, plan the layout, and get it printed. If you are reading this in December, for example, your favorite Rap magazine has more than likely already "closed" (that is, decided on everything to be included, and are no longer taking advertisers) on the issue that will be on sale in March.   The obvious drawback to the lead time challenge is that if you want coverage of your artist to coincide with the release of the record, you have to give a magazine as much as 3 months advance notice. This may be way before anyone has even heard of your record, or before it's even been mixed! Realistically, however, since it takes about as much time for a promotion campaign to really get going, if you send out the tapes to the magazines at the beginning of your promotion, it might just work out that any coverage that you're lucky (or persistent) enough to get will coincide with the time that you actually start making some noise.   So, be aware of it, but don't let the lead time issue influence your plan of action too much.

SELLING TO GET AIRPLAY—Target, Tools & Techniques

Target: Radio Stations, Video Shows, Record Pools
Tools: Promo copies of your release
Technique & Tips:

Promoting To Radio

Most Music Directors do want to play good music. They can also be a bit more knowledgeable about what their listeners want to hear. Notice I said "can". Sometimes, their ears have been jaded by listening to their own station for years, and might be out of touch with what is hot and new on the streets. Don't blame them, educate them! If you've got enough positive response to really be sure you have something worth listening to, there will be someone else in high places who will agree with you. Your job is to find that person, get them on your side, build on that and start a chain reaction. Don't limit yourself to just one geographic area (or even one country). You now have lists of radio stations and stores all over the country. You may find yourself living in Maine, with a record that the Hip Hop crowd in Miami thinks is phat! If that happens, promote in Miami and sell it to them!

Your radio promotion must include targeting college radio stations. Unfortunately, as we've said before, the industry on a whole, including more than likely, your distributor, have been slow to acknowledge the power of college radio stations in affecting and effecting record sales. Many distributors and stores won't consider a record worthy if it is being aired on college radio only. For Rap especially, which has found a more open-minded reception there, promoting at the college level may be more critical to your success. Targeting college radio initially in your campaign will facilitate getting on charts such as The Gavin (weekly) Report whose reporter list is primarily (about 70%) college stations. From there, people on the commercial side of the industry may start to take notice. Many Rap acts have had their start on college radio, and then moved to commercial radio and charts. The "Rap Friendly" station list is where you'll find an abundance of the key college stations.

Promoting To Video

In the video world of the smaller Rap shows, the individuals involved are less influenced by corporate sponsors. They are vying for the attention and recognition of the public, but for less monetarily based reasons as the radio stations, the stores and the national video shows. Their viewer base does not translate directly into dollars in their pocket (not usually, anyway). Most of the V-Jays or Video Jocks are nine-to-fivers who, one day a week, are filling a need for Rap video programming in their area.

The material reward was not what coaxed them in. For many, it was a love of expression through video which brought them into this end of the business. The shows can be a natural extension and an outlet for their craft as video producers or directors. Quite a few, in addition to hosting shows, have video production companies as well. Promoting to a VJ, therefore, may not involve all the same pressures that come from a financial "bottom line". It may be more of a "creative thing" which will need to be handled with a slight difference.

One VJ, realizing and sympathetic to the fact that he was dealing with an inexperienced independent label, was generous enough to explain the finer points of what my promotion assistant and I needed to do to get his attention and what we were competing with from the major labels (i.e. free CD's, posters etc.). The essence of his advice was that one should develop that "rapport" which we spoke of earlier. (The free CD's don't hurt, either). The key to the effectiveness of your (or your promotion person's) efforts is the personal interaction with the people who are being promoted to.

Promoting To Pools

Record Pools are comprised of mostly club DJ's and some radio DJ's who pay a fee to be members. Record labels provide promotional copies of new releases to the pools (usually enough to "service" all the members of the pool) to get exposure in the dance clubs and on the radio shows which these DJ's work. Many pools will provide an excellent service of tracking the play that your record is getting. Pools usually strive to maintain a good relationship with labels since the backbone of their operation is in fact the "service" (supply of records) from the labels.

Rap, which has historically had its origins and found its strength and true fans apart from the mainstream, was never a music tailored for the radio.   It was of an experience which wasn't impressed by Arbitron (a radio ratings company) numbers and video play lists. However, as radio and video grew into Rap, the true fans were joined by a greater number of converts. These converts, by their sheer numbers affected radio station programming and video rotation. The heads of the labels now producing Rap used these media to set the standards for how Rap should be promoted. As many major Rap labels, pseudo-indies, and even some real indies make the switch with the technology, many pools complain about a growing indifference by the labels to their craft. This indifference takes the form of reduced service from the labels who see more return on investment in servicing radio stations and video shows over the Pools.

The life of the record as well as the longevity of the artist's career rests with establishing a Foundation of support from "the underground". The true fans of many Rap artists reside within the communities which feel that the artist is one of them, shares their background, their tastes, habits and fun. Nowhere is that sense of familiarity and kinship more effectively transmitted than where many Rap fans go to release the week's tensions, to socialize and to keep up with what's happening : the dance floor. It would be wise, as an independent Rap label to maintain ties with the club scene in which Rap has its roots.

SELLING TO GET SALES

Target: Retail stores, Distributors, Public
Tools:
Music (CD, cassette, MP3)
Video in correct format
Media Kit, including
Press Release
Sales Sheet
Website

Technique:
"Send it out, then go after it!"

What exactly is Promotion? Promotion is the job of getting people to know about your record.

The actual act of Promotion will involve: getting the record to the key people (who both influence and satisfy public demand) and following up with phone calls, personal visits (when possible), faxes, and any and everything else to keep the name of the group, the name of the song, the name of the company, and your name in their minds. The more people who know about and hear your record, the more records you can sell. Just hearing it (Radio), however, isn't enough. The record has to be available to be bought (Retail). Solving the Radio and Retail challenge is the basis of good promotion.

The reason this is such a tricky challenge is : many radio stations are reluctant to add a new record just on the basis of how it sounds . They want to know if people are buying it, how it's doing saleswise.   At the same time, at the retail level, many store owners/buyers are reluctant to stock a new record unless it is getting airplay. They fear it will take up valuable wall or shelf space and won't sell.

Luckily, moosecalls aren't what's in, slammin' music is.   So your record, if it's good, does have its place on the airwaves; you just need to remember what the Music Director's and Store Owner's bottom lines are. Keep it in mind when you talk to them about adding your record to their rotation lists, or to their shelves.

So back to the challenge of retail and radio promotion. Both the Music Director and Store owner have legitimate concerns. They are in business and want to stay in business. What this means is that you will have to be more creative, persistent, professional and committed if you want to get into business. It may seem at times that others are trying specifically to keep YOU out of business, and from being successful. Whenever you feel this way, that's your signal that you have to try harder.

SELLING TO YOUR OWN TEAM

Target: Artists, Managers, Staff, and yourself

Tools: Your words, your thoughts, your vision

Technique:

You may never have looked at it in quite this way, but part of the formula for changing the game with your record label is keeping your team motivated, inspired and committed. When you can paint a vivid picture of desirable future, you gain a person's interest. When you can enroll them in your vision, you gain their support. When you can show them how they stand to benefit in that vision, you can move them to action. When they see their own dreams coming true by their association with you, you gain their commitment. Immediate compensation is not always the deciding factor in a person's decision to commit to your dream. Know this and know the power of being a good leader.

Equipped with the information on how to sell, you are now ready to implement it all in a unique strategy I call "Momentum Marketing."

Momentum Marketing

What is Momentum Marketing?
Answer: a way to get massive publicity and get the whole world talking about you on a shoestring budget

'Momentum Marketing' (M 'n M) is a technique for creating a snowball marketing campaign for your product or service without spending millions or even thousands of dollars. Whether you're marketing a book, an invention, an event, or a service, Momentum Marketing can be used effectively to let the world know what you're doing. MM is used by savvy marketers around the world, and you may even be using it right now to get attention focused on what you're doing.

In scientific terms, Momentum is defined as mass x velocity (m x v)and is a measure of the size of an item, the motion of the item, and the direction the item is moving in. In this report, your goal is to increasing the momentum of your marketing campaign. In simpler terms, in order to be successful, you want to increase the (mass)es of people who know about your product, and to increase the speed at which the news gets to them so you can sell your product to them

The Theory Behind The Plan
To fully understand how and why momentum marketing will work for you, we'll need to go into a bit of theory. So get your thinking caps on! Here's your first test: Answer the following question.

Which would you rather have: a penny doubled each day for a month or 10,000.00?
If you haven't already encountered that question before, you might be tempted to take the 10,000 dollars. After all, 10,000 is 10,000 and a penny is only a penny. And even if you suspect that doubling a penny each day might in fact amount to a big number, most people might intuitively realize just how much is at stake. The correct answer, provided you want the option that will make you richer, is to take the penny option. The chart below will illustrate what happens to that penny each day for 30 days.

day 1 - 1 cent		day 16	- 327.68
day 2 - 2 cents		day 17	- 655.36
day 3 - 4 cents		day 18	- 1310.72
day 4 - 8 cents		day 19	- 2621.44
day 5 - 16 cents		day 20	- 5242.88
day 6 - 32 cents		day 21	- 10,485.76
day 7 - 64 cents		day 22	- 20,971.52
day 8 - 1.28		day 23	- 41,943.04
day 9 - 2.56		day 24	- 83,886.08
day 10 - 5.12		day 25	- 167,772.16
day 11 - 10.24		day 26	- 335,544.32
day 12 - 20.48		day 27	- 671,088.64
day 13 - 40.96		day 28	- 1,342,177.28
day 14 - 81.92		day 29	- 2,684,354.56
day 15 - 163.84		day 30	- 5,368,709.12

**A geometric progression is one that generates each new term by multiplying by a fixed ratio, usually named r. If the first term is a, then the second term is a*r, the third term is a*r*r = a*r^2, and so on.*

Seen for what it is, this example is truly astounding! A single penny, doubled for an entire month yields a final day's return of over 5 million dollars! (And a total accumulated return of about 10 million!) This is based on a concept called Geometric Progression*. It's growth which progresses not arithmetically, by single units, but geometrically, by the square of some number. (see mathematical definition below). Like the progression of rewards on the popular game show, "Who Wants To Be A Millionaire" which goes from 100 to a million in just 12 questions, the concept of geometric growth is indeed a powerful one.

Visually, you might picture a snowball that takes thirty days to roll down a hill gathering mass as it rolls. By day 30 its size is massive! Or, in keeping with the concept of momentum, let's say the numbers represent a car traveling and accelerating down a road. Each day it doubles in speed such that by day 30 it's traveling faster than the speed of light!

Now before you get too excited, keep in mind that the reason many people never realize the full potential of a Momentum Marketing campaign is simply this: They don't have the patience to see it through. Look back at our example, for a moment, and notice how the rewards grow. A week after you've started, your daily take is still just 64 cents. Fifteen days later, fully half way through the process, your daily take is just 163.00, just 0.00305% of what it will be on the final day. (That's LESS than 1/2 of 1/10 of 1 percent!) Two-thirds of the way through, at .88, your day's reward is just about 1/10 of a percent of what the reward will be on the final day. So for many people, since it's difficult to gage how the momentum is growing, they abandon the campaign before they reach day thirty!

Now imagine if these numbers represented the number of people who bought your product. Or, let's be conservative, and say it represents simply the number of people who HEAR about your product. And let's say that only 1% of these people purchase your product for 25.00. So 53,687 people buying your product means sales of 1,342,177.25. Not bad for thirty days of hard work don't you think? This is precisely what we are going to do through momentum Marketing. However, you're going to work a little smarter. And, instead of trying to reach the people yourself, you're going to employ the gatekeepers who collectively can reach all these people.

Who Are Gatekeepers?

GateKeepers are people who, by virtue of their profession or business, have access to great numbers of people. They, in effect, guard the gates to reaching your public. Gate Keepers include magazine/newspaper editors, event promoters, radio show hosts, publicists, heads of organizations, e-zine publishers and anyone who is constantly in touch with great numbers of people. These are the people who you'll want to have in your corner as they have the power to influence purchasing decisions for many people at one time. If you think hard enough, you probably know a gatekeeper or two already. The head of a local community organization, your church minister, the little league coach. You may not have to look very hard to find that one person who can start the ball of your MM campaign rolling.

The 10 Steps to a Momentum Marketing Campaign

1. Set Goals & create wish list of Media Outlets
Which magazines, shows, etc. do you want to be featured in?

2. Using the Marketing Log, make a list of the Gatekeepers you currently know.
These are the people who have a direct channel to the public or the particular audience you want to reach. These include radio hosts, editors, event promoters, organization presidents, and others of notoriety and influence. Who's in your orbit? Who appear to be the key players? This list can and should change as you proceed down the runway. These are simply the people who are standing on either side of the runway as your plan proceeds down the runway. They're not flying the plane. They're not on the plane with you. And they won't necessarily be there when the plane takes off, unless they run alongside you as you pick up speed. The key is to and recognize when the scenery is changing. It means you're moving. If seen in this light, I believe more people would have success as new people, circumstances and situations come into their lives. The challenge for most people is that they don't change and grow fast enough to keep pace with the required change in thinking, behavior, beliefs and actions that success demands.

3. Contact the GateKeepers

4. Fax or email press release, send media kit & or deliver samples to new gatekeepers

5. Follow up to request "Desired Action"

6. Ask Gatekeepers (hosts/reviewers) for quotes; add to testimonial sheet of media kit

7. Request at least 2 names of others in their circles

John,
Do you have a relationship with, or know of any other radio show hosts or editors
I might use your name to contact to request an interview or suggest a story idea?

8. Extend list of gatekeepers in Momentum Marketing Log
Work in waves. Start with 10 or 12 gatekeepers. As you work with getting interviews and reviews with this first wave, you'll also be creating a list of the next wave of gatekeepers whom you will fax the testimonials, reviews and announcements of the first wave.

9. Contact new gatekeepers

10. Go to step 4, and repeat process

The Hip Hop Label's Momentum Marketing Checklist

IMPORTANT: Do not overlook any item in this checklist. The success of your campaign is at stake!

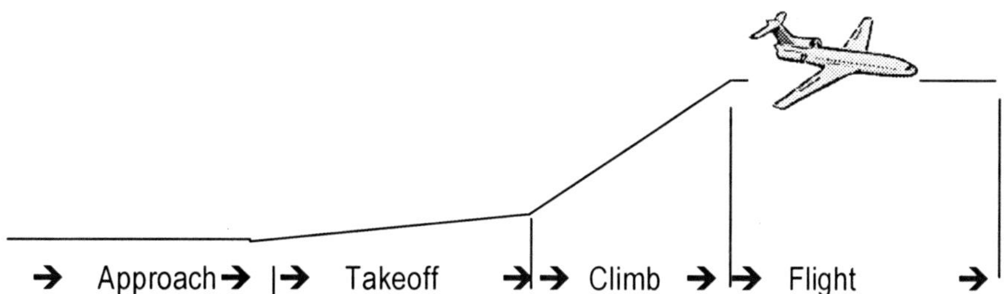

The Big Picture

In order to succeed at your independent label, there are three areas of the big picture that must be in order: The Person, The Product & The Plan.

The Person

We spent the first chapter making sure that everything about you, The Person, the way you think, what you expect of yourself, your standards, your work ethic, your people skills, your commitment, your vision, your ideals, and your ability to bounce back, are all in tact and of an exemplary nature. We can't afford to have the success of our project compromised because you're not up to doing what has to get done.

Are you ready?

The Product

We've assumed that "The Product"—the music that is at the heart of your label—is actually worthy of all of this effort. It often happens that the people involved in a label get so caught up that they lose the objectivity required to assess whether or not the music is worthy. Sometimes, team members are afraid to say nay for fear of being seen as a dream killer. It's easy to get trapped because everyone's dreams are vested in the success of the venture. However, you must be able to answer, "Yes! 100%" to the following questions.

Is the music the best that it can be? Is there something that should be changed? *(If so, fix it now! If you don't have the time to do it right, how will you have the time do it over?)*

Does the music have that certain something that captures a mood, feeling, mindset, or the thoughts and experiences of those who listen to it?

Does it make people stop, listen and nod? Get up and dance?

Is it radio-friendly? (If not, create a version that is!)

Am I 100% behind this artist and his music? *(If in doubt, get the heck out!)*

The Plan

Finally, the most important aspect is making sure the plan is sound. Within "The Plan" are elements that can seem overwhelming, and rightly so. There's a lot going on simultaneously that needs to be coordinated in order to succeed. First, let's be clear about what we want to have happen. Our goal is to boost sales to the specific amount indicated below by using the Momentum Marketing Campaign and the Tools to create, sustain and advance momentum during the 12 month period following the release of the single/album.

Set a specific goal of how many items I wish to sell. Enter Goal: [_____________________]

Tools

Assume: these tools are in the bag.
-Video
-1000 copies of the single
-1000 copies of the album
-Media Kit
-Website (Up and running and prepared to take orders. Site has 30-second samples of three of the album cuts that visitors can download.

Send	*Contact Lists*	*Attract Customers*
Music (CD, cassette, MP3) Video in correct format Media Kit, including Company info Fact sheet Bios Press Release Articles Graphics/Visuals Testimonials	Top 20 Wish List Gatekeepers Retail Store List Radio Station List Video Program List Magazine List Website List Standard letters for -New contacts -Retail -Radio -Video -other Momentum Mktg Log	Website, including "Join/Signup" form "Order now" link Order-taking function Top 20 Wish List Subscriber list of emails Weekly update Template Method to send emails to list *Other Helpful Tools Though not necessary, the following items may make doing the work of your MM campaign a little easier. - Design Software - Scanner

Preparation

For the purposes of this strategy, we're going to assume that we have the following tools in the bag.

We created a video that we will use to market the group;

We have 1000 copies of the single and 1000 copies of the album already completed

We have the names and contact information for 100 video shows across the country which we got from hiphopbiz.com (shameless self-promotion)

We have a media kit, press release

Our website is up and running prepared to take orders

Our site has several 30-second samples of three of the album cuts that visitors can download

Step 1. Assessing the challenge

Here's the challenge we're faced with. We're selling a product. This product is sold visually and audibly. We must cut through the clutter of other record labels big and small, who are also competing for the attention of the public, and find a way to force people to stop and pay attention.

Step 2. Finding the story

At this point, I would want to know more about the label, the artist, what makes them unique, what their history is, what story is hiding in their background, their stage names, the group name, their message, the label, the relationship to their community, and every other aspect that might be relevant. I would look to see if I notice any relationship or significance in the timing of this group. In other words, is what they're saying relevant to any national debate, any news item, any trend, or any world event? The reason I do this is because at some point, we'll have to create a "hook", some type of angle, or advantage that has our artist and who they are stand out in the minds of the media, tv/cable and radio hosts, webmasters, magazine editors, video show hosts whom we'll be targeting.

I'm asking myself, "what's the story here?" What makes this group, this label, this record unique in some way. What can we "sell?" Why would anyone care that our album is about to drop. I never rely solely on the music as the strength of a record. As a marketing person, I'm always thinking of the story.
I use this to create a media kit that is on the website as well as in hard copy format

Step 3. Identifying the Variables

These are things to keep in mind about a Momentum Marketing Campaign and its success.

½ Your goal is to keep impressing and keep attracting new subscribers, new converts, new supporters, new disciples, new customers, new clients, new gatekeepers who will jump on the "Brand Wagon" you're creating. Once on, they talk to those in their circle of influence and create more momentum.

½ This initial "approach" can take weeks, months or years.

½ "Take-off" only happens when you have the right combination of speed and wing position. Even an appearance on a major media outlet may not result in "takeoff" if it happens at the "wrong" time. You need both a track record (enough distance traveled), speed (new people hearing about you), and position (credibility, appearance and a record of those appearances)

½ Being able to communicate your track record is important to "takeoff" (phase 2). Websites and email are a great way to keep the momentum going while acting as a permanent record, a "mini-me"dia kit of your accomplishments

½ This entire plan can be rendered unnecessary by making and exploiting the right contact at the right moment in the approach. (i.e. if you make an alliance with the right DJ, or get reviewed in the right magazine at just the right moment right before take-off speed)

½ The speed of approach may affected by
1. Gatekeepers' response time
2. Delivery times for your promotional packages
3. Magazine Lead Times, event promotion times, etc.
4. Holidays, Seasons, etc.

½ This is not an exact science. Your success may be affected and influence by a unique and unpredictable combination of contacts, chance, timing, economic conditions, geography, consumer mood and a host of other factors that no one can predict. That's why you'll need a "Secret Weapon"

½ Secret Weapon: Your secret weapon throughout all of this is your ability to spot opportunity.

½ Call, communicate with tastemakers at least once per month in the first quarter
       twice per month in the 2nd quarter
       every ten days in the 3rd quarter
       once per week in the 4th quarter

Tips for Winning over anyone you contact

Call, communicate with tastemakers at least once per month in the first quarter
twice per month in the 2nd quarter
every ten days in the 3rd quarter
once per week in the 4th quarter

Tips To Get More Appearances, Interviews And Sales

1. Keep past gatekeepers informed of your progress (they may have you back for another interview)
2. Impress new gatekeepers of the momentum you're gaining (they'll want to be part of the excitement)
3. Create "disciples"—these are the people who will be spreading the word about your artist/music/label

Other Things To Do

Attend Networking Events to meet new gatekeepers
Keep a growing list of customers
Email your customers with specials. (It's been proven to be easier to get an existing customer to make an additional purchase than it is to get a new customer.)

What needs to happen on a daily basis

On a daily basis, you will be Creating, Sustaining and Advancing Momentum, coordinating Branding Efforts and developing, coordinating, delegating, monitoring & maximizing your own and other people's efforts related to

½ Publicity (PR) Campaign (press, media, reviews)
½ Advertising (traditional and
½ Street level/ "Guerilla" promotion and marketing
½ Sales Promotion (outreach to stores and distributors)
½ Product Development (product image must be consistent with artist/company image)
½ Public Affairs/Public (outreach must be consistent)
½ Networking (Phone calls, emails to key people, gatekeepers, etc.)
½ Calling in Favors (part of networking and building relationships and goodwill)
½ Managing and Capitalizing on the Unknowns
½ Recognizing the Value in everything that Happens (good or bad)

SUCCESS!!! How You'll Know if You're Succeeding

As you proceed with your MM campaign, here's how you'll know that you're doing well. A few things will start happening:

½ interviews get scheduled
½ appearances get booked
½ record gets played
½ visitors to website increase and join more frequently
½ sales to the public/distributors/retailers increase

Conclusion

So there you have it: a step-by-step plan for achieving massive exposure on a shoestring budget. Your only expenses are some mailing costs, printing and perhaps some long distance phone charges.

Momentum Marketing Action Plan—PUBLICITY

Focus	Key Position	Needs *What THEY need* *see bottom line*	Desired Action *What YOU need*	Phase 1 "Approach" Actions/Tasks for months 1-3	Phase 2 "Takeoff" Actions/Tasks for months 4-6	Phase 3 "Climb" Actions/Tasks for months 7-9	Phase 4 "Flight" Actions/Tasks for months 10-12
Video Programs	½ Host ½ Producer	-Latest videos -great guests -Viewers -Sponsors	-video in rotation -endorsed offer	-initial contact -update once/mo	follow up update every 2 wk	follow up update every 10day	follow up update every wk
Radio Station	½ Mix DJ ½ Music Dir ½ Prog Dir ½ Host	-Latest music -great guests -Listeners -Ratings -Advertiser$	-add to playlist -interview artist	-initial contact -update once/mo	follow up update every 2 wk	follow up update every 10day	follow up update every wk
Magazine	½ Editor ½ Writer ½ Freelancer	-Good stories -content -Subscriber$ -Advertiser$	-Review song -interview artist	-initial contact -update once/mo	follow up update every 2 wk	follow up update every 10day	follow up update every wk
E-zine	½ Editor	-Subscribers -Content -Advertiser$	-Mention in ezine -Endorsed offer -act as affiliate	-initial contact -update once/mo	follow up update every 2 wk	follow up update every 10day	follow up update every wk
Club	½ Owner ½ DJ	-word of mouth -Exposure -Patron$	-play track ev nite	-initial contact -update once/mo	follow up update every 2 wk	follow up update every 10day	follow up update every wk
Record Pool	½ Director	-Cd, Vinyl -DJ member$	-access to DJs	-initial contact -update once/mo	follow up update every 2 wk	follow up update every 10day	follow up update every wk
Key Website	½ Webmaster	-Visitor$ -Content	-exposure -endorsed offer	-initial contact -update once/mo	follow up update every 2 wk	follow up update every 10day	follow up update every wk
Event Promoter	½ Owner	-hot acts	-headline				
Writers	½ Writer	-good stories	-good PR				
Advocate/Disciples	½ Fans	-					

The Key to getting what you want from EVERY interaction:

1. Show them how helping you gets them what they need
2. Offer them a way to make money with an endorsed offer
3. Gain access to their list/subscribers/listeners/fans/database

Momentum Marketing Action Plan for SALES

Outlet	Key Position	Needs *What THEY need*	Desired Action *What YOU need*	Phase 1 "Approach" Actions/Tasks for months 1-3	Phase 2 "Takeoff" Actions/Tasks for months 4-6	Phase 3 "Climb" Actions/Tasks for months 7-9	Phase 4 "Flight" Actions/Tasks for months 10-12
Retail Store	½ Onwer ½ Buyer	-Latest music -Customers -Sale$	-Direct Orders -Orders to Distributor	-initial contact -update once/mo	follow up update every 2 wk	follow up update ev 10d	follow up update every wk
Distributor	½ Buyer ½ Sales Agent	-Support -	-Push it to Retail	-initial contact -update once/mo	follow up update every 2 wk	follow up update every 10day	follow up update every wk
Affiliates	½ Webmaster	-Support -Training	-Sales	-initial contact -update once/mo	follow up update every 2 wk	follow up update every 10day	follow up update every wk
Subscribers/Fans	½ Customer ½ Disciple	-Entertainmnt	-Direct Orders -Tell their friends *CALL in and/or -Request in stores -Request on radio -Request on Video -Request in clubs	-initial contact -update once/mo	follow up update every 2 wk	follow up update every 10day	follow up update every wk
Other Stores							

Key to getting what you want from EVERY interaction:

1. Give them what they need
2. Build relationship
3. Ask for what YOU need

Momentum Marketing Action Plan for the TEAM

Who	Key Position	Needs *What THEY need*	Desired Action *What YOU need*	Phase 1 "Approach" Actions/Tasks for months 1-3	Phase 2 "Takeoff" Actions/Tasks for months 4-6	Phase 3 "Climb" Actions/Tasks for months 7-9	Phase 4 "Flight" Actions/Tasks for months 10-12
Artist	½ Artist	Fame/Fortune	-Direct Orders	-initial contact -update once/mo	follow up update every 2 wk	follow up update ev 10d	follow up update every wk
Management Co	½ Manager ½ Staff	-Support	-Push it to Retail	-initial contact -update once/mo	follow up update every 2 wk	follow up update every 10day	follow up update every wk
Label	½ Owner ½ Staff	-Support -Training	-Sales	-initial contact -update once/mo	follow up update every 2 wk	follow up update every 10day	follow up update every wk
Promotion Dept	½ Staff ½ Disciple	-Entertainmnt	-Direct Orders -Tell their friends *CALL in and/or -Request in stores -Request on radio -Request on Video -Request in clubs	-initial contact -update once/mo	follow up update every 2 wk	follow up update every 10day	follow up update every wk
PR Company	½ Staff						
Street Team	½ Staff						

Key to getting what you want from EVERY interaction:

1. Paint a picture of the vision; include them in it

Other Important Considerations

Mailing Costs And Telephone Bills

In promoting your record, mailing costs and telephone bills will be your biggest expense apart from actual product development.   Unfortunately, there's not much you can do to reduce your phone bills, except stop calling. Find and use the long distance carrier that offers the cheapest rates. The rates don't vary by too much, but since you'll be making a lot of calls, it does add up.

As far as the mailings, you do have some choices. United Parcel Service (UPS) provides a cheaper alternative to almost all of the express delivery companies and to a certain degree, even the U.S. Postal Service (USPS). Their rates range anywhere from $1.88 to $3.00 per package for the items you'll usually be mailing (records or video tapes) depending on where it's going and how much it weighs. If you must have the prestige of overnight hand delivery, UPS offers that too, and they now offer Saturday delivery (call your local office for details).

The U.S. Postal Service (USPS) offers a flat rate Priority Mail Service.   For $2.90, they will deliver anywhere in the U.S. within two business days. The $2.90 is quite competitive with what UPS charges for out of state and beyond, but is a bit high when compared to what UPS charges for local deliveries. It has been my experience that UPS works out cheaper in the long run. However, for the mass mailings you'll be doing, if speedy delivery is a factor, you may want to do a combination of both UPS (for in state) and USPS (for out-of-state).

Another option to cut mailing costs is to use US Postal Service Third Class rate. If you can afford a longer delivery time, this option can shave a few more cents off.

Reporters And The Charts

It is virtually every musician's and record company owner's dream to see their record on the charts. A chart position offers an undeniable validation of one's creativity and hard work. The charts one sees in prominent magazines like Billboard, Cashbox, Urban Network, and Gavin Report, fall into one of two categories: Retail or Radio. (There's that combination, again!) Some, like those in Hits Magazine offer charts that are a combination of the two. Video Charts are also gaining more attention as new acts and labels take the "video first" route to success.

Retail Charts

From a label's viewpoint, the retail charts would receive the most promotion focus. The retail charts give an indication of actual sales of your record.   As with airplay indexes, since it would be virtually impossible to collect and process information from each of the approximately 8,500 stores (or the 5,000 radio stations) across the country each week, only particular stores are monitored. For Rap, there are about 60-100 of these reporter stores whose consumers' buying habits are used to determine what's hot and what's not. Your "Rap Stores" list has those stores!

Radio Charts

The Radio charts, like the Retail Charts are compiled using certain representative barometers of public taste. Certain stations are more influential than others and carry more weight in affecting a record's chart position and chart progress. Since there are less than a handful of stations with an exclusive Rap Music format, a Rap record's radio chart position will be determined by predominantly "Urban/R&B" radio stations whose formats include Rap. This fact may help to explain why it seems only the "crossover" artists enjoy wide acceptance and position on the charts. For those within Rap's circles, however, there is an awareness of the power of the "mix shows" (typically a 1 or 2-hour feature of many R&B stations which showcases rap releases spun and mixed by a local diskjockey) and College radio stations in generating public demand.   The industry at large has been slow in acknowledging College Radio's power in affecting and effecting sales of Rap Music.   Since college radio doesn't usually answer to corporate sponsors in determining their playlists (that very fact being why distributors and retailers don't rate them as influential), it is the wise Rap label executive who uses and profits from their untapped power.

Keep in mind that despite their prestige, "The Charts" aren't the final measure of success. A record company can be very profitable without ever having an act make the charts. There are many artists who have actually gone gold in particular regions without ever being known on a national level. Also, though there is a definite correlation between the two charts, for Rap they can be opposite sides of different coins. NWA's album, EFIL4ZAGGIN, for example, topped the national retail sales charts in 1991, despite receiving little to no commercial radio airplay. Ice Cube consistently accomplishes the same feat with every album. In the past, and still today there has been a noticeable avoidance of Rap by some commercial radio. Don't let this deter you from what you've set out to accomplish. Rap is one of the few music forms that can accomplish impressive sales without radio support. In fact, a publicized avoidance (ie. banning) of your music by radio for whatever reason, can actually be the best promotional gimmick around to generate interest in and sales of your record. As a record label, in your promotional targeting, your objective should be clear: target the areas where the response to your music is greatest, regardless of their chart influence. (Rap lovers in Wilber, Nebraska have money, too!) Nor should you target only the top stations and stores trying to make a quick jump onto the charts; the competition is stiff (don't you think everyone else with a record is thinking of and acting on that very idea?)

Soundscan

Soundscan is a national system of reporting which uses the barcode to track retail sales. With the introduction of Soundscan , much of the mystery, hype and bribery were taken out of the compiling of the retail sales charts. Over the counter sales are code-scanned at the cash register, and are then automatically reported directly to the computers at Soundscan. Now, powerful promotion people have less ways of influencing the charts by "convincing" retail reporters to adjust their lists before mailing or calling them in to the trades. However, since many Mom & Pop stores have not incorporated the barcode reading technology at their checkout counters, the Soundscan system is much more reliable for tracking and analyzing sales trends in larger stores and chains. Nonetheless, as use of the technology becomes more widespread ALL labels, big or small will be playing on a more level field, and all it takes is a barcode. Of course good promotion helps too, but you're now a little better equipped in that area as well.

SUMMARY of Chapter 10: *"Selling"*

- In the game of succeeding at your hip hop record label, selling is the name of the game.

- **Selling** is what you want to do; it's your ultimate goal

- **Marketing** is how you do it (i.e. Promotion, Publicity and Advertising are forms or techniques of marketing which help you to sell more); There's overlap among all forms of marketing. Some advertising looks like publicity; some advertising might be called creative marketing, etc.

- **Branding** is what you will accomplish in the process; Branding happens whether you focus on it or not. If it's done effectively and consciously, you'll create a strong brand identity and sell more. If not done effectively, then your sales will suffer because of a poorly perceived brand.

- There's an art to selling that you can use to sell to generate sales, get media coverage, get radio and video airplay, and even motivate your team.

- The tools of selling include your media kit, video, samples of your product, website and every means of communication you have at your disposal.

- Momentum Marketing is the name of a strategy you can use to build exposure and create a buzz around your artists' music.

For selling

- *Buzz Your MP3* by Brian Freeman (Author) (Digital)

- *The Complete Guide to Internet Promotion for Musicians, Artists, & Songwriters* by Tim Sweeney, John Dawes

- *This Business of Music Marketing and Promotion* by Tad Lathrop, Jim Pettigrew

Chapter 11
"Effective Distribution of your CD"

<u>Remember the Game Plan</u>

<table>
<tr>
<td>

Now it's time to distribute your product!

</td>
<td>

Monitor your OPERATIONS
Find, sign and develop talented ARTISTS
Create your PRODUCT on CD or other media
MARKET, Promote & Advertise it…
½ SELL IT to stores, distributors and to the public
Maximize additional streams of INCOME
RECOUP your expenses
PAY the players
Make a PROFIT.
GROW your business

</td>
</tr>
</table>

The Big Picture

Your mission is to sell your product. There are three channels you can use to do so. You can sell to the public directly. You can sell to the stores directly. Or, you can sell to distributors. As an independent label, you'll probably be using a combination of all three methods.

Selling to the Public

This is a very simple and direct concept. Depending on how you structure your business, and whether or not you have a major distributor, it may also be the easiest way to sell your product. There are two things to do. 1.Anywhere you or your artist appear, make sure you have product with you ready for sale. And, 2. Drive traffic to your website (see Chapter 6).

Selling to Stores

The major challenge here is in establishing the relationships with the stores. Many larger stores prefer to deal with distributors. However, if you have an in-demand product, you might have more leverage to establish a direct relationship with key stores in key cities.

Selling to Distributors

This part of the game is probably the most critical, and can also be the most frustrating. Your task, however, is actually quite simple in concept.   You have to convince any distributor that he/she can make money by handling your product. Notice I didn't say you have to get them to like your music. It would be nice if all you had to do was have them listen to it, they'd obviously agree it was slammin', they'd order a million copies and you could retire. The reality is that what they think of your music is secondary to what the buying public thinks. There are many distributors making a healthy profit selling music they themselves don't like or even understand.

In the *Hip Hop Entrepreneur Lists of Exposure* is a list of independent distributors you can target. Call each of them and find out who the Rap Singles or Rap CD buyer is. Then mail them a copy or two of your music.

MINDCHECK

Standing Out In The Crowd

Competition in the music industry is fierce. Distributors (as well as music directors, record pool directors and magazine editors) are flooded with product from all over the country. I've talked to radio DJs who have shown me the piles of records and tapes sometimes as many as 25 each day! What this means is you have to stand out from the crowd. Image, presentation, packaging all help to create a positive impression around you, your company, and your artists.   Since they are in the business of selling music, most buyers for distribution companies will actually listen to what is sent to them.   However, sometimes the sheer volume makes it difficult to get around to everything that's sent.   Once they do get around to listening to it, they may not have a chance to listen entirely to everything that's on the tape or record. (So put your best stuff first, or make sure you call their attention directly to the track you want them to focus on.). When you call (every other day or so), be "pleasantly persistent", but respect the fact that the distributor may have a small staff. The buyer you are trying to win over, in addition to getting 25 other calls just like yours, may have to do inventory checks, go to meetings, talk to other accounts etc. He or she, every once in a while, may be just having a bad day. So be considerate. Even if you think you're
getting "the treatment", be pleasantly persistent. Nine times out of ten, if they think your stuff is whack, they'll tell you straight out. Don't worry about them beating around the bush. They are in this to sell records, not spare feelings. Sometimes if a buyer is "busy" every time you call, he or she probably didn't get around to listening to your record when they promised they would, and are just tactfully buying themselves some more time. Stay committed!

When you finally do get around to talking to a potential distributor, hit them with your accomplishments first. You should also have included a brief letter listing any accomplishments when you first mailed your music out. Even if they listened to your music, and they themselves didn't like it, the fact that it's getting airplay somewhere, for example, might save you from getting the axe. Whip out the list of accomplishments and favorable responses and run them down.

Once you get past this hurdle, and you've convinced the buyer that there might really be something going on with your record, you might find yourself invited for a meeting with the distributor. The distributor will want to get some more information before making that final decision to handle your "line" (i.e. Line of Product, see Mindcheck below). Among the first things a distributor will ask you is if you're barcoded. Since you took my advice in the How to Start a Business section, a cool and casual "Of course" will do. They'll then want a street address (not a P.O. Box) to ship returns to. They'll also want to know what formats or configurations (cassette, CD or vinyl) your product will be available on, as well as what price they will have to pay for each configuration. (See Profit & Markup Section.) Keep in mind that you are a company now. You're not just a guy with a record. Your pitch should include telling the distributor what "we" are planning to do with the company, how "we" are plan to market and promote the record, to give them a sense of the future.

An important note: the agreement to distribute your product WILL NOT be a written agreement between you and the distributor. Also, your distributor will most likely request exclusivity for the particular region that they distribute to. The reason for this is simple. Many distributors in a given region often service the same retailers. If your record is available from two distributors in the same area, a store owner/buyer may not remember which one of the two your record was ordered from and return them or charge them to the wrong distributor: an accounting headache for the distributor and for you as well.

Before you choose any distributor, make sure you have confidence in his competence and his ability to sell your record. You may want to contact several stores and speak to the buyers to find out their opinions on specific distributors before you make your choice.

Where's My Money?

When a distributor decides to take your product, he or she will speak in terms of "handling your line"-- referring to your product line, that is, your catalog, or your other (future) releases. You may not have thought about it before, but you've made it this far, don't back out now. From the distributor's point of view, he wants to make sure that no one, especially him, gets the short end of the stick. His terms of payment to you are sixty days. Both he and you know, that sixty days from the day you delivered your records to his warehouse, you'll be calling him with a little question: WHERE'S MY MONEY!!? O.K, so this is the scenario: 2 months ago, he requested 1000 records from you as an initial order based on the strength of the record, as well as the initial response he got from some of his key accounts. He sent the records out to the stores that ordered it. You continued to get airplay, you even saw your record in some of the local stores and had a little celebration. From the day they left his warehouse, he hasn't really been in contact with your records. The only time he may have heard of it again was if there were reorders. But let's suppose for this exercise, that there were no reorders, but that there were no returns either. Let's assume also that he pays you. Next month, however, when the stores get around to doing their inventory, we find that 500 of those thousand records didn't actually sell, and get returned to his warehouse. What happens then? Your distributor will probably call you with a little question of his own: WHERE'S MY MONEY?! Many distributors have gotten burned this way, and are very wary about being burned again. Your plan to be around tomorrow is his insurance against something like this happening. From his point of view, if you had an ongoing account, with, for instance, another record that was selling, he would just deduct the money you owe him from your check for the second record , and everything would be O.K. To guard against the scenario described above, your distributor may pay you in installments so as to stretch payment out over several accounting periods.

The Distribution Process

Assuming that you've secured independent distribution for your release, here are the steps involved in getting your record on the shelves of your local store through your distributor.

Announcement

Several weeks before your record is actually released, your distributor will want to know the following about your release:

1. Title
2. Artist
3. Selection/Barcode #
4. Available formats, and
5. Expected release date of your record.

This information will be included in the regular correspondence or catalog updates the distributor provides to his/her accounts. If you've made any fliers or posters, you may ask the distributor to include these in the mailing as well.

Pre-Soliciting/Pre-Selling

In the pre-soliciting stage, the distributor starts to generate orders for your record. He or she may send a compilation tape with that week's new releases (yours and other labels') or cassette samples to all the store accounts. Upon listening to the music, the stores will place their (usually small) initial order based on their feeling as to its sale potential. This process may take about 3-4 weeks from the time you supply the samples to the time your distributor notifies you of an initial order.

The Purchase Order (P.O.)

After compiling the orders from the stores, the distributor's buying department will issue a "Purchase Order" to your company requesting an initial amount of product. They may mail it, fax it, or just request it over the phone (ask for the paperwork also if they phone it). However they get it to you, make sure you get a purchase order number as well. The purchase order will include the selection number, quantity and formats requested, and the wholesale price agreed upon at your initial meeting.

Satisfying the Order

Most distributors will expect product to be delivered about 4 weeks from the time you receive the purchase order. If you've been cautious, that still gives you enough time to give the order to print the jackets and inserts, have them shipped to the pressing plant, have the pressing plant press and duplicate your records and ship them to the distributor. If you've already pressed your records and tapes, you can ship them out the same day. Try not to split orders. By this I mean, if your distributor places an order for a certain number of cassettes and records, and you have enough records on hand, but not enough cassettes, hold on to the order until everything is ready, and then ship them out. Your distributor will appreciate you saving him the extra paperwork. Another reason to wait, is that some distributors themselves won't send your order to the retail accounts until everything is ready. It would require massive amounts of paperwork to keep track of which stores got tapes, which got lps, and how many, and who needs to be sent what and how many and in which format at a future date. (whew!) Better to have the records sitting in your warehouse, (or living room) than in his. When placing your order with the printing company or pressing plant or tape duplication house, keep in mind that certain times of year are more hectic than others. Right before a major conference or seminar, or around the time that most major labels are releasing product, are bad times to expect speedy completion of your order. Plan ahead.

Shipping

Most distributors will pay the inbound freight (that is, the cost of shipping it to them) on all orders. When either you (usually through UPS) or the pressing plant ships product to the distributor, the distributor's purchase order number should accompany the shipment, and if possible, it should be written on each box in the shipment. If some or all of the shipment will be used as promotional copies, make sure you or your pressing plant identifies the ones to be used as such. The usual promo-copy identification practice is to punch holes in or clip the corners of the promo copies. It's a good practice to prevent records you've allocated as promotional from ending up on store shelves being offered for sale.

Collecting Your Payment

In most cases, in order to get paid, you'll have to submit an invoice at the appropriate time (60 days) to initiate the process of payment. Remember, you are now asking the distributor to part with money, expect a few obstacles and delays here. Keep in mind also, his wariness about being burned by returns. There are no tricks here or secret advice I can give. Hopefully, your distributor's integrity and reputation will be enough to prevent any bad experiences in this area. I've devoted a lot of space to the challenge of getting distributors since this will be a critical milestone in the ultimate success of your company. It's up to you to make it happen!

What To Do If You Can't Get A Distributor

In the hierarchy of the independent distribution world, the distributors are at the top, then come the onestops, then the retail outlets. If you find yourself with a good record but unable to convince any distributor to handle it, try a different level in the hierarchy. As a small label, you might have better luck dealing with a onestop. Some will be willing to deal with you, others (in one of the many more catch-22's of the business) will only buy your record if they can get it through a distributor (so that they don't get burned by returns). Since the onestops are often the distributor's larger accounts, this can actually give you a way to get in. If you can generate a real buzz and a real demand for your record that makes its way to the ears of the onestop buyer, he may be able to exert some pressure up the ladder to get the distributors to deal with you. Likewise, if the retail outlets (stores) are asking the onestop to supply them with this "hot new record that everyone's asking about", you can be sure that you'll start to see some action.

At worst, you can start out using the "MC-Hammer" route to success. As the story goes: Hammer started out selling his records to the public and to the smaller stores from out the back of his car. This is still a reality even today. It means effectively being your own distributor. A few of the artists in the Reggae, Calypso, and other Caribbean music scenes in New York, for example, still sell their music this way. This self-distribution process entails the tedious job of "selling on consignment". That is, a store will agree to take several copies of your record "on account". (You'll want to do this with as many stores as you can. Usually, the "Mom & Pop" stores, and other indie-friendly outlets will be more willing. However, there are some big shots who still look out for the struggling artist--Tower Records, for example was still taking indie product on consignment as of early 1992.) The tedious part comes when you have to physically make the rounds to all of these stores to find out if your records sold, and to get paid. Obviously, your means to success through self-distribution are limited. However, it can be the first step in building a following, and a history, and some real sales which can pave the way for your growth into the big time.

With a good distributor behind you, you'll have the means to get your record in stores. THE MEANS, NOT THE GUARANTEE. Pay close attention here. Most young labels make the mistake of thinking that all their prayers will be answered by hooking up with a distributor. Your distributor should be viewed as just one part of YOUR promotion campaign.

What Distributors REALLY Do

If distributors were promotion companies, then they'd be promotion companies.

Distributors supply a demand.

This is how most distributors actually define what they do. Many new labels tend to overlook these points and expect some miraculous sales to result from their distributor's promotion. Though it is in every distributor's best interest to promote the records they handle, it is YOUR responsibility to create the demand for your record.

"You Mean I'm NOT Special???"

Many distributors pride themselves on the personal service and attention they provide to each of their label accounts. Many of them do just that. However, from a purely business standpoint, there is a reality that you can't wish away. Keep in mind that your distributor has other accounts (accounts which were keeping him in business before you came along), with the same concerns, questions and desire for profit that you have. They all make demands on the distributor's time during the course of business hours. You might want to ask yourself a very simple question. Where do you rank in profit benefit to your distributor? Are you the million seller account for whom he should drop everything and speak to when you call?   Are you the consistently selling account who is keeping the distributor's rent and overhead paid? Or, have you just stepped onto the scene with no past and an undecided future.   The truth is, you've got some work and some proving ahead of you if you want to be as high a priority as any of the regulars. Eventually, if you maintain a consistent relationship with your distributor long enough, you'll start to see a change in how you are perceived.

<u>**SUMMARY of Chapter 11: *"Distribution..."***</u>

- One of the important keys to your success as a record label is securing distribution for your product. You can distribute directly to the public, to stores , work with distributors or use a combination of all three methods.

- Familiarize yourself with the distribution process that most distributors employ when dealing with independent labels.

<u>**RESOURCES for Chapter 11: *"Distribution...""***</u>
(BOOKS, AUDIO PROGRAMS, MAGAZINES, ORGANIZATIONS & WEBSITES)

For understanding the Music Industry Game of distribution
- *This Business of Music*

- *Fight the Power* by Chuck D; some great ideas on independent distribution

- *Confessions of a Record Producer* by Moses Avalon; insider info on major label distribution

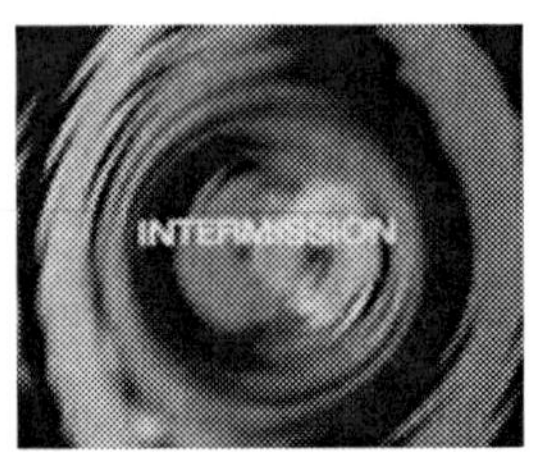

HALF-TIME!
"A Review of Strategy"

CHAPTER 12

"Piecing it all Together"

A BUSINESS STARTUP, RELEASE, AND PROMOTION TIMETABLE

A BUSINESS STARTUP, RELEASE, AND PROMOTION TIMETABLE

I. DO IMMEDIATELY: Personal Preparation & Business Startup

Choose to grow; Get any additional resources from Hip Hop Entrepreneur Reading List at

Choose your game (Ego or Economic; Ethics or Everything Goes!)

Set your goals (**6 month, 1 year, 2 year and 5 year goals**)

Decide on Business structure.

<u>Choose your company name</u>. (Choose separate Publishing Company name also.) Research company name to see if it is already being used. Your county clerk's office has listings of all registered companies. Visit local Chamber of Commerce, County Clerks or relevant local and state office to conduct name search. The Performance Rights Organization you choose (BMI, ASCAP) will also search for prior use of your Publishing company name.

Reserve your domain name. See tips for choosing an effective URL.

Design your logo [Visit the HipHopBiz.com website for Links to Service & Resource Options we recommend]

Trademark your logo if you choose.

Obtain and complete a DBA or "Fictitious name" form (if required in your state). Remember to include Publishing company name on DBA form as a subsidiary company, if allowed.

Decide on your business and shipping addresses. Obtain a Post Office box if necessary. (Include Publishing company name on your P.O. Box application form as a recipient of mail.)

Have letterhead, envelopes and business cards printed.

Open a business checking account. Include Publishing company name on bank forms (very important) as an alternate payee.

Contact Uniform Code Council and apply for membership.

Contact BMI or ASCAP for Publisher forms. Register publishing company. Make sure artist registers as well.

Contact Copyright Office to get appropriate forms. Make sure artist copyrights music.

Obtain Contact IRS, SBA and your State for suggested forms, kits and pamphlets.

Locate and start account with suppliers (Pressing plant, tape duplicator, printing company or "All-in-one" company.)

II. DO WHILE THE TRACK IS BEING PRODUCED

Register song with performing rights organization. (BMI or ASCAP)

Have photography done. Order 8X10's.

Decide on your selection number.

Order barcode.

Design the 12" jacket, cassette or CD insert.

Design 12" label, cassette imprint, or CD text.

Prepare artist press kit.

Get any input and feedback on record during this stage if possible.

III. DO JUST AFTER THE FINAL MIX OF RECORD

Begin Momentum Marketing Campaign [See Momentum Marketing]

Have mastering done and get test presses OR make tapes of final mix. (You may want to hold off on the mastering until you get more feedback on the tapes from your pre-release recipients.)

Set a release date. (Don't sweat it if you miss it. Things happen, especially if this is your first time.)

Provide copies (tape or test press) to distributors.

Provide copies to pool directors.

Provide copies to any clubs or show promoters.

Provide copies to magazines along with press kit. Send to key people whose opinions are important.

If you've held off on mastering, the next phase begins once everyone is happy with any re- mix. It would be best to be sure of the strength of the track before making it available to your distributor for pre-selling. (A retailer's bad first impression may be hard to change.)

If you've already done your mastering and have no plans to go back into the studio, the next phase begins once your initial order comes in from your distributor.

IV. DO ONCE YOU GET YOUR INITIAL ORDER FROM THE DISTRIBUTOR

Decide on the amount of your initial pressing.

Give your printer the mechanicals and the green light. Have printer ship directly to pressing plant. If you're using an "all-in-one" all you need to do is hand over the D.A.T. or two-track, the mechanicals (or rough layout), the barcode, pay your money and wait.

IV. DO ONCE YOUR RECORDS/TAPES/CD'S ARE MANUFACTURED

Since your printing company should have been keeping you up to date with the progress of your project, there should be no surprises, misspellings, omissions (check the spine for selection #) or anything else to damage your company's professional image.

Provide your distributor with initial order and any promos needed.

Do your mailings to Pools, Stores, Radio, Retail, and then...

Continue Momentum Marketing Campaign

Follow up, Follow up

AND NOW.....BACK TO THE GAME!

Chapter 13:
"Other Ways To Make Money With Your Label's Music"

<u>Remember the Game Plan</u>

There are many other ways to make money in the music industry!

Monitor your OPERATIONS
Find, sign and develop talented ARTISTS
Create your PRODUCT on CD or other media
MARKET, Promote & Advertise it…
SELL IT to stores, distributors and to the public
½ Maximize additional streams of INCOME
RECOUP your expenses
PAY the players
Make a PROFIT.
GROW your business

Making More Money With Your Music (For Artist And Label)

It is the unwise business person who puts all of his/her eggs in one basket. The music industry provides other ways to capitalize on the public's demand for your Rap music. Following are overviews of and advice concerning each of the indicated areas of interest. They are listed here primarily to initiate action on your part in that particular direction. Gather as much information as you can in each area so as not to be taken advantage of.

Performances

Traditionally, this is where most new artists generate their income. Since your record company might still be "recouping" its expenses well into the life of your record, the artist and manager should be exploiting every other area of the artist's career. Make sure you perfect your stage performance. Many Rap artists, relying solely on the power of the word and slammin' beats, have neglected this part of pleasing their public. Should you choose to hire a professional to help out in this area, there are dance companies which specialize in helping the artist bring more into their live performances.   There are which specialize in performance choreography with a Hip Hop-centric emphasis. Remember, how your artist backs up his/her record on stage can form the basis of a loyal pool of customers for your product and a demand for your performance.

Performance Royalties

Once your record hits the big time, and is being played on major stations across the country, the performance right organization that tracks airplay (BMI or ASCAP) will initiate the process of payments (usually quarterly) for the performance of your music. The literature you'll request from them will explain the process in more detail.

Movie Soundtracks

Usually a song is licensed to a movie production company for a one-time fee. There will usually be two licenses sought by the production company: A "synchronization license" which is sought from the copyright owner (usually the artist) and a "master use license" which is sought from the owner of the master recording of the music (usually the record company). Keep abreast of what's going on in the film industry to increase your chances of getting your music exposed this way. One way to do this is to join the Black Filmmaker's Foundation (212-941-3944).

Whereas a mechanical license permits a user to mechanically reproduce an underlying musical coposition on a compact disc, prerecorded tape, phonorecord, or other audio only format, the synchronization license permits the accompaniment of a moving image with the underlying musical piece. Consequently, the "synch" license is required for videos, motion pictures, television, commercials, and other visual formats that are combined with musical works. The synch license is generally a grant from the publisher or his/her licensor to the producer of the visual work which authorizes the utilization of the underlying musical composition. Similar to a mechanical license, any proceeds go to the benefit of the publisher and/or writer (i.e. the owner of the copyright in the underlying work). Licensing agencies such as the Harry Fox Agency and AMRA issue synchronization licenses on behalf of their affiliated publishers and give fee quotations for such synchronization.

The "synch" license itself does not permit the use of any specific recording of the particular musical composition. A separate recording or master use license is required for such a use or, in the alternative, a new recording of the work would have to be produced.

If a performance is captured live on a medium such as television, the first airing of that show containing that performance does not require a synch license (though it will require a "performance license"). Subsequent broadcasts of that same performance, however, would require the appropriate synchronization license.

Fees and advances for synch licenses vary greatly depending upon the prospective use (e.g. whether the song will be used as a title song of a movie or in a commercial), the prominence of use (background music or featured performance), the popularity of the song and/or the songwriter, the media in which the song is to be used (e.g. television, motion pictures or even a video arcade game), the budget of the potential licensee, and the amount of goods that are to be initially manufactured, as well as other factors. For motion picture use payment in full, from the producer to the licensor is the norm.

Furthermore, new technological uses have created new markets and the potential for greater earnings through synchronization. In addition, questions have arisen regarding such new technological uses as cable, pay per view, pay television, satellite rebroadcast, home video, interactive video, and the internet.

In the past, one of the most troublesome areas in synchronization license fee negotiations had been home video. In the mid 1980's when home video quickly became a mass consumer market, it was a relatively new phenomena and thus there were no real firmly established standards. Along those same lines, similar issues have arisen for existing media, as many agreements for previously licensed musical works were negotiated prior to the advent of the "video age." Therefore, many licenses granted were sometimes limited to the existing technology by reference as they sometimes failed to include language allowing broader use for newer media, thus posing a similar challenge at the advent of internet technology.

Due to such limitations or failures, rights owners had to turn to the courts to determine whether an initial synch license, entered into many years ago, included the previously unanticipated release of the film or program on new medias such as home video, or the internet. A 1988 Circuit Court decision seems to indicate that such a license does not.

Faced with the possibility of litigation, users of licensed music must consider going back to the source of the original synch license for new rights or risk the consequences. For example, old agreements which provided for eight millimeter films for home use now probably need to acquire new home video synch licenses and/or internet use licenses.

It is now more common for contracts to include a catch-all phrase such as ". . . any and all media now known or hereafter invented when addressing to scope of the synch license" This phrase, or similar language, is used by attorneys and production companies to keep up with and anticipate technological developments. Thus, uses in such newer technologies as laser optical disc, compact disc video, or live audio and video streaming, can be accounted for even if not specifically anticipated when negotiating the original synch license.

Commercials/Endorsements

Let your ethics be your guide.

Many companies, in an effort to target certain groups of potential customers in their advertising, are using Rap artists and/or Rap music to "sell" their products. Controversy exists as to whether Rap artists (or any artist, for that matter) should endorse products which are potentially harmful to the kids and population at large to whom the artist appeals and to whom the products are aimed. There are companies that have had a history of neglecting the communities or concerns of the people who comprise their customer base; companies that have concentrated their targeting of potentially harmful products within certain neighborhoods rather than others. Quite a few Rappers have openly expressed their unwillingness to endorse the products of these companies.

Since for those companies, the return on the advertising dollar is significant, the compensation for the endorsements can at times be quite inviting to the new artist. The controversy will continue as each artist will have to let their conscience guide them through the dilemma. You won't have to worry about this right away. For now, your first concern should be building a big enough name for yourself (or your artist) so that you can have this dilemma.

Merchandising

If the image of your artist or your company becomes popular enough, and you can generate some income for your company through merchandising.   A merchandising company will request rights to market the names and/or logos of the artist or the company.   The onetime merchandising fee that you are paid will authorize them to put the artist's (or your company's) logo on hats, t-shirts, jackets, and whatever else there's a market for.   Since the merchandising company will be the one producing the items, you as the label, will receive royalties from the sale of the products.   A royalty rate in the area of 20% is not unusual. If your artist is on tour, the merchandiser may want to have the exclusive right to sell the t-shirts, hats, jackets at the venues where the artist is performing.

Foreign Sales

Even if you don't have a licensing arrangement with a foreign based company, you can still sell your record overseas through Import/Export companies.   There's a major advantage to making sales this way. Unlike distributors here at home, when an Import/Export company purchases copies of your record for sale overseas, it's a cash sale.   No consignment, no returns.   It's their responsibility and that of their overseas account to sell the records. The U.K., Japan, (and maybe soon the restructured Soviet countries) have growing markets open to what Rap has to offer. Many distributors and onestops are involved in overseas markets, and may be able to recommend some import/export companies that deal in countries in which they themselves do not.

<u>**SUMMARY of Chapter 13: *"Other Ways To Make Money..."***</u>

• As an independent label, you can earn money through performances, commercial endorsements, performance royalties, movie soundtracks, merchandising and foreign sales.

<u>**RESOURCES** for Chapter 13: ***"Other Ways to Make Money"***</u>
(BOOKS, AUDIO PROGRAMS, MAGAZINES, ORGANIZATIONS & WEBSITES)

For Licensing
> • *The Licensing Book* by Andy Krinner

CHAPTER 14:
"Money Matters"

Recouping Expenses, Paying the Players and Making a Profit

Remember the Game Plan

<table>
<tr>
<td>

Let's talk money!

</td>
<td>

Monitor your OPERATIONS
Find, sign and develop talented ARTISTS
Create your PRODUCT on CD or other media
MARKET, Promote & Advertise it…
SELL IT to stores, distributors and to the public
 Maximize additional streams of INCOME
½ RECOUP your expenses
½ PAY the players
½ Make a PROFIT.
GROW your business

</td>
</tr>
</table>

Recouping Expenses

Recouping costs simply means making sure that you are reimbursed for the money your spent developing the product. This standard industry practice is a basic fact of doing business. As a label owner
Tip: Keep track of expenses as well as income based on project or artist, so that it's easier to do your accounting.

Paying the Players

There are many ways that you can "Pay the players" on your team. Whether staff members, independent contractors or artists for hire, your commitment to compensating your team is what will set you apart from other labels. The challenge many labels—and, in fact, many companies in general-- face is that their expenses are usually greater than revenues. By the time money comes in from the sale of product, the label has most likely been operating under a tremendous amount of debt. Therefore, it usually is not in a position to pay royalties as might otherwise be desired.

Hopefully, however, once you institute the profit-making tips in the next section, you'll be able to any of a number of methods (Paypal, direct deposit, writing checks directly) of getting money in the hands of your key players.

The 7-point Strategy for Making a Profit

There are only two ways to earn a profit in business: charge more or spend less.

1. Maximize streams of income

Introduce other items with lower unit production costs

Sell music in digital format

2. Reduce overhead and fixed costs

Introduce The Cost Cutting Measures in Chapter 7

3. Decrease unit cost per item sold

Take advantage of quantity discounts

Order in bulk

4. Sell Services to deep pockets

5. Sell Your Company

6. Work with affiliates. Find an affiliate who is already reaching your audience that can sell 10,000 units on your behalf. ask yourself the question - how could i sell 10,000 units in 90 days? the best may is to partner with someone is already reaching 100,000 people who fit your demo.

7. Reduce taxable income

Following is an example of how to do just that.

Doing Your Taxes as a SOLE PROPRIETORSHIP
Explanation Of Sample Entries For Black Gold Records

Sample startup forms and tax returns for Derek I. Black have been provided. Derek is currently working as a Sales Manager for a small clothing company. His yearly salary from this job is $25,000. He has always been interested in music and (with loans from his friends and family, and a cash advance from his credit card) decided to launch his own company in January of the past year. Derek is single, lives alone, and runs his label, Black Gold Records, from his apartment. He originally pressed 5000 units (CDs, records and cassettes) which, with photography, separation, printing, etc., cost about $5000 to manufacture.

By the end of the year, (after 12 months of operation), Derek had collected checks from his distributor, income from website sales, and sales at live appearances in the amount of $30,500. Records totaling about $100 were returned as "unsold" or "defective".

The completed sample forms related to Derek's sole proprietorship provided here are:

Form SS-4 (Application for Employer Identification Number)
Form 1040 (Federal Income Tax Return)
Schedule C (Profit or Loss from a Business)
Form 8829 (Business use of the Home)
Form SE (Self Employment Tax)
Following are explanations of how Derek filled out some of the line items on the forms. The scenario presented here as been made quite simple for the purpose of illustrating basic principles of income reporting and tax computation. Your situation may vary.

NOTE: "N/A" stands for "not applicable" and means that the specific question does not apply to Derek's situation.

Form SS-4

There are several circumstances under which you might need to file for an Employer Identification Number (EIN). In Derek's case, he is a sole proprietor who expects to have employees. In the event he opted to immediately start his business as a corporation, he would also need an EIN in order to file the necessary forms, for instance, to become an S-Corporation.

Form **SS-4** (Rev. December 2001) Department of the Treasury Internal Revenue Service	**Application for Employer Identification Number** (For use by employers, corporations, partnerships, trusts, estates, churches, government agencies, Indian tribal entities, certain individuals, and others.) ► See separate instructions for each line. ► Keep a copy for your records.	EIN OMB No. 1545-0003

1 Legal name of entity (or individual) for whom the EIN is being requested
DEREK I. BLACK

2 Trade name of business (if different from name on line 1)
BLACK GOLD RECORDS

3 Executor, trustee, "care of" name

4a Mailing address (room, apt., suite no. and street, or P.O. box)
P.O. BOX 618

4b City, state, and ZIP code
NEW YORK NY 10008

5a Street address (if different) (Do not enter a P.O. box.)

5b City, state, and ZIP code

6 County and state where principal business is located

7a Name of principal officer, general partner, grantor, owner, or trustor

7b SSN, ITIN, or EIN

8a Type of entity (check only one box)
- ☒ Sole proprietor (SSN) _______
- ☐ Partnership
- ☐ Corporation (enter form number to be filed) ►
- ☐ Personal service corp.
- ☐ Church or church-controlled organization
- ☐ Other nonprofit organization (specify) ►
- ☐ Other (specify) ►
- ☐ Estate (SSN of decedent) _______
- ☐ Plan administrator (SSN) _______
- ☐ Trust (SSN of grantor) _______
- ☐ National Guard   ☐ State/local government
- ☐ Farmers' cooperative   ☐ Federal government/military
- ☐ REMIC   ☐ Indian tribal governments/enterprises
- Group Exemption Number (GEN) ►

8b If a corporation, name the state or foreign country (if applicable) where incorporated — State / Foreign country

9 Reason for applying (check only one box)
- ☒ Started new business (specify type) ► *RECORD LABEL*
- ☐ Hired employees (Check the box and see line 12.)
- ☐ Compliance with IRS withholding regulations
- ☐ Other (specify) ►
- ☐ Banking purpose (specify purpose) ►
- ☐ Changed type of organization (specify new type) ►
- ☐ Purchased going business
- ☐ Created a trust (specify type) ►
- ☐ Created a pension plan (specify type) ►

10 Date business started or acquired (month, day, year)
JAN 1ST

11 Closing month of accounting year
DECEMBER

12 First date wages or annuities were paid or will be paid (month, day, year). **Note:** If applicant is a withholding agent, enter date income will first be paid to nonresident alien. (month, day, year) ► *MAY 1ST*

13 Highest number of employees expected in the next 12 months. **Note:** If the applicant does not expect to have any employees during the period, enter "-0-".
— Agricultural / Household / Other

14 Check one box that best describes the principal activity of your business.
- ☐ Construction ☐ Rental & leasing ☐ Transportation & warehousing
- ☐ Real estate   ☐ Manufacturing   ☐ Finance & insurance
- ☐ Health care & social assistance ☐ Accommodation & food service ☐ Other (specify)
- ☐ Wholesale–agent/broker ☒ Wholesale–other ☐ Retail

15 Indicate principal line of merchandise sold; specific construction work done; products produced; or services provided.
RECORDED MUSIC

16a Has the applicant ever applied for an employer identification number for this or any other business? . . . . ☐ Yes ☒ No
Note: If "Yes," please complete lines 16b and 16c.

16b If you checked "Yes" on line 16a, give applicant's legal name and trade name shown on prior application if different from line 1 or 2 above.
Legal name ►   Trade name ►

16c Approximate date when, and city and state where, the application was filed. Enter previous employer identification number if known.
Approximate date when filed (mo., day, year) / City and state where filed / Previous EIN

Third Party Designee — Complete this section only if you want to authorize the named individual to receive the entity's EIN and answer questions about the completion of this form.
Designee's name
Designee's telephone number (include area code) ( )
Address and ZIP code
Designee's fax number (include area code) ( )

Under penalties of perjury, I declare that I have examined this application, and to the best of my knowledge and belief, it is true, correct, and complete.

Name and title (type or print clearly) ► *DEREK BLACK, PRESIDENT*
Applicant's telephone number (include area code) ( )

Signature ► *Derek Black*   Date ►
Applicant's fax number (include area code) ( )

For Privacy Act and Paperwork Reduction Act Notice, see separate instructions.   Cat. No. 16055N   Form **SS-4** (Rev. 12-2001)

Schedule C (Profit or Loss From Business)—Page 1

SCHEDULE C (Form 1040)	Profit or Loss From Business	OMB No. 1545-0074
Department of the Treasury Internal Revenue Service	(Sole Proprietorship) ▶ Partnerships, joint ventures, etc., must file Form 1065 or 1065-B. ▶ Attach to Form 1040 or 1041. ▶ See Instructions for Schedule C (Form 1040).	**Millennium** Attachment Sequence No. 09

Name of proprietor: **DEREK I. BLACK** Social security number (SSN): **123 45 6789**

A Principal business or profession, including product or service (see page C-1 of the instructions): **SALE OF RECORDED MUSIC** B Enter code from pages C-7, 8, & 9: ▶ **7 1 1 5 1 0**

C Business name. If no separate business name, leave blank. **BLACK GOLD RECORDS** D Employer ID number (EIN), if any: **1 3 0 0 0 0 0 0 0**

E Business address (including suite or room no.) ▶ **PO BOX 618**
City, town or post office, state, and ZIP code **NY NY 10008-0618**

F Accounting method: (1) ☐ Cash (2) ☑ Accrual (3) ☐ Other (specify) ▶ ....

G Did you "materially participate" in the operation of this business during 2002? If "No," see page C-3 for limit on losses . ☑ Yes ☐ No

H If you started or acquired this business during this year check here .... ▶ ☐

Part I Income

1	Gross receipts or sales. **Caution.** If this income was reported to you on Form W-2 and the "Statutory employee" box on that form was checked, see page C-3 and check here ▶ ☐	1	30500 00
2	Returns and allowances	2	100 00
3	Subtract line 2 from line 1	3	30400 00
4	Cost of goods sold (from line 42 on page 2)	4	6750 00
5	**Gross profit.** Subtract line 4 from line 3	5	23650 00
6	Other income, including Federal and state gasoline or fuel tax credit or refund (see page C-3)	6	
7	**Gross income.** Add lines 5 and 6 ▶	7	23650 00

Part II Expenses. Enter expenses for business use of your home **only** on line 30.

8	Advertising	8	300	19	Pension and profit-sharing plans	19	
9	Bad debts from sales or services (see page C-3)	9		20	Rent or lease (see page C-5):		
10	Car and truck expenses (see page C-3)	10		a	Vehicles, machinery, and equipment	20a	
11	Commissions and fees	11	1000 00	b	Other business property	20b	
12	Depletion	12		21	Repairs and maintenance	21	
13	Depreciation and section 179 expense deduction (not included in Part III) (see page C-4)	13		22	Supplies (not included in Part III)	22	150
14	Employee benefit programs (other than on line 19)	14		23	Taxes and licenses	23	
15	Insurance (other than health)	15		24	Travel, meals, and entertainment:		
16	Interest:			a	Travel	24a	500
a	Mortgage (paid to banks, etc.)	16a		b	Meals and entertainment		
b	Other	16b		c	Enter nondeductible amount included on line 24b (see page C-5)		
17	Legal and professional services	17	700	d	Subtract line 24c from line 24b	24d	
18	Office expense	18	1500	25	Utilities	25	1000
				26	Wages (less employment credits)	26	
				27	Other expenses (from line 48 on page 2)	27	9163

28	**Total expenses** before expenses for business use of home. Add lines 8 through 27 in columns ▶	28	14313
29	Tentative profit (loss). Subtract line 28 from line 7	29	9337
30	Expenses for business use of your home. Attach **Form 8829**	30	330
31	**Net profit or (loss).** Subtract line 30 from line 29. • If a profit, enter on **Form 1040, line 12,** and also on **Schedule SE, line 2** (statutory employees, see page C-6). Estates and trusts, enter on Form 1041, line 3. • If a loss, you **must** go to line 32.	31	9007
32	If you have a loss, check the box that describes your investment in this activity (see page C-6). • If you checked 32a, enter the loss on **Form 1040, line 12,** and also on **Schedule SE, line 2** (statutory employees, see page C-6). Estates and trusts, enter on Form 1041, line 3. • If you checked 32b, you **must** attach **Form 6198.**	32a ☑ All investment is at risk. 32b ☐ Some investment is not at risk.	

For Paperwork Reduction Act Notice, see Form 1040 instructions. Cat. No. 11334P Schedule C (Form 1040) Millennum Ed.

Schedule C (Profit or Loss From Business)—Page 2

Part III — Cost of Goods Sold (see page C-6)

33 Method(s) used to value closing inventory: a ☑ Cost   b ☐ Lower of cost or market   c ☐ Other (attach explanation)

34 Was there any change in determining quantities, costs, or valuations between opening and closing inventory? If "Yes," attach explanation . . . . ☐ Yes   ☑ No

35 Inventory at beginning of year. If different from last year's closing inventory, attach explanation	35	0
36 Purchases less cost of items withdrawn for personal use	36	6750
37 Cost of labor. Do not include any amounts paid to yourself	37	—
38 Materials and supplies	38	—
39 Other costs	39	—
40 Add lines 35 through 39	40	6750
41 Inventory at end of year	41	0
42 Cost of goods sold. Subtract line 41 from line 40. Enter the result here and on page 1, line 4	42	6750

Part IV — Information on Your Vehicle.
Complete this part **only** if you are claiming car or truck expenses on line 10 and are not required to file Form 4562 for this business. See the instructions for line 13 on page C-4 to find out if you must file.

43 When did you place your vehicle in service for business purposes? (month, day, year) ▶ ...... / ...... / ......

44 Of the total number of miles you drove your vehicle during this year, enter the number of miles you used your vehicle for:

a Business 12,000   b Commuting ....   c Other 3,000

45 Do you (or your spouse) have another vehicle available for personal use? . . . . ☐ Yes   ☑ No

46 Was your vehicle available for personal use during off-duty hours? . . . . ☑ Yes   ☐ No

47a Do you have evidence to support your deduction? . . . . ☑ Yes   ☐ No

b If "Yes," is the evidence written? . . . . ☑ Yes   ☐ No

Part V — Other Expenses. List below business expenses not included on lines 8–26 or line 30.

VIDEO PRODUCTION	5000
WEBSITE HOSTING	600
INTERNET ACCESS	263
GRAPHIC DESIGN	300
TRANSPORTATION	1000
PROMOTION	2,000
48 Total other expenses. Enter here and on page 1, line 27	**48** 9163

233

Schedule C (Profit or Loss From Business)

After reading the instructions in Publication 334, Derek decides on his accounting method and inventory valuation method. He fills out all of the requested information in the top section

B. The code that best describes a record label is 711510 "Independent Artists, writers and performers"
D. This is the employer ID number he received after submitting form SS-4 (See Appendix)
F. Accounting method is "accrual"; Businesses that keep an inventory must use the accrual method.

Part I Income
Line 1.   Derek's income from website sales, live appearances and distributors total $30,500.

Line 2. Returns total $100. This includes customer returns as well as an amount charged to his account by the distributor.

Line 4. Derek uses the worksheet on page 2 of Schedule C to figure Cost of Goods Sold.
> *From page 2:*
> Line 35 Since this is Derek's first year, his inventory (value of records in stock) at the beginning of the year was $0.(since he had no records or tapes or cd's)
> Line 36 The 3,000 CDs, 1000 12"s and 1000 cassettes cost Derek $6,750 to manufacture.
> Line 41 Between his distributor and his promotion, Derek got rid of everything that was pressed or duplicated. His ending inventory on Dec 31 was valued at $0. (If Derek hadn't received the check for the full amount of records given to the distributor, he would have had to value his closing inventory at the amount of the unsold records sitting in the distributor's warehouse. It's not considered sold until the check arrives.)
> Line 42 Cost of Goods Sold, therefore, is $6,750. The "cost of goods sold" is simply how much was spent to actually produce and manufacture the products.

Line 5.   Derek's gross profit--$23,650--is the difference between his net sales and his cost of goods sold.

Part II
Lines 8 thru 27 list other expenses Derek incurred by running the business. Since he kept good records of his expenditures during the year, it was easier to itemize them.

Line 28.   His total expenses for the year including video production, promotion, utilities etc., were $14,313

Line 29.   Derek's tentative profit is $9,337
[That's $23,650 (line 7) minus -$14,313 (Line 28) equals –9,337]

Line 30.   Since Derek had a gross profit, he will be able to deduct additional expenses for using his home as his place of business (see Form 8829). If, for example, his gross income were zero or negative, he would have not have been able to deduct any expenses for business use of his home.

Line 31   His net profit for the year, therefore is **$9,007!**

Form 8829 Expenses for Business Use of Your Home

Form **8829**	**Expenses for Business Use of Your Home**	OMB No. 1545-1266

Department of the Treasury
Internal Revenue Service (89)

▶ File only with Schedule C (Form 1040). Use a separate Form 8829 for each home you used for business during the year.

▶ See separate instructions.

Millennium

Attachment Sequence No. **66**

Name(s) of proprietor(s): DEREK I. BLACK

Your social security number: 123 45 6789

Part I Part of Your Home Used for Business

1	Area used regularly and exclusively for business, regularly for day care, or for storage of inventory or product samples (see instructions)	**1**	400 S.F.
2	Total area of home	**2**	1200 S.F.
3	Divide line 1 by line 2. Enter the result as a percentage	**3**	33 %

- For day-care facilities not used exclusively for business, also complete lines 4–6.
- All others, skip lines 4–6 and enter the amount from line 3 on line 7.

4	Multiply days used for day care during year by hours used per day	**4**		hr.
5	Total hours available for use during the year (365 days × 24 hours) (see instructions)	**5**	8,760	hr.
6	Divide line 4 by line 5. Enter the result as a decimal amount	**6**	.	
7	Business percentage. For day-care facilities not used exclusively for business, multiply line 6 by line 3 (enter the result as a percentage). All others, enter the amount from line 3 ▶	**7**	33 %	

Part II Figure Your Allowable Deduction

8	Enter the amount from Schedule C, line 29, **plus** any net gain or (loss) derived from the business use of your home and shown on Schedule D or Form 4797. If more than one place of business, see instructions		**8**	9337

See instructions for columns **(a)** and **(b)** before completing lines 9–20.

			(a) Direct expenses	(b) Indirect expenses		
9	Casualty losses (see instructions)	**9**				
10	Deductible mortgage interest (see instructions)	**10**				
11	Real estate taxes (see instructions)	**11**				
12	Add lines 9, 10, and 11	**12**				
13	Multiply line 12, column (b) by line 7			**13**		
14	Add line 12, column (a) and line 13				**14**	0
15	Subtract line 14 from line 8. If zero or less, enter -0-				**15**	9337
16	Excess mortgage interest (see instructions)	**16**				
17	Insurance	**17**				
18	Repairs and maintenance	**18**				
19	Utilities	**19**		1000		
20	Other expenses (see instructions)	**20**				
21	Add lines 16 through 20	**21**		1000		
22	Multiply line 21, column (b) by line 7			**22**	330	
23	Carryover of operating expenses from last year's Form 8829, line 41			**23**	0	
24	Add line 21 in column (a), line 22, and line 23				**24**	330
25	Allowable operating expenses. Enter the **smaller** of line 15 or line 24				**25**	330
26	Limit on excess casualty losses and depreciation. Subtract line 25 from line 15				**26**	9007
27	Excess casualty losses (see instructions)			**27**		
28	Depreciation of your home from Part III below			**28**		
29	Carryover of excess casualty losses and depreciation from last year's Form 8829, line			**29**		
30	Add lines 27 through 29				**30**	0
31	Allowable excess casualty losses and depreciation. Enter the **smaller** of line 26 or line 30				**31**	0
32	Add lines 14, 25, and 31				**32**	330
33	Casualty loss portion, if any, from lines 14 and 31. Carry amount to **Form 4684**, Section B				**33**	
34	Allowable expenses for business use of your home. Subtract line 33 from line 32. Enter here and on Schedule C, line 30. If your home was used for more than one business, see instructions ▶				**34**	330

Part III Depreciation of Your Home

35	Enter the **smaller** of your home's adjusted basis or its fair market value (see instructions)	**35**	
36	Value of land included on line 35	**36**	
37	Basis of building. Subtract line 36 from line 35	**37**	
38	Business basis of building. Multiply line 37 by line 7	**38**	
39	Depreciation percentage (see instructions)	**39**	%
40	Depreciation allowable (see instructions). Multiply line 38 by line 39. Enter here and on line 28 above	**40**	

Part IV Carryover of Unallowed Expenses to next year

41	Operating expenses. Subtract line 25 from line 24. If less than zero, enter -0-	**41**	0
42	Excess casualty losses and depreciation. Subtract line 31 from line 30. If less than zero, enter -0-	**42**	

For Paperwork Reduction Act Notice, see page 4 of separate instructions.

Cat. No. 13232M   Form **8829** Millennium Version

Form 8829 Expenses for Business Use of Your Home

The procedure for completing form 8829 is described briefly below

Part I

Derek has practically converted his small apartment into an office. He sleeps on a convertible in the living room, and has turned his bedroom into his office. The amount of space he uses for his office, equipment and inventory storage is approximately 400 square feet. Since the total space in his apartment is approximately 1200 square feet, the area used for business is 400 divided by 1200 = 33%

He makes the entries indicated, after reading the instructions.

NOTE: There are two types of expenses one can have when running a home business: Direct, and Indirect. Direct expenses are those which are incurred solely for the business. Indirect expenses are those which are actually for the entire home, but which benefit the business indirectly. Rent and utilities, for example, would still have to be paid whether you ran a business out of your home or not. Therefore, they are considered "Indirect" and only the percentage of the expense that benefits the business may be deducted.

For illustrative purposes, we'll limit the entries on the form to a single Indirect expense on line 19.

Line 19.   The electric portion of Derek's utility bill totals $1000 for the year.

Line 21. So, in this example, we'll assume he spent a total of $1000 for the year maintaining his apartment.

Line 22 Since he uses 33% of his apartment for business, he can enter 33% of the $1,000 as expenses
for business use of his home. (0.33 X $1000 = $330)

Line 34 We see that the amount of **profit** one can deduct for business use of the home is determined by how what percentage of that expense goes to home upkeep goes to

Schedule SE Self Employment Tax

As an entrepreneur, Derek is required to pay Self-Employment tax. This is a pre-determined amount of his net profit. If his net profit were under $400 for the year, he would not have been required to file this form.

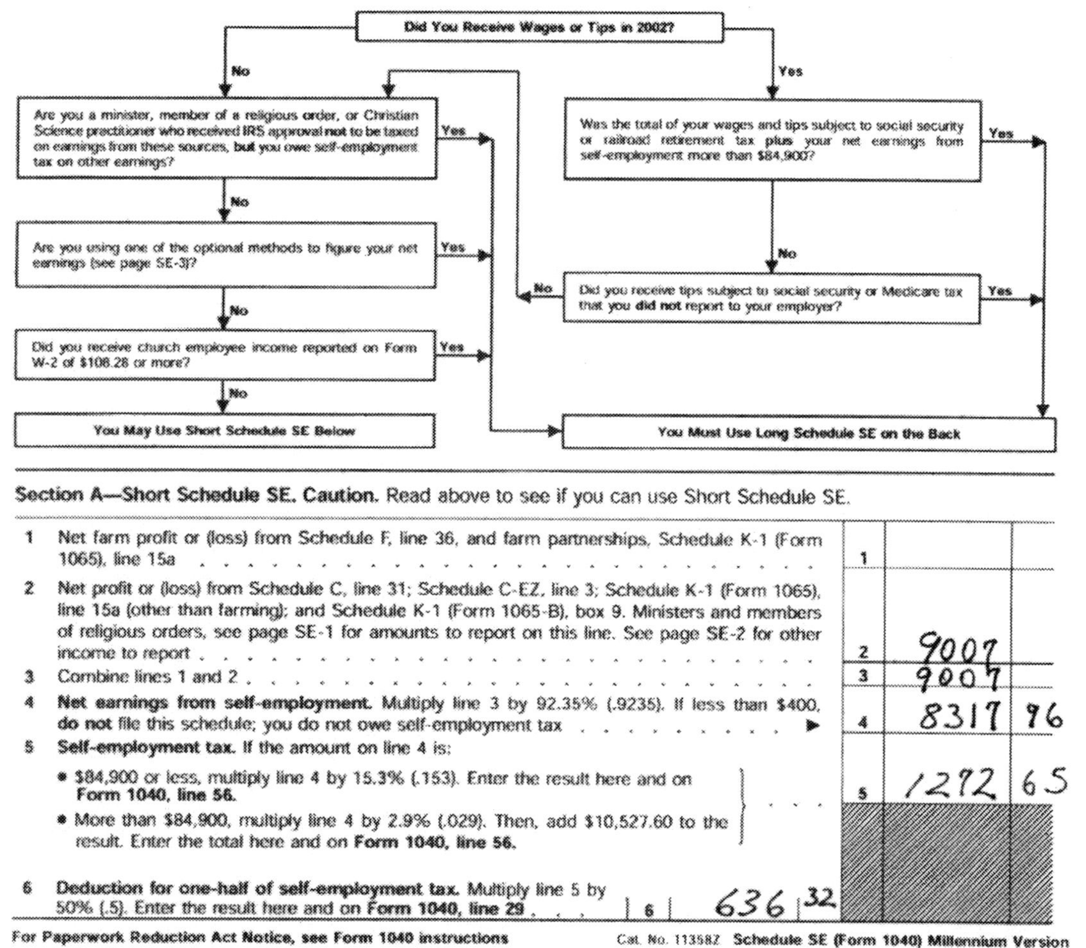

Form 1040 US Individual Income Tax Return

Form 1040

Department of the Treasury—Internal Revenue Service

U.S. Individual Income Tax Return for Change The Game Millennium Edition

For the years 2000 and beyond!

OMB No. 1545-0074

Label (See instructions on page 21.)

Use the IRS label. Otherwise, please print or type.

Your first name and initial: DEREK I.   Last name: BLACK

Your social security number: 123 45 6789

If a joint return, spouse's first name and initial   Last name

Spouse's social security number

Home address (number and street). If you have a P.O. box, see page 21.: 100 KILIMANJARO ST   Apt. no. 5A

City, town or post office, state, and ZIP code. If you have a foreign address, see page 21.: RESTON VA 22123

▲ **Important!** ▲ You must enter your SSN(s) above.

Presidential Election Campaign (See page 21.)

Note. Checking "Yes" will not change your tax or reduce your refund.

Do you, or your spouse if filing a joint return, want $3 to go to this fund? ▶   You: ☐ Yes ☑ No   Spouse: ☐ Yes ☑ No

Filing Status

Check only one box.

1. ☑ Single
2. ☐ Married filing jointly (even if only one had income)
3. ☐ Married filing separately. Enter spouse's SSN above and full name here. ▶ _______
4. ☐ Head of household (with qualifying person). (See page 21.) If the qualifying person is a child but not your dependent, enter this child's name here. ▶ _______
5. ☐ Qualifying widow(er) with dependent child (year spouse died ▶). (See page 21.)

Exemptions

6a. ☑ **Yourself.** If your parent (or someone else) can claim you as a dependent on his or her tax return, **do not** check box 6a

b. ☐ **Spouse**

c. **Dependents:**

(1) First name Last name	(2) Dependent's social security number	(3) Dependent's relationship to you	(4) ☑ if qualifying child for child tax credit (see page 22)
			☐
			☐
			☐
			☐
			☐

If more than five dependents, see page 22.

No. of boxes checked on 6a and 6b: **1**

No. of children on 6c who:
• lived with you _______
• did not live with you due to divorce or separation (see page 22) _______

Dependents on 6c not entered above _______

Add numbers on lines above ▶ **1**

d. Total number of exemptions claimed

Income

Attach Forms W-2 and W-2G here. Also attach Form(s) 1099-R if tax was withheld.

If you did not get a W-2, see page 23.

Enclose, but do not attach, any payment. Also, please use Form 1040-V.

7	Wages, salaries, tips, etc. Attach Form(s) W-2	7	25,000
8a	Taxable interest. Attach Schedule B if required	8a	100
b	Tax-exempt interest. **Do not** include on line 8a 8b		
9	Ordinary dividends. Attach Schedule B if required	9	
10	Taxable refunds, credits, or offsets of state and local income taxes (see page 24)	10	
11	Alimony received	11	
12	Business income or (loss). Attach Schedule C or C-EZ	12	9007
13	Capital gain or (loss). Attach Schedule D if required. If not required, check here ▶ ☐	13	
14	Other gains or (losses). Attach Form 4797	14	
15a	IRA distributions 15a b Taxable amount (see page 25)	15b	
16a	Pensions and annuities 16a b Taxable amount (see page 25)	16b	
17	Rental real estate, royalties, partnerships, S corporations, trusts, etc. Attach Schedule E	17	
18	Farm income or (loss). Attach Schedule F	18	
19	Unemployment compensation	19	
20a	Social security benefits 20a b Taxable amount (see page 27)	20b	
21	Other income. List type and amount (see page 29)	21	
22	Add the amounts in the far right column for lines 7 through 21. This is your **total income** ▶	22	34107

Adjusted Gross Income

Line	Description	Amount		Total
23	Educator expenses (see page 29)	23		
24	IRA deduction (see page 29)	24		
25	Student loan interest deduction (see page 31)	25		
26	Tuition and fees deduction (see page 32)	26		
27	Archer MSA deduction. Attach Form 8853	27		
28	Moving expenses. Attach Form 3903	28		
29	One-half of self-employment tax. Attach Schedule SE	29	636	32
30	Self-employed health insurance deduction (see page 33)	30		
31	Self-employed SEP, SIMPLE, and qualified plans	31		
32	Penalty on early withdrawal of savings	32		
33a	Alimony paid b Recipient's SSN ▶	33a		
34	Add lines 23 through 33a	34		636 32
35	Subtract line 34 from line 22. This is your **adjusted gross income** ▶	35		33470 68

For Disclosure, Privacy Act, and Paperwork Reduction Act Notice, see page 76.

Cat. No. 11320B   Form **1040** Millennium Edition

Form 1040 US Individual Income Tax Return—Page 2

Form 1040 created exclusively for Change The Game Millennium Edition

Page 2

Tax and Credits

Standard Deduction for—
- People who checked any box on line 37a or 37b or who can be claimed as a dependent, see page 34.
- All others:
  - Single, $4,700
  - Head of household, $6,900
  - Married filing jointly or Qualifying widow(er), $7,850
  - Married filing separately, $3,925

Line	Description		Amount
36	Amount from line 35 (adjusted gross income)	36	33470 68
37a	Check if: ☐ **You** were 65 or older, ☐ Blind; ☐ **Spouse** was 65 or older, ☐ Blind. Add the number of boxes checked above and enter the total here ▶	37a	
b	If you are married filing separately and your spouse itemizes deductions, or you were a dual-status alien, see page 34 and check here ▶ 37b ☐		
38	**Itemized deductions** (from Schedule A) **or** your **standard deduction** (see left margin)	38	4700
39	Subtract line 38 from line 36	39	28770 68
40	If line 36 is $103,000 or less, multiply $3,000 by the total number of exemptions claimed on line 5d. If line 36 is over $103,000, see the worksheet on page 35	40	3000
41	**Taxable income.** Subtract line 40 from line 39. If line 40 is more than line 39, enter -0-	41	25770 68
42	Tax (see page 36). Check if any tax is from: a ☐ Form(s) 8814 b ☐ Form 4972	42	3566
43	**Alternative minimum tax** (see page 37). Attach Form 6251	43	
44	Add lines 42 and 43 ▶	44	3566
45	Foreign tax credit. Attach Form 1116 if required	45	
46	Credit for child and dependent care expenses. Attach Form 2441	46	
47	Credit for the elderly or the disabled. Attach Schedule R	47	
48	Education credits. Attach Form 8863	48	
49	Retirement savings contributions credit. Attach Form 8880	49	
50	Child tax credit (see page 39)	50	
51	Adoption credit. Attach Form 8839	51	
52	Credits from: a ☐ Form 8396 b ☐ Form 8859	52	
53	Other credits. Check applicable box(es): a ☐ Form 3800 b ☐ Form 8801 c ☐ Specify ______	53	
54	Add lines 45 through 53. These are your **total credits**	54	0
55	Subtract line 54 from line 44. If line 54 is more than line 44, enter -0- ▶	55	3566

Other Taxes

Line	Description		Amount
56	Self-employment tax. Attach Schedule SE	56	636 32
57	Social security and Medicare tax on tip income not reported to employer. Attach Form 4137	57	
58	Tax on qualified plans, including IRAs, and other tax-favored accounts. Attach Form 5329 if required	58	
59	Advance earned income credit payments from Form(s) W-2	59	
60	Household employment taxes. Attach Schedule H	60	
61	Add lines 55 through 60. This is your **total tax** ▶	61	4202 32

Payments

If you have a qualifying child, attach Schedule EIC.

Line	Description			Amount
62	Federal income tax withheld from Forms W-2 and 1099	62	3454	
63	2002 estimated tax payments and amount applied from 2001 return	63		
64	**Earned income credit (EIC)**	64		
65	Excess social security and tier 1 RRTA tax withheld (see page 56)	65		
66	Additional child tax credit. Attach Form 8812	66		
67	Amount paid with request for extension to file (see page 56)	67		
68	Other payments from: a ☐ Form 2439 b ☐ Form 4136 c ☐ Form 8885	68		
69	Add lines 62 through 68. These are your **total payments** ▶	69		3454 00

Refund

Direct deposit? See page 56 and fill in 71b, 71c, and 71d.

Line	Description		Amount
70	If line 69 is more than line 61, subtract line 61 from line 69. This is the amount you **overpaid**	70	
71a	Amount of line 70 you want **refunded to you** ▶	71a	
b	Routing number ______ ▶ c Type: ☐ Checking ☐ Savings		
d	Account number ______		
72	Amount of line 70 you want **applied to your next year's estimated tax**	72	

Amount You Owe

Line	Description		Amount
73	**Amount you owe.** Subtract line 69 from line 61. For details on how to pay, see page 57 ▶	73	748 32
74	Estimated tax penalty (see page 57)	74	

Third Party Designee

Do you want to allow another person to discuss this return with the IRS (see page 58)? ☐ **Yes.** Complete the following. ☐ **No**

Designee's name ▶ ______ Phone no. ▶ (   ) Personal identification number (PIN) ▶

Sign Here

Joint return? See page 21. Keep a copy for your records.

Under penalties of perjury, I declare that I have examined this return and accompanying schedules and statements, and to the best of my knowledge and belief, they are true, correct, and complete. Declaration of preparer (other than taxpayer) is based on all information of which preparer has any knowledge.

Your signature: *Derek Black* Date: ______ Your occupation: OFFICE MANAGER Daytime phone number: (718) 464-3754

Spouse's signature. If a joint return, **both** must sign. Date: ______ Spouse's occupation: ______

Paid Preparer's Use Only

Preparer's signature ▶ ______ Date: ______ Check if self-employed ☐ Preparer's SSN or PTIN: ______

Firm's name (or yours if self-employed), address, and ZIP code ▶ ______ EIN: ______ Phone no. (   )

Form **1040** Millennium Edition

Form 1040 US Individual Income Tax Return

Derek now has all the information he needs to complete his 1040 as he has in previous years. He used to file 1040-EZ when he was a student, but since getting a job and starting his business, he must use the appropriate forms to make the tax laws work for him.

The most significant difference between this and previous years, is that now Derek enters the $9,007 profit he gained in his business on Line 12 of his 1040.

WHAT IT ALL MEANS:
From each paycheck from his Sales Manager job, the IRS has been deducting taxes based on Derek's yearly income of $25,000. They deducted about $3454 (Line 62) from his annual salary.

However, because of Derek's business income, the amount he should have been taxed on was $25,000 plus the $9,007 he earned from the business . In other words, because of his business, instead of being in the $25,000 a year tax bracket, he is actually in a higher tax bracket of $33,470.

Fortunately, however, after figuring his standard deduction of $4,700 (Line 38) and his exemptions of $3,000 (line 40), according to the tax tables, he finds finally that he is actually in the $25,770 tax bracket (line 41) and that the IRS should receive $3,566 in taxes on his "taxable income" and $636 in self-employment taxes for a total of $4,202.32.

Since $3,454 had already been deducted from his salary, he finds he only needs to pay an additional $748 in order to satisfy the IRS.

As his income grows, and turns more of a profit, Derek will need to look for different ways to shelter his income from taxes.(through various investments and bonds, for example).

Make sure you understand the concept behind the tax laws, and make them work for you!

SUMMARY of Chapter 14: *"Money Matters"*

Doing your taxes is an essential part of keeping more of what you make.

RESOURCES for Chapter 14: *"Money Matters "*
(BOOKS, AUDIO PROGRAMS, MAGAZINES, ORGANIZATIONS & WEBSITES)

½ *For understanding the tax laws*
- Pub 334 Tax Guide for Small Business
- Pub 17   Your Federal Income Tax
- Pub 533   Self Employment Tax
- Pub 587   Business Use of Your Home
- Pub 917   Business Use of Your Car
- Pub 463   Travel, Entertainment and Gift Expenses
- Pub 529   Miscellaneous Deductions
- Pub 1045   Information for Tax Practitioners (contains catalog/order blank for these and every publication and form available through the IRS.

 After reading the publications mentioned above, you will find out if your business-related tax return should include additional forms or information. You should also order the IRS YBTK (Your Business Tax Kit) which includes sample forms, publications and other information.   There is a separate YBTK for your choice of structure. Phone 1-800-424-3676 (forms only). The IRS also sponsors Small Business Tax Workshops to help you in filing returns. The IRS office in your state will have information on dates and times.

½ *Forms and Publications for Sole Proprietorship Returns*
- Form 1040
- Schedule C   Profit or Loss From A Business
- Schedule C-EZ   Net Profit From Business
- Schedule SE   Social Security Self-Employment Tax
- Form 8829   Expenses for Business Use of Your Home

½ *Forms for Partnership Returns*
- Form 1040
- Form 1065   US Partnership Return of Income
- Schedule K-1   Partner's Share of Income, Credits, Deductions, Etc.
            (Provided to the partners by the "Partnership")

½ *Forms for Corporations*
Individuals will file appropriate individual tax returns. Corporation's forms are:
- Form 1120   US Corporation Income Tax Return
- Form 1120A   US Corporation Short-Form Income Tax Return
- Form 1120S   US Income Tax Return for and S-Corporation, along with
- Schedule K-1   Shareholder's Share of Income, Credits, Deductions, Etc.

Kits, publications, forms, and   services vary widely from state to state. Usually each state has a "Department of Taxation and Finance" or "Department of Revenue" which administers the small business programs as well as the collection of taxes. Give them a cold call. Contact the SBA office in your state or for a catalog/forms write to: SBA P.O. Box 30 Denver   CO   80201

PART 5: POST-GAME WRAP UP

CHAPTER 15
"Growing Your Business"

Remember the Game Plan

Consider this a part of growing your business.

Monitor your OPERATIONS
Find, sign and develop talented ARTISTS
Create your PRODUCT on CD or other media
MARKET, Promote & Advertise it...
SELL IT to stores, distributors and to the public
Maximize additional streams of INCOME
RECOUP your expenses
PAY the players
Make a PROFIT.
½ GROW your business

How to REALLY Change Conditions in Your Life and Business

No matter which of the milestones you aspire to—making more money, matching your income in order to quit your job, or becoming a millionaire, there are specific things you will have to do in order to make it happen. You'll need to apply something called The Condition Formulas.

These Condition Formulas, based on the work of L. Ron Hubbard, provide proven formulas you can use to move from one level of success to the next.

The following is an excerpt from "Ethics and Conditions" (based on Hubbard's work) which explains in a bit more detail. First, a few definitions.

DEFINITION:
Condition: a state of existence. Organizationally, it is an operating state.

An organization or its parts or an individual passes through various states of existence. These, if not handled properly, bring about shrinkage and misery and worry and death. If handled properly they bring about stability, expansion, influence and well-being. Any organization or person or area of a person's life is, at any given time, in a particular condition.

As an example, if you made $10,000 last year and only $2,000 this year, you obviously are slipping; if you made $11,000 this year you are pretty stable; if you made $50,000, this year you are affluent--all compared to the $10,000 you made last year.

Product: someone or something that has been brought into existence; the end result of a creation. A product is a finished, high-quality service or article in the hands of the consumer as an exchange for a valuable. It is not a product at all unless it is exchangeable.

Statistics: a number or amount compared to an earlier number or amount of the same thing. It is simply the relative rise or fall of a quantity compared to an earlier moment in time. Statistics refer to the quantity of work done or the value of it in money. Statistics are the only sound measure of any production or any job or activity.

Any activity can be given a statistic. For example, if a farmer harvested 15,000 bushels of wheat one season and 10,000 bushels of wheat the following, his production and therefore, his statistic ("bushels of wheat harvested") is falling. If you made more money this year than you did last year, your statistic of "income" is rising.

The CONDITION of any activity can be measured by statistics. Statistics must reflect the actual desired product. An example of an incorrect statistic, say for a shoe salesman, would be "number of hours worked" or "number of shoes correctly fitted." Those statistics would not allow the salesman to measure his PRODUCT as they would not reflect what he should be producing (i.e., shoes sold).

The correct statistic for a shoe salesman, on which would reflect the actual desired PRODUCT, could be "number of shoes correctly fitted and sold." He could keep this statistic on a daily or even hourly basis.

Statistics can be plotted on a graph against time. A statistic is simply an index of things as they have been and they inform you of the relative need of action.

So based on those definitions, here is a chart with an overview of the conditions and their formulas.

Statistic	Condition	Formula
When one finds his statistic in such a low range that it shows no real products are being achieved or those that are being worked on are moving so slowly that the activity is nonviable, a condition of Non-Existence exists. Additionally, when someone begins a new job or activity, he starts off in the condition of Non-Existence because he has not yet produced anything in that capacity which can then be exchanged for income.	NON-EXISTENCE	1. FIND A COMMUNICATION LINE. (By communication line is meant the route along which a communication travels from one person to another or any sequences through which a message of any character may go.) 2. MAKE YOURSELF KNOWN. 3. DISCOVER WHAT IS NEEDED OR WANTED. 4. DO, PRODUCE AND/OR PRESENT IT.
A Danger condition exists when the statistics show a continuing steady decline or a steep, steep fall.	DANGER	1. Bypass habits and normal routines. 2. Handle the situation and any danger in it. 3. Assign yourself a danger condition. 4. Find out what you are doing that is contrary to the ideals or best interests of the group or activity and use self-discipline to correct it and get honest and straight. 5. Reorganize your life so that the dangerous situation is not continually happening to you. 6. Formulate and adopt firm policy that will hereafter detect and prevent the same situation from continuing to occur.

The Senior Danger formula is the formula an executive, himself, applies when he assigns a junior or area under his control a condition of Danger. It is assigned when A. When a statistic plunges downward very steeply. B. When an executive suddenly finds himself or herself doing the job of the head of the activity because it is in trouble. C. An Emergency condition has continued too long.	SENIOR DANGER	1. Bypass (ignore the junior or juniors normally in charge of the activity and handle it personally). 2. Handle the situation and any danger in it. 3. Assign the area where it had to be handled a danger condition. 4. Assign each individual connected with the danger condition a junior danger condition and enforce and ensure that they follow the formula completely. 5. Reorganize the activity so that the situation does not repeat. 6. Recommend any firm policy that will hereafter detect and/or prevent the condition from recurring
When a statistic remains unchanged over a period of time, it is a condition of Emergency. Additionally, when a statistic is seen to be gradually declining over a period of time, it is in a condition of Emergency.	EMERGENCY	1. Promote. That applies to an organization. To an individual you had better say produce. 2. Change your operating basis. 3. Economize. 4. Then prepare to deliver. 5.stiffen discipline.
A Normal condition exists when there is a routine or gradual increase (expansion) of a statistic. It must be a regular, routine, gradual increase.	NORMAL	1. The way you maintain an increase is when you are in a state of normal operation you don't change anything. 2. Do not take any savage disciplinary actions. 3. If a statistic betters, look it over carefully and find out what bettered it and then do that without abandoning what you were doing before. 4. Every time a statistic worsens slightly, quickly find out why and remedy it.
A condition of Affluence exists when there is a steep increase in a statistic. Whether it's up steeply for one week or up steeply from its last point week after week after week, it's Affluence.	AFFLUENCE	1. Economize 2. Pay every bill. 3. Invest the remainder in service facilities; make it more possible to deliver. 4. Discover what caused the condition of affluence and strengthen it.

	POWER	1. The first law of a condition of power is don't disconnect. 2. The first thing you have got to do is make a record of all its lines. (the first thing you have to do is write up your whole job or activity. By doing so, you make it possible for another person to take over your job if, for example, you get promoted.) 3. The responsibility is write the thing up and get it into the hands of who is going to take care of it. 4. Do all you can to make the job or activity occupiable.
The condition of Power is a Normal statistic in a stellar range so high that it is in total abundance, no doubt about it. The statistic is a brand-new range in a Normal trend.		
Correctly applying the condition of Power Change makes it possible for a person to successfully take over a job his predecessor left behind.	POWER CHANGE	Go through the exact same routine every day that your predecessor went through, sign nothing that he wouldn't sign, don't change a single order.

As a new record label, therefore, you will be starting from a position of Non-Existence. Therefore, there are four major categories of steps you should be engaged in once you finish this book and begin implementing your plan:

1. FIND A COMMUNICATION LINE.

List all the relevant magazines, websites, organizations, pr companies, media outlets, potential customers, distributors, manufacturers related to your business. Who should you be in communication with, in an ideal scenario to be a successful record label? The more thorough you are, the more successful you will be.

2. MAKE YOURSELF KNOWN.

Create your press release or introductory letter and contact all of the people and companies on the list above.

3. DISCOVER WHAT IS NEEDED OR WANTED.

Find out what your customers, suppliers, media companies need from you in order to do business with you or expose your company.

4. DO, PRODUCE AND/OR PRESENT IT.

Quite simply, give them what they ask for.

As simple as they appear to be, these Condition Formulas are profoundly effective. I implement them for every project I embark on, and have used them to help my clients turn their passions into profit! (You can order the full text of Ethics and Conditions on the PassionProfit.com products page.)

The Next Phase: How to Get a Record Deal

So, as promised, I'm including this section for those who are starting their record labels with the purpose of selling it, or getting bought by a major label. Wendy Day of Rap Coalition and I both agree that there are three ways to get a record deal:

1. Get put on
2. Create a buzz
3. Sell units

They're all somewhat related and tied to each other, but let's look at them as independent strategies. But, let's explore each of these strategies a little further so that you can incorporate one or more into your operations.

Get "Put On"

Getting "put on" simply means having someone in the industry who is already established opening the door for you. Snoop Dogg was "put on" by Dr. Dre. The Wu-Tang Clan rise to prominence is one of the most popular examples of this concept. Initial success within the Clan was used to aid the success of all the other members. Getting put on relies on an undisputable fact of life and of business: people do business with people they know. It's only natural that given the opportunity, that a successful individual would first help those who are closest to him, whom he knows and trusts. Your mission, therefore, in order to use "getting put on" as a strategy for getting a record deal, is to foster, develop and nurture as many real relationships as possible.

Create a buzz

Creating a buzz in order to get a record deal assumes that by creating enough of a public and media groundswell of attention, notoriety and interest in your label and artists, that it will lead to being noticed by the A&R scout at a major label, who'll then contact you and offer you the deal of a lifetime. It does indeed happen. Of course, you don't have to wait on luck for the labels to find out about you, you can strategically incorporate them into your marketing efforts and "buzz building" so that you're sure they're hearing about you. Many of the suggestions in the chapter on selling can help you create that buzz you're looking for. Keep in mind, however, that while creating a buzz is about hyping yourself, your artists and your label, that the people must believe the hype. In other words, it all has to be based on truthful and real accomplishments.

Sell units

Selling units must also be combined with creating a buzz (i.e. effective marketing) to make this strategy work for you. For although word of financial success has a way of getting around, it's important that the right people know about your success. The great thing about this strategy is that very act of selling units is a way of creating a buzz. In other words, the more people who are buying your music, the more people are listening and most likely playing it for their friends. And, it's the best way, since it puts some money in your pocket at the same time. If you're selling units, it means you're doing something right. And once you have this proven track record of sales, you can actively use it in your pitches to major labels. Make sure that everyone you talk to knows about your sales history.

The bottom line question that every record label will ask when deciding whom to sign is very simple: "will it sell?" If you come to the negotiation table with a proven answer to that question, then half the battle is won.

At the same time, you might find that the financial rewards and independence of doing things as an independent are so lucrative and satisfying that you might opt to continue this route without going major!

One Success Story shows how it's done!

Editor's note: Because of the nature of the music industry and the sanctity of relationships, the names of the key players in the following interview have been changed. It is my wish to simply impart information without revealing the exact personalities and companies involved.

Mico Goodgold owns an independent record label. We caught up with Mico in New York.

When did you start your label?
MICO: We actually started in late 1998. We incorporated in the first quarter of 1999, and got more clarity as far as where we wanted to go in mid 2000. So, we didn't really start playing the game until a little over 2 years ago. And it's just the last 7-8 months that we've been going pretty hard.

Where are you right now? What successes can you point to?
MICO: Well everything is a process, you know. Right now we're in negotiations with Columbia Records, Jive and Universal. They all like the artist's tracks and are interested in doing something with us.

Exactly how did you make that happen in just these few short months? Many up-and-coming labels toil for years without ever making into the offices of major label executives. You have relationships with three. Was that always the plan?
MICO: It's funny, we actually started in the game simply shopping X's music. We saw the major label deal as being the gold medal—the be all and end all. As things progressed, however, we realized that we needed to sell something. Our plan right now is that if we can't secure a major deal by the time we planned to release the single, then we'll put out an independent album

The A&R reps you're in negotiations with…Did you know any of these people before you started the label?
MICO: No

So, take us through the process. The purpose of this interview is to help others to do what you did.
MICO: Well at (Major 1) we're speaking on a regular basis with [Person 1A], the Executive VP of Urban Music, as well as Persona 1B, who is the Director of A&R Research. I sent out a mass email to about 100 industry contacts telling them about the new artist, and that we'd like to send a package. The majority didn't want to do face to face, and simply ignored the email. But a few responded.

You said you sent out a mass email. How did you get the email contact information?
MICO: We met a lawyer at one of our release parties. He liked our image. He and I hit it off, and he simply did me a favor by giving me a copy of an A&R Networking Registry that included some insider information and phone fax, email addresses.

What are the elements that you see as being pivotal in your success story?
MICO: Well, the story isn't written yet. It's still a work in progress until we get the check! But, there are three things that I would point to that are significant in our story up to this point.
1. Meeting with that lawyer who gave us the contact info was the first turning point.
2. Having DJ X as a consultant is the second. His reputation in the industry is really opening a lot of doors for us, and
3. the fact that our artist had a childhood relationship with [MajorArtist] is helping as well.

Everything is about the relationship. I can't stress that enough. It's interesting because we actually played our Artist's music for Label 2 about 2 and a half years ago. They like it, but didn't hear a hit record at the time. I kept the relationship warm over 2 years. And then now,

The next significant development is that we "hired" a consultant who's been in business for 22 years. He's a dj in a club, and does mixes for a local radio station. Someone like him, who is entrenched in business, can do wonders for the building of other relationships.

How did you find him?
MICO: I met him through Rick, another contact. It was just a chance meeting at Jimmy's Uptown café in Harlem. Rick ricky introduced to Johnathan Donker

How much are you paying him?
Not nearly what he's really worth. But, fortunately, he has faith in the artist, he trusts me, so he's willing to work for a lower monthly retainer with promise for a greater reward on the back end.

So what part of your story is NOT teachable? In other words what do you think is the unique gift or talent that you brought to the mix that resulted in your success?
I think the most important thing about the route that we took is the FOLLOW UP. You've got to stick to your guns. Persevere. The people who I'm now in frequent contact with are not easily accessible. If I were easily discouraged by how hard they are to get to, I would have given up a long time ago.

The next thing, I believe, is the level of professionalism that I and my partners projected. My communications, my letters were well written, well thought out. They were direct and to the point. When you read it, you weren't unclear as to what we accomplished, what we wanted to have happen next, my experience and our team credentials and potential for getting us there.

What advice can you give to up and coming labels
MICO: Have a clear idea of what you want to accomplish. Keep shopping your product. What shopping does is it creates relationships that might bear fruit sometime down the line. Use email to communicate initially. It's a non-threatening and cheap method of getting to A&R reps. You can follow up with more expensive kits, samples, etc. once the relationship is established. Get out there and meet people. Pool resources with your artists, their contacts and their contacts contacts, and never give up!

Your "exit" strategy

Every good business plan has what's called an "exit strategy". I mentioned in the opening sections that the only reason to start a business is to sell it. An exit strategy, as the name implies, details how you plan to exit your business. Some typical options for exit strategies include

• Selling all or a portion of the business
• Passing the business on to a family member
• Selling to an Employee Stock Ownership Plan (ESOP)
• Taking the company public
• Liquidation

Valuing your company (A General Guide)

Valuation Methods:

- Income-based. These forward-looking methods are general enough to be applied to most types of businesses.

     Discounted cash flow: This method involves forecasting earnings into the future (usually by three to 10 years) to determine the present value. Discounted cash flow is a good valuation method for fast-growth businesses; it can also be used if you're valuing your business for the purpose of bringing in a partner.

     Capitalization of cash flow: For this method, which is best used for mature companies with stable earnings, the value of one normalized earning period is used to predict future value.

- Market-based. If you're valuing your company in order to sell it, you'll want to look at how other businesses in your industry are valued.

     Capital market (or guidance company): This method looks at multiples of publicly traded stocks, and works best for any companies that are large enough to be comparable to publicly traded firms. For example, this method would be more appropriate to use for a chain of retail stores than a single-unit retail company.

     Transaction: Better for smaller companies, this method examines what other businesses in your industry have sold for.

- Cost- or asset-based. This valuation method adds up all the individual components of your business to find its value. Manufacturing or asset-holding companies, which have few intangibles, can get the most from this method.

Increasing your Value

As mentioned in the opening chapter, the only reason you should start any business is for the sole purpose of selling it. According to experts, you can improve your chances of being able to attract major Here are five tips contrasted with how label interest and sell your company in the following ways.

1. Cross the $1-million mark

companies have an easier time attracting buyers once they pass the $1-million-in-revenues threshold.

2. Build a staff of five or more

statistics suggest that the hardest businesses to sell are those with fewer than five employees.

3. Create a corporate identity

The goal of this tactic is to distinguish you and your personal identity from your company. If people associate the label with producing good music, then In the industry, it's often the individual with the "ear" who is the prize. Puffy, who strikes a deal with Arista Records, it's the production skill, contacts and ear for finding a hit sound that's the asset. In the case of a Death Row Records, though the same can be said of Suge Knight, the label itself had a powerful image even in his absence.

4. Accumulate Assets

Your masters, contracts with artists, equipment, real estate, proprietary technology, marketing lists or any other way you can demonstrate internal value for your company will go a long way in setting a higher price for your company.

5. Build a board of directors

Having a strong board of directors signals to the world that you're serious about business than to set up a strong board. Include major label contacts, former A&R people, established producers, famous people, business experts, and anyone who can add some legitimacy to your operation, its vision and goals.

SUMMARY of Chapter 15: *"Growing Your Company*

• The Condition Formulas are a powerful tool you can use to change conditions in your life as well as your business.

• According to Wendy Day of Rap Coalition, there are 3 ways to get signed to a major
1. Get put on
2. Create a buzz
3. Sell units

• In anticipation of the day when you want to implement your exit strategy and/or sell your business, take the necessary steps to increase the value of your business: cross the $1-million mark, build a staff of five or more, create a corporate identity, accumulate assets, and build a board of directors

RESOURCES for Chapter 15: *"Growing Your Company*

BOOKS, AUDIO PROGRAMS, MAGAZINES, ORGANIZATIONS & WEBSITES
For valuing your company
      • *The Business Of Business Valuation* by Gary E. Jones and Dirk Van Dyke
      • *The Small Business Valuation Handbook* by Lawrence Tiller

CHAPTER 16:
"A Few Final Words"

■ ■ ■ ■

I hope the business information proves helpful to you in starting and running your Rap label. It is intended to get you thinking and acting in a certain direction towards more realistic goals, and with a professional and knowledgeable attitude.   It isn't possible to cover adequately in one book every aspect of running a business. The obstacles that business (and life as well) will throw at you are unpredictable, at best. The key to overcoming these obstacles is not by having 7000 different gameplans to counter every possible contingency. You only need one. That one game plan which can be used no matter what the obstacle is your attitude, i.e, how you react. Remember, you'll never be able to control the actions of other people or the outcome of events that are out of your hands.   The only thing you have control over is how you react to these actions and events. Not everyone will like your record. If a distributor says your record is weak, you have a couple of options. You can close up shop spend the day crying, or you can take the attitude that a business interaction with this distributor wasn't meant to be, view it as a temporary setback meant to guide you in another direction and move on.   One of these options has a better chance of getting you what you want.

As they often say, preparedness is sometimes the best defense. If you've prepared yourself with the knowledge that things can go other than how you want them to, and you've decided beforehand that whatever happens you'll get back in and try harder without breaking, then you'll have half the battle won already. The other half of the battle is left up to your belief in yourself and how much you really want what you say you want.

With that said, I'll offer just....

....Some Final Words About.....

Lawyers

Pay them now, or pay them later. With as much emphasis as the written word will allow: It is a wise move to hire a lawyer to write or look over the contracts you sign into. Many new labels have struggled with and developed new artists, only to have them whisked away by larger companies with sharp lawyers who can rip apart loosely worded agreements. By the same token, many new artists have effectively signed themselves into bondage by not having a lawyer looking out for their best interest.

Management

An artist needs a manager. An artist needs a manager who is committed to the artist's career when things aren't going so well, in addition to when they are. When looking for a manager, remember that enthusiasm and creativity rate just as highly as reputation and plush office space. Respect for, and an understanding of your music should also be looked for. As a label president, be aware of the "surrogate manager" syndrome which sometimes accompanies signing an unmanaged artist. You, as the surrogate, will be looked to to provide ALL the things that an artist wants and needs in his/her career, from clothing to guidance. It is in the label's interest to insist that a new artist be competently managed. If you can afford to wait (though sometimes a bit impractical), you might want to make this a pre-requisite to signing any new talent, as many larger companies do.

Image And Appearance

Before anyone opens your product; before you open your mouth in a meeting, the image and appearance of what the consumer or the businessperson sees in front of them sets the stage with certain expectations. True, no amount of good packaging can make a bad record good. But, if you have a good record on the inside, why hurt your chances of being listened to with bad packaging on the outside. Likewise, distributors, radio station directors, and magazine editors are all affected in some way by a professional image. Many people carry their biases with them into the workplace. Keep this in mind and realize that while a distributor may deal with you on the strength of your product, HOW he deals with you might be more influenced by how you present yourself.

Artist Commitment

Amidst stories of "overnight" stardom and images of wealth within the music industry, it is understandable that a new artist might have visions of making a quick buck. It is understandable as well the disappointment which invariably follows for all but a privileged few. Regrettably, what many fail to realize is the real degree of hard work and personal commitment that must occur and exist. The term "paying one's dues" encompasses the numerous rejections, disappointments, growth and experience which one goes through.   It might and usually does take years of pushing with all of one's strength before the door finally starts to move. The new artist must realize that if he or she isn't committed to self enough to keep coming back after each disappointment, then no one else will. You, as the artist, must be twice as committed to your career as everyone else you deal with. You as the label, must be twice as committed to your company and its future as everyone else you work with. .If things don't go the way you want them to, self pity and complaints about your record company, or your management, or the industry in general won't get you the Grammy. You are ultimately responsible for your own career.

Your Commitment

Much of your success will come from developing and accumulating your own experience. It will come from jumping in and developing your own "feel" for how things work, what's important, and what you need to do to make it come together for you. It will come from developing your intuition about everything from the potential of a song, to which areas you should target, to when you should release a record, etc. None of these things can be taught. They have to be lived. Choosing to start your own label, or
promoting your own record is a step in the direction of independence. Maintaining the enthusiasm is an exercise of commitment. So, what is commitment? Commitment is not being deterred by the fact that things may not always go the way you envision. Commitment is knowing that as hard as you try, and as much as you've accomplished, there's always another mile that has to be traveled. Commitment is knowing that you, and no one else, should control the direction of your ship. Commitment is expecting and pursuing the "yes" at the end of a hundred "no's". (Remember: no one person can keep every door closed to you.) Commitment is the late nights, the sacrificed parties, the work-filled weekends. Commitment is following up with the small leads with as much enthusiasm as the big ones. Commitment is knowing that there is only one question with only one answer : Did I get the job done? Yes!   At each point when you feel like giving up, remember the stories of the successful individuals. (See "Books to Get".) They succeeded only because they went the extra mile realizing that "within each defeat is the seed of an equivalent victory". Remember, staying committed and motivated is another part of the formula for success, and may be the most important.

A Higher Purpose

Your commitment to the game will come from your "why", ie. your reason for embarking on this journey. When all is said and done, but hopefully way before then, you'll ask yourself a very important question: Why am I doing this? What's the purpose of starting this record label? Why am playing this game? What do I hope to accomplish? Is there a bigger picture? Do I want to change the world? Do I simply want to make money to change my immediate financial condition? Do I have a message I want to offer society?

I suggest to you that your true success will come when you align yourself with a higher purpose. Other Hip Hop entrepreneurs have found a higher purpose by feeding the homeless and financially challenged (Luke does it every Thanksgiving), giving to or starting their own charitable organizations (see Russell's Rush Foundation), guiding the next generation (check out LL Cool J's summer camp for kids) and many more noble actions too numerous to mention here.

What's going to be your legacy?

The State of Radio in the New Millennium: An opinionated commentary

As I complete this new edition of Change The Game, the state of commercial radio is one of the hottest topics on the minds of concerned Hip Hop Entrepreneurs. After the FCC (Federal Communications Commission) lifted the restriction of how many radio stations a single entity could own in different markets, many of the radio stations across the country are being bought out. One corporation in particular, Clear Channel Communications, owns over 1,200 radio stations across the country. In the minds of many, the result of such ownership is an ominous change in the control of the nation's airwaves.

As Daddy-O of Rap pioneer group Stetsasonic says, "Hip Hop used to be a regional creation." According to Daddy-O, he made music for the 5 square block area he called his neighborhood. Run DMC made music for Hollis, MC Hammer made music for Oakland, and Luke made music for Miami. Each artist and each region had a unique flavor and perspective that it offered to the overall Rap music scene. You could travel to Miami, for example and hear artists unique to that region, that you didn't hear in New York. These days, however, with central, monopoly-like ownership of radio stations, the radio playlists on stations in Boise, Idaho are now exactly the same as those in Dallas, Texas. Critics of this type of expansion say that it makes the flavor of Hip Hop too homogenous and limits the opportunities for up and coming artists in that region.

Coupled with that reality is the fact that the decisions as far as the content of what to play is being centralized as well. This too, critics say, has a negative effect on the music, for if a record on a playlist is considered offensive, it's now offending more people in different markets all around the country. Fewer and fewer individuals are controlling tastes, perceptions and the content for more and more people.

So, what can you do?

The answer is really quite simple. Since cash is the bottom line in the decisions of such companies, the average consumer/listener has much more power than they may realize. Radio stations make their decisions based on advertising dollars. DJs can be fired, songs can be removed from playlists, and current programming decisions can be altered based on a radio station's listeners. If a station realizes that the content of their playlist is offensive to their listeners, AND they are made aware that these same listeners are turning to other stations as a result (an action that will be reflected in the offensive station's ratings), then, in order to remain competitive and to lure advertising dollars, they'll have no choice but to change their ways.

Such actions on the part of consumers, though not widely practiced, are quite doable. To prove this, there are different initiatives that aim to take back control of the local airwaves by sending a message to radio stations. Once such movement, appropriately entitled Turn Off Offensive Radio, based in New York, and which has the support of The Hip Hop Entrepreneur Company. If you wish to find out more, call their hotline at (718) 398-1766.

RAP MUSIC, YOUR COMPANY, AND THE FUTURE

As a Hip Hop Entrepreneur, you are part of a new breed of young business owners who are taking something that is uniquely their own, and using it to pave a path towards economic empowerment. You are rising to the challenge of taking the voice of today's urban youth to the forefront of national and international awareness, and doing so in a financially beneficial way.   It is my wish that you use the information provided within these pages to further careers, establish businesses and realize the dreams that will keep the voices heard, the culture alive, and the future hopeful.

Rap Music, with its origins in the oral tradition of Africa, its infancy in the BeBop of America in the 1940's, and its early maturity in the 80's, is a relatively young music form as it comes of age in the media and commercially and technologically driven age of the 90's. As Rap goes through its growing pains, and as the industry develops, we can expect to see more new developments and changes to the art form: experimentation, counterfeiters (i.e. funk fakers), stereotyping, labeling and all the expressions of the
metamorphosis that characterize growth. The opportunities for you as a taste maker or taste-satisfier for the Rap audience are limitless. The challenges which will be yours in taking Rap to its ultimate destiny are numerous. The responsibility that comes with being an executive within your field of creativity or expertise are empowering within themselves. The benefits to doing all of this successfully are within your
reach.

You, as a member of a community which listens to, supports, and respects Rap, have an obligation to expand the horizons of the art form to have it prosper in legitimacy alongside other genres.

The first step in the journey, is the realization of the power that you as an executive have in shaping the minds of young listeners. The power to change and influence thoughts and dreams.   With this power, comes a certain amount of responsibility. You will be responsible for representing the music, its artists, and your company, and yourself in a way which supports and emphasizes your commitment to the goals you have set. You will be charged with presenting the music and the images associated with it to the public. What you choose to present, and how you choose to present it will determine how well you
answer to the responsibility.

Rap Music is a form of expression and entertainment within Hip Hop culture. Being of the culture, by its very nature, it can, should, and will reflect the ideas and images of importance to the culture. It will at once be entertaining, thought provoking, unifying, militant, while at the same time indicative of the range of emotions that are a part of the people of the culture. It will laugh with its people, and it will cry with them; it will ask questions with its people, and it will search for answers with them; it will scream in frustration at the reality of its people, and it will seek escape with them.   It need not apologize for being what it is and doing what it does. It is.

Music can uplift as well as entertain. It can paint pictures of a possible future as well as a current reality. We should expand the limits of what is considered "true" to the art form as we and the music grow into maturity. As we develop in our own understanding, we should develop in our music those new ideas and ways that come with growth.   For many, "true" or "real" Rap is that which is steeped in the reality of urban America. For these fans, "hardcore" is synonymous with street, with violence, with abuse, with desolation, with hopelessness, with survival in a world of antagonism. These are all elements of reality. But it is just half the story. Musical enjoyment and expression can come in different forms. Music can speak of solutions as well as highlighting life's challenges; it can show the happiness of life as well as the sadness, and it can speak of hope as well as despair.

Over the years, Rap has suffered the slings and arrows of negatively slanted publicity and coverage. It has been stigmatized as epitomizing the very evils and wrongs from which in protest it grew. It has even been charged with inciting the violence which has always existed as a natural part of the American experience and of which those close to the Hip Hop experience have been the victims of rather than the perpetrators.   This image of itself from which Rap now suffers threatens to contaminate the very minds of those who support it.   It threatens to limit the horizons of those who use it as a yardstick for measuring the width of their dreams.

As such a powerful medium of expression, today's youth look partly to Rap and Rappers to help in defining what is real for them. Their expectations of what life will offer to them, and what they can offer to life are sought within the lyrics and interviews of their favorite artist. Those of us who keep Rap alive must be aware of this, and set examples that make their experience as wide as possible. Those of us who keep Rap alive must keep it alive to grow and to become.... not just to be.

PEACE.

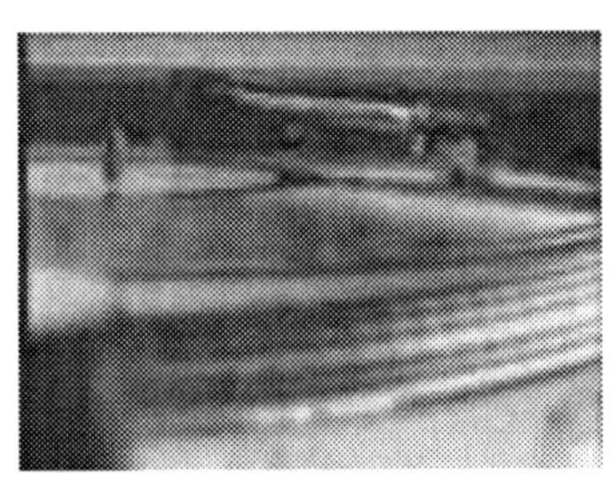

Change The Game
APPENDIX:

QUESTION: Why aren't things working out as planned?
ANSWER: You need to Use the Record Label Trouble Shooting Guide!
Tips for getting your label working correctly and profitably

Situation/Challenge	Possible Causes	Possible Solutions
I can't find good people to work with	You're choosing from among your friends, relatives, and people in your immediate circles who may not really be qualified.	•Join networking organizations. Be prepared to move outside of your comfort zone. As you grow personally, you'll start to attract a different caliber of individual. •Offer value; find out your partners' reasons and motivations for being involved in your venture, and create a trade that satisfies THEIR needs as well.
My artists are not meeting their deadlines.	Your artists have a fear of success You're not communicating a sense of urgency to them	• Find new artists
I can't get a distributor to handle my product	It could be the music, your presentation, or you're not succeeding in impressing them with both	•Get some objective feedback on your music, artist/company image, • Ask distributors who've rejected you for honest feedback • Spruce up your media kit • keep trying • See Mico's Story in How to Get Signed by a Major
How can I fill the positions in my org chart if I have no money to pay these people?	You're not being creative enough in solving this challenge	• Barter for services • Look overseas for cheap labor • Enroll people in your vision • Offer stock options/ownership
My distributor isn't paying me in a timely manner	He's shady or is simply low on cash.	• Use a baseball bat (just kidding) • This one is really tricky. There are probably some good economic reasons why the distributor isn't making payments...(See Chapter 11 for a full explanation of your options)
My website isn't getting any traffic	You're not doing the right things to promote it. Website promotion is an ongoing activity	• See "Getting Visitors" in Launching Your Label on the Internet Chapter 6)
People are visiting my website but I'm not making any sales	You're not giving them a reason to part with their money.	• Offer samples of the music • Create a bundled package • offer incentive (free t-shirt) • offer free shipping • post listener feedback on the site
Things are moving too slowly	You haven't built up enough momentum to reach "takeoff" speed.	• Focus on doing more selling to the media and phase 1 activities

Situation/Challenge	Possible Causes	Possible Solutions
Cash flow is always tight to non-existent.	You're not diversified enough	•Create alternate income streams …(See Chapter 13 for a full explanation of your options
I need money to manufacture my CDs	You're broke	•Go Cheap (See ways to finance your company in Chapter 4)
I can't seem to manage all the tasks and people in my organization	You need the right management tool	• Try the "Passion Profit Turning Pro Operations Manual" included in the Passion Profit I-Supplement on Profit available at www.PassionProfit.com

Of course, these challenges and solutions do not represent all the possible scenarios that can arise when running a record label. The Record Label Trouble Shooting Guide is simply meant to remind you that there is indeed a solution to every challenge that you will face. You're mission is to find it. Don't let challenges deter you from reaching your goals. They are a necessary part of the journey. If you can't find the answers and solutions within the pages of this book, you can brainstorm with your team, consult with advisors, or ask the Hip Hop Biz Answerman at www.hiphopbiz.com. Be flexible. Be creative. Be open to step outside of your comfort zone. Be willing to take a detour on your journey. But whatever you do, DO NOT GIVE UP!

EXCLUSIVE ARTIST AGREEMENT

THIS AGREEMENT, made and entered into at _______________________ by and between:
COMPANY: ____
(hereinafter referred to as "COMPANY")

-and-

ARTIST: ____
(hereinafter referred to as "ARTIST")

DATE: ____

WHEREAS, COMPANY is in the business of producing, exploiting, distributing and marketing Phonograph Records, and WHEREAS, ARTIST is a vocalist and performer and is interested in having COMPANY produce phonograph recordings and audio visual devices embodying ARTIST's performances and to exploit, distribute and market same in an many parts of the work as may be economically and commercially practical.

NOW, THEREFORE, in consideration of the representations and warranties and mutual promises hereinafter set forth it is agreed as follows:

1.DEFINITIONS

(a)"Advance" - a prepayment of royalties. Company may recoup advances from royalties to be paid to or on behalf of you pursuant to this or any other Agreement.

(b)"Album" or "LP" - one or more twelve-inch 33 1/3 rpm records, or the equivalent, at least thirty-five (35) minutes in playing time, sold in a single package.

(c)"Audiophile" records - (other than video-records) marketed in specially priced catalogue series by reason of their superior sound quality or other distinctive technical or artistic characteristics. (All records made for digital playback are audiophile records.)

(d)"Budget Line" - a record bearing a suggested retail list price which is at least three dollars ($ 3.00) or more less than the suggested retail list price of the top line records embodying performances of pop artists released by Company or its Licensees in the Territory concerned.

(e)"Compact Disc" - a laser (video) read disk containing performances of one or more musical compositions.

(f)"Compositions" - a single musical compositions, irrespective of length, including all spoken words and bridging passages and including a medley.

(g)"Controlled Composition" - a Composition wholly or partly written, owned or controlled by you or any other Person to whom you are related or in whose business affairs you have a direct or indirect interest.

(h)" Disco or 12" Single" - a disc of not less than twelve (12) inches in diameter, or the equivalent in a non-disc configuration, and having not less than five (5) minutes in playing time, sold in a single package.

(i)"Inception of Recording" - the first recording of performance or other sounds with a view to the eventual fixation of a Master Recording. "Master Recordings From The Inception of Recording" include, without limitation, all rehearsal recordings, "outtakes", and other preliminary or alternate versions of sound recordings which are created during the production of Master Recordings made under this Agreement.

(j)"License" or "licensee"- includes, without limitation, subsidiaries, wholly or partly owned, and other divisions of Company or its licensee is).

(k)" Master Recording" - every recording of sound, whether or not coupled with a visual image, by any method and on any substance or material, whether now or hereafter known, which is used or useful in the recording, production and/or manufacture of records or video-records. A "Master Recording" shall be a master recording made hereunder embodying your performance.

(I)"Matrix" - any device now or hereafter used, directly or indirectly, in the manufacture of records and which is derived from a Master Recording.

(m)"Mid-priced Line" - a record bearing a suggested retail list price which is at least two dollars ($2.00) but no more than two dollars and ninety-nine cents ($2.99) less than the suggested retail list price of the top line records embodying performances of pop artists released by Company or its licenses in the Territory concerned.

(n)"Multiple Record Set" - an Album containing two (2) or more 12-inch 33 1/3 rpm records packaged as a single unit, or the equivalent.

(o) "Net Sales" - ninety (90%) percent of gross sales for which Company receives payment and which are not returned or for which an exchange is not made; however, if any licensee pays Company upon a lesser amounts of Net Sales, then for records of video-records sold by that licensee such lesser percentage shall be applicable.

(p)"Person" and "Party" - any individual, corporation, partnership, association or other organized group of persons or legal successors or representative of the foregoing.

(q)"Records" and "Party" - any individual, corporation, partnership, association or other organized group of persons or legal successors or representatives of the foregoing.

(r)"Recording Costs" - all amounts representing direct expenses paid or incurred by Company in connection with the production of Master Recordings under this Agreement which are customarily considered "recording costs" in the record industry. Recording Costs include, without limitation, the amounts referred to in Paragraph 5, travel, food, transportation, music videos, rehearsal, and equipment rental expenses, advances and/or fees paid to producers, payments to directors, choreographers, engineers, lighting personnel, scenic designers, costumers, all other technical and creative personnel, studio and engineering expenses in connection with Company's facilities and personnel otherwise, the costs of mastering and remixing, and the costs of lacquer, copper and other equivalent masters, and immigration clearances.

 (s) "Restricted Composition" - for the purpose hereof, is a composition which shall have been recorded by you fro a Master Recording made under this Agreement or any other agreement with Company.

(t)"Single" - a disc Record of seven (7) or twelve (12) inches in diameter, or the equivalent in a non-disc configuration, containing not more than two sides.

(u)"Suggested Retail List Price"

(i)the suggested retail list price in, at Company's election, the country of manufacture or sale of records sold in he United States and in any other country where company manufactures and sell records for its own account as opposed to licensing such rights to third parties; and, for records sold elsewhere, the suggested retail list price in the country of manufacture or sale, whichever shall be the basis upon which Company is paid by its licensees (exclusive of all taxes, discounts, duties and packaging). In those countries where a suggested retail list price is not permitted or widely used, the term "suggested retail list price" shall mean the generally accepted retail list price in that country. The suggested retail list price for records sold by third parties under Company's authority or permission shall be that upon which company's royalties are calculated.

(ii)Notwithstanding (i) immediately above, Company may change the method by which it computes royalties (for some or all of the Territory) from a method based on suggested retail list prices to some other method, (the "New Method"). If Company adopts a New Method, such New Method shall be deemed incorporated herein in lieu of the present method of computing royalties with respect to all records derived from the masters thereafter sold, ran appropriate reference in respect to the New Method shall replace the current references to the suggested retail list price, and the royalty rates provided for herein shall be adjusted to the appropriate royalty which would be applied to the New Method so that upon the first change to the

New Method, the dollars and cents royalty amounts payable with respect to the top-line Albums being sold by company (or its Licensees) would be identical to that which was payable immediately prior to such change. All other royalty rates shall be proportionately adjusted. The royalty adjustments to be made pursuant to this Paragraph shall be based on net dollars and cents royalty amounts and shall take into account any factors (including, without limitation, Company's (or its Licensees') regular "free goods" policies before and after Company's adoption of the New Method affecting such net royalty amounts.

(v)"Video-record" - a video-cassette, video-disc or functionally similar technology, whether now or hereafter known, capable of emitting aural and visual signals simultaneously and intended for use in the home with electronic or mechanical playback equipment.

(i)Unless otherwise specified in the Agreement, a Master

Recording shall consist of a continuous performance of a particular arrangement or version of Composition, and shall be not less than three (3) minutes in playing time. If any album (or other group of Master Recordings) produced by, or produced hereunder in partial or complete fulfillment of a Recording Commitment expressed as a number of sides or Masters include Master Recordings of more than one (1) arrangement or version of nay Composition, all of those recording will be deemed to constitute one (1) side or one (1) Master.

(ii)an audio-visual Master Recording made hereunder, though sometimes referred to in this Agreement as a "Master Recording", shall not apply in reduction of Your Recording Commitment hereunder.

(x)"Wholesale price" - the wholesale royalty base price at which Company is accounted to by its Licensees, if applicable.

2. TERM FOR INDEPENDENT DISTRIBUTION

In the event that company is effecting the distribution of records embodying your performance hereunder in the United States directly or through so-called "independent distributors" who purchase finished records from Company and resell them, then the following subparagraphs of this Paragraph 1 shall define the Term" hereof:

(a)The term hereof (Term) shall consist of an initial period (Initial contract Period) ending on the latter of (i) one (1) year, commencing upon the date hereof, or, (ii) that date which is six (6) months following the date Company has completed the Master Recordings which comprise your Recording Commitment for that Contract Period, unless sooner terminated in accordance with the provisions of this Agreement.

(b)You hereby irrevocably grant to Company four (4) separate consecutive options to extend the Term for a "Second", "Third", "Fourth" and "Fifth" contract Period" respectively. Each such exercised Contract Period shall commence on the date immediately following the end of the preceding Contract Period, and shall end on the latter of: (i) one year thereafter, or, (ii) that date which is six (6) months following the date upon which Company completes Master Recordings which comprise Your recording Commitment for the Contract Period, unless sooner terminated, extended or suspended as provided herein. Each such option shall be deemed to be exercised by Company unless company shall give you notice to the contrary prior to the date that the then current contract Period would otherwise expire.

(c)The Initial contract Period together with any exercised Option Contract Periods, if any, rights for which are exercised by Company, shall be referred to as " the Term".

3.APPLICATION OF DISTRIBUTION AGREEMENT

(a)If at any time during the Term hereof (i) company enters into an agreement with a third party record distribution company (the " Distribution Company") under which records embodying your performances are to be manufactured and sold in the United States (a "Distribution Agreement") by such third party and (ii) the terms of the Distribution Agreement require that Company deliver to the Distribution Company rights relating to or derived from you which are different from those contained in this Agreement, then such different terms in the Distribution agreement shall nevertheless be deemed a part of this Agreement during the Term of the Distribution Agreement even if he result is that obligations imposed upon you differ from and/or are more difficult for you to perform that those set forth in this Agreement. Such Distribution Agreement may not, however, impose terms less favorable to you than those offered by this Agreement.

It is the intention of the parties that:

(i)The Term of this Agreement shall be deemed to be identical in length to the term of the Distribution Agreement. In no event shall the Term hereof expire or terminate prior to the expiration of the Distribution Agreement between Company and the Distribution Company. If the Distribution Company shall exercise an option to extend the term of the Distribution Agreement or to suspend the term thereof, the Term hereof shall automatically deemed suspended or extended for an equal period of time.

(ii)If the term of the Distribution Agreement shall expire or be terminated, the Term hereof shall nevertheless continue for an additional period of six (6) months during which the Company shall have the exclusive right to secure a new Distribution Agreement (a "Successor Distribution Agreement"). If Company shall enter into a Successor Distribution Agreement, then the term hereof shall continue for a period of time identical to the complete term of the Successor Distribution Agreement and shall end on the same day as the Successor Distribution Agreement. In no event shall the Term hereof expire or terminate prior to the expiration of the Successor Distribution Agreement. If the Successor Distribution Company shall exercise an option to extend the term of the Successor Distribution Agreement or to suspend the term thereof, the Term hereof shall automatically be deemed suspended or extended for an equal period of time.

(iii)In the event that the Distribution agreement shall expire or be terminated and Company does not enter into a Successor Distribution Agreement, company may, at its election, continue to record Master Recordings embodying Artist's performances for the longer of the unconsumed balance of the Term hereof as set forth herein or the unconsumed balance of the term of the Distribution Agreement and to itself exploit the Master Recordings made hereunder.

(iv)In no event, however, shall the Artist be bound to record Master Recordings hereunder for a period which is of greater duration than the current maximum legally acceptable term applicable to personal service agreements under the statutes of the State the laws of which are being utilized to construe this Agreement.

4.SERVICES

During the Term of this Agreement, Artist shall render exclusively to Company throughout the world Artist's services as a recording artist for the purpose of making Master Recordings and as otherwise set forth herein. For the purposes hereof, "services as a recording artist" shall mean and include, but shall not be limited to, the rendering of performances fixed by any method, mode or device, whether now known hereafter developed, regardless of whether such method, mode and/or device is capable of fixing sound alone or sound fixed together with visual images.

5.RECORDING COMMITMENT

(a)If there is no Distribution Agreement in effect:

(i)During each Contract Period of the Term, Company shall record and you will perform for the recording of master Recordings sufficient to constitute two (2) Singles (the "minimum Recording Commitment") with, at Company's request, dub mixes, Disco or 12" Single mixes and other variations of the Compositions embodied therein.

(ii)During each Contract Period, Company shall have the right to require that you render services and perform for the recording of a number of Master Recordings in addition to the Minimum Recording Commitment applicable to that Contract Period sufficient to comprise two (2) LPs (the "Overcall Recordings"). company's option for the Overcall Recording may be exercised by Company at any time by sending you notice at any time before the end of the Contract Period concerned. Any request for Overcall Recordings shall be for the number of Master Recordings or Sides designated by Company, in increments determined by Company. Nothing contained herein shall be construed so as to require Company to release an LP. The Minimum Recording Commitment taken together with the Overcall Recordings requested for any Contract Period hereof shall be referred to as "Your Recording Commitment".

(b)If a Distribution Agreement is in effect, then you shall record no less than a number of Master Recordings as the Distribution Company shall require delivered (also referred to as "Your Recording Commitment" herein).

(c)Each time Company notifies you that it requests you to record Master Recordings hereunder, you will complete you performances for the requested Master Recordings within one (1) month following Company's notice to you that it requires same, or within the time frame required by the Distribution Company.

6.RECORDING PROCEDURE

(a)In connection with Master Recordings to be made hereunder, the following matters shall be determined by Company:

(i)selection of the producer:

(ii)selection of material to be recorded (including the number of Compositions to be recorded):

(iii)selection of the dates of recording and the studio where recording is to take place, including the cost of recording therein;

(iv)the scheduling and booking of all studio time;

(v)the recording budget therefore;

(vi)the selection of arrangers, musicians, background vocalists, copyists, contractors, engineers and all other technical personnel;

(vii)the designation of compositions to be released on Singles, Disco-Singles; and Albums:

(viii)all artwork used in advertising materials, promotional materials, record sleeves and record jackets; and

(ix)all other creative elements to be utilized or embodied in recording activity conducted hereunder or to promote the records derived form the Masters.

(b)Each Master Recording made hereunder shall be subject to Company' s approval as commercially and technically satisfactory for the manufacture and sale of records. You agree to re-record each Composition until Company is satisfied, in its sole discretion, that a Master has been produced which is technically and commercially satisfactory for the manufacture and sale of records. You shall be deemed not to have completed your services in respect of any Master made hereunder until Company has acknowledged in writing that a Master has been so produced.

(c)You shall be available to perform at all recording sessions scheduled hereunder provided that you have been given not less than sever (7) days prior notice of session times, dates and places.

(d)No Composition recorded hereunder and no Master fixing that performance shell apply in reduction of Your Recording commitment to Company if it is of a "live performance", a Joint Recording, of a Composition previously recorded by you, or of a Composition which you are legally prohibited from recording. In the event Company requests or accepts as part of your recording commitment a Multiple Record Set, same shall be deemed to be a number of Masters sufficient to comprise only one (1)LP for the purposes of Your Recording Commitment hereunder.

(e)Any Masters which are not recorded in all respects in accordance with the terms and provisions hereof shall not, unless Company otherwise consents in writing, apply toward the fulfillment of Your Recording Commitment hereunder. Furthermore, in the event that Company shall make any payments with respect to non-complying Masters, and such non-compliance is the result of acts or omissions on your part, then you shall, upon Company's demand, promptly reimburse Company for any such payments. If you shall fail to reimburse Company, Company shall, in addition to all of Company's other rights and remedies in such event, have the right to deduct an amount equal to such payments from any payable by Company to you hereunder or under any other agreement between you and your affiliated companies and Company or its affiliated companies.

(f)If you or any Person retained by you or under your control shall for any reason whatsoever delay the commencement of completion of, or be unavailable for, any rehearsal or recording session, or fail to perform in a professional manner at any such session, you shall, upon Company's demand, promptly reimburse Company for any expenses or charges actually incurred or paid by Company by reason thereof. If you fail to so reimburse Company, in addition to any and all of Company's other rights and remedies, shall have the right to deduct an amount equal to such expenses or charges from any moneys payable by Company to you hereunder or under any other agreement between you and Company or its affiliated companies.

7.RECOUPABLE AND REIMBURSABLE COSTS.

(a)In the event that Company becomes a signatory to a collective bargaining agreement with any labor organization having jurisdiction of recording hereunder, Company shall pay to you minimum union scale payments required to be made to you under agreements between Company and applicable collective bargaining organizations with which Company is affiliated. Company shall also pay ail costs of instrumental, vocal and other personnel specifically approved by Company for the recording of Master recordings made hereunder, and all other amounts required to be paid by Company pursuant to any applicable law or any collective bargaining agreement between Company and any union representing persons who render services in connection with such Master Recordings.

(b)All amounts described in Paragraph 7 (a) above plus those referred to in Paragraph 4(s) hereof are herein sometimes called "Recording Costs" and shall constitute Advances. Payments to the AFM Special Payments Fund and the Music Performance Trust Fund based upon record sales (so-called "pre-record royalties") shall not constitute Advances.

(c)The amounts applicable to any Joint Recording which are payable by you or chargeable against your royalties under this Paragraph will be computed by apportionment as provided in Paragraph 11 (e) (ii).

8.ADDITIONAL ADVANCES.

All moneys paid to or on behalf of you during the Term of this Agreement, inclusive of advertising and promotional expenses incurred by Company but excluding royalties paid pursuant to Paragraph 11, shall constitute Advances unless otherwise expressly agreed in writing by an authorized officer of Company.

9.RIGHTS IN RECORDINGS.

(a)Each Master and or Audio-visual Recording made under this Agreement or during its Term, from the Inception of Recording, will be considered a "work made for hire" for Company or its assignees or designees. If a such Master Recording is determined not to be a work made for hire it will be deemed transferred to Company by you. All such Master Recordings and all matrices and records manufactured from them, together with the performances embodied on them, shall be the sole property of Company, its assignees and successors in perpetuity, free from any claims by you or any other person; and Company shall have the exclusive right to or any other person; and Company shall have the exclusive right to copyright those Master Recordings in its name as the author and owner of them and to secure any and all renewals and extensions of such copyright throughout the world. You will execute and deliver to Company such instruments of transfer and other documents regarding the rights of Company in the Master Recordings subject to this Agreement as Company may reasonably request to carry out the purposes of this Agreement, and Company may sign such documents in your name and made appropriate disposition of them.

(b)Without limiting the generality of the foregoing, Company and any person authorized by Company shall have the unlimited, exclusive rights, throughout the world.

(i)to manufacture records and video-records in any form and by any method now or hereafter known delivered from the Master Recordings made under this Agreement or during its Term;

(ii)to sell, transfer or otherwise deal in the same under any trademarks, trade names and labels, or to refrain from such manufacture, sale and dealing;

(iii)to reproduce, adapt and otherwise use those Master

Recordings in any medium or in any manner, including but not limited to use in audiovisual works;

(iv)to cause or permit the public performance of such Master Recordings, or derivatives thereof through any and all media; and

(v)to exploit such Master Recordings and derivatives therefrom through any and all means whether now or hereafter known, all without payment of nay compensation to you except the royalties, if any, which may be expressly prescribed in this Agreement for the use concerned. In the alternative Company may, at its election, refrain from doing any or all of the foregoing.

10.NAMES AND LIKENESSES; PUBLICITY

(a)Company and any license of Company shall have the right and may grant to others the right to reproduce, print, publish or disseminate in any medium, your name, portraits, pictures and likenesses in connection with Master Recordings made under this agreement (including, without limitation, all professional, group, and other assumed or fictitious names now or thereafter used by you), and biographical material concerning you, as news or information, for the purposed of trade, or for advertising purposes. The uses authorized by the preceding sentence include, without limitation, the use of those names, portraits, pictures, and likenesses in the marketing of records. During the Term of this Agreement you shall not authorize any Person other than Company to use your said name (s) and likenesses (or any professional, group or other assumed or fictitious name used by you) in connection with the advertising or sale of:

(i)records; or

(ii)blank recording tape or tape recording equipment.

(b)(i) You hereby grant to Company the exclusive right during the Term hereof and throughout the Territory to use and/or sublicense to others the use of your name (s) (both real and professional), mark, logotype, likenesses and/or performances for merchandising and other commercial purposes, whether or not related to the manufacture and ale of records, embodying the photographs, images, graphics and other artwork embodied on any packing materials relating to records manufactured hereunder including, without limitation, in connection with the sale (whether through "flyers", "bouncebacks", and similar Album inserts, or otherwise) of T-shirts and other apparel, posters, stickers and novelties. Upon Company's request, you shall execute a license agreement in the licensing of name and likeness rights for merchandising purposes, though the failure on your part to do so shall not diminish Company's rights with respect to the merchandising of the aforesaid properties. If you fail to do so, you hereby irrevocably appoint an officer or Company as your agent for the purpose of executing such documents.

(ii)Company shall have the right to approve the servicemark ("Mark") under which you shall render entertainment services during the Term. Company and you hereby approve the use of the Mark. Such Mark is and will be COMPANY'S sole and exclusive property and you warrant the represent that you own all rights in and to the Mark throughout the world and that there are and will be no competing claims with respect you your right to use the Mark in all areas of entertainment industry. You may not alter the service mark under which you render professional services as performers and recording artists without Company's prior written consent. Company shall have the sole and exclusive right, but not the obligation, to apply for and obtain in its name a federal registration of the Mark in connection with the use thereof in all areas of the entertainment industry, including without limitation, in connection with the recording and sale of records, the establishment of fan clubs, the rendition if concert and live performances, and the sale of clothing and other merchandise. If Company does so, the costs of obtaining such registration shall be an Advance hereunder, except as agreed among the members of Artist, in a signed unity given to company.

(c)Company agrees to credit to your collective royalty account twenty-five (25%) percent of the net income actually received in hand by Company (as opposed to Company' s licensees, agents or other representatives) from the exploitation of the rights granted to it hereunder by virtue of (b) (i) and (b) (ii) above. For the purposes hereof, "net income" shall mean the gross income actually received by Company which is derived directly and solely from such use of the rights granted to it under said subparagraphs less a five (5%) percent administration fee computed upon gross income, and less direct expenses actually incurred by Company relative thereto including, but not limited to:

(i)costs of collection;

(ii)commissions and/or royalties payable to third parties;

(iii)cost of manufacture and design;

(iv)cost of packing, shipping, storing, postage and insurance; and

(v)advertising and promotion expenses. The aforesaid royalty shall not be paid to any individual named as "Artist" who is not still member of the Artist at the time a royalty accounting is due hereunder.

11.ROYALTIES

Conditioned upon full and faithful performance of all the terms and conditions hereof, your collective royalty account shall be credited with royalties on Net Sales of records as hereinafter set forth against which shall be charged all Advances and other permissible offsets hereunder, as follows:

(a)(i) Company shall credit to your royalty account for

Net sales of records sold for distribution in the United States embodying solely the Master Recordings a royalty equal to six (6%) percent of the suggested retail list price of such records.

(ii) In the event any cassette which solely embodies ARTIST's newly-recorded studio performances required to be recorded and delivered hereunder shall have net sales paid for recorded and delivered hereunder shall have net sales paid for through normal retailer channels in the United States in excess of 500,00 copies, the applicable Basic U.S. cassette rate shall be increased by one-half (1/2%) percent, but only with respect to those net sales (through normal retailer channels in the United States) in excess of 500,00 royalty bearing copies of such LP.

(iii)The base royalty provided hereinabove shall be payable only with respect to Master Recordings completely produced by You. In the event that You do not completely produce a Master Recording hereunder and Company agrees to pay a royalty to a third party to produce or cc-produce such Master Recording, then the royalty payable to such third party shall be deducted from the percent of the suggested retail list price for records of the type referred in one (1) immediately above, and otherwise computed in the same manner as your royalties are computed hereunder.

(iv)In respect of Master Recordings embodied on albums, Tape or Singles which are sold for distribution outside of the United States, Company shall credit your royalty account with a royalty computed at one-half (1/2) of the rate otherwise applicable under subparagraph ja) and its subsections, as may be applicable.

(B)Notwithstanding the foregoing, with respect to records sold for distribution in the United States:

(i)the royalty rate in respect of records sold through any direct mail or mail order distribution method (including without limitation, record club distribution), and/or sold through retail stores in conjunction with special radio or television advertisements (including, without limitation, records of the type presently distributed by Company) shall be one-half (1/2) of the otherwise applicable royalty rate as calculated in accordance with the foregoing provisions, or one-half 11/2) of the net royalty which Company shall receive from any licensee distributing such records, whichever is less:

(ii)the royalty rate in respect of the sale of records on a mid-priced line or a budget line shall be one-half (1/2) of the otherwise applicable royalty rate as calculated in accordance with the foregoing provisions;

(iii)the royalty rate in respect of records sold for use premiums or in connection with the sale, advertising or promotion of any other product or service shall be one-half (1/2) of the otherwise applicable royalty rate as calculated in accordance with the foregoing provisions, and shall be based upon the price received by Company for such records sold by Company or upon the price utilized by Company's licensee in accounting to Company for such records sold by Company's licensees, as may be applicable;

(iv)the royalty rate in respect of records sold to the United States Government, its subdivisions, departments or agencies (including records sold for resale through military facilities), and in respect of records sold to educational institutions or libraries, shall be one-half (1/2) of the otherwise applicable royalty rate as calculated in accordance with the foregoing provisions;

(v)the royalty rate in respect of Masters licensed by Company for phonograph record use on a flat-fee basis for all other types of use (other than phonograph record use) on a flat-flee or non-royalty basis shall be an amount equal to twenty-five (25%) percent of the net flat-fee or net non-royalty, as the case may be, received by Company in respect of each such use.

(vi)the royalty rate in respect of records sold by Company or its licensees in the "compact disc" configuration or as audiophile records shall be the applicable royalty rate provided for in Paragraph 11 (a) or (b) above, but for the purpose of calculating such royalty, the suggested retail list price for Company's then current regular top-line similar records.

(vii)the royalty rate in respect of records sold by Company to distributors or others for less than Company's regular wholesale price, or at a discount therefrom, but for more than fifty (50%) percent of such regular wholesale price the royalty shall be reduced in the same proportion as the reduction in such regular wholesale price.

(C)(i) Notwithstanding anything to the contrary contained hereinabove, no royalties shall be payable or creditable on records furnished as "free" or "bonus" records to members, applicants, or other participants in any record club or other direct mail distribution method; on records distributed for promotional purposes to radio stations, television stations or networks, to record reviewers or other customary recipients of promotional records: on so-called "promotional sampler records" distributed without charge or for sale at a substantially lower price than the regular price of Company's Albums, on records sold as scrap or as so-called "cutouts": and on records distributed on a so-called "no charge" or 'free" basis (such as, but not limited to, records commonly described in the record industry as "free goods" or "freebies") or sold at less than fifty (50X) percent of their highest applicable wholesale price to distributors, subdistributors, dealers or others, whether or not the recipients of such records are affiliated with Company and whether or not such records are intended for sale by the recipient thereof.

(ii) in computing the number of records sold hereunder, Company shell have the right to deduct returns and credits of any nature, including, without limitation; (1) those on account of any return or exchange privilege, (2)defective merchandise, and (3) errors in billing or shipment.

(iii)for the purpose of computing royalties hereunder there shall be deducted from the applicable wholesale price (or other applicable price, if any, upon which royalties are calculated) of phonograph records hereunder:

(1)there shall first be deducted therefrom any amount equal to any exercise, sales, value-added or similar taxes;

(2)there shall be deducted from the suggested retail list price (or other applicable price, if any, upon which royalties are calculated) of phonograph records hereunder, an amount equal to ten (10%) percent thereof for sales in disc form (including 12" Singles packaged in single fold jackets without any special elements (such as, but not limited to. inserts or attachments): twelve and one-half (12 ½%) percent thereof for all other long playing or extended play records in disc form: and twenty (20%) percent thereof for reel to reel tapes, cartridges cassettes or other record devices (other than discs but including so called "compact discs" and other audiophile records);
(3)there shall be deducted from the suggested retail list price of video records fifteen (15%) percent thereof: and

(4)Notwithstanding the subparagraphs immediately above, if on licensee distributing records hereunder shall deduct a greater amount as a packaging allowance, then with respect to records sold by such licensee, Artist's royalties shall also be subject to such greater packaging allowance.

(d) Notwithstanding any of the foregoing Royalties shall be computed and paid upon Ninety (90%) percent of Net Sales; provided, however, that if any licensee distributing records hereunder shall compute and pay royalties to Company on less than Ninety 190%) percent of Net Sales, your royalties hereunder with respect to such records shall be computed and paid on the same percentage of Net Sales as such licensee shall utilize in computing and paying royalties to Company;

(e)Notwithstanding any of the foregoing:

(i)the royalty payable to Company hereunder with respect to any phonograph record embodying Masters hereunder together with other master recordings shall be computed by multiplying the otherwise applicable royalty rate by a fraction, the numerator of which shall be the number of selections contained on the Masters made hereunder embodied on such phonograph records and the denominator of which shall be the total number of selections embodied on such phonograph record;

(ii)the royalty payable to you and the Recording Costs with respect to any Master recorded hereunder jointly by you with another artist or musician to whom Company is obligated to pay royalty in respect of such Master ("Joint Recordings") shall be computed by multiplying the otherwise applicable royalty rate and recording costs by a fraction, the numerator of which shall be one (1) and the denominator of which shall be the sum of one (1) and the total number of such other artists or musicians whose performances are embodied thereon.

(iii)No royalty shall be due you an any record sold hereunder or any other type of exploitation of the Master Recording until such time as Company is finally paid on such sale.

(f)If COMPANY shall cause or permit the commercial manufacture, distribution and sale of a video embodying the Artist's performances, then for Net Sales of video records in the United States embodying solely performances of the Artist produced hereunder, COMPANY shall credit your royalty account with the lesser of five (5%) of the wholesale price of such video records or thirty five (35%) of COMPANY'S net royalty receipts therefrom. Said royalty shall be adjusted in the same prorata manner as the same prorata manner as provided in Paragraph 11 and its subsections fro sales other than through normal retail channels. The royalty rate on a video record containing your performance hereunder and other audiovisual works will be determined by apportionment based on actual playing time on the video record concerned.

(g)Notwithstanding the preceding royalty provisions:

(i)if Company is distributing records on an independent basis in the United States and enters into a Distribution Agreement with one (1) or more third parties pursuant to which such third parties distribute records derived from the Master Recordings inside or outside of the United States and pay Company a royalty therefore; or

(ii)if Company enters into a Distribution Agreement for the distribution of records in the United States, or the United States and Canada, and retains for itself the right to directly license Master Recordings in other parts of the world on a royalty basis, then in either of such events your royalty shall be computed under such Distribution Agreement (s) upon the same basis and in the same manner as Company's royalties are computed for records sold by said Distribution Companies. Your royalty account shall be credited by Company on exactly the same basis as Company is paid in accordance with net sales by that third party. Your royalty shall be subject to the same prorata reductions (including but not limited to records sold in configurations other than

Albums, for foreign sales, club sales, budget sales, coupling, mail order sales, premium sales, government sales, post exchange sales and mid priced line sales), the same deductions therefrom (including but not limited to returns, reserves for returns, packaging allowances, taxes, sales discount, "free" and promotional records), all definitions pertaining to royalty computations and distributions, and all royalty handling provisions and the same adjustment to royalties, except that (1) your basic royalty applicable to sales of records inside or outside of the United States shall be the applicable rate set forth in Paragraph Il(a) above

(iii)when Company is paid and a share of net royalty receipts or net receipts by its licensee, your share of Company's share of net royalty receipts shall be forty 40% percent thereof if you are the sole producer of a particular Master and thirty (30%) percent thereof if you are not the sole producer thereof: and

(iv)notwithstanding the provisions of Company's agreement with its licensee (s), Company shall nevertheless have the right to deduce from your royalties all Advances. You shall not be entitled to any portion of advance payments received by Company in respect of the Masters except to the extent of your entitlement by virtue of Net Sales of records from the payer of said advance payment.

(h)(i) Notwithstanding the foregoing, in the event that Company enters into a Distribution Agreement for worldwide distribution of Master Recordings made hereunder, then your royalty account shall be credited with royalties on Net Sales of records as hereinafter set forth against which shall be charged all Advances and other permissible offsets hereunder of sums which equal forty (40%) percent of company's net royalty receipts from such distribution Company in respect of the sales of records and other exploitation's of the Master Recordings made hereunder. For the purposes hereunder, the term "net royalty receipts" shall mean gross receipts (exclusive of advance payments, regardless of designation or reason paid, issued by a Distribution Company) actually received in hand by Company (as distinguished from a Distribution Company, agent, representatives or licensee) from the sale of records by a Distribution Company (or entities authorized by such Distribution company) embodying the Masters following the deduction of all out of pocket and thereto fore unrecovered expenses which Company shall have incurred in connection with the Artist, the Masters and the Distribution Agreement.

(ii) The royalty provided in (i) immediately above shall be payable only with respect to Master Recordings completely produced by you. In the event that you do not completely produce a Master Recording hereunder and Company agrees to pay a royalty to a third party to produce or co-produce such Master Recording, then the royalty payable to you with respect to such Master Recordings shall be thirty (30%) percent of Company[s net royalty receipts in respect of such Masters in lieu of forty (40X) percent thereof.

(i)If the reference "you" hereunder applies to more than one (1) individual, then the royalties expressed hereinabove shall be an aggregate amount of royalties payable to all such individuals collectively, and prorate shares thereof shall be paid to each such individual. If, however, any individual currently comprising the Artist at some point in time is no longer a member of the Artist at the time a Master Recording is recorded hereunder, then that individual shall not have the right to receive royalties with respect to such Master Recording, unless agreed otherwise by Artist, in a signed unity given to members of the Company.

12.ROYALTY ACCOUNTING

(a)Company will compute your royalties as of each June 30th and December 31st for the prior six (6) months in respect of each such six month period in which there are sales or returns of records on which royalties are payable to you. On the next September 30th or March 31st Company will send you a statement covering those royalties and will pay you any royalties which are due after deducting unrecouped Advances. Company will not act unreasonably in maintaining royalty reserves against anticipated returns and credits. Company shall not be required to pay a royalty to you for any record upon which Company does not receive payment. If Company makes any overpayment to you, you will reimburse Company for it. Company may also deduct it from any payments due or becoming due to you. If Company pays you any royalties on records which are returned later, those royalties will be considered overpayment.

(b)Sales of records for distribution outside the United States are called "foreign sales" below. Company will compute your royalties for any foreign sale in the same national currency in which Company's licensee (s) pays Company for that sale, and Company will credit those royalties to your account at the same rate of exchange at which the licensee pays Company. For the purpose of accounting to you, Company will treat any foreign sale or any sale by a distribution Company as a sales made during the same six month period in which Company receives its licensee's accounting and payment for that sale. If any Licensee deducts any taxes from its payments to Company, Company may deduct a proportionate amount of those taxes from your royalties. If any law, any government ruling, or any other restriction affects the amount of the payments which a licensee can remit to Company, Company may deduct from your royalties an amount proportionate to the reduction in the Licensee's remittances to Company. If Company cannot collect payment for a foreign sale in the United States in United States Dollars, Company will not be required to account to you for that sale. If such cases Company may, at its election, elect to accept payment in foreign currency or in a foreign country, and Company may deposit to your credit (at your expense) in such country in a depository selected by Company payments so received applicable to royalties hereunder. Company shall be required to notify you of such deposit. Deposit and notice as aforesaid shall fulfill the obligations of Company as to royalties due you hereunder.

(c)Company will maintain books and records which reports the sales of records, and the calculation of net receipts derived from the exploitation of Master Recordings on which royalties are creditable to you. You may, at your own expense, engage a certified public accountant not then engaged in an outstanding examination of Company's books and records for a third party, only for the purpose of verifying the accuracy of the statements sent to you under Paragraph 11. You may make such an examination for a particular statement only once, and only within one (1)year after the date when Company is required to send you that statement under Paragraph 12. You may make those examinations only during Company's usual business hours, and at the place where it keeps the books and records to be examined. If you wish to make an examination you will be required to notify Company at least ten (10) business days before the date when you plan to begin it. You will not be entitled to examine any manufacturing records or any other records that do not specifically report sales, charges against Royalties, or other distributions of records hereunder, or calculation of net receipts, on which royalties are payable to you. You acknowledge that Company's books and records contain confidential trade information. You warrant and represent that neither you nor your representative (s) will communicate to others or use on behalf of any other Person any facts or information obtained as a result of such examination of Company's books and records.

(d)If you have any objections to a royalty statement, you will give Company specific notice of that objection and your reasons for it within one (1) year after the date when Company is required to send you that statement under Paragraph 12. Each royalty statement will become conclusively binding on you at the end of that one 11) year period, and you will no longer have any right to make any other objections to it. You will not have the right to sue Company for royalties on records sold or net receipts derived by Company during the period a royalty accounting, or to sue company for royalties on records sold or net receipts derived by Company during the period a royalty accounting covers, unless you commence the suit within that one (1) year period. If you commence suit on any controversy or claim concerning royalty accounting rendered to you under this Agreement, the scope of the proceeding will be limited to determination of the amount of the royalties due for the accounting periods concerned, and the court will not have the authority to consider any other issues or award any relief except recovery of any royalties found owing. Your recovery of any such royalties will be the sole remedy available to you by reason of any claim related to Company's royalty accounting. Without limiting the generality of the preceding sentence, you will not have any right to seek termination of this Agreement or avoid the performance of you obligations under it by reason of any such claim. If the reference "you" hereunder applies to more than one (1) individual, then the examination right set forth herein shall be deemed a collective right, it being agreed that Company shall not be required to allow such examination to be conducted by more than one (1) individual comprising "you" in any year period referred to above.

13.LICENSES FOR COMPOSITIONS

(a)(i) You will obtain at COMPANY'S expense and election, and for Company's benefit, mechanical licenses covering Compositions embodied on the Master Recording at a payment rate no greater than the royalty rate equal to the minimum compulsory license rate applicable under the copyright law of the country concerned at the time of release; or if there is no minimum compulsory license rate applicable in a particular country, at the lowest prevalent rate being, paid to mechanical copyright owners at the time of release in the country concerned for Compositions of comparable length which are performed by other artist who have attained Record sales comparable to sales by Artist in the country concerned. You grant COMPANY an irrevocable license, under copyright, to reproduce each Controlled Composition on Phonograph Records and distributed by them in the Territory.

(ii) For that license, Company will pay mechanical Royalties of three-fourths of the minimum statutory rate then in effect per Composition for Records sold in the United States and Canada, on the basis of Net Sales. The Mechanical Royalty on any Record sold through a Club Operation will be the amount fixed in the preceding sentence. If the Composition is an arranged version of public domain work, the Mechanical Royalty on it will be half of the amount fixed in the first sentence. No Mechanical Royalties will be payable for any Records described in Paragraph (d).

(b)The total Mechanical Royalty for all Composition on any Album, including controlled Compositions, will be limited to the number of Compositions on each album times the amount which would be payable on it under section 13, (a) (1) (2) if it contained only one (1) Controlled Composition. The total Mechanical Royalty on any "single" Record will be limited to twice that amount.

(c)You also grant to Company an irrevocable license, under copyright, to reproduce each Controlled Composition in motion pictures and other audiovisual works ("pictures"), and to distribute and to perform those pictures throughout the world for the purpose of marketing Phonograph Records, and to authorize others to do so.

(d)If the copyright in any controlled Composition is owned or controlled by anyone else, you will cause that Person to grant Company the same rights described in paragraphs 13 (a) 13 (d), on the same terms. If the copyright in any Controlled composition is transferred, the transfer will be made subject to this Agreement.

14.MUSIC PUBLISHING; CONTROLLED COMPOSITIONS

You hereby irrevocably and absolutely assign, convey and set over to Company (or its designee), or will cause Company (or its designee) to receive an assignment, of One Hundred (100%) percent of the right, title and interest (including worldwide copyright and all extensions and renewals thereof) in and to each and every Controlled Composition which is recorded hereunder. You agree to execute and deliver to Company, or to cause to be executed and delivered to Company (or its designee) a separate Songwriter's Agreement in the form of the standard songwriter agreement then being utilized by Company, or its publishing affiliate or designee, in respect of each such Controlled Composition. If you shall fail to promptly execute such agreements, you hereby grant to Company their right to sign same on your behalf, through company's failure to exercise the rights granted to use such authority shall not diminish Company's rights as set forth within this Agreement.

15.WARRANTIES; REPRESENTATION; RESTRICTIONS; Indemnities

You warrant and represent:

(a)) You have the right and power to enter into and fully perform this Agreement.

(b)Company shall not be required to make any payment of any nature for, or in connection with, the acquisition, exercise or exploitation of rights by Company pursuant to this Agreement except as specifically provided in this Agreement.

(c)You are or will become and will remain, to the extent necessary to enable the performance of this Agreement, a member in good standing of all labor unions, guilds, membership in which may be lawfully required for the performance of your services hereunder.

(d)No materials, as hereinafter defined, or any use thereof, will violate any law or infringe upon or violate the rights of any Person. "Materials", as used in this Article, means:

(i)All Controlled Compositions;

(ii)each name used by you, individually or as a group, in connection with Master Recordings, other recordings and records made hereunder; and

(iii)all other musical, dramatic, artistic and literary materials, ideas, and other intellectual properties, furnished or selected by you and used hereunder in connection with the packaging, sale, distribution, advertising, publicizing or other exploitation of the Master Recordings and derivatives thereof.

(e)During the Term of this Agreement, you will not enter into any agreement which would interfere with the full and prompt performance of your obligations hereunder, and you will not perform or render any services as a performing artist, a producer, or otherwise, for the purpose of making Master Recordings, records or video records for any Person except Company.

(i)A "Restricted Composition", for the purposes hereof, is a Composition which shall have been recorded by you for a Master Recording made under this Agreement or any other agreement with Company.

(ii)You will not perform or produce a master recording embodying any Restricted Composition for any Person except Company for the purpose of making Master Recordings, records, or video records at any time before the later of the following dates:

(1)the date five (5) years after the date upon which the Master Recording made hereunder embodying that Composition has been completely produced: or

(2)the date two (2) years after the expiration of the Term of this Agreement.

(iii)You shall not authorize or knowingly permit your performances to be recorded for any purpose without an express written agreement prohibiting the use of such recording on records in violation of the restrictions prescribed in subparagraph (ii) immediately above.

(g)If you become aware of any unauthorized recording, manufacture, distribution or sale by any third party contrary to the foregoing re-recording restrictions, you will notify Company of it and will cooperate with Company in the event that Company commences any action or proceeding against such third party.

(h)During the Term of this Agreement you will not render any musical performance (audiovisual or otherwise) for the purpose of making any motion picture or other audiovisual work ("Picture" below) without having secured Company's prior written consent. If Company does consent to your performance in a Picture, such consent shall not be deemed to waive or otherwise affect any of Company's other rights under this Agreement, including, without limitation, its rights under paragraph 15 (e) above.

(I)Your Services are unique and extraordinary, and the loss thereof cannot be adequately compensated in damages, and Company shall be entitled to injunctive relief to enforce the provisions of the Agreement.

(j)You shall sign any and all documents which Company determines in the exercise of its reasonable judgment hereunder are necessary or desirable to effectuate the intention of this Agreement, including, without limitation, the execution of so-called "letters of inducement" in favor of any Distribution company or licensee.

(k)There are curt-entry in existence no Master Recordings embodying your performance which have not been released in the United States on records.

(I)You will at all times indemnify and hold harmless Company and any licensee of Company from and against any and all claims, damages, liabilities, costs and expenses, including legal expenses and reasonable counsel fees, arising our of any breach or alleged breach by you of any warranty, representation, covenant or agreement embodied in this Agreement, due you in an amount bearing a reasonable relation to your relation to your potential liability to Company under this subparagraph.

16.REMEDIES

(a)If you do not fulfill any portion of Your Recording Commitment within the time prescribed in Paragraph 4 for any reason whatsoever, Company will have the following options:

(i)To suspend the running of the Term of this Agreement and/or to suspend Company's obligations to make payments to you under this Agreement until you have cured the default;

(ii) to terminate the Term of this Agreement at any time, whether or not you have commenced during the default before such termination occurs; and

(iii)to require you to repay to Company the amount, not then recouped, of any Advance previously paid to you by Company. Company may exercise of those options by sending you the appropriate notice. If Company terminates the Term under clause 16Ia) (ii) company will be deemed to have fulfilled all of its obligations under this Agreement. No exercise of an option under this Paragraph will limit Company's right to recover damages by the reason of your defaults, its rights to Exercise any other option under this Paragraph, or of its other rights.

(b)(I) If Company refuses to allow you to fulfill the Minimum Recording Commitment for any Contract Period and such refusal is no way attributable to acts or omissions under this Agreement on your part, then you shall have as your sole remedy in such instance the right to terminate the term of the Agreement.

(ii) If you elect to terminate the Term, you shall be required to notify Company within thirty (30) days following the end of the contract Year during which company has failed to record the applicable Minimum recording commitment (the "Notice Period). Company shall have a period of thirty (30) days following its receipt of such notice (the "Cure Period") in which to commence to record the then unrecorded Minimum Recording Commitment applicable to that Contract Period.

(iii)If, during the Cure Period, Company shall fail to commence recording of the unrecorded Minimum Recording Commitment, Term hereof relating to unrecorded Master Recording shall end as of the end of the Cure Period. If you fail to timely notify Company during the Notice Period, you shall be deemed to have waived your right to do so, and the Term hereof shall continue uninterrupted for the next Contract Period, if applicable.

(iv)If the Term hereof shall be properly terminated by you in accordance with the provisions of the Paragraph, the Term of this Agreement relating to unrecorded Master Recordings shall terminate with the effect that all parties will be deemed to have fulfilled all of their obligations hereunder except those obligations which survive the end of the Term (e.g., warranties, re-recording restrictions and obligations to pay royalties), and Company shall pay you on demand at the applicable per Master rate referred to in Paragraph 5 above applicable to all unrecorded Master Recordings comprising the Minimum recording Commitment applicable Period as full settlement of its obligation in connection therewith, which payment shall constitute an Advance.

(c)If because of: an Act of God, inevitable accident; fire; lockout; strike or other labor dispute: riot or civil commotion; government or governmental instrumentality (whether federal; state, local or foreign); failure of technical facilities; failure or delay of transportation facilities; illness or incapacity of any performer or producer: or other cause of a similar or different nature not reasonably within Company's or its Licensees' control; Company or such Licensee is materially hampered in the recording, manufacture, distribution or sale of records, then, without limiting Company's rights, company shall have the option by giving you notice to suspend the running of the then current Contract Period for the duration of any such contingency plus such additional time as is necessary so that Company shall have no less than sixty (60) days after the cessation of such contingency in which to exercise its option, if any, to extend the Term of this Agreement for the next following Option Period.

(d)Company shall have the right to terminate the Term of this Agreement with respect to any individual comprising the Artist at any time on thirty (30) days written notice. In such event and only if such termination is without cause, the individuals so terminated shall continue to be entitled to share of royalties hereunder only with respect to aster recordings on which his/her performances are embodied. Any terminated member of Artist shall be required to comply with the provisions of the third sentence of Paragraph 16© and all of Paragraph 16 (d).

17.LEAVING MEMBERS

(a)Your obligations under this Agreement are joint and several. All references to the "you" include all members of the group inclusively and each member individually, unless otherwise specified. A breach of any term or provisions or a disaffirmance or attempted disaffirmance of the Agreement for a reason by any one of the individuals comprising your members shall, at company's election, be deemed a breach by all members comprising the group.

(b)Additional individuals may become members of your group only with Company's prior written consent. Company shall have the right to designate such new members. You shall cause any individual so approved by Company to be bound by all terms and provisions of the Agreement, and you shall, upon our request, cause such individual to execute and deliver such documents as Company may deem necessary or expedient to evidence such individual's Agreement to be bound.

(C)(I) If any of your members ("leaving member") ceases, refused, neglects, ceases or fails to perform as a member of the group for any reason whatsoever, you will notify Company thereof promptly. The leaving member will be replaced by a new member, if Company so agrees in writing. Upon replacement, all members of Artist including the leaving member (s) shall in writing determine an allocation of all Royalties payable to Company to Artist among new and leaving members. Upon failure to do so advise Company, Company shall pay all Royalties to only correct members of Artist. The new member will be deemed substituted as party to this Agreement in the place of the leaving member and you will cause the new member to executed and deliver to Company such instruments as Company, in its judgment, may require to accomplish that substitution. Thereafter, you will have no further obligation to furnish the services of the leaving member for performances under this Agreement, but you (and the leaving member individually) will continue to be bound by the other provisions of this Agreement, including, without limitation, subparagraphs (b), (c) and (d) of this Paragraph. You will not permit any musician to perform in place of the leaving member in making Master Recordings under this Agreement unless that musician has executed and delivered to Company the substitution instruments referred to above.

(ii) Company will have the right to terminate the Term of this Agreement with respect to the remaining members of the Artist by notice given to you at any time before the expiration of ninety (90) days after Company's receipt of your notice provided in (a) above. In the event of such termination, all of the members of the Artist will be deemed leaving members as of the date of such termination notice, and paragraph © will apply to all of them, collectively or individually as Company elects.

(iii)Company shall have the option to engage the exclusive services of each leaving member as a recording artist ("Leaving Member Option"). The Leaving Member Option may be exercised by Company by notice to the leaving member at any time before the expiration of ninety (90) days after the date of:

(1)Company's receipt of your notice under section (a) above; or

(2)Company's termination notice pursuant to section (b) above, as the case may be. If Company exercises that Option, the leaving member(s) concerned will be deemed to have executed Company's standard form of term recording Agreement for the services of an individual recording artist on an approved budget basis without recording fund provisions and containing the following provisions:

(i)the term will commence on the date of Company's exercise of such Leaving Member Option and may be extended by Company, at its election exercisable in the manner provided in Paragraph 1 of this Agreement, for the same number of additional Contract Periods as the number of option contract Periods, if any, remaining pursuant to Paragraph 1 at the time of Company's exercise of the Leaving Member Option (but at least two (2) such additional periods in any event);

(ii)the Minimum Recording Commitment for each Contract Period of such Term will be Master Recordings Sufficient to comprise two (2) 12" singles or its equivalent, with an overall option equivalent to that granted to Company in paragraph 3 of this Agreement;

(iii)the royalty percentage rates in respect of records and video records embodying performances recorded during that term will be the same provided herein; and

(iv)if your royalty account under this Agreement is in an unrecouped position at the date of Company's exercise of the Leaving Member Option, a pro-rata of the amount of that unrecouped balance, determined by computing the percentage of the original group being retained by Company will constitute an Advance recoupable from those royalties.

(d)No leaving member shall have the right thereafter to use any professional name or servicemark utilized by other of your members at any time during the Term of this Agreement, or any servicemark similar thereto. Furthermore such leaving member shall not have the right to promote herself, or allow himself to be promoted as, "formerly of (the Mark)' or by any similar label.

18.AGREEMENTS, APPROVAL & CONSENT

As to all matters treated herein to be determined by mutual agreement, or as to which any approval or consent is required, such agreement, approval or consent will not be unreasonably withheld. Your agreement, approval or consent, whenever required, shall be deemed to have been given unless you notify Company otherwise within ten (10) days following the date of Company's written request to you therefore.

19.NOTICES

Except as otherwise specifically provided herein, all notices hereunder shall be in writing and shall be given by personal delivery, registered or certified mail or telegraph (prepaid), at the addresses shown above, or such other addresses as may be designated by either Party. Notices shall be deemed given when mailed or when transmitted by telegraph, except that notice of change of address shall be effective only from the days of its receipt. A copy of all notices directed to company shall be sent simultaneously to or such notice shall be ineffective.

20.PUBLICITY SESSIONS

You shall be available from time to time, at Company's request and expense and upon reasonable notice of not less than seven (7) days, to appear for photograph, promotional films, posters, cover art, to appear for interviews with representatives of the communication media and publicity personnel and to perform other reasonable promotional functions during the Term thereof. You shall not be entitled to compensation therefore other than minimum union scale payments set forth in applicable collective bargaining agreements to which Company is a signatory, if such a scale exists for the specific appearances requested. Any payment made to you hereunder shall constitute an Advance. Any expenses incurred by Company including the pre-productions, production, post-production or acquisition of any video or film embodying Artist's performances shall be deemed an Advance hereunder.

21.MISCELLANEOUS

(a)You will, prior to the release of the first record hereunder, prepare an act to professional quality and will during the Term of this Agreement, actively pursue a career as an entertainer in the live engagement field.

(b)This Agreement contains the entire understanding of the Parties relating to its subject matter and supersedes any prior agreements, written or oral, between the parties or their successors. No change or termination of this Agreement will be binding upon Company unless it is made by an instrument signed by an officer of Company. A waiver by either party of any provision Agreement shall be governed by the laws of the State of Florida applicable to contracts entered into and performed entirely within the State of Florida. The Florida courts (state and federal), only, will have jurisdiction of any controversies regarding this Agreement; any action or other proceeding which involves such a controversy will be brought in those courts and not elsewhere. Any process in any such action or proceeding may, among other methods, be served upon you by delivering it or mailing 1, by registered or certified mail, directed to the address first above written or such other address as you may designate pursuant to Paragraph 19. Any such process may, among other methods, be served upon you or any other Person who approves, ratifies, or assents to this Agreement to include Company to enter into it, by delivering the process of mailing it by registered or certified mail, directly to the address first above written or such other address as you or the other Person concerned my designate in the manner prescribed in Paragraph 19. Any such delivery or mail service shall be deemed to have the same force and effect as personal service within the State of Florida.

(c)In entering into this Agreement, and in providing services pursuant hereto, you have and shall have the status of independent contractors and nothing herein contained shall contemplate or constitute you as Company's agents or employees.

(d)You acknowledge that Company has given you the right and opportunity to have this agreement, and the attachments hereto, reviewed by an attorney of your choice having competence in the music and entertainment industries, and you have done so. You further acknowledge that said attorney has reviewed with you the terms and conditions of this Agreement and its attachments, and that he has advised you that it is in your best interest to execute said Agreement.

IN WITNESS WHEREOF, the parties have set their hands to this Agreement as of the day and date first above written.

ARTIST: ARTIST: ARTIST:

_________________ _________________ _________________

_________________ _________________ _________________

SS#   SS#   SS#

ANSWER: Use the Momentum Marketing Log

MOMENTUM MARKETING LOG

Title: ___________________ **Artist:**___________________ **Release Date:** _______

Contact		Intro	Kit/Demo	Call	Quote	Lead	Follow-up	Follow-up	Follow-up	ACTION	Comment
				√							

QUESTION: How should I divide the publishing share of ownership on the Performance rights organization clearance form. (Ascap, BMI, SESAC)?

Example: Black Gold Records is the record label. Golden Words Publishing is the publishing branch of the label which has been registered with BMI.   The group which has been signed is called Rapsody, and consists of two members A. Brown, and B. Sable. The musical work which is being cleared is entitled "Fuzz Buster". Both members of the group contributed equally in writing the song.

Note how the percentage shares were computed. There are three entities sharing ownership of the music in question. The figures are a total of the copyright percentages as well as the publishing percentages. As per the instructions, the total percentage shares should total 200%. Typically, an artist will relinquish 50% of Publishing rights to the label while retaining all of the writer's share. The remaining 50% of publishing rights must then be shared between the writers. Hence the 25% share indicated below.

The final percentage share breakdown, therefore, is as follows:

A. Brown	B. Sable	Golden Words Publishing
50% of writer's share	50 % of writer's share	0% of writer's share
25% of Publishing	25% of Publishing	50% of Publishing
75% Total	75% Total	50% Total

BMI Locations

New York
320 West 57th Street
New York, NY 10019-3790
(212) 586-2000

Nashville
10 Music Square East
Nashville, TN 37203-4399
(615) 401-2000

Los Angeles
8730 Sunset Blvd. 3rd Flr West
West Hollywood, CA 90069-2211
(310) 659-9109

London
84 Harley House
Marylebone Rd
London NW1 5HN, ENGLAND
011-0044 207486 2036

Miami
5201 Blue Lagoon Drive
Suite 310
Miami, FL 33126
(305) 266-3636

Atlanta
P.O. Box 19199
Atlanta, GA 31126
(404) 261-5151

Puerto Rico
255 Ponce de Leon
East Wing, Suite A-262
BankTrust Plaza
Hato Rey, Puerto Rico 00917
(787) 754-6490

Question: How much does it cost to incorporate? (courtesy of Bizjump.com)

Answer: See chart below. Other Bizjump processing fees apply

MANDATORY STATE FEES

STATE	Processing Time	Express	Standard Corp	LLC
ALABAMA	30	7	$125	$115
ALASKA	10	1	$280	$280
ARIZONA	60	14	$275	$265
ARKANSAS	10		$ 80	$ 80
CALIFORNIA	30	5	$145	$115
COLORADO	20	5	$130	$130
CONNECTICUT	5	1	$380	$165
DELAWARE	7	1	$ 74	$ 70
District Of Columbia (D.C.)	14	1	$150	$130
FLORIDA	10	1	$ 80	$165
GEORGIA	10	1	$230	$205
HAWAII	20	5	$180	$180
IDAHO	10		$120	$120
ILLINOIS	15	1	$130	$430
INDIANA	10		$120	$120
IOWA	10		$ 80	$ 80
KANSAS	7		$105	$180
KENTUCKY	10		$100	$ 70
LOUISIANA	15		$150	$ 90
MAINE	10		$125	$125
MARYLAND	60	2	$128	$138
MASSACHUSETTS	20	1	$275	$510
MICHIGAN	10	2	$ 90	$ 90
MINNESOTA	12		$185	$185
MISSISSIPPI	8		$ 80	$ 80
MISSOURI	2	N/A	$ 88	$135
MONTANA	5		$120	$100
NEBRASKA	8		$225	$295
NEVADA	8	1	$225	$225
NEW HAMPSHIRE	10		$120	$125
NEW JERSEY	9	2	$135	$160
NEW MEXICO	10		$130	$ 80
NEW YORK	60	12	$170	$235
NORTH CAROLINA	12	1	$180	$255
NORTH DAKOTA	10		$155	$155
OHIO	30	14	$125	$125
OKLAHOMA	10		$ 80	$130
OREGON	10	2	$ 80	$ 70
PENNSYLVANIA	20	1	$250	$100
RHODE ISLAND	15		$180	$180
SOUTH CAROLINA			$210	$110
SOUTH DAKOTA	10		$120	$120
TENNESSEE	30	7	$150	$250
TEXAS	10	3	$325	$225
UTAH	15	2	$105	$105
VERMONT	15		$105	$105
VIRGINIA	10	5	$111	$138
WASHINGTON	15		$225	$225
WEST VIRGINIA	7		$107	$130
WISCONSIN	10		$115	$160
WYOMING	10		$130	$130

Question: Where can I find specific business start up info for my state?

Answer: To find out what forms, licenses, etc. you'll need for your state, first check the SBA's website for links to specific contact information for Small Business http://www.sba.gov/starting/sbdclocations.html. Also,

Alabama - http://www.ador.state.al.us/licenses/authrity.html
Alaska - Not available at this time
Arizona - http://www.revenue.state.az.us/license.htm
Arkansas - http://www.state.ar.us/online_business.php
California - http://www.calgold.ca.gov/
Colorado - http://www.state.co.us/gov_dir/obd/blid.htm
Connecticut - http://www.state.ct.us/
Delaware - http://www.state.de.us/revenue/obt/obtmain.htm
District of Columbia - http://www.dcra.dc.gov/
Florida - http://sun6.dms.state.fl.us/dor/businesses/
Georgia - http://www.sos.state.ga.us/corporations/regforms.htm
Hawaii - http://www.hawaii.gov/dbedt/start/starting.html
Idaho - http://www.idoc.state.id.us/Pages/BUSINESSPAGE.html
Illinois - http://www.sos.state.il.us/departments/business_services/business.html
Indiana - http://www.state.in.us/sic/owners/ia.html
Iowa - http://www.iowasmart.com/blic/
Kansas - Not available at this time
Kentucky - http://www.thinkkentucky.com/kyedc/ebpermits.asp
Louisiana - Not available at this time
Maine - http://www.econdevmaine.com/biz-develop.htm
Maryland - http://www.dllr.state.md.us/
Massachusetts - http://www.state.ma.us/sec/cor/coridx.htm
Michigan - http://medc.michigan.org/services/startups/index2.asp
Minnesota - http://www.dted.state.mn.uss
Mississippi - http://www.olemiss.edu/depts/mssbdc/going_intobus.html
Missouri - http://www.ded.state.mo.us/business/businesscenter/
Montana - http://www.state.mt.us/sos/biz.htm
Nebraska - Not available at this time
New Hampshire - http://www.nhsbdc.org/startup.htm
New Jersey - http://www.state.nj.us/njbiz/s_lic_and_cert.shtml
New York - http://www.dos.state.ny.us/lcns/licensing.html
New Mexico - Not available at this time
Nevada - http://www.state.nv.us/binn/
North Carolina - http://www.secstate.state.nc.us/secstate/blio/default.htm
North Dakota - http://www.state.nd.us/sec/
Ohio - http://www.state.oh.us/sos/business_services_information.htm
Oklahoma - http://www.okonestop.com/
Oregon - http://www.filinginoregon.com
Pennsylvania - Not available at this time
Rhode Island - http://www.corps.state.ri.us/firststop/index.asp
South Carolina - http://www.state.sd.us/STATE/sitecategory.cfm?mp=Licenses/Occupations
South Dakota - http://www.state.sd.us/STATE/sitecategory.cfm?mp=Licenses/Occupations
Tennessee - Not available at this time
Texas - http://www.tded.state.tx.us/guide/
Utah - http://www.commerce.state.ut.us/web/commerce/admin/licen.htm
Vermont - http://www.sec.state.vt.us/
Virginia - http://www.dba.state.va.us/licenses/
Washington - http://www.wa.gov/dol/bpd/limsnet.htm
West Virginia - http://www.state.wv.us/taxrev/busreg.html
Wisconsin - http://www.wdfi.org/corporations/forms/
Wyoming - http://soswy.state.wy.us/corporat/corporat.htm

Question: What forms do I need to trademark logos and copyright my work?

Answer: See explanation below

For Trademarks: Visit www.USPTO.gov, complete online; print form; mail to USPTO

For Copyrights:
The Library of Congress allows you to copyright
Literary Works
Visual Arts
Performing Arts
Sound Recordings
Serials/Periodicals

using the following forms
  Form TX- For published or unpublished non-dramatic literary works
  Form TX with instructions
  Short Form TX - Simplified version of Form TX
  Form PA - For published or unpublished works of the performing arts
  Form PA with instructions
  Short Form PA - Simplified version of Form PA
  Form SR - For published or unpublished sound recordings
  Form SR with instructions
  Form VA - For published or unpublished works of the visual arts
  Form VA with instructions
  Short Form VA - Simplified version of Form VA
  Form GR/PPh/CON - Group registration of published photographs continuation sheet
  Form SE - For serials (newspapers, magazines, newsletters, annuals, journals, etc.)
  Form SE with instructions
  Short Form SE - Simplified version of Form SE
  Form SE/Group - For registration of a group of serials
  Form G/DN Non Fill-in version - For registration of a group of daily newspapers
  Form RE - For claims to renewal of copyright
  Form RE with instructions

Basic Registrations (Fee to accompany an application and deposit for registration of a claim to copyright)
Form TX or Short Form TX $ 30
Form VA or Short Form VA $ 30
Form PA or Short Form PA $ 30
Form SE or Short Form SE $ 30
Form SR $ 30

For further information on current fees, call the Copyright Public Information Office at (202) 707-3000, 8:30 a.m. to 5:00 p.m. eastern time, Monday through Friday, except federal holidays. The TTY number is (202) 707-6737. See also Circular 4, Copyright Office Fees. Or, you may write for information to
Library of Congress Copyright Office 101 Independence Avenue, S.E. Washington, D.C. 20559-6000

Question: What forms do I need to clear a sample?

Answer: Submit this form in writing to the original publisher of the music being sampled

CLEARANCE REQUEST FORM

Requested by: _______________________________   Date: ______________

1. Original Work

Title of original work ____

Writer(s) of original work____

Publisher(s) of original work____

Original artist____

Original record company____

Brief description of original work within new work____________________

2. New Work (Proposed Release)

Title of new work____

Catalogue Number____

Format (album/single etc.) ____

Does it contain any other samples? (list samples) ___________________

Writer(s) and writer(s) affiliation of new work______________________

Publisher and publishers affiliation of new work_____________________

Artist ____

Distribution ____

Proposed release date ____

Number of units to be manufactured Proposed release date ____________

3. Provide any further information we may find useful
Include Recording of original work/artist:
Brief description of original work within new title, including duration of use:

4. Contact Information
Name ____
Address _______________________________________
Telephone ___________________Email ______________Fax ________________

Question: Help! I need to license my music to an independent film producer!

ANSWER: Here is a MUSIC SYNCHRONIZATION LICENSE form

For and in consideration of Producer's agreement to pay a license fee in the sum of $__________ and other good and valuable consideration to the undersigned publisher (CalvinWorks Publishing (ASCAP) "Publisher"), Publisher hereby grants to the producer, Fred Film Works, Inc., and its successors, assigns, and licenses (herein referred to as "Producer"), the nonexclusive, irrevocable right, license, privilege and authority to:

(a)   Record the musical composition identified below (including the music and/or lyrics thereof in any arrangement, orchestration or language), but only in the synchronization or timed relation with the motion picture identified below;

(b) Make any number of copies of said recordings;

(c) Sell, license, distribute, subdistribute, export, and import said recordings and/or copies from and into any country or territory throughout the universe; and

(d)   Perform said musical composition throughout the universe but only in synchronization or timed relation with the motion picture identified below, upon and subject to the terms and conditions set forth

1. The musical composition covered by this license is:

          Composition: Fred's Nightmare   Publishers share: 100% worldwide

2. The present working title of the motion picture with which said recording will be used is Fred's Nightmare. As used herein, the term "motion picture" refers to said motion picture and all versions thereof now or hereafter in existence, whether in English or foreign language, television, or any other form, (but not including remakes or sequels), and trailers, promotional films, television and radio spots, clips and excerpts of said motion picture or any version thereof.

3. The territory covered by this license is the universe.

4. The music publishing company designated for the musical composition will be CalvinWorks Publishing (ASCAP). CalvinWorks Publishing will own 100% of all worldwide music publishing rights for the Score as described herein. Producer agrees to specify Calvin Composer (ASCAP) as 100% writer and CalvinWorks Publishing (ASCAP) as 100% publisher for all music composed by Calvin Composer on performing rights cue sheets. Producer agrees to prepare accurate performing rights cue sheets and file with ASCAP and provide a copy to Composer no later than 30 days after the sound mix of the film.

5. This license shall remain in full force and effect for the duration of all copyrights in said musical composition, including any renewals and extensions without Producer having to pay any additional consideration thereof.

6. The recording rights granted in (a) above may be exercised by any and all means, methods, and systems of recording sound in synchronization or timed relation with motion pictures, whether now known or hereafter devised.

7. Publisher warrants that it has the right to grant this license, that it owns and controls one hundred percent (100%) of the right, title and interest in and to said musical composition and that the use of said musical composition hereunder will not violate the rights of any third party. Publisher shall indemnify costs, losses, damages and expenses (including reasonable attorneys

fees) arising out of any breach or failure of any warranties or covenants made by Publisher herein.

8. Subject only to the rights herein above granted to Producer, all rights of every kind and nature in said musical compositions are reserved to said Publisher, together with all rights of use thereof. However, in no event shall Producer have less rights than a member of the public would have in the absence of this license.

9. No failure by Producer to perform any of its obligations hereunder shall constitute a breach of this license, unless Publisher has given Producer written notice of such non-performance and producer fails to cure such non-performance within thirty (30) days of its receipt of such notice.

10. Publisher's rights and remedies in the event of a breach of this license shall be limited to Publisher's right, if any, to recover damages in an action at law.

11. Producer agrees to give credit to the composer, full card in the main titles to read: Music Composed and Conducted By Calvin Composer

12. Producer agrees not to manufacture or distribute sound recordings (including soundtrack albums, promotional CDs, and any and all methods of sound recording) separately from actual positive prints of the motion picture and directly integrated media (such as digital recordings to be used in theaters as part of a theater's digital sound reproduction system).

13. This license shall be governed by and subject to the laws of the State of California applicable to agreements made and to be wholly performed therein.

14. This license is binding upon and shall inure to the benefit of the respective successors and/or assigns of the parties hereto.

15. This represents the entire agreement between Producer and Publisher with regard to said musical composition.

Question: How Can I Pay the Players?

ANSWER: Here is a form you can use to authorize direct deposits into your players' accounts.

Electronic Funds Transfer Authorization

Telephone: (   ) _________________I hereby authorize my employer to directly deposit my pay in the bank account(s) listed below in the percentages specified. (If two accounts are designated, deposits are to be made in whole percentages of pay to total 100%.) I have attached a voided check or deposit slip for each account specified below. This authorization is to remain in force until the company has received written authorization from me of its termination or change.

Also, I grant [Your Business] the right to correct any Electronic Funds Transfer resulting from an erroneous overpayment by debiting my account to the extent of such overpayment.

Name: ____

Address: ____

Signature: ___________________________________   Date: ____________

Company Use Only: Effective Date _______________________________

Account #1   Checking_______________ Savings____________ (Check only one)

Financial Institution: ____

Street Address: ____

City, State and Zip Code: ______________________________________

Telephone: (   ) __________________

Personal Account Number: ______________________________________

Percent of pay to be deposited into this account: ____________________%

Company Use Only: Bank/ABA Number ____________________________

Account #2   Checking_______________ Savings____________ (Check only one)

Financial Institution: ____

Street Address: ____

City, State and Zip Code: ______________________________________

Telephone: (   ) __________________

Personal Account Number: ______________________________________

Percent of pay to be deposited into this account: ____________________%

Company Use Only: Bank/ABA Number ____________________________

Question: It's time to sell or partner with a major. How much is my business worth?

ANSWER:

BUSINESS VALUATION FORM

CALCULATE BOOK VALUE

1. Add up the value of tangible assets

a.	Cash on Hand	$__________
b.	Inventory	$__________
c.	Accounts Receivable	$__________
d.	Land and building	$__________
e.	Improvements to leased property	$__________
f.	Equipment, fixtures, furniture	$__________
g.	Supplies, vehicles	$__________
h.	Miscellaneous	$__________
	Total Assets	$__________

2. Add up liabilities

a.	Loans, mortgages long-term debt	$__________
b.	Accounts, notes, taxes payable	$__________
	Total liabilities	$__________

3. Subtract liabilities from total assets to calculate book value $__________

CALCULATE ANNUAL NET INCOME

4. Enter annual net revenues $__________

5. Enter annual cost of goods sold $__________

6. Subtract line 5 from line 4 to get gross annual profits $__________

7. Add up annual expenses

a.	Owner's and employees' waes	$__________
b.	Rent, utilities, phone	$__________
c.	Supplies, vehicles	$__________
d.	Repair and maintenance	$__________
e.	Insurance, accounting and legal fees	$__________
f.	Advertising	$__________
g.	Travel an entertainment	$__________
h.	Interest, taxes	$__________
i.	Miscellaneous	$__________
	Total annual expenses	$__________

8. Subtract total expenses from gross profits to get annual net income $__________

CALCULATE GOOD WILL

9. Enter the avg rate of return for your industry. (or use 10%) $__________

10. Compute return on tangible assets (line 9 x total assets) $__________

11. Calculate earnings due to good will (line 8 minus line 10) $__________

12. Capitalization Multiplier (5 for high risk 7 for low risk) $__________

13. Good Will (multiply line 11 by line 12) $__________

CALCULATE TOTAL VALUE

About the author:

Walt Goodridge is known as the "Passion Prophet."

A graduate of Columbia University, Walt is a former civil engineer who walked away from his career to follow his passion for music, writing, and helping others. He has been an artist manager, record label owner, inventor, poet, network marketer and consultant. He is the author of 10 books including *Turn Your Passion Into Profit (Information, Inspiration and Ideas to Help You Make Money Doing What You Love)*, and owns and operates a dozen websites. He is the creator of "Walt's Friday Inspirations", a popular weekly email of "the thoughts that create success" that he sends to the over 26,000 people who subscribe. Walt writes for *Entrepreneur Magazine* and *Black Enterprise*, and has been featured in *Time Magazine, the Dallas Morning News, Essence, The Kip Business Report* and numerous publications and websites. Walt offers personalized coaching and conducts workshops around the world to help others make money doing what they love!

CD

SHOW ME THE DOLLARS!
with Alvin Hartley

Alvin Hartley has successfully negotiated millions in sponsorship dollars and services from Coca-Cola, Burger King, Pepsi, Calvin Klein, Coors Light, Verizon and MCI to name just a few.

Now, for the first time ever, in our most popular expert series edition, he reveals the mindset and methodology he uses. This audio CD features Walt and Alvin in a revealing conversation!
ITEM: EXPERT001
CD: $19.95

E

PASSION-CENTERED BUSINESS PLAN TEMPLATE
available as :
1. RTF (Rich Text Format) files; "Word File"; Use Microsoft® Word® or most word processing programs
ITEM: BUSPLAN001

E

ALWAYS ON TOP
with Kamau Austin

How to get the Highest Possible Search Engine Position For Your Small Business Website.EVERY TIME!! Stop paying Per Click Cut your advertising budget to $0 or close to it! Beat the Search Engines at their own Game

Always on Top includes tons of information about how the search engines work, why some sites get to the top while others don't and much more. Quite simply, if you follow what Kamau suggests, you'll see a rise in ranking, visits to your site and ultimately sales. –Walt
ITEM: EXPERT003
e-BOOK: $27.00

CASS

THERE'S NO BUSINESS LIKE YOUR OWN BUSINESS
Two Time Oprah Guest and USA Today columnist Gladys Edmunds shares a balanced and wholistic approach to success that will be a timeless resource!
ITEM: GLADYS001
SIX CASSETTES: $47.00

CD

HOW TO GROW A MILLION DOLLAR COMPANY
with Andrew Morrison

CNN Expert and Oprah Guest, Andrew Morrison grew his first company to 3 Million dollars in sales before his 30th birthday! This audio cassette features Andrew Morrison in a revealing conversation with Passion Prophet Walt Goodridge.
ITEM: EXPERT002
CASSETTE: $19.95

P E

21 QUESTIONS THAT WILL BUILD YOUR BUSINESS IN 90 DAYS!
with Andrew Morrison
Get the Book with the Questions That Will Transform Your Business!

ITEM:QUESTIONS001
PAPERBACK: $49.95

"Simply Brilliant! Andrew distills a lifetime of business wisdom into a practical set of questions most business owners never think to ask. Thoughtfully answering just one of these powerful questions can instantly improve your business, income and your life!" --- **Ramon Williamson, Author, *of Six Simple Things That Can Change Your Life***

P=Paperback
E=ebook
CD=Compact Disc
CASS=Cassette

CL=Clothing

NEW!!!

LIFE RHYMES
The Complete Collection!
Life Rhymes cover practically every facet of life! There's always one you can share with a loved one to give them some encouragement, some words of understanding, or just a little kick in the pants!
ISBN: 0974531316
ITEM: LR001; 475 PAGES
paperback: $34.95

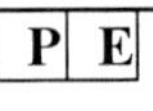

THE TAO OF WOW
Many consider this Walt's most inspired work! Discover your Wow Factor, Become a Wow Master and the learn the secret to getting anything you want in life! Experience Walt's Life Rhymes in way you've never seen them before!
ISBN: 096292024X
ITEM: TAO001
PAP-$14.95; E-BOOK: $4.95

You know him as the Passion Prophet, or the founder of HipHopEntrepreneur.com, but Walt is a virtual internet-celebrity as the creator of Walt's Friday Inspiration Life Rhyme email. Life Rhymes are "...positive, situational, success-oriented, lyrical, rhyme-based poetry designed to inspire new ways of thinking." Changing the way you think is an integral part of turning your passion into profit. Walt has written a brand new life rhyme EVERY week without fail for an unprecedented 385 week stretch! These unique, and totally original creations have been thrilling fans every Friday consistently* for an amazing 7 years! Experience Walt's unique brand of Inspiration in several formats

LESSONS IN SUCCESS
Way back in 1998, before there was Lyrics for Living, Walt published the first collection of Life Rhymes 1-50. Featuring his "days of homelessness" story, "sheriff ducking 101", and "How to Deal with Creditors calling", this volume will provide a few chuckles as you read the stories behind his unique brand of inspiration!
ISBN: 0962920274
ITEM: WG001
PAPERBACK: $14.95
(QUANTITIES LIMITED)

LYRICS FOR LIVING
Vol 2
Volume 2 includes Walt's Life Rhymes #51-100. Teachers are using them to teach students. Some credit them wih changing their lives. Includes commentary and a few of the real stories behind them. Own this second in an increasingly popular series!
ISBN: 0962920258
ITEM: LL002
paperback: $10.00

COME INTO OUR WHIRL
The first collection of poetry by an online community of poets was published in 1997 by the PoetsNiche— one of Walt's sites. Features poems from the sites international community and contributions from Walt!
ISBN: 0962920266
ITEM: PN001
PAPERBACK: $19.95

(QUANTITIES LIMITED)

P=Paperback, E=ebook, CD=Compact Disc, CASS=Cassette, CL=Clothing

The PassionProfit Company

Everyone has a passion.
Every passion can be turned into profit.
You <u>can</u> make money doing what you love!

--Walt Goodridge, The "Passion Prophet"

Visit us online at www.PassionProfit.com!
Order Form
Order online at PassionProfit.com!

Call (212) 831-1854
Fax to (212)658-9232

Mail to:

The Passion Profit Company
PO BOX 618
NEW YORK, NY 10008-0618
USA

ITEM	QUAN	Description	Format	Size	Color	Price

SHIP TO

Name:

Address

City   State   Zip

Province/

COUNTRY

Phone:

EMAIL:

BILL TO (If different than Ship to Name and Address)

Name:

Address

City   State   Zip

Province/

COUNTRY

Subtotal

Subtract Coupon or Member Discount   — $_______

NY State Residents Only   + $_______
8.50% Sales tax
Subtotal _______ X (0 .085)=

Processing Charge   +   **$3.00.00**

Shipping Charge   + $_______
Total Number of of items ____ x 0.95=

Plus International Shipping   + $_______
Charge=Email or call us for this.

Miscellaneous Charge or Discount

TOTAL ORDER

Thank you for your support and patronage!
Orders are normally processed and shipped
within 72 hours of receipt in our offices.

[_} VISA(16)   [_] MasterCard   [_}AMEX (15) [_}Discover

Expiration mm/yy

Signature

X_______

____